Jim & Sh

May

MW01528275

the reading of Bedrock Faith!

Time is of the Essence –
Jesus is Coming Soon!

Esther Seaton-Dummer

BEDROCK FAITH

ESTHER SEATON-DUMMER

WESTBOW PRESS
A DIVISION OF THOMAS NELSON

Copyright © 2012 by Esther Seaton-Dummer.

All rights reserved. No part of this book may be used or reproduced by any means, graphic, electronic, or mechanical, including photocopying, recording, taping or by any information storage retrieval system without the written permission of the publisher except in the case of brief quotations embodied in critical articles and reviews.

Scripture taken from the King James Version of the Bible.

Scripture taken from the New King James Version. Copyright 1979, 1980, 1982 by Thomas Nelson, inc. Used by permission. All rights reserved.

New Living Translation ®, copyright © 1996, 2004 by Tyndale Charitable Trust. Used by permission of Tyndale House Publishers. All rights reserved.

THE MESSAGE: The Bible in Contemporary Language © 2002 by Eugene H. Peterson. All rights reserved.
The Living Bible

WestBow Press books may be ordered through booksellers or by contacting:

WestBow Press
A Division of Thomas Nelson
1663 Liberty Drive
Bloomington, IN 47403
www.westbowpress.com
1-(866) 928-1240

Because of the dynamic nature of the Internet, any web addresses or links contained in this book may have changed since publication and may no longer be valid. The views expressed in this work are solely those of the author and do not necessarily reflect the views of the publisher, and the publisher hereby disclaims any responsibility for them.

Any people depicted in stock imagery provided by Thinkstock are models, and such images are being used for illustrative purposes only.

Certain stock imagery © Thinkstock.

ISBN: 978-1-4497-6246-9 (sc)
ISBN: 978-1-4497-6245-2 (hc)
ISBN: 978-1-4497-6247-6 (e)

Library of Congress Control Number: 2012914515

Printed in the United States of America

WestBow Press rev. date: 9/10/2012

Artwork by Daniel L. Dummer

danieldummer@gmx.com

Thank you to Daniel who willingly shared his unique talent with all of us here. Blessings on you for your time and artistic view on each thing I asked for.

Poem – "Unbroken" by Brian McBride

Brian, age 16, is a gifted author, who is publishing his first book.

Thank you to Brian for contributing his poem, further enhancing the message of ***Bedrock Faith.*** I am looking forward to seeing your first book, ***Paradox*** in print.

Endorsements for Bedrock Faith

***Bedrock Faith** is a must read for today's Pastors, Spiritual Leaders and all believers. It is a passionate and powerful wakeup call for a slumbering Church. Many denominations that once experienced the tangible Presence of the Lord and the Power of a Holy Spirit Pentecost are now being referred to as an "Old Wineskin Movement." The author refocuses our eyes clearly upon our Lord and Savior Jesus Christ, the ROCK of our Salvation and Lord of His Church. She not only exposes the spiritual weaknesses and failures of today's lukewarm religious culture, she is used of the Lord through spiritual wisdom and prophetic gifting to return all of us back to a Glorious Church. **Bedrock Faith** gives us a fresh opportunity to "Hear what the Spirit is saying to the Church." Is anyone listening???*

- Ormel Chapin; Revivalist; Founder of Pastors PowerUp International

*Esther's writing style is like looking at the many facets of a diamond from every angle, allowing the light to glitter off of it. She is comparable to John Bevere in thoroughness and to David Wilkerson on Biblical correctness. **Bedrock Faith** is an essential for every honest and sincere Christian who desires to get it right and honor God with their lives.*

- Loren L. Dummer—Lead Pastor; Gateway Worship Center; Oregon

*What a challenging and encouraging book. **Bedrock Faith** is full of spiritual depth and insights. It is great for personal study or teaching. A must read.*

- Debra McBride—Pastor/Teacher

Bedrock Faith's** message is clearly the key to the heart of God—to get it right, to do right and to be right before God. As you read the pages of **Bedrock

***Faith**, your grip will tighten and you will find yourself standing more firmly than ever on the Unmovable, Unshakeable Truth of God's Word!*

- Mary Seaton—Veteran Pastor/Teacher; Morning Star Worship Center; Oregon

*If your faith is shaky, **Bedrock Faith** will help to tear down the shakable things and build a good foundation of truth. If you feel your faith is strong, it will remind you to strengthen your stand to prepare for the days ahead.*

- Donna Conley—Youth Pastor/Teacher—

*The message of **Bedrock Faith** hits right down the line. Tighten your belt and gear up! It is filled with wisdom and depth. It is worth reading more than once. We are looking for more from this author.*

- Jim and Chris H—Deacon and Nursing Home Ministry

***Bedrock Faith** is a much-needed book for our time. It pierces to the heart of where we should live. There is no middle road with **Bedrock Faith**. Yes and Amen!*

- Beverly W.—Pastoral Prayer Team

*All I can say is, "Wow!" **Bedrock Faith** is life-changing. It makes you take a serious inward look.*

- Jessica K—Sunday School Teacher

*I have never been able to get into a book and read with passion—but **Bedrock Faith** drew me into the message. It touched my heart and made me focus on what I need to do to serve Jesus with my whole life.*

- Joey C.—New Believer

Bedrock Faith *will bring each and every person who enters its pages all the way to an encounter with Jesus, changing every soul with that encounter. It has greatly impacted my life in much-needed ways.*

- Lydia A.—Pastoral Prayer Team

Bedrock Faith *is a great book of truth, exposing our hearts and the heart of the church.*

- Christopher C.—Age 17

Bedrock Faith *is a powerful message of truths taken from the Bible and put together to make a book to solidify your faith in the Lord. Every word of it rang with the truth of God and I highly recommend it if you want your faith to become all the more strong.*

- Michael M.—Age 14

Bedrock Faith *is a powerful and raw message and is a Word of Truth. It captivated me from the first sentence. Every word is etched with and embodies the truth of the Bible. I wholeheartedly recommend this message to anyone who seeks to make firmer their stance on the Bedrock of Faith.*

- Brian M.—Age 16

Acknowledgments

To the ***Rock of my Salvation, Jesus Christ,*** for the strength of the place I have found and yet find in you. Thank you for believing in me, for continuing to use me to edify and build up your precious people. I am honored.

To ***Loren Dummer,*** husband of mine, my greatest fan in this life. Thank you for being the kind of man that readily reads and enjoys what I write, offering valuable feedback and some great nuggets of truth that shows up as "*quotes*" on the pages of ***Bedrock Faith***. Also, thank you for being the vessel God can use to speak to His Church.

I also want to give a shout out to my incredible children, ***Donna, Debra and Daniel***. You all inspire me. Love you so much!

And for the prayers of ***God's people*** here and abroad—thank you so much from the bottom of my heart. I could not do what I do without the innumerable prayer warriors who pray for me.

DEDICATION

I want to take this space in ***Bedrock Faith*** to acknowledge an incredibly faithful, God-fearing, God-honoring host of people who have separated themselves apart from the world, religion and secularism, and who have not handled the Word of God deceitfully or for material gain.

> ***2 Corinthians 4:1-2***—*Therefore seeing we have this ministry, as we have received mercy, we faint not; But have renounced the hidden things of dishonesty, not walking in craftiness, nor handling the word of God deceitfully; but by manifestation of the truth commending ourselves to every man's conscience in the sight of God.*

I think of my father, Delbert Seaton, and the years he spent laboring, spending himself for God's people. Here are the vows my father made to the Lord over sixty years ago when he entered the ministry:

1. He would leave his children a heritage in the Lord.
2. He would never violate his vows to his wife, bringing shame to her, his children or the church.
3. He would never put money in the balance with ministry.

Thank you dad for keeping every vow you made to God, my mother, your children and the church. What an example of integrity!

I also think of my mother, Mary Seaton, as well, a lady who has held God's Word in her hands and heart for over sixty years and knows where the Rock is, pointing many, many to safe ground. The value she has placed on God's Word to herself and what she has shared with others is also an example of integrity.

You both are the example of what I'm talking about here for I know there are thousands of others like you!

I have no doubt my godly parents represent a multitude of God's faithful servants who have labored in spite of the storms, adversity and persecution. Not every martyr for the cause of Christ is dead or in some dank prison; many have laid their lives down for the gospel of Jesus Christ and yet proclaim the truth of God's Word in multitudes of fields of labor.

Thank you pastors, evangelists, missionaries, Sunday school teachers, elders, bishops, professors, apostles, prophets and other unnamed Christian leaders,—serving all around the world in small and large places where Christ's church is equipped by the faithful warriors of the Cross of Jesus, and commissioned to carry the gospel torch to others.

Thank you all for keeping the true *"Light"* turned on, the *"Fire"* burning hot and the *"Well"* dug deep for the hungry and thirsty and wayward of the world. You have, *in spite of a failing religious system*, set the bar high, raised the standard for others to follow as you follow Christ, moving the true Church of the Lord Jesus Christ forward!

I say to you all . . . *Hold your course . . . Keep the Faith . . . Finish Well!*
God bless you all!

Table of Contents

"Cowardice asks the question—is it safe?
Expediency asks the question—is it politic?
Vanity asks the question—is it popular?
But conscience asks the question—is it right?
And there comes a time when one must take a position that is neither safe, nor politic, nor popular; but one must take it because it is right."

Dr. Martin Luther King, Jr.

BEDROCK

The firm foundation or basis: the fundamental principles, as of a teaching or belief

Prologue

Standing Firm in a Shaking World

Hebrews 12:26-29

When God spoke from Mount Sinai his voice shook the earth, but now he makes another promise: "Once again I will shake not only the earth but the heavens also." This means that all of creation will be shaken and removed, so that only unshakable things will remain.
Since we are receiving a Kingdom that is unshakable, let us be thankful and please God by worshiping him with holy fear and awe. For our God is a devouring fire.

A person would have to be living in a bubble to not see, know and understand that our whole world is shaking like it has never shaken before. It would be wrong of me or anyone else to take the current events of the world and sensationalize them just to get a platform to build a ministry. But, it would also be wrong to ignore the world-shaking events as if they have nothing to do with anything, thereby bringing people into a false sense of security and peace.

There is a place for us to stand in the midst of the storm and the ensuing confusion that surely comes and be a voice of truth that positions people rightly before the Lord.

It is imperative that God's people align themselves to what God knows or does so there is neither fear nor apathy working to immobilize us.

There are those that are all about *doomsday*, while others are about, *peace, peace*, but we are to be about the message of redemption of our Christ to many people who are lost in trauma while others are equally lost in living it up in safety. The unsaved in either place are lost at the edge of the worst event in their life—death without ever knowing God or His Son's plan to redeem and rescue them.

Even with all the wars, droughts, famines, the days we are living in are not just touching a region, but an entire world. Every king and every kingdom is feeling the movement. Every sinner is feeling the tremors. The empires of man are even now seeing the fault lines in their foundations, destabilizing the structures they've put in place. The things people have trusted in are failing them, right and left. They are scrambling to find something that isn't shaking and failing them.

Every believer should be feeling for those who tremble outside the Ark of Safety.

We know we have entered a truly prophetic season of awakening. At the same time the foundations of the world are shaking, there is another kind of rumbling—there is a powerful move of God developing at an ever-increasing rate in the nations of the world. There have been markers of that movement of God towards His people on earth and their resounding of His voice back to the heavenlies.

- ***Intercession*** has rooted itself deep into the hearts of a people determined to take hold the horns of the altar on behalf of the lost, to see the harvest come in.
- ***Worship*** has deepened and opened doors of understanding to the holiness of God and yet His nearness to His people.
- ***Warfare*** has gripped the heart of a people who are tired of sitting idle while the devil has his way in the hearts and lives of their loved ones, the cities they live in, the nations of the world, governments, courts and yes, the church.
- ***The Word of God*** has opened up in waves of revelation of the hidden mysteries of the Kingdom, things that were never tapped into even in past revivals. There are things that were prepared for and kept hidden until this day when it suddenly opened up

to those who were willing to mine the depths to find the vein of gold.

There has been a church, the living, and breathing, moving Church of the Living God that has been strengthening herself, preparing herself and moving to impact her world in these last days. She is a glorious church, redeemed by the blood of the Lamb, walking in a corrupted world, without spot of wrinkle or any such thing, declaring the salvation of the Lord.

It is that church that will stand, even during times of shakings.

God wants His people to be the strongest, the most prepared of all people. He wants His church to shine forth in the dark and difficult times as a people from a Kingdom of Light that cannot be shaken. He wants them to shine out in the darkness; to outshine every governmental, secular organization currently operating. He wants them to reveal to a world that is fast losing hope in other things, that there is a Christ who loves them and wants to redeem them in these days of increasing turmoil, fear and war.

He wants us to be available to Him because of the one thing we have that many others do not—A Rock to stand on—one that is impossible to be shaken by anything happening on earth, from the beginning of her history to the current day until the end of time.

This is the Rock to which we fix ourselves in faith.

But, I believe there is still a church world that has yet to notice there are storm clouds gathering that are going to trouble their world, up close and personal. Many, for some reason, have chosen to live with inside their own walls as if they will escape all hardship.

The first church came into existence in the fires of adversity, persecution and a great expansion of God's Kingdom through souls being saved. Everyone who served God had to decide if they were willing to live a life that was cross-wise to the existing culture they lived in. Their choices many times were a choice to live as one dead to their rights to live.

The Last Days believers, church, will be of the same caliber as the first—faithful, true and loyal to the cause of Christ, *no matter what.* They too will see the ingathering of a massive harvest of new souls into the Kingdom of God, not just in the midst of, but possible because of the shakings that have begun and will yet increase as it comes closer to the return of the Lord.

Many times in history, things came to stay and never went back to the way they used to be. America and other nations of the world will no doubt experience an awakening for the sake of the souls yet in need of Jesus, but there is absolutely no guarantee that the next election won't plunge us deeper into a chasm too deep to get out. There is no guarantee our dollar will last the year.

The only guarantee we have is Jesus.

We have had people say, *"They always live on the negative side, unnecessarily alarming others with all this talk about preparing for hard times . . ."* Well, folks, the hard times are upon us. It's time for the revival church, in particular, to get a reality check and wake up to the facts—our world is shaking and many within the church are still living as if this is just a passing thing.

There's a time to blow the trumpet in Zion and sound the alarm on God's Holy Mountain—and that time is now!

- ***I am alarmed*** when the "prophets" are still crying, *"Peace, peace, peace,"* when there is none except in Jesus.
- ***I am alarmed*** at the number of people that have been led to believe that church membership, water baptism, church attendance and charitable giving are equal to salvation.
- ***I am alarmed*** that people are still disputing over styles of worship instead of worshipping God.
- ***I am alarmed*** that the structures of man continue to be established without a thought for the original plan God had for His church.
- ***I am alarmed*** at the apathy and complacency that still resides in the church.

- ***I am alarmed*** at the level of compromise that seals the fate of so many who believe they are okay with God because they believe in Him.
- ***I am alarmed*** that God moved to visit His people and He could not get inside the doors.
- ***I am alarmed*** that there are still people that will reject the message of preparation, repentance and holiness.

We need to quit telling people what they want to hear and begin to tell them what they need to hear. I am not happy about the things going on either, not in the world or what I still see at work in the church, but a good dose of *wake up and smell the coffee* is needed.

- ***Our faithfulness*** to our church is not going to save us.
- ***Our denomination*** is not going to save us.
- ***Our bank accounts and retirement funds*** are not going to save us.
- **Our government** is not going to save us.

The only One who can save us is Jesus! And to stand in that salvation through every storm, in Him alone is imperative!

When a prophetic timetable begins to open up and be fulfilled according to God's Word, it is time to get our eyes on the Lord and Savior, Jesus Christ, the Rock of our Salvation.

Part I

I will Build My Church

Matthew 7:24-27

"Anyone who listens to my teaching and follows it is wise, like a person who builds a house on solid rock. Though the rain comes in torrents and the floodwaters rise and the winds beat against that house, it won't collapse because it is built on bedrock. But anyone who hears my teaching and ignores it is foolish, like a person who builds a house on sand. When the rains and floods come and the winds beat against that house, it will collapse with a mighty crash." NLT

CHAPTER 1

BEFORE

John 1:1a

"In the beginning was the Word . . ."

Before anything and everything else was made—before all created things—before the sun, moon, stars—before the Milky Way and the earth—before the devil and evil—before mankind—before idols and idol worshippers—before the nations, presidents, kings and queens and world rulers—before governments, senates, congresses, elections, winners and losers—before you, your church, your denomination—before all the words that have ever been spoken by mankind—before sickness, disease, doctors and drugs—before preachers and sermons, worship leaders and songwriters—before deacons, teachers, prophets, evangelists, apostles and pastors and other church leaders—before revival, revivalists and awakenings—before intercessors and prayer movements—before John the Baptist,

The Word was with God (John 1:1b)

We must never forget this truth—Jesus was before!

If we forget it, we might think too much of the devil's power, other men's power or even our power *or* we may think too much of the damage done by evil and forget the Redeemer.

- Before the earth—***He was Creator***
- Before darkness—***He was Light***
- Before man—***He was Breath***

- Before evil—***He was Holy***
- Before sin—***He was Redeemer***
- Before sickness—***He was Healer***
- Before bondage—***He was Deliverer***
- Before the Bible—***He was the Word***
- Before lost—***He was the Way***
- Before deception—***He was Truth***
- Before the church—***He was the Head***
- Before death—***He was Life***
- Before government—***He was the King of Kings and Lord of Lords***

And so much more than that . . .

- Before hate—***He was Love***
- Before depression—***He was Hope***
- Before weakness—***He was Strength***
- Before sadness—***He was Joy***
- Before loss—***He was Restoration***
- Before turmoil—***He was Peace***
- Before fear—***He was Shelter***
- Before shame—***He was Lifter of your Head***
- Before rejection—***He was Acceptance***
- Before empty—***He was Fullness***

And He is still yet more . . .

- Before hungry—***He was Bread***
- Before thirsty—***He was Living Water***
- Before wayward—***He was Shepherd***

An ultimately . . .

- Before religion—***He was I Am***

He's a Rock, a High Tower, the Provider, the Revelator; Grace and Mercy

He's all we need!

> ***Revelation 1:8*** (Emphasis Added)—*I am Alpha and Omega, the beginning and the ending, saith the Lord, which is, and **which was,** and which is to come, the Almighty.*

Jesus is an *eternity* Jesus.

He didn't start in the manger and end at the cross.

All that He was, He is yet to this day, and will be to the end of time *as we know it on earth*, and will be the same, yesterday, today and forever!

> ***1 Peter 1:18-20*** (Emphasis Added)
>
> *18 Forasmuch as ye know that ye were not redeemed with corruptible things, as silver and gold, from your vain conversation received by tradition from your fathers;*
>
> *19 But with the precious blood of Christ, as of a lamb without blemish and without spot:*
>
> *20 Who verily was foreordained **before** the foundation of the world, but was manifest in these last times for you,*

He was before

God did not send a little empty shell of a human being to Bethlehem, He sent Jesus, *the one in whom the fullness of the Godhead dwelt bodily.* (Colossians 2:9) Everything was already in Him; His coming to earth just revealed all He was to mankind, and He's so much more than we can presently see.

There are no words on earth that can ever describe the majesty of this Jesus who came, lived, suffered and died for mankind. His blood was not that of bulls and goats; His was precious, holy blood, the blood of the Lamb of God who came to take away the sins of the world. This is the Jesus who was sent. This is the Jesus who came.

This is the Jesus who is the Bedrock of our Faith; God incarnate!

John who bore witness of him cried out, saying, *"This was he of whom I spoke, He that cometh after me is preferred before me: for he was* ***before*** *me. And of his fullness have all we received, and grace for grace."*(John 1:15-16) (Emphasis Added)

It is absolutely essential that we understand the Truth about Jesus; He was and is and will yet be for all eternity—*Before us.*

Even though a world gone wrong has taken everything He has said and done from Genesis 1:1 to the present day and ran with it without even acknowledging Him, we must not. The one and only reason the world and the apostate church are on shifting sand is because they have no standing with Jesus who is the Bedrock of our Faith.

Jesus is the foundation of all things.

> ***Acts 17:28-29****—For in him we live, and move, and have our being; as certain also of your own poets have said, for we are also his offspring. Forasmuch then as we are the offspring of God, we ought not to think that the Godhead is like unto gold, or silver, or stone, graven by art and man's device.*

And the Word was God (John 1:1c)

When Jesus is denied and rejected, the earth under our feet begins to shift from Rock to sand and all our houses we have built in our name will surely crumble.

When Jesus is accepted and obeyed, the earth under our feet begins to shift from sand to Rock and the house we build there will surely stand.

CHAPTER 2

PERILOUS TIMES

Genesis 1:1-2

In the beginning God created the Heaven and the earth.
And the earth was without form, and void . . .

In the days of antiquity, *before creation*, the Word tells us the condition in which the earth lay. It was a planet that was in complete and utter ruin.

Genesis 1 tells us that

- ***The earth was without form***—a place of confusion, a place that was worthless and laid to waste.
- ***And it was void***—a total undistinguishable ruin. It was not even a shell of its former self. Any trace of what it once was had been obliterated.
- ***And, worse than that—darkness was upon the face of the deep***—it was not just a surface darkness. The darkness was a heavy blanket of misery, destruction, death, ignorance, sorrow and wickedness.

The earth was a place of deep agitation—an abyss.

It was primal chaos before creation, nothing but a disorderly, dark mass of nothing. The perplexity and agitation was the force that controlled the environment, as it were.

This worthless planet was void of the presence of God—but God's Spirit moved and said, *"Let there be Light."* It was no accident or freak of nature that put the light in first. Light draws a line and separates darkness from itself. There is no battle for dominance when light is present for it dispels the darkness.

It was by the Word of God the world was formed and filled by God's Spirit. God did it all with expectation that this glorious creation, imbued with the Seed of His Word, reproduce after its kind.

And then, after all the earth was in place in all her glory and beauty, the last remaining crown God would place would be someone like Himself—mankind, starting with Adam and then Eve.

And sadly, it was in this ideal place, created and held in place by God's Word and given life by God's Spirit, a place of fellowship with God—man fell into sin and death entered the human race and a curse fell upon everything.

The serpent had infiltrated the garden and perverted God's Word and darkened the nature of mankind through the original seed of mankind. He was smooth with his words and brought a mixture to the true and pure Word of God. She came into agreement with and began to dialogue with this alluring creature.

The serpent lied and *she was smitten and then bitten* and then death entered her veins—as if a rattlesnake had pressed its fangs into her heart. From that moment forward, her life was darkened and chaotic. Of course, she shared the bite of the poison with her husband, Adam, and they were expelled from God's glorious presence.

It is amazing that God can give something so wonderful, pure and clean to mankind and in only a matter of time they return it to the mass of chaos it was before creation.

God knew that man would need a redeemer and God knew what to do to redeem—He would send a Savior!

Genesis 3:14-15—(Emphasis Added) *And the Lord God said unto the serpent, Because thou hast done this, thou art cursed above all cattle, and above every beast of the field; upon thy belly shalt thou go, and dust shalt thou eat all the days of thy life: And I will put enmity between thee and the woman, and between thy seed and her seed;* ***it shall bruise thy head, and thou shalt bruise his heel.***

Isaiah 53:3-6—(Emphasis Added) *He is despised and rejected of men; a man of sorrows, and acquainted with grief: and we hid as it were our faces from him; he was despised, and we esteemed him not. Surely he hath borne our griefs, and carried our sorrows: yet we did esteem him stricken, smitten of God, and afflicted.* ***But he was wounded for our transgressions; he was bruised for our iniquities: the chastisement of our peace was upon him;*** *and with his stripes we are healed. All we like sheep have gone astray; we have turned everyone to his own way; and the Lord hath laid on him the iniquity of us all.*

1 Peter 1:18-20—(Emphasis Added) *Forasmuch as ye know that ye were not redeemed with corruptible things, as silver and gold, from your vain conversation received by tradition from your fathers; But with the precious blood of Christ, as of a lamb without blemish and without spot: Who verily was* ***foreordained before*** *the foundation of the world, but was manifest in these last times for you,*

Revelation 13:8—(Emphasis Added) *And all that dwell upon the earth shall worship him, whose names are not written in the book of life of the* Lamb ***slain from the foundation of the world.***

The Void in Me

We have established a Biblical foundation of truth in regards to historical things of antiquity; the world, nations, events and people and how God felt about the Void of God's Word in them. We have seen through scripture and real life the cataclysmic effect upon anything that is voided by man by rejecting the Word of God by the work of His Spirit.

We know God's Word is powerful, sharp and quick and effective and is not void.

> ***Isaiah 55:11****—So shall my word be that goes forth out of my mouth: it shall not return unto me void, but it shall accomplish that which I please, and it shall prosper in the thing whereto I sent it.*

It is evident God sent His Word in Jesus Christ to earth and further established His Word through the inspired Scriptures, not just containing the Word of God *but in fact is the Word of God.* And it is also evident from history past and the present day we live, that mankind has the power to either accept or reject and invalidate the Word spoken to him by free will.

All around us people's lives are blatantly falling apart.

- ***We know*** that alcohol and drug abuse is at an all-time high—and not just on skid row but also in corporate America and Hollywood and the neighbor next door and maybe even in your families.
- ***We know*** that many, in and out of the church are addicted to pornography and are in moral failure mode on many other levels.
- ***We know*** that adultery, divorce and abuse ravage many homes, including many you know.

It is not just the people of low estate, poor, uneducated and unemployed—there are people in high places, living the high life, people teaching our kids at school, leading the nation's churches, sitting in government seats, judges benches—people who for all appearances are successful, happy and living a good life—*but destitute*—derelict of true hope and happiness—living in a shell of degrading humanity.

The decisions of those sitting in churches reflect a void as degradation has hit the church with a tidal wave of opposing arguments.

Stats on marriage, divorce, abortion, sexuality, pornography, abuse, adultery, drinking, smoking and recreational drugs—reflect the truth that a great void of God's Word has developed—*one in which God's Word has been rejected as,* non-relevant, out-dated, narrow-minded, unloving and harsh

. . . And it is shocking that this is the attitude of many in the church today.

Jesus' claim as the *only way* has been refuted by the great religious minds, but also the small arguments of our minds also find *another way when* we want it.

> ***John 14:6b***— *. . . I am the way,* the truth, and the life: *no man cometh unto the Father, but by me.*

The greatest void of all is to have known the ways of righteousness and turned from truth to darkness.

Any statistic on just about any subject will reveal deep problems for mankind, the church and families in the modern world we live in. I am talking about lives that are spiritually empty, *void of the Word of God,* without foundation, light, lost and undone without God or His Son, living on the edge of eternity with only one breath between them and hell.

The nations, *multitudes in the valley of decision,* will be swallowed by the developing world system of darkness, lies and deception.

Everyone is bewailing the death of common sense, wondering at *what in the world is going on* around them as they watch people do some of the most outrageous things. Sometimes there are no words to express the sense of shock at what is currently being reported on the daily news.

But should we not bewail those who are being sucked into the whirlpool of deception, lies and darkness, *a place where the Word of God has been opposed and rejected*, creating the greatest void of all?

It is such intense spiritual darkness that will parallel the days of Noah and Sodom and Gomorrah as spiritual darkness will attempt to totally engulf humanity and take them back to the moral morass of chaos once again. God's Word, *(not the notion of God),* Jesus Christ *(not the Jesus of our imagination)* and the Scriptures *(not our interpretation of what God has said)* from Creation to Christ have been nullified in: Government, Education, Religion, Homes and marriages, the Raising of children and other Choices of the Heart

Our cities are filled with people who are living in a void.
Our family members exist in a void.
People sitting next to us on church pews are dwelling in a void.

And some reading this, though you love Jesus and want to serve Him, have *places of void*, places God's Word is not preeminent.

I have met many of God's people who are living with voids in their lives that God would love to breathe His Spirit into; places of fear, rejection, self-pity, insecurity; grief, sorrow, pain; confusion, hopelessness, depression, darkness; sickness, weakness. These are places where pressures build, pain is experienced, troubles come, and persecution happens, sickness brings you low, disasters happen; life goes wrong and loss is suffered.

And there are those who have been living with a seed of darkness in their heart, growing and swelling with words designed to increase darkness—but God desires to turn the light of truth on and dispel the darkness of the soul. These are places of hurt, resentment, unforgiveness; places of anger, revenge, hatred, betrayal, offenses, grievances; places of complaints and murmuring; places of accusation—*even against God . . .*

- *If you're the healer, why . . . ?*
- *If you're the provider, why . . . ?*
- *If you're God, why do bad things happen?*
- *Why did God do this to me?*

- *If I'm a child of God, why is everything going wrong?*
- *I've prayed and prayed and nothing's happening!*
- *Where are the signs of your appearing?*

Maybe there are some who have places void of God's peace and truth that God's Spirit desires to fill; places of strife, division, contention; places of legalism, religion, critical spirit; places of self-righteousness, self-deception, pride; places of arguments, imaginations and opinions. These are places where people, who say they love God's Word, read God's Word and hear God's Word, may also argue with God's Word in key areas of their life.

Many times because we think a certain thought when we hear God's Word and feel Him trying to work in our lives, we may get in direct conflict with the Word that would penetrate. We do know how to argue our point—and most of those arguments are inside where no one else knows the struggle we are in to just let God have His way.

For some there are void places that God's Spirit wants to fill; places of secret sins, presumption; control, manipulation and failure. There are places where you have been documenting your life by your failures rather than the victories in Christ Jesus and His Grace, legalistically going over them as a prosecuting attorney before a judge, seeking some kind of stiff sentence that will tell you how bad you have been. Have you been giving a daily list to Jesus of *your miserable attempts* to live an overcoming life and then beating your own back with a lash of self-incrimination?

Every human void is filled with darkness and deep turmoil until God's Spirit breathes new life.

Let God's Word by His Grace fill that void. He desires to *brood over the face of this dark water* and bring the Word of light and life home to your spirit. You keep repenting for failure as if every attempt you make and fail is sinful. God says, "*Fall on the Grace of God.*" He is able to lift you up and help you stand in your weakness. He is strong where you are weak.

Jesus said our bellies were to be filled with Rivers of Living Water which is the Spirit of God, but sometimes what churns in us is not God at all but places void of His establishing, healing Word.

There are voids in lives; specific places that have either not been penetrated because they are closed, barred and protected ***or*** places the Word has been rejected, shoved aside, ignored and refused entrance.

It is time for the people of God to get their bellies filled, allow the Light to penetrate the dark voids of our lives and remove the wilderness of our hearts where we wander in a famine of God's Word—*a Soul Drought.*

> ***Psalms 119:11***—*Thy word have I hid in mine heart, that I might not sin against thee.*

> ***Psalms 119:105***—*Thy word is a lamp unto my feet, and a light unto my path.*

We need to understand today that every void in our life that is not filled with the Word *is without form and void,* where darkness covers the face of the deep—a place of raging waters and inner turmoil.

We may *have our face on*—a good front—the outside secured—but we know there are places deep inside that the Light of God's Word has not been able to enter to create a new heart. God's Spirit breathed upon the face of the deep and there was a fullness of the Spirit of God where that breath moved. The deep, hidden, dark, turmoil places of the earth received the breath of God's Spirit and were made new.

God's breath is still moving today, but we must receive it.

> ***John 1:1-5***—*In the beginning was the Word, and the Word was with God, and the Word was God. The same was in the beginning with God. All things were made by him; and without him was not anything made that was made. In him was life; and the life was the light of men. And the light shineth in darkness; and the darkness comprehended it not.*

In the Beginning—*Before* everything else was—*Before* you and the problems you face—*Before* your family, your sons and daughters, mothers and father, brothers and sisters . . . *Before* everything existed . . . was the Word!

> ***Matthew 4:4***—(Emphasis Added) *But he (Jesus) answered and said, "It is written, Man shall not live by bread alone, but by every word that proceeds out of the mouth of God."*

"Consume the Word until the Word consumes you."
Smith Wigglesworth

"All we need in Christ, we shall find in Christ. If we want little, we shall find little. If we want much, we shall find much. But if, in utter helplessness, we cast our all on Christ, He will be to us the whole treasury of God."

Henry Benjamin Whipple

> ***Revelation 19:11-13*** (Emphasis Added)—*And I saw heaven opened, and behold a white horse; and he that sat upon him was called Faithful and True, and in righteousness he doth judge and make war. His eyes were as a flame of fire, and on his head were many crowns; and he had a name written, that no man knew, but he himself. And he was clothed with a vesture dipped in blood . . .*

And his name is called The Word of God.

CHAPTER 3

GROUND ZERO

Philippians 2:5-8

Let this mind be in you, which was also in Christ Jesus:
Who, being in the form of God, thought it not robbery to be equal with God:
But made himself of no reputation, and took upon him the form of a servant, and was made in the likeness of men:
And being found in fashion as a man, he humbled himself, and became obedient unto death, even the death of the cross.

- Ground Zero—a scene of great devastation

My mind goes back to a television program called, *"Extreme Makeover—Home Edition,"* and a particular story:

A family had suffered the loss of their home by fire and had to move in with relatives. Soon they got a trailer house and were beginning to settle in and adjust. One day the father took three of his children to the river with him for a swim. He took his little girl, about age 7, and putting her on his shoulders went out into the water. Waiting on the shore were his two sons, ages 9 and 19.

As he waded out something happened. He dropped off into deep water and began to struggle. He told his little girl to hang onto his neck real tight as he struggled to get control. The little girl screamed. The oldest brother saw the problem from shore and went in to help. He got his little sister to a safe place in the river where she could get in by herself. He then turned back to help his dad. As he tried to help, they both drowned.

The story was concluded with this mother and her two remaining children getting a new home. The local fire department made a plaque in the son's honor and put hung in a prominent place in the house. It greatly moved the mother and her children to see it there to help remind them that he had made the ultimate sacrifice—giving his life to save another.

- The elder brother was safe on the shore.
- He saw the water overwhelming his loved ones.
- He put his life on the line to rescue them.
- He made the ultimate sacrifice for them.

This is a human story that reveals a truth; in each of us is the capacity to save a drowning person, someone trapped in a burning car, someone who is having a heart attack, someone who is dying; to make that split second decision to put ourselves on equal ground with them—*Ground Zero*—their place of devastation; to enter into their world and reach out to help.

From the time of creation the world has been being taken over by the original chaos of the beginning. The raging waters of history have taken a toll on people who had no one to rescue them. The best they could do was to come year after year and make a sacrifice to try to push back judgment for the time being.

- We see the world in Noah's day and wonder, *"How could it become so fallen?"*

Look at the overwhelming flood of wickedness and filth that had covered the earth:

> ***Genesis 6:5***—*And God saw that the wickedness of man was great in the earth; every imagination of the thoughts of his heart was only evil continually.*
>
> ***Genesis 6:11***—*The earth also was corrupt before God, and the earth was filled with violence.*

- We also see the cities of Sodom and Gomorrah and the sin and degradation that had come like a billowing flood of hedonism.

  Ezekiel 16:49-50—(Paraphrased) *Behold, this was the iniquity of Sodom . . . pride, fullness of bread, abundance of idleness was in her neither did she strengthen the hand of the poor and needy. They were haughty, committed abomination before me:*

They ended up *without form* and *void* and *darkness* was upon the face of *their* deep.

The chaos and darkness and indescribable ruin of the day the Twin Towers were destroyed in an act of violence by terrorists will live on for many reasons. It represents two things: the evil of man and the hero side of man. Those with dark hearts were willing to spend their lives for their cause *and* those first responders were willing to spend their lives for their cause.

And in the heart of the fiery heat of the battle for life there were those who laid down their lives for another; *heroes who we will never forget.*

- The man dressed in a fine suit, only moments before sitting at a desk earning a living, was now blackened by the smoke of disaster as he made his way to help a momma, a daddy, a son, a daughter, a wife, a husband get back home, knowing in his heart he would not come back to his own family.
  - *He ran to the roar of the fiery heat and paid the ultimate price.*
- The lady in her fine clothes, now covered in ash and with hair singed, shielded another, trying to cover a friend, a neighbor, a fearful co-worker with her own body.
  - *Her heart was gripped with the terror of the moment, but ran to the roar of the battle for life and paid the ultimate sacrifice.*
- Firefighters, in full gear, ran without thought for their lives into the heat of the battle and laid down their lives.

  - *They were trained to do battle and did not fail in fear, but took their heart to the limit in honor and paid the ultimate sacrifice.*
- Others at ground zero lived to tell the story of the horrors of that day, coming out of the fray with the smell of smoke on them.
  - *They, as it were, had gone to the edge of hell to pull some back and made a difference in lives.*
- Policemen, without thought also laid their lives on the line, thinking only of saving a human being.
  - *They were not paid to fight fires, but stepped over the line and entered a realm of battle for the living, putting their own lives in jeopardy, with some paying the ultimate sacrifice.*

And there were those on the airplane that rushed into the face of darkness and paid the ultimate price to save many from certain destruction.

Many, many nameless, faceless, unsung heroes; thousands of low-wage workers who mopped up toxic dust in the aftermath, who did remarkable things for others, totally forgetting their own mortality and running to the roar to save another.

And the nations of the world grieved and stared in wonder at the heroes of that day and the terror of the darkness.

It was a day that stopped the whole world in its tracks.

People, with that *saving and rescuing nature of God* created into them had rescued others, not realizing they were in His likeness as they jumped into the river to save the drowning person, pulled a person from a burning car or ran into a burning house to try to save someone.

There was another day that stopped the world in its tracks. a man called Jesus Christ, who left a mark that has been etched on human hearts since the beginning. He stepped over the line and came down to meet those in need of rescue.

Jesus! It's the greatest story ever told of a world-wide rescue that would cover thousands of years. There has never been a day like the day Jesus entered this old, sinful, fallen world, in the form of a little baby boy, lying in a manger in Bethlehem.

It was the form He took, *humble, innocent, and helpless like a little lamb, God Incarnate wrapped in the flesh of humanity*, that was so remarkable.

Philippians 2:6-7 speaks of this man, "*Who, being in the form of God, thought it not robbery to be equal with God: But made himself of no reputation, and took upon him the form of a servant, and was made in the likeness of men.*"

He was one who could have told the world, *"I AM equal with God,"* but He made himself of no reputation!

The Word of God in this same scripture setting tells us we are to be of the same mind. Jesus was mild, meek, humble and lowly. He was born in a barn, lived in a place people questioned as being significant . . . "*Can any good come from this place?*" He was despised by the religious orders and routinely hunted like an animal, with people laying in wait to kill Him.

While human rescue can be done by a compassionate person who does not know Jesus—there is one rescue that takes someone who steps into the world of great darkness and brings the light of the gospel to a dying people.

Our *elder brother*, Jesus, was safe on the shores of heaven. He could hear the cries of the drowning masses of humanity.

The psalmist cries out in Psalms 69:1-3 "*Save me, O God; for the waters are come in unto my soul. I sink in deep mire, where there is no standing: I am come into deep waters, where the floods overflow me. I am weary of my crying: my throat is dried: mine eyes fail while I wait for my God.*"

For Jesus, He saw, not one or two, but the masses of humanity in deep trouble, drowning in their sins, overwhelmed by the angry billows of life.

Jesus, safe on heaven's shore, made a decision to jump into the waters of life and rescue the perishing *and it cost him His life.* There was no other way. He didn't tip-toe around the edges but went in to deep, dark waters, the seas of humanity to die so they could live.

The depths of waters he dove into were sin's dark waves. He placed Himself at the mercy of the waves to get redemption to those who would choose to be saved.

He could not sit and watch while they died so he became a *"drowning man"* in their stead, helping them out while giving up His life.

> ***John 15:13***—*Greater love hath no man than this, that a man lay down his life for his friends.*

Back to the plaque that was made in the honor of the elder brother's memory; today we have plaques hanging in homes, churches, printed on the front of Bibles, hanging around people's necks and on rings on their fingers—*the Cross.*

This memorial plaque is in the honor of the One who paid the ultimate sacrifice by laying down His life, not just for a man, but for the world.

It is one thing for one of us to die to save another individual, our equal, but to take upon yourself the entire race of human beings, from creation to the end of time, and immerse yourself in their collective sins, pain, sickness and loss and fallen human nature, is something that only One has ever done.

Jesus came down and took the lowest seat to die the lowest death; the death of a criminal for you and me!
Jesus paid it ALL at Ground Zero; the Cross of Christ.

CHAPTER 4

BECAUSE

Luke 4:18
(Emphasis Added)

The Spirit of the Lord is upon me, ***because*** *he hath anointed me to preach the gospel to the poor; he hath sent me to heal the brokenhearted, to preach deliverance to the captives, and recovering of sight to the blind, to set at liberty them that are bruised,*

Jesus had just closed the book and sat down. He had read from Isaiah 61 concerning the Spirit of the Lord anointing Him.

He had spoken to them about what the anointing was for:

- Preach the gospel to the poor
  - Feeding a beggar who, cringing before those from whom he begs, toils daily to find something to eat
- Heal the brokenhearted
  - Bind up, as in placing a compress for healing, bringing comfort to the crushed in heart
- Preach deliverance to the captives
  - Opening a dungeon to set free through salvation a prisoner of war
- Recovery of sight to the blind
  - To restore sight to the physically or mentally blind
- Set at liberty those that are bruised.
  - Bestow forgiveness and freedom to those who are crushed by sin and its consequences.

Look at this mandate and see the true reason for the anointing: to address the darkness, the void, the pain and confusion of mankind, *not just the mass*, but for the individual, for you and me.

When we read the words, *poor, brokenhearted, captive, blind and bruised*, we see people who are in need of a Redeemer. The anointing was upon the life of Jesus to save, heal and deliver people from a pit of despair, loss, pain, blindness and captivity.

I have known of ministries that act as if the anointing is to help build their reputation as one who can *heal the sick*, or as in some cases, put on shows of *casting out demons*. Some have even used the anointing and charged entrance of folks to partake of what Jesus gave away freely.

I believe Jesus' heart breaks for the abuse and misuse of the Holy Spirit and even those that falsify the gifts of the Spirit to gain a following for profit.

Jesus came to set the captives free and it was free to "*whosoever will.*" (John 3:16) Jesus' purpose was to meet people at *Ground Zero*, and rescue them out of the devastation that life had become for them.

- *He came* to break the chains of sin and sickness and call people forth from the grave.
- *He came* to heal the wounded and broken and sick, to fill the destitute and needy with the purpose for which they were born.
- *He came* with a mandate and God empowered Him to the fullest to do what He sent Him to do.

He wants to do the same with His Church. The anointing upon Jesus empowered Him by The Holy Spirit of God, to do the things that caused people to marvel and wonder and yes, even hate Him.

When Jesus asked His disciples *who they say He is* Peter answered saying, "*Thou art the Christ, the Son of the Living God.*" (Matthew 16:16) *Christ* in scripture means *the anointed Messiah, the Son of God*

Jesus came to save, heal and deliver—*that was what the anointing on His life was about.*

> ***Matthew 11:5***—*The blind receive their sight, and the lame walk, the lepers are cleansed, and the deaf hear, the dead are raised up, and the poor have the gospel preached to them.*

- ***He came because*** of the blind men.
- ***He came because*** of the demoniac in the tombs.
- ***He came because*** of the man with the withered hand.
- ***He came because*** of the lady with the bowed back.
- ***He came because*** of the lame man.
- ***He came because*** of the woman taken in adultery.
- ***He came because*** of the woman with the issue of blood.
- ***He came because*** of the rejects of society.
- ***He came because*** of the dead.
- ***He came because*** of the deaf and dumb.
- ***He came because*** of the lepers.
- ***He came because*** of you and me—to save, heal and deliver us.

He stood in that anointing, *as the Messiah*, when he called to the tomb of his dear friend, *"Lazareth, Come forth,"* and the man who had been dead for four days rose and walked out free.

There is an anointing that isn't contingent on circumstances, storms, trials, or persecution but is totally contingent upon the Holy Spirit and a person who is submitted to His Father's will.

Jesus, *no matter what was going on in His life*, whether He was being honored or cursed, was anointed!

- ***He was anointed*** when He knelt in the Garden of Gethsemane and yielded to His Father's Will.
- ***He was anointed*** when Judas kissed him in betrayal.
- ***He was anointed*** when He was arrested and taken to trial.
- ***He was anointed*** when He took the stripes for our healing upon His back.
- ***He was anointed*** when they pressed the crown of thorns into his head.

- ***He was anointed*** when He carried His cross to Golgotha
- ***He was anointed*** when His hands and feet were pierced.
- ***He was anointed*** when He turned to the thief on the cross and said, "*Today you shall be with me in Paradise.*"
- ***He was anointed*** when He cried out, "*Father, forgive them, for they know not what they do.*"
- ***He was anointed*** when He cried out, "*My God, My God, why have you forsaken Me?*"
- ***He was anointed*** when He *gave up the ghost* and died.
- ***He was anointed*** when they laid Him in the tomb and rolled the stone over the entrance and sealed it.

> ***Acts 13:29b—30*** *". . . they took him down from the tree, and laid him in a sepulcher. But God raised him from the dead."*

And, praise God,

- ***He was anointed*** when He was raised in resurrection power, defeating death and overwhelming the grave.

> ***1 Corinthians 15:14***—*And if Christ be not risen, then is our preaching vain, and your faith is also vain.*

Jesus Christ didn't just have anointed hands—His very being was permeated with the anointing of the Spirit of God.

> ***Romans 8:11***—*But if the Spirit of him that raised up Jesus from the dead dwell in you, he that raised up Christ from the dead shall also quicken your mortal bodies by his Spirit that dwelleth in you.*

So what is our mandate? It is to prepare our hearts for the anointing on every level. If we desire to walk where Jesus walked and do what Jesus did, we have to be like Jesus was.

Now, that's Bedrock Faith in its Finest Hour!

CHAPTER 5

THE MASTER BUILDER

Matthew 16:18b

". . . upon this ***Bedrock*** *I will build my church; and the gates of hell shall not prevail against it.*

Jesus had spent three and one half years pouring His life, vision, doctrine, the Kingdom into a small group of men He had chosen to be Apostles. This was part of the plan for God sending His Son to earth—to put in place a source of His Power on earth once Jesus returned to heaven.

Think of Jesus' powerful declaration coming out of His mouth, His voice, His eyes ablaze with passion, and His resolute will fixed on His call. He was preparing to create on earth a people who would bear His image to the world. It was a pivotal time in earth's history as prophecy began to unfold.

God was entrusting the earth to a living, breathing organism called the Church; the Church Jesus would build.

Jesus did not just start being a builder on earth as a man who was a carpenter's son, one who was going to take hammer and nails and build His Church.

Remember, Jesus was there at creation. He was there when man was first formed. He was there when man took the first breath God gave him. His building skills on earth were not based on things He learned on earth about building; He came as the Master Architect, the Master Builder.

Back to chapter one—everything was in Him to completely fulfill His Father's Will on earth, just as it was in heaven.

His tools were going so different from anything the builders of the Temple had ever seen or known. He was going to use the Apostles to lay the foundation and His disciples all down the generations as building blocks.

People have always been the building blocks of the Church.

1 Peter 2:5 tells us that we are stones that are alive, *"built up a spiritual house, an holy priesthood, to offer up spiritual sacrifices, acceptable to God by Jesus Christ."*

We see again in ***Ephesians 2:20-22*** this same truth expressed: *"Together, we are his house, built on the foundation of the apostles and the prophets. And the cornerstone is Christ Jesus himself. We are carefully joined together in him, becoming a holy temple for the Lord. Through him you Gentiles are also being made part of this dwelling where God lives by his Spirit." NLT* [2]

1 Corinthians 6:19-20 also asks a question while describing a truth to us: *"What? Know ye not that your body is the temple of the Holy Ghost which is in you, which ye have of God, and ye are not your own? For ye are bought with a price: therefore glorify God in your body, and in your spirit, which are God's."*

Even Peter's *(a piece of rock)* confession of his faith as being in *"Christ, the Son of the Living God,"* was a revelation of God upon which Jesus immediately found His *first stone* for the new thing called, *The Church* in ***Matthew 16***

There is no question in the mind of God that Jesus is not only the builder of His Church, but He is the Head of His Church.

Colossians 1:18 tells us, *"And he is the head of the body, the church: who is the beginning, the firstborn from the dead; that in all things he might have the preeminence.* (First in rank or influence; before)"

The church did not start with man and will not finish with man.

Jesus has preeminence!

- **Preeminent**—above or *before others*; (Chapter One) superior; surpassing: *Synonyms:* distinguished, peerless, supreme.

He is of the highest rank—higher than any *other architect* of the church

- **Architect**—the deviser, maker, or creator of anything:

The Church is a revelation of God on earth that is bound not to a building but to a people. When God sent His only begotten Son, He sent the Master Builder of the Church. His purpose with the New Testament Church was the same as it was with the Children of Israel; to bring a people to Himself that was separate and prepared to House His Glory on earth.

We didn't think He meant our church or denomination did we?

F.B Meyer made this comment: *"There is nothing, indeed, which God will not do for a man who dares to step out upon what seems to be the mist; though as he puts his foot down he finds* ***a rock*** *beneath him."*

This is how the continual lineage of faith in believers since the day Jesus declared His church to man, is built; people who believe Jesus and put their trust in Him alone. *That Rock* has been established and is waiting for *whosoever will*, to plant their feet in obedience to Jesus teachings. ***Matthew 7:24***

The Message says it this way, *"These words I speak to you are not incidental additions to your life, homeowner improvements to your standard of living. They are foundational words, words to build a life on. If you work these words into your life, you are like a smart carpenter who built his house on* ***solid rock."*** [3] (Emphasis Added)

Salvation through Jesus Christ puts you there and obedience to Him keeps you there—founded, grounded and secure in the Bedrock of your Faith.

God did not place His dear Son in *just any old place*; He put Him in *a prophetic city* with a *prophetic manger* in a *prophetic time.*

- ***He didn't send Jesus*** so we can have a nice Christmas; He sent Him so He could come as Light to darkness.
    - o ***Matthew 4:16****—The people which sat in darkness saw great light; and to them which sat in the region and shadow of death light is sprung up.*
- ***He didn't send Jesus*** so we can celebrate a colorful Easter; He sent Him so He could destroy the works of the devil.
    - o ***1 John 3:8b****—For this purpose the Son of God was manifested, that he might destroy the works of the devil.*
- ***He didn't send Jesus*** so we can have nice church services; He sent Jesus to wash and cleanse a people to be presented a glorious church, without spot or wrinkle or any such thing.
    - o ***Ephesians 5:27****—That he might present it to himself a glorious church, not having spot, or wrinkle, or any such thing; but that it should be holy and without blemish.*
- ***He didn't send Jesus*** to build a powerless Church; He sent Him to empower her to be filled with the Spirit of the Living God.
    - o ***Acts 1:8****—But ye shall receive power, after that the Holy Ghost is come upon you: and ye shall be witnesses unto me both in Jerusalem, and in all Judaea, and in Samaria, and unto the uttermost part of the earth.*

In the same way He had breathed the breath of life into Adam, He was going to breathe the breath of His Spirit into His Church. God has never created anything that is dead. In all that He created, from the smallest life to the greatest, He created life.

While man builds his church *his way*—Jesus is building His Church *His Way*!

Jesus was facing a religious giant of man's opinions and dogma the day He made the declaration that *He will build His Church*, but all He needed was just one man who believed in Him enough to confess Faith in Him.

Back to the question Jesus asked of His disciples as recorded *in **Matthew 16:13-19***, a question that must still be answered by each of us today: He asked, *"Who do men say that I the Son of man am?"*

- ***Their answer*** would define the building material of the first churches foundation.
- ***Our answer*** will give definition to the church in the same way.

I don't know if we truly understand how important *the confession of our faith* in Jesus Christ is in a world such as ours.

When Jesus asked, *"Who do you say I am?"* Peter gave the right answer in a religious world of many opinions about Jesus; He said, *"You, Jesus, are the Christ, the anointed Messiah, the Son of the Living God."* Jesus answered him saying, *"Flesh and blood has not revealed it to you but my Father in heaven."* Peter was hearing with the ears of the Spirit who Jesus truly was.

That is the need of the Church today, to have ears to hear what the Spirit is saying to us because it is God's Spirit that always leads us to Jesus.

Make no mistake about it; *the true-glorious-without-spot-or-wrinkle-or-any-such-thing-church* is rising up strong, victorious and powerful in these last days. The first Christians lived in one of the most strategic and powerful times for the Church, a time when the enemy would have aborted all plans and her destiny right in the season of her birth, *if he could have.*

It's not that he didn't try; it's that he failed!

In spite of all the efforts by evil men and all the diabolical plans of the devil and the resistance of the religious world, *the Church was born!*

It has remained a force to be reckoned with since its inception.

There is a lifeline of the Church of the LORD Jesus Christ, *a glorious lifeline*, one that has continued, in spite of all that men and devils have tried to do to destroy the Church.

Jesus also speaks of His undefeatable church in ***Matthew 18*** saying, "*The gates of hell shall not prevail against it.*" His Church is invincible, unable to be removed or destroyed. Jesus assures us that no matter what the devil throws against His Church it will not prevail.

Every inconceivable evil is within those gates: seductions, bewitching, deception, error, perversity, wolves in sheep's clothing, false prophets, false teachers, heresy, tables of devils, damnable doctrine of devils, pride, division, vain arguments, strife, and nuances of all these in different garments, personalities and manifestations sent to deceive.

The church Jesus builds in not able to be infiltrated by the resources of hell. *Oh, yes, the devil will try;* he has no choice but to try and stop you, but *God, by His Holy Spirit* has put everything under Jesus' feet and given us everything we need to be overcomers. ***Ephesians 1:20-23***

The Church Jesus builds has the full resources of Heaven because God backs *His* Church

Though hell has raged and beat against the doors and went on murderous rampages all down through history—there is a church that is alive and well on planet earth—it is the Glorious Church of the Lord Jesus Christ.

- ***The problem is***—not everything that calls itself a church is The Church!
- ***The question is***—are you a part of *a church* or *The Church?*

Holy Men of God prophesied by Holy Unction and with Divine Foresight, the birth of Jesus Christ, the Messiah, who would come—the one who would transition the religious world into the new covenant.

When Jesus said, "*I will build my Church,*" it was as true and powerful as God saying, "*I will send my Son.*" Words spoken by Jesus were never void or chaotic, but powerful and true and meant to come to pass, *just He spoke them.*

Jesus does have His Church!

And the church continues to this day . . . The churches we see around the world today are a product of what Jesus set in motion. I don't get too mixed up in the discussion of what really constitutes the church simply because mankind has not always got it right. I simply turn back to the Word of God and see the first principles Jesus put in place and the fact that believers from the beginning have had a meeting place to gather for worship, prayer, equipping and serving their world they live in.

I don't care whether it has a steeple, a store front window or a thatched or tin roof, as long as Jesus built it. There is nothing wrong or biblically unsound in finding a group of people meeting some place they deem suitable for the church of a city, town, village, neighborhood, jungle . . .

There has been and always will be a church that is real; *organically grown by the Eternal Seed of God's Word.*

Since Jesus Christ set the church in order, there have been countless times in history when God, by His Spirit, spoke to man/woman to go to a certain place and establish His Church i.e., a meeting place where the saints of that city, region, town, village, would meet to be equipped and worship the Lord. Those places of worship would be set as a lighthouse in a dark place to shed the light of the gospel of the Lord Jesus Christ and to expand the Kingdom of God.

Churches all around the nations were prophesied before they came to pass and into the public view.

Micah 5:2 could read prophetically: "*But you,* (enter your church or ministry here), *though you are little among the larger cities and churches of* (enter your place here), *out of you shall come forth a mighty move of God that shall bring light to a dark region and people who live in that darkness.*"

Prophesy is a fire in the spirit of the one who receives it. They cannot help but speak it forth, regardless of the personal cost to them. They tried to and did kill some of the Prophets because of what they spoke.

Someone, somewhere, had a little prophetic seed dropped in their spirits and it nurtured in their hearts.

This is where every fresh move of God has begun, prophetically in the heart of a man or woman of God. I don't know if we have understood this yet, but God planted churches by the Living Breath of Prophecy to live!

- ***Jesus*** was a child of prophecy—*born by decree of God.*
- ***John the Baptist*** was a child of prophecy—*born by decree of God.*
- ***The Church*** is a child of prophecy—*born by decree of Jesus Christ.*

God never brought anything to life to watch it die, *except Jesus Christ* and He died that we might live.

I can remember my father, all of my life, being led by God to go a certain place to establish a church. He heard God, *plain and simple as that*! I remember how he held something new and fresh in his spirit as God began to drop the thing not yet born into his heart for a small desert town called, Parker, Arizona.

It was prophetic before it was a reality.

But soon, according to the Word of God delivered to a man of God's heart, he began to enact the will of God, as God developed within the heart of my father His plan. Oh, it was not some huge boom from heaven where a deep, resonate voice sounded to that little dry plot of ground; it was more like a *"step by step I will lead you."*

- He rented an armory from a Senator, ***by faith.***
- He bought a lot at the corner of the desert, ***by faith.***
- He purchased an old building belonging to the library, ***by faith.***
- He cut it in half and hauled it in two pieces down Navajo St., ***by faith.***
- He put it back together and remodeled it, ***by faith.***
- He preached, visited, led, ***by faith.***
- He expanded the Kingdom of God, ***by faith.***

And now, *because of that faith walk*, based on a prophetic word *(meaning, God spoke to him)* there is a church sitting on that piece of ground in that little desert town, though he has long ago left the area. Parker Assembly of God was born, *just as God had said it would.*

Others would have wondered why a man would go to the middle of a very hot desert, where there was nothing and build a church. It was the Spirit of Prophecy that drove him forward.

No doubt what God has spoke to you about His will for your life and ministry was just a seed that grew by the Spirit of Prophecy before you ever broke ground for the birth of the vision.

God breathed and His Church—*meaning the on-going, generation after generation of believers*—was conceived by the Supernatural Power of the Holy Ghost and built by Jesus Christ.

Jesus is the one who turned the lights and water on in His Church, bringing power and life by His Spirit to all through those who believe in and declare His name.

***NOTHING* that God births is *EVER* conceived by man, but *ALWAYS* by the Holy Ghost.**

Remember when the angel of the Lord came to Mary and spoke to her? In ***Luke 1:35*** He says, *"The Holy Ghost shall come upon thee, and the power of the Highest shall overshadow thee: therefore also that holy thing which shall be born of thee shall be called the Son of God."*

The Womb of Mary and a Supernatural Conception by the Holy Ghost brought reality to the prophecy to birth Jesus on the earth. It was also by the spoken Word of Jesus Christ to His disciples and a supernatural conception by the Holy Ghost at Pentecost, the Church was birthed.

What God is doing today, all over the world, in multitudes of ministries, churches, etc . . . is as Mary who said yes to the Holy Ghost. You have allowed and hosted the Holy Ghost to come upon you, to have the power of the Highest to overshadow you, so that the holy thing born of you would be called *Jesus* to the world around you.

Jesus was born to bring glory to His Father
The Church was born to magnify Jesus

There is no Jesus represented to your world until *the Mary Church* of this hour agrees to be used of God to carry this prophetic child to term. You have to agree once again to be willing to stand apart from all others and stand in a hard place—*just as Mary did.*

As soon as it was known that Mary was carrying a child, they tried to execute Mary, to destroy from the face of the earth, removing all evidence of the womb and its fruit—*the Messiah.*

Don't let anyone abort the will and purposes of God for your church!

You carry something precious in your spirit and when it comes forth, it will transform your city and a region that sits in darkness. When the church begins to understand that we are carrying Jesus to a lost and dying world, we too must be willing to pay the price of condemnation for what we bear within our spirits.

The Church declares what many do not want to hear: "*This child I am carrying, this visitation resulting in my vision of Christ's coming, is of the Holy Ghost!*"

Luke 2:7 records the birth of Jesus who came prophetically right on time, in the exact place spoken by God through prophecy. And it was God who broadcast it to the first people to hear of His Son's birth.

I have sat in hospitals waiting for my grandchildren to be born. The gift shop sells little pink or blue cigars that says, *"It's a boy"* or *"It's a girl,"* purchased by new fathers.

Oh, how our human announcements pale in comparison to God's the day His Son was born on earth; He sent an angelic choir to sing to the shepherds!

Luke 2:15-16 tells us of the shepherds making a decision to go to Bethlehem and see the thing which had come to pass that the Lord had made known to them. We know they went and found the baby lying in a manger.

Look at the same elements that existed then as do now—the shepherd's are in proximity of a move of God being birthed. They are doing what shepherd's do—watching over the flock of God. Then when it is made known to them that just down the street, God has moved into a small, *off-the-beaten-path-place*, into a little church that no one really goes to, what did they do?

They went with haste to find Jesus!

This is the kind of heart God is seeking in this Church today, *one that goes with haste to find Jesus;* those who will humbly kneel down in the straw of the altars and worship Him. It may be your church or our church where this move of God is taking place but worship must exude in that place where He may be found.

Whether anyone accepts it or not, regardless of how many people welcome it, or how many people/churches deny entrance to it, there is a very real move of God being birthed today.

Something has been born of the Spirit in our time, *as surely as* Jesus was born in Bethlehem. Jesus is coming to His Church in our day, *as surely as* Jesus entered into His Temple in the early days!

> ***Isaiah 55:6***—*Seek ye the LORD while he may be found, call ye upon him while he is near:*

The question is: Will we *go with haste* to see the thing that has come to pass, which the Lord has made known to us?

If there was a birthplace for the Church—it would be Bethlehem.

Jesus was the *first Church plant* in a little town called Bethlehem.

He came just as He was prophesied.

There are many powerful ministries, which may appear small and insignificant, or even relegated to *not really being a ministry*, but they have been prophesied, conceived and born non-the-less. And they yet remain a force to be reckoned with.

Why do you think the devil has tried to kill you, to stop the move of God in you, to stone to death or abort the purposes of God through you?

You are not dead and though weapons have been launched against you from your prophetic beginning to the season you are now in, *you live*—because God recognizes you as the Church Jesus built!

CHAPTER 6

NOT MY WILL

Matthew 6:10

Thy kingdom come. Thy will be done in earth, as it is in heaven.

The will is by definition: *"The mental faculty by which one deliberately chooses or decides upon a course of action."*

- ***I wonder*** if we realize that just one little choice could eternally alter our standing with God, for the good or the bad.
- ***I wonder*** if we realize that just one little argument with God about something He is asking of us holds great power over our future, depending on who wins and who yields?

We all have a mind and a will from which we decide what we are going to do and how we're going to get there. We are good at setting goals and planning and placing things into *our mental committees* to enact *our will*. But, when you are talking about God, the creator of all things and His great and Infallible Mind deciding upon a course of action and exhibiting His will, it is a totally different thing. And, unfortunately, this is where man most often clashes with God.

The *bright thoughts* of our own minds and the actions that come from our will are actually darkness to God and battle against His Will.

Ephesians 4:17-18 (Emphasis Added)

> *17 This I say therefore, and testify in the Lord, that ye henceforth walk not as other Gentiles walk, in the* ***vanity of their mind,***
>
> *18 Having the understanding darkened, being* **alienated** (Estranged, to be a non-participant) *from the life of God through the ignorance that is in them, because of the* ***blindness of their heart:***

I was taken with the word, ***"Estranged."*** The dictionary definition means, *"To turn away in feeling or affection; alienate the affections of."* It is a word we hear in human relationships but this scripture reveals that walking in the vanity of our minds alienates and estranges us from God.

That is what our mind is capable of.

<u>**There are three things spoken of in this portion of scripture:**</u>

- ***Vanity of their mind***—Transient and depraved *(corrupt, wicked, or perverted)* thoughts of the intellect.
- ***Understanding darkened***—the deep thoughts of the mind being made obscure
- ***Blindness of their heart***—the callousness of the thoughts and feelings

This can occur on two levels—personally and yes, even corporately, as a body of believers grows apathetic towards the things of God. Whether this occurs in the inner sanctum of our own hearts or in the church, we are in trouble.

Jesus held the secret to the churches success; it was and is and will always be about God's will. He entered into a time of prayer where the will of His Father was being finalized in His life, just before His arrest and crucifixion.

Few of us have truly put ourselves in the place of Jesus in that time of heart-breaking resolve as He bent His will to that of His Father.

> ***Luke 22:42*** (Emphasis Added)—*Saying, Father, if thou be willing, remove this cup from me: nevertheless* ***not my will, but thine, be done.***

- **Will**—What one wishes or has determined shall be done; of the purpose of God to bless mankind through Christ; of what God wishes to be done by us.

Jesus was submitting His will to the will of His Father, so that what God desired to do through Him would be accomplished. This level of submission would make it so that mankind could be blessed with redemption. And for us, when our knees are bowed to the will of God, it will bring us to the place that God can do what He wishes through our lives to touch others.

Jesus knew what He brought with Him to earth—*a plan*—one that, *if followed* according to His Father's will, would open wide heaven's gates to multitudes to be reconciled to the Father.

The church needs to understand this expediency—get the gates open, *according to the plan.* If any of us think even for a moment, that we know how to *run our lives, run the church,* and *enact our plans,* we will surely forfeit something so precious that Jesus held true to ***and*** died upholding—***the Father's Will.***

- ***If*** Jesus would have followed any path, *other than what God gave Him*, He would have forfeited the power of the cross—the only thing that would bring mankind back to God.
- ***If*** He stood in any methodology or wisdom of man, man would have remained trapped in mental darkness and never have seen the light of the glorious gospel of Jesus Christ.

The Apostle Paul had learned this lesson well as we see in ***1 Corinthians 2:4-5***. He said, *"My speech and my preaching was not with enticing words of man's wisdom, but in demonstration of the Spirit and of power: That your faith should not stand in the wisdom of men, but in the power of God."*

- ***If Jesus*** stood in the strength of His own glory; He would not have been able to say, *"If you've seen Me, you've seen my Father, for My Father and I are one."*
- ***If*** the church stands in their own glory others will not see The Glory of God.

The choices are before us—the temporal glory of man *or* the enduring Word of the Lord.

1 Peter 1: 25 says, *"The word of the Lord endures forever. And this is the word which by the gospel is preached unto you"*

- ***If Jesus*** would have relished and flaunted charm and charisma, He would have not been able to walk in the anointing of ***Isaiah 61***, as prophesied and fulfilled in ***Luke 4.***
- ***If the church*** does not understand that all of our wit and charm and personal charisma will not heal the sick, raise the dead, set at liberty those held in captivity, cleanse the lepers or cast out demons, then we will totally miss the anointing to do the works of our Lord.

We see in the Word that there was ample opportunity for Jesus to go *another route.*

- ***He could have*** taken the devil's offer in the wilderness—a quick trip to the top—instant success, as far as man's eyes could see.
- ***He could have*** taken Judas' way into power—instant fame and enjoyed the time of being held in men's esteem.
- ***He could have*** conceded to the crowd's desire to crown Him an earthly king—a crowd pleaser, led astray by the *Hallelujah*'s and accolades of mankind to the destruction of His ultimate destiny.
- ***He could have*** listened to Peter's desire that He not die—accepted His friend's intervention and remain on earth and enjoyed being a *"career Jesus."*
- ***He could have*** called 10,000 angels to put and end to the matter of the cross, using His heavenly clout to overthrow earthly powers and proven to everyone what a powerful person He was; greater than anyone else.

He knew that any compromise on His part would compromise the plan of God for mankind—any alternative mindset would circumvent the plan of God.

Compromise, by definition means, *"a middle way between two extremes: an accommodation in which both sides make concessions."*

Compromise is a *mentally lukewarm state* in which one is neither hot nor cold in their values.

It is possible for any of us to succumb to the power of human persuasion—*that of others **and** our own inner voice that speaks great words of success to us*—and risk compromising so as to forfeit the Father's will for us.

The High Road of man's thoughts of success looks like a very low road to undiscerning minds.

Jesus understood this—He was a humble servant—removing Himself from His high estate. ***(Philippians 2:6-8)*** The *path of the greatest resistance* is often seen as a failure in the eyes of those who would judge one on such a journey. Others will not understand the willingness to face the warfare and the ridicule and the appearance of being a total failure in the eyes of man—all for the blessing from God who says, *"Well done, good and faithful servant."****(Matthew 25:21; 23)***

The true church that Jesus builds is separated unto God and often misunderstood because the *standard success ideologies* rate it as a failure—according to human standards of *testing the fruit.*

<u>Inventory according to men would look something like this;</u>

- ***Good church fruit is when*** the *numbers are up.*
- ***Good church fruit is when*** the *bank accounts are full.*
- ***Good church fruit is when*** you *play by others rules and conform to the norm.*
- ***Good church fruit is when*** the *departments of the organization are all in place.*

- ***Good church fruit is when*** the *annual reports are filled out and they show an increase.*
- ***Good church fruit is when*** *everyone speaks and thinks well of you, at home and abroad.*

<u>Inventory according to God would look like this:</u>

- ***Good church fruit is when*** prayer is in the House.
- ***Good church fruit is when*** The River of God is there.
- ***Good church fruit is when*** the Glory of God dwells there.
- ***Good church fruit is when*** Jesus is the Head of His Church.
- ***Good church fruit is when*** there is Unity in the bonds of peace.
- ***Good church fruit is when*** souls are being added to the kingdom.
- ***Good church fruit is when*** the humble meet God at an altar of sacrifice.
- ***Good church fruit is when*** Spirit and Truth worship is ascending to heaven.
- ***Good church fruit is when*** the uncompromised Word of God is being preached.
- ***Good church fruit is when*** Jesus is the declared King of Kings and Lord of Lords.

The true church, the one of whom Christ is the Head, does not make corporate sense by any stretch of the imagination. It upsets a good part of *the shareholders*, by giving no one a vote.

What makes total sense to God still baffles mankind.

1 Corinthians 1:26-29 (Emphasis Added)

26 For ye see your calling, brethren, how that not many wise men after the flesh, not many mighty, not many noble, are called:

27 But God hath chosen ***the <u>foolish things</u>*** (trifling, insignificant, or paltry) *of the world to confound the wise; and God hath chosen* ***the <u>weak things</u>*** (lacking in force,

> inadequate) *of the world to confound the things which are mighty;*
>
> *28 And* ***base things*** (without estimable personal qualities; of little or no value) *of the world, and* ***things which are despised****,* (regarded with contempt and scorn) *hath God chosen, yea, and things which are not, to bring to naught things that are:*
>
> *29 That no flesh should glory in his presence.*

We, as *"go-getters-for-Jesus"* have failed to understand a simple truth—a lot of what we do, in the church we have built, does not even have the Father's approval because it does not resemble the house we are to be building called *"The Church."*

Sometimes it isn't even that we've embraced the world or idolatry—*though that is a problem too*—it's just that we haven't embraced Jesus' Design for His Church.

It has been a total *take-over* and *make-over* of what Jesus died for to name as His own—to define by His Word, His Will and His Way.

Slowly but surely, the church has released the Hand of God, *one finger at a time*, until He no longer is touching His church the way He planned and so longs to do.

We can learn volumes from understanding how *obediently precise* Jesus was to His Father's will during His time on earth.

He was being clocked by a time piece much different from earth's clocks.

2 Peter 3:8*—But, beloved, be not ignorant of this one thing, that one day is with the Lord as a thousand years, and a thousand years as one day.*

Jesus was on His Father's time, doing His Father's Will, His Father's Way.

Many people have been in a rush to do in a short time what God has been laying a sure foundation for over the years. We don't even have to work hard at imagining the ***greatest***, ***biggest*** and ***best,*** and rush to the end zone of our plans, but what God did through Jesus is still being enacted by His Will daily in the lives of other submitted servants of the Cross.

The church that was established by Jesus is still the same church we are today. There has not been *a church then* and *a church now* that has been set in place.

The church has been a *"by design"* continual flow of God's move, a progressive and uninterrupted work on the earth for centuries—with always a remnant doing it God's way.

The biggest stronghold that God has to always take apart at the seams has been *the church we have built,* according to our own legends, doctrines and history—those ideological concepts and men's traditions and doctrines which exist in the mindset of the church.

God has a long and effective history of redeeming mankind out of captivity—out of the messes His people have made of their faith; He's the only one who knows how to do it.

In the same way Jesus placed His life in the hands of His Father, so must we, ***if*** we are to fulfill our call to be the church in this darkening hour of tolerance, compromise and cold love.

- ***He knew*** what He was doing when He tackled this modern-day church in the hour that we live.
- ***He knew*** exactly what needed to be done to bring us back to the heart of the Father.
- ***He knew*** the path He would take us on.
- ***He knew*** the difficulties of that journey.
- ***He knew*** that all would not make it because the way would be hard and long.
- ***But He knew*** that a remnant would arrive safely to the place He's taking them.

- ***He knew*** the remnant would rebuild the old waste places.
- ***He knew*** they would restore the walls and retrieve the holy things from the hands of the enemy and put them all back in the temple of God—*personally and collectively.*

Just as in days of old when an enemy king came and stripped the temple of all God mandated to be placed there, ***the church has specifics that are just as mandated to be in place*** . . .

- Jesus Christ as the Head of His Church;
- The Glory of God in the House of God;
- The Breath of Holy Spirit moving without human restraint;
- The uncompromised preaching of the Word of God;
- Spirit and Truth Worship;
- Unity of the Believers;
- Holiness unto the Lord;
- The Fear of God;
- Humble Service to the Lord;
- Discipleship to Equip the Believers for the Kingdom of God;
- The Release of God's Spirit to Work in Power and Glory

. . . my, my, how far short of the Glory of God we have fallen. We have a lot to return back to the Lord . . .

> ***Jeremiah 24:7****—And I will give them an heart to know me, that I am the Lord: and they shall be my people, and I will be their God: for they shall return unto me with their whole heart.*

God desires to take individuals and whole churches, *from the pulpit to the pew*, on the trip of return, back to the Holy Place where we would restore the sacrifices, *not of blood*, but of presenting our bodies as a living sacrifice unto the Lord ***(Romans 12:1-2)*** to serve God in obedience, with pure hands and clean hearts as priests unto God.

> ***Heb 12:28****—Wherefore we receiving a kingdom which cannot be moved, let us have grace, whereby we may serve God acceptably with reverence and godly fear:*

Romans 12:1-2*—I beseech you therefore, brethren, by the mercies of God, that ye present your bodies a living sacrifice, holy, acceptable unto God, which is your reasonable service.*

This is truly the Bedrock of our Faith in its finest form!

We are no different than our contemporaries of old who took the same journey we are now invited to take. Israel got somewhat testy with God and exhibited a lot of impatience with Him and the leader God gave them. They simply did not understand the place God was taking them.

He was not taking them to the Promise Land—*He was bringing a people to Himself.*

Exodus 6:7*—And I will take you to me for a people, and I will be to you a God: and ye shall know that I am the Lord your God, which bringeth you out from under the burdens of the Egyptians.*

That's all God wants from us—for us to be a people that have returned to Him, wholeheartedly

Chapter 7

I surrender all

Matthew 7:21

Not everyone that saith unto me, Lord, Lord, shall enter into the kingdom of heaven; but he that doeth the will of my Father which is in heaven.

"The will of God is always a bigger thing than we bargain for, but we must believe that whatever it involves, it is good, acceptable and perfect."
Jim Elliot

People of God, we are in the *Battle of a Lifetime,* and there will be winners and losers whose placement will be related directly to their standing with God in these deceptive days. God says, ***"Surrender all."*** It's a sweet, yet demanding, invitation to yield to God's will for all of us.

The word, ***Surrender*** means, *"To yield something to the possession or power of another."* ***Yield***, a similar word means, *"To give up or surrender oneself, to give up or over; relinquish."* Another word, ***submission,*** has come under fire in the past years and has even been declared by some in the church as *a spirit of control* from which they must break free. People are proclaiming they are free of the church and all its controls, declaring; *"Only God tells me what to do."*

Regardless of what people may or may not say, the Word of God stands as the final word over every man, woman, youth or child.

> ***Hebrews 13:17*** (Emphasis Added)—*Obey them that have the rule over you, and* ***submit yourselves*** *(surrender): for they watch for your souls, as they that must give account, that they may do it with joy, and not with grief: for that is unprofitable for you.*
>
> ***1 Peter 2:13*** (Emphasis Added)—***Submit yourselves*** *to every ordinance of man for the Lord's sake: whether it be to the king, as supreme;*
>
> ***Ephesians 5:20-21*** (Emphasis Added)—*Giving thanks always for all things unto God and the Father in the name of our Lord Jesus Christ;* ***Submitting yourselves one to another in the fear of God.***

- **Submitting yourselves**—to subordinate; to obey: be under obedience submit self unto.
    - **Subordinate:** Placed in or belonging to a lower order or rank; of less importance; secondary.

So, we see Jesus submit to His Father's will. Even though *He thought it not robbery to be equal with God,* He put Himself in the form of common man and became subordinate. And we are so glad He did . . . *how wonderful for Him to be so humble and thoughtful to do things God's way so He could be a pure sacrifice so we can be redeemed from our sins*—but what about us?

I am so glad Jesus kept His focus and learned submission to His Father's Will.

How different our world would be today if He "*did it His way,*" as the song declares. We have all been given a wonderful grace gift from God—an opportunity to make some decisions that will revolutionize our lives, make changes that will follow us from here to the end of our journey on earth.

We need to remember the spirit of the antichrist kingdom is one of rebellion—which is even now accelerating with time and flaunting itself in the streets of the cities of the nations of the world.

1 Timothy 1:8-11(Emphasis Added)

8 But we know that the law is good, if a man use it lawfully;

9 Knowing this, that the law is not made for a righteous man, but for the lawless and disobedient, for the ungodly and for sinners, for unholy and profane, for murderers of fathers and murderers of mothers, for manslayers,

10 For whoremongers, for them that defile themselves with mankind, for menstealers, for liars, for perjured persons, and ***if there be any other thing that is contrary to sound doctrine;***

11 ***According to the glorious gospel of the blessed God,*** *which was committed to my trust.*

To vacillate between two things is to not fully yield to the demand of the one that wants the full surrender.

Look at the definition to vacillate: to waver in mind or opinion; be indecisive

James 1:6-8

6 But let him ask in faith, nothing wavering. For he that wavereth is like a wave of the sea driven with the wind and tossed.

7 For let not that man think that he shall receive any thing of the Lord.

8 A double minded man is unstable in all his ways.

God desires that His people are steady on their feet, to not lack an understanding heart that knows where to stand in times of decision.

The thing about it is this: The devil is okay with church attendance, Christian duties and such, as long as we don't fully give in to God—he's willing to take us *half-way* because he knows that *half-way is a compromise of our faith* in Christ and will ultimately cost us so much more than we gain.

***But God* is not willing to allow us to take Him half-way—He wants ALL of you—He wants all of me.**

He speaks to try to get us in the right place with Him because our life depends on it . . . our answers to Him will have a direct impact on us. He's moving on into the Last Days with or without us fully following Him, but He would like to take us with Him, to be able to finish in and through us what He started.

> ***1 Kings 18:****21* (Emphasis Added)—*And Elijah came unto all the people, and said,* ***"How long halt you between two opinions? If the Lord be God, follow him: but if Baal, then follow him."*** *And the people answered him not a word.*

This is a picture of so much of the church world today and yes, individuals as well—stuck betwixt and between serving God and serving themselves and their own interests—unwilling to say what needs to be said . . . to release what needs to be released.

Altar calls have gone unanswered because people were not ready to give an answer to God's call to *surrender all to Him*, or they stood physically in the right place while in their hearts they were still making deals, mentally, about what they would and would not concede.

What God is revealing is this: He's not talking about a ***weakness*** in you that you struggle with, but a ***will*** in you that is not surrendered. It's a place in which you are still *the boss*, *the king* over a kingdom in your heart that has not been yielded to Him—a place He does not have the rule over.

He wants your will to yield to His Will. Why?

Because there will always be winners and losers in this Battle and He wants you to win—to go forth to do HIS WILL.

<u>I want to take you on a journey that will bring this message home to your heart.</u>

We have all seen a surrender flag. It is waved by one who is giving up—yielding to the other side.

- ***Imagine*** with me how many time a surrender flag has been waved in the spirit as the battle of the heart has been fought at altars all down through generations.
- ***Imagine*** how many time hearts have soared with commitment and the flag has been waved as people have sang the songs of commitment and surrender.
- ***Imagine*** how many times the surrender flag of the heart has waved in your life-time as you have faced your own battles between your will and God's will.

Think about this—the white flag of surrender, which represents our heart's consent to follow Jesus, is in your hand all the time. It represents your commitment, your faith, your decisions to concede in areas of your life and you ***wave it in worship***, ***amen it in sermons***, ***hallelujah it in praise***, ***unfurl it as a sign*** that your life is yielded to the Lord.

Now imagine with me a surrender flag, knotted on both corners. These knotted, fisted areas are a part of the flag that is not unfurled. It doesn't matter how many times you wave such a flag, if there's an area that is not released to wave freely, there is still an area of *hold-out*, and area of the will that is not yielded to surrender to the conquering King, Jesus.

There are those, *maybe us at times*, that refuse to give up particular areas of our lives and will *hold out* until the bitter end.

- **Hold out—*Phrase***—to continue to exist; last: to refuse to yield or submit:

Picture with me Jesus carrying His surrender flag, *not one necessarily in His hand, but one deeply entrenched in His heart,* with Him throughout His life.

<u>What areas of His life did this level of surrender impact?</u>

Every prayer, every encounter, every message, every answer He gave—His entire life from before birth through persecution, rejection, beatings, piercings, to the cross, to the grave and back—every breath and step He took resonated with His Father's Will fully embraced.

His surrender flag represented the *quality of life laid down* for the Cause—a life fully surrendered to His Father's will.

Now, Imagine Jesus carrying a banner that is of the same caliber as one of ours—one that will represent His mission on earth to do His Father's Will

Imagine Him walking out His call to His cause with a flag that is like those held in the hand of God's people today. I cannot answer the question about the level of surrender for you nor you for me because each of us must give an answer to God concerning His will for our lives.

Many people may believe in part that God's will has to do with some level of ministry or placement—but actually God's will is about us being submitted to Him in many ways that affect the ministry or placement we may have—Just like Jesus . . .

If Jesus came to this point in His life without having fully embraced His Father's will, He would have stumbled His way to Calvary, with His feet tangled in arguments about the way things were being done. Our will can find many ways to circumvent the Will of God and be justified in the thoughts of the heart.

If Jesus was not submitted in His will, He would have never been submitted to the cross.

To start the mission God gave Him required He know WHY He came.

John 12:24 tells us that if there is no death, there is no new life. That is a strange parable, but Jesus spoke these words in this verse: ***"Except a corn of***

wheat fall into the ground and die, it abides alone: but if it dies, it brings forth much fruit." (Emphasis Added)

We all must come to this conclusion as well—unless we die, there is no fruit and to die, there must be an embracing of the greater picture—the cause!

Jesus states in verse 27 "Now is my soul troubled; and what shall I say? Father, save me from this hour: ***but for this cause came I unto this hour."*** (Emphasis Added)

Jesus came to cast the prince of this world out, but it could have never happened without the ultimate surrender—Jesus yielding His body to death. The Father's will was finished through Jesus Christ and the devil was defeated.

Imagine further an un-yielded flag being carried by Jesus into the wilderness of His temptation. The devil came at Him with counter-offers, to try to dissuade Him from His destiny—but Jesus would have none of that. He knew why He had come and fought against the insidious offers of Satan to dislodge His loyalty to His Father's will.

A flag carried by many churches carries today would have been a sham in the face of such a demonic onslaught, because any area we are holding back on will come to defeat us when we are faced with such temptations to concede.

And think of Jesus carrying this banner that *represents more of a stronghold of human will than surrender to God . . .* can you see Jesus taking this surrender flag with Him into the Garden of Gethsemane?

"Oh yes, most of the flag is unfurled," **He could have said—but any part held back will be the death of the cause.**

The Garden was a pivotal place in Jesus' life—a place where His will would have to concede to the Father's Will to drink the cup. It was a place of soul-wrenching agony.

> ***Matthew 26:39*** (Emphasis Added)—*And he went a little further, and fell on his face, and prayed, saying, O my Father, if it be possible, let this cup pass from me: nevertheless* ***not as I will, but as thou wilt.***

Oh how we need our own Gethsemane—a place where we wrestle and bring our will to a place of submission to the Father's Will.

How stubborn God's children are in holding out a part of their life, and how much will be forfeited if a full surrender is not made.

Now walk with Jesus as He holds onto a surrender flag like one in the hands of the church today and see Judas, one who sat at the table with Him.

- Judas was a man of conflicted wills, trying to follow Jesus but *"holding out a piece reserved for himself"* coming to the end of his walk with Jesus in disgrace.
- See the soldiers coming to arrest Jesus to drag Him off to court, falsely accused.
- What kind of reaction will He give when the kiss of betrayal comes to touch His face?
- What kind of man will He be when ***the cause*** for which He was sent begins to unfold into such a scene of the pain of betrayal by one of His trusted men?
- Is He going to clinch His fist and harbor unforgiveness, bitterness and anger?

Or will He go like a lamb to the slaughter?

> ***Acts 8:32-33*** . . . *He was led as a sheep to the slaughter; and like a lamb dumb before his shearer, so opened he not his mouth: In his humiliation his judgment was taken away: and who shall declare his generation? For his life is taken from the earth.*

"Father, not my will, but Yours be done . . ."

Think of what kind of Savior He would have been if He had carried His flag with a ***half-submitted will, almost fully yielded to the cause***, beaten and mocked as the scourge was laid upon His back.

He was right where His call had brought Him,
but would He give it all in full surrender to His Father's Will?
"Father, not my will but Yours be done!"

And think of the pressure and pain of walking the Via De la Rosa; Jesus carrying His flag of surrender with just one area of hold out to His own will, being mocked and thronged by an angry crowd, screaming for His death.

The pressure is building—the inner conflict of following His Father's Will on earth as it is in heaven is beginning to take a toll on Him—***IF*** He's carrying a surrender flag like mine. Because of an undecided area of inner conflict as to how far He is willing to go . . . Jesus with a part of His life clinched hard in His hands like we sometimes do, would waver in His resolve between two places in His mind—wanting to let go and fulfill His Father's will and wanting to run from the event of His death.

But the Master is the Servant and the cry from the depths of His Spirit rings true . . .

"Father, not my will but yours be done . . ."

None of us know what level of persecution at the hands of angry people we will face, *if any*, but to be like Jesus we have to have our own Garden where we have died to our own will, where our flag is unfurled in full and sweet surrender.

Hear His voice echoing down through the ages, leading the way for us to follow him all the way . . ." ***My meat is to do the will of him that sent me, and to finish his work." John 4:34***

Just imagine what kind of Jesus He would have been if He had carried a part of His will still intact throughout His life . . . He would have never made it this far . . .

There He is, my Jesus! The One who laid it all down from the beginning of the foundations of the world . . . The One who has come to do His Father's will on earth, as it is in heaven . . . carrying a banner fully unfurled as His identity with His Father.

He's carrying it to His death, focused on only one thing—finishing what His Father sent Him to do.

- ***Can we say*** today that we have such a banner of full surrender, fully unfurled, ready to lay down our life for the cause of Christ, so that the Father's Will through us can be on earth as it is in heaven?
- ***Or are we*** tight fisted with our will, holding back hidden places of inner conflict where a battle has raged?
- ***Have we*** clinched our fist when God is calling us to fully and completely die to our will?

Imagine Jesus being stretched out still hanging onto a piece of His will as the nails are being driven into his hands and feet. ***It's impossible*** to have a piece still held onto and to fully stretch yourself out on behalf of another, much less the world's sinners.

What kind of man would lay down His life for such as you and me?

- ***Do we*** still have any area of our life where we are becoming more tight-fisted with our will in any area God has been dealing with?
- ***Are any of us*** resisting fully dying to ourselves so Christ might live in us and through us?
- ***Are we*** yielded to completely laying it all down to follow Him all the way, no matter where He leads us?

Is there a place in your life that overrides the Father's Will?

It would have been impossible for Jesus to lay down His life while still holding onto *a half-way surrendered life, holding back a part, only going part way, keeping an option open*—to enact His will *if He wanted to* . . . but He didn't want to!

> ***Matthew 26:53****—Thinkest thou that I cannot now pray to my Father, and he shall presently give me more than twelve legions of angels?*

Think about Jesus hanging there upon the cursed tree between two thieves and Roman soldiers at His feet gambling on and tearing apart His identity, mocking Him at the foot of the cross. He could have never gone that far with a surrender flag such as the worldly church offers clutched in His hand. Is there any hope for we who vacillate and waver sometimes in the area of our will? Yes, there is hope. We can make up our minds to be the kind of surrendered person Jesus was.

The world has yet to see what God can do with and for and through and in and by the man who is fully and wholly consecrated to Him. I will try my utmost to be that man.
D.L. Moody

God's church finds her feet, hands, heart, arms and body movement in you and me to the degree that God has us and we have Him as King over the kingdoms of our heart.

What does it mean to surrender all, really, completely?

Many people down through history have fought, won and lost wars, with one side surrendering. They may have given up but *they didn't change their mind about what they were battling for.*

World War II was won by America and allied forces, but the enemies of America remained solid in their inner conflicts with our nation. Even while signing the Armistice Agreement, the hearts of those who put the pen to the paper in what would appear to be solidarity to end the war, had hearts of varying degrees of anger, seething emotions.

When it comes to surrender, unlike a natural military that waves the white flag to indicate they give up the fight and yield as a national military unit or branch to the other force they have been battling, where everyone simultaneously lays down their arms, ***the church surrenders one person at a time.***

There is a painting of the end of a major battle in which a single man is standing in a field of bodies littering the ground all around him. The painting is called, "Last Man Standing." This is a picture of what it looks like sometimes at the end of a time of conflict with the heart of man and God. Man still stands in some area of his life, though much may be crucified

Because of this lack of unity of surrender to the conquering King, Jesus, the battle continues, not only in the hearts, but in the church with varying degrees of occupation being done within the hearts of many.

The church all sits on the same pews, stands in the same altars but from heart to heart, there are differences that make or break the churches power to be what Jesus called her to be.

In the many years of leading God's people, as any minister to the church can also attest to, we have seen people in the church who have *never come clean with God*, never yielded to His call, though making a show of doing so publically.

It really doesn't matter how many times a person walks the aisle of a church and kneels at an altar, until the heart yields all its kingdom to the victor, ***the white flag means little to the one waving it.***

It can be a concession that is made momentarily, but not full surrender of the reason for the battle of the wills.

Many of those who walked the aisle *(I am not just talking about an altar in a church, but any place a person meets God—a car, school, home, workplace, etc . . .)* have fallen back to serving their own interest, rather than Jesus. Many cried buckets of tears, testified and got baptized, but many also returned to their old way of living, talking, doing and dressing.

- **Surrender—*verb (used with object)*—**To give oneself up, as into the power of another; submit or yield.

Jesus wants to anoint His people to overflow into their world, but the anointing never goes on flesh nor upon human will, but upon that which is prepared for sacrifice and service to the Lord.

Many times people want more from God than they are willing to give Him. Jesus will not be able to fully use a person who is not fully surrendered in all the kingdoms of their heart. If you or I refuse or fail to let go of the fisted areas of our hearts and lives, that is a piece of us that cannot die to the cause for which Christ has called us.

I believe Jesus is telling us, His church, that we will not be able to face the season that is upon us without a full surrender of our will.

WE must be able to say with our Lord, ***"Not my will, but thine be done—on earth, as it is in heaven."***

If we are carrying a surrender flag that is still knotted with our will, ***it's time*** to unclench the fist that is holding on so tight to something we have been unwilling to release to Him and let the banner of full surrender unfurl.

Remember? I said an altar is simply a place of meeting God, on His terms. It can be right now while reading this chapter, wherever you are. Has God's Spirit has been dealing with you on something—something that you are still in control of or conflicted in your will about?

It's time to let go and let God have HIS WAY in your life, ministry, church, family . . .

The constant battle of the wills—***ours and God's***—will lead to the wrong kind of death. The fleshly will is supposed to die so the Spirit can thrive—but holding out empowers the flesh and quenches the Spirit.

Can we simply bend our will to the Father's Will and to His Cause?

The end of our journey will be just like Jesus'

"Well done, good and faithful servant!"

CHAPTER 8

GIVE US BARABBAS

Luke 23:18

And they cried out all at once, saying,
"Away with this man, and release unto us Barabbas."

Jerusalem was a religious city, a place of the Temple and synagogues. We can find a parallel with our world today as we look around us and find multiplied many times over the concepts and ideas of religion. Jesus came into the world, making claims that greatly angered people until there was a mob rule to kill him for standing against their religion.

Let's talk about religion. I am going to take this time, in the midst of massive religions all over the world, to declare the truth of Jesus. Oh yes, everyone has a concept about Jesus—just like they did back in the days he walked earth—but so much of what people think is erroneous and many times blatantly deceptive.

Some today say He was a good man, a teacher, a prophet—but many will not say He is *"Jesus Christ the Son of the Living God,"* sent to redeem mankind from their sin, opening the door of salvation, healing and deliverance through His death and resurrection.

Because of that—the world has more religion today than they do relationship with Jesus Christ as their only Lord, Master and Savior.

<u>All of our ministry we have heard it:</u>

- *"Why are there so many religions, so many churches, gods, denominations, cults, covens . . . ?"*
- *"Don't all roads, belief systems, gods, worship and sacrifice lead to God, just so people are sincere in what they believe?"*
- *"If there is One God, why are there so many religions?"*

There are massive religious beliefs today, *as there always have been.*

The day Jesus was arrested, tried, flogged, mocked and crucified was a day of a religious war.

He was crucified in a world of differing beliefs.

He was an enemy to the current trends and ideas of man about *the Messiah.* The *priests* of the region—who were all using their *pulpits* to declare their teachings—were angry at this man who upset their religious world. It was, to them, about Jesus who came delivering a message of absolutes—*"I am the way, the truth, the life. No man comes to the Father but by Me."* You can imagine how controversial His message and life was. Then again . . . you can just look at the battle today over His name and claim today.

Intolerance is nothing new—the religious world was very intolerant of Jesus and those who followed Him.

So, if there is One God—why are there so many religions? Because there are so many people in darkness—people avoiding the Light—people defying God's Son as the Only Way—Deceived people, deceivers, betrayers—people who refuse to worship God and instead chose the darkness of the fallen world—people who refuse the narrow door of Salvation found in Jesus Christ alone.

Many people declare that the Jesus door is too narrow—but the truth is—religion is as narrow, dogmatic and legalistic . . . but many see it as tolerant and wide because they do not have to deal with their sin.

Bottom line, people want a religion that allows them to live the way they choose. And yet, unfortunately, those trapped in all kinds of religions are in terrible bondage.

God is not indecisive or flexible—trying to make up His mind which way He wants to do things. It is man who has taken hold of the holy—puts God under a human microscope and dissected Him into different beings for different people.

Every part of me—my head, mind, fingers, toes, internal organs, outward skin, eyes, ears, nose, mouth, body, spirit—is Esther. My parts make up the whole person that I am.

If there was some gruesome murder and I was dissected into pieces and sent all over the world, every piece of me would still be me—carrying my unique DNA. God is not made up of man's pieces, chopped up and sent all over the world. Wherever God is—He is whole—not some Frankenstein monster made in the imaginations of man or some creature stepping out of the swamp of man's mind.

He is God—totally, fully, completely in every way, every fragment, every word, deed, commandment, law and complete in His love for man and complete in His Door of Salvation through Jesus Christ.

Humanity today acts like spoiled kids who refuse their parents good gifts, throws it back in their faces, spit on them, and say, "*I am going to do things my way*!" It doesn't matter how much that parent loves that child—they cannot make them love and obey them if they choose *another way.*

We have places for those who break the rules of laws in our homes, nations and yes, even in faith. They get fenced in because of their willful way until they can learn to obey the rules of society and home. Our prisons today are full of people that are learning the hard way that their way was not right.

And there is a wage for those who try it on their own without Jesus—bondages, prisons of all kinds hold people in their control. Sin makes a mark on the life of the one who refuses the redemption of Jesus. Bottom line—man is the fallen one, under the darkness of this present age without Jesus. He needs a savior, a redeemer—He needs cleansed not only of his sins, but of his ways. He needs Jesus, so God sent Him to mankind—to you and me.

But there are many that will not enter that door—because He's controversial.

Yes, God has presented for mankind a narrow door to access Him, in contrast to hell's ever-widening door, which opens even more grandly to accommodate those who push and crowd through its gates. As the world continues to philosophize and meditate on its greatness, they have ignored the ***One Way*** out of the maze.

God's door, Jesus Christ, is a gift to mankind and yet He has been met, from the days He walked earth, with great rejection by the *"Give me Barabbas"* crowd.

Being narrow is not bad as some might think . . .

- It has a certainty and sure-footed feel to it, which does not leave those who embrace it feeling like they are *on the sinking sand of wavering and uncertainty.*
- Having one's mind *made up* is a pretty good feeling, even when being called, *narrow-minded.*

. . . At least you know for sure *what and who* you believe.

> ***2 Timothy 1:12***—*For the which cause I also suffer these things: nevertheless I am not ashamed:* ***for I know whom I have believed,*** *and am persuaded that he is able to keep that which I have committed unto him against that day.*

Jesus Christ is the Controversial Door—but oh what a door of access He is . . .

The door in Jesus, though many want to paint it ugly, is actually a beautiful door, though narrow. People do truly stumble over His claims, as being the only door, and miss the rest of the story . . .

Jesus said

- *I am the bread of life—**John 6:35***

- *I am the light of the world—**John 8:12***
- *I am the door of the sheep.* ***John 10:7***
- *I am the good shepherd: the good shepherd gives his life for the sheep.* ***John 10:11***
- *I am the resurrection, and the life—**John 11:25-26***
- *I am the way, the truth, and the life—**John 14:6***
- *I am the true vine—**John 15:5***
- *I am the vine—**John 15:1***
- *I am the first and the last—**Revelation 1:17-18***
- *I am the root and the offspring of David, and the bright and morning star.* ***Revelation 22:16***

Jesus whole purpose in coming was to open the door of salvation back to God where man had shut it in the face of God through sin. Death had entered by that door of sin and disobedience and now Life had come through the door of obedience and purity in Jesus.

On the day Jesus was on trial a cry went up concerning a choice they were asked to make. The violent voices gave a single cry as the choice was given when asked the question as to who should be released and who crucified . . .

"Jesus or Barabbas?"

We read in ***Luke 23: 18-25*** their reply, ***"Away with this man, and release unto us Barabbas."***

Notice the dismissive attitude behind the way they spoke the words, *"Away with **this man**."* They did not call Jesus by name but by a generic flip of the wrist, they wrote Him off as a *"no name-non-person-nobody."* They at least named Barabbas, the criminal—giving him more credence than the Son of God.

Pilate was willing to release Jesus and spoke again to them.

But they cried, saying, "Crucify him, crucify him."

Pilate asked a third time, *"Why, what evil hath he done? I have found no cause of death in him: I will therefore chastise him, and let him go."*

The response they gave really matches the call for the "*Death of Jesus*" today, as attempts are still being made to erase Him from society. The Bible tells us that they instantly, with loud voices, required that Jesus be crucified.

They cried out then, as is still the cry from many today, as they chose a way other than Jesus, "*Away with Him—give us Barabbas!*"

- Away with Him—***give me my idols.***
- Away with Him—***give me my religion.***
- Away with Him—***give me my relationships.***
- Away with Him—***give me my style of worship.***
- Away with Him—***give me my way!***

Proverbs 16:25—*There is a way that seems right unto a man, but the end thereof are the ways of death.*

Barabbas was an alternative door they chose to walk through that day. He represented an utter rejection of Jesus as the Messiah, the Redeemer, The Master and Lord of all, King of Kings, Barabbas represented a hatred of Jesus.

> ***Isaiah 53:6***—*All we like sheep have gone astray; we have turned everyone to his own way; and the Lord hath laid on Him the iniquity of us all.*

Their voices calling for Barabbas was a release of what was in their heart—a release of their will against God's Will.

Men still choose sin over redemption, the error of his ways over truth, death over life. Mankind gambles with the most precious thing he has—his eternal soul.

"Who do you say that I am?"

Our answer determines our eternity.

CHAPTER 9

PASSION

Mark 15:37-39

And Jesus cried with a loud voice, and gave up the ghost.
And the veil of the temple was rent in twain from the top to the bottom.
And when the centurion, which stood over against him, saw that
he so cried out, and gave up the ghost, he said,
Truly this man was the Son of God.

- **Passion:** The sufferings of Christ between the night of the Last Supper and his death; A powerful emotion, such as love, joy, hatred, or anger; an intense, an intense, overpowering emotion.

The atmosphere was electric with the spiritual tensions that filled the city. Sides had been drawn. Everyone had made a decision. Jesus was the object of much idle chatter while others engaged in angry dissertations of why He must die.

Others huddled behind closed doors gripped with their love for this man called Jesus but tinted with fear that bound them like chains to the place of hiding.

The drama that surrounded the days that led up to Jesus arrest and ultimate crucifixion couldn't have been filled with more intrigue, passion and emotion. Everyone connected to Jesus, *on any level*, were consumed with an odd mixture of passions that battled for the stage of time. Tempers flared, while hatred was given vent with great vengeance as *the plan came together* with the death of Jesus.

Many were consumed with deep grief as everything seemed to be falling apart around the one they loved and believed in.

- ***But no one really*** understood the story that was playing out behind the gates of hell where even the demons were gripped with passionate hatred and revenge for this *Jesus.*
- ***None*** could spit His name out in mockery and with such zeal as those who once worshipped Him in Glory—***"Jesus—the Son of the Living God!"***

Mark 5 (Emphasis Added)—*"What have I to do with thee,* ***Jesus, thou Son of the most high God?*** *I adjure thee by God, that thou torment me not."*

- ***And no one*** really understood the outpouring of love that was washing over the planet called earth as God's love was being shed upon their hearts.

This love was painful because it involved a sacrifice—a giving to those who were gripped with hatred for the Lamb.

John 3:16-17

16 For God so loved the world that he gave his only begotten Son, that whosoever believeth in him should not perish, but have everlasting life.

17 For God sent not his Son into the world to condemn the world; but that the world through him might be saved.

- ***And no one*** could have begun to understand the emotions of Jesus—the passionate love for mankind that took Him to Calvary. They did not feel the agony of His death at the hands of an angry mob or the feelings of devotion to His Father to complete the plan.

Passion?
Oh, yes, *Jesus knows* about Passion.
***He knows* the Joy of the Cross!**
***He knows* the power of Love for lost humanity!**
***He knows* the passionate power of forgiveness!**

Yes, there were those that were aware of their part, but did not have a clue how it was to impact humanity for eternity.

God's plan was being fulfilled in love but humanity missed the fact that the Messiah, the Lamb of God, without blemish, was being prepared for the Passover Sacrifice and then sacrificed right in front of their eyes.

Most did not recognize this one who had been given as a gift of God from Heaven. Even those who followed him the closest missed the perfect plan that they were a part of.

For many others, all they could do was battle Him—*to the death!*

The people on the streets, Mary, the mother of Jesus, John, the Centurions, the mockers, and the two thieves who were also crucified on either side of Him took a stand that day.

Jesus, in His Passion for lost mankind, cried out <u>*and*</u> a passionate cry also came from the mouths of those surrounding Him.

Passion has a voice . . .

- ***Passion cried***, *"Father, if you be willing, remove this cup from me: nevertheless not my will, but yours be done."*
- ***Passion cried***, *"Why sleep you? Get up and pray, lest you enter into temptation!"*
- ***Passion cried***, *"Judas, do you betray the Son of man with a kiss?"*
- ***Passion cried***, *"Crucify Him!"*
- ***Passion cried***, *"Father, forgive them; for they know not what they do."*
- ***Passion cried***, *"He saved others; let him save himself, if he be Christ, the chosen of God."*

- ***Passion cried***, *"If you are the king of the Jews, save yourself!"*
- ***Passion cried***, *"If you are Christ, save yourself and us."*
- ***Passion cried***, *"Lord, remember me when you come into your kingdom."*
- ***Passion cried***, *"Today you shall be with me in paradise!"*
- ***Passion cried***, *"Father, into your hands I commend my spirit!"*
- ***Passion cried***, *"Certainly this was a righteous man."*

It was a stage like no other. Everyone took a place but little did they know the magnitude of what they were a part of.

Voices rang out into the heavens as the passion of God and man spilled over and out upon the earth—*mingled for eternity.*

To this day, people have filmed the story of Jesus over and over, so many times more than any other story ever told. The focus on Jesus has been intense from the time He entered earth as a baby, up to now.

- This is the man that people still cannot stop talking about, making movies about, presenting plays and writing songs about.
- Even the atheists spend all their life focused on Him!
- Some of the greatest witnesses of Jesus have been those who do not believe in Him because they constantly talk about Him.

The world is obsessed with Jesus Christ.

The ***Passion of Christ*** is truly a phrase that depicts the fire and fervor that has always surrounded the mention of Jesus' name. People are not neutral concerning Him—never have been, never will be. His name provokes passionate action on everyone's part.

His name brings everyone to a decision unlike any other—do you accept or reject Him as the Savior of the world, the Son of the Living God?

There have been millions of martyrs since the beginning of time—people who died for what they believed—but no death so notable, documented, dissected and preached from the pulpits of the word of the lovers and haters of Jesus.

He is inescapable!

Oh, yes, there have been a multitude of messianic-type men, teachers and prophets, but which of them, even though many claimed to be God or Messiah, ever had the publicity that Jesus Christ has had, with the world trying its best to prove Him wrong or right? Or which of them ever shed their life's blood for all of humanity, without thought for themselves? There is no other man such as this!

Anyone today who gets in the proximity of Jesus on any level, in any way, will make a decision. It will be one that will invade their human mind, emotions and spirits.

Apathy has a voice, as does fear.
Complacency, though idle speaks a message.

It's Easter—Resurrection Sunday! Ah, the dresses, hat, celebrations, dinners and games that are played—all because Jesus died and rose again. Yearly many gather all over the world to celebrate that Jesus lives. Some without even understanding why they are inexplicably drawn to acknowledge this day, will get up and go to church on Sunday or a Sabbath Service. They will nod in Jesus direction, letting Him know they are still aware of Him.

Voices will once again be raised to the heavens.
God will hear.

The earth will resound with the passionate voices of everyone once again—like clockwork!

- ***Some*** will curse His name.
- ***Others*** will praise Him!
- ***Some*** will yawn in His face.
- ***Others*** will mock Him, as it was done in the days of old.
- ***Some*** will give Him a nod of appreciation.
- ***Others*** will raise their voices in shouts of gratitude.

For believers, The Passion of our Lord and Savior should provoke us to greater love and worship for Him.

He is our Redeemer!
He is our Healer!
He is our Deliverer!

Can we not raise our voices in rejoicing for the Victory of the Cross, the Power in His Blood and the Authority in His name, Jesus? Everyone's talking about Jesus, so why don't we?

Let's bring our passion and love for Jesus to a new level—one that goes outside the church, outside of our worship and into the city streets, to proclaim the Name of Jesus!

CHAPTER 10

BY HIS OWN BLOOD

Hebrews 9:11-12
(Emphasis Added)

But Christ being come an high priest of good things to come, by a greater and more perfect tabernacle, not made with hands, that is to say, not of this building; Neither by the blood of goats and calves, but ***by his own blood*** *he entered in once into the holy place, having obtained eternal redemption for us.*

People shed the blood of animals all over the world in religious rituals—from pagan rituals to those who attempt to cover their sins. In some places people, wring the neck of a rooster and a hen to sprinkle the blood over the head of men and women to symbolically cover their sins.

This all indicates to me that man seeks a way of salvation—even when they are getting it wrong.

> ***Hebrews 10:4****—For it is not possible that the blood of bulls and of goats should take away sins.*

We see that for all man's efforts and substitute religious activities, he cannot save himself.

There are not enough works, not enough chickens, not enough bulls, sheep or goats that can remedy what is wrong with the world and the church—*everyone needs Jesus and His shed blood!*

The Blood of Jesus was greatly honored in past revivals. It is from these revivals the songs on the blood were written. Now, once again, the LORD is bringing the Power of the Blood to the attention of the believers.

We need to learn to Honor the Blood for through the Blood we have power over all the might of the devil—*no matter where—no matter how—not matter in whom*—he shows up.

While praying for an upcoming prayer conference called ***Going up to High Places***, God impressed upon a prayer warrior the image of a therapist's couch. I knew God was speaking to an issue He has—*counseling has replaced just about everything*—the altars, repentance and Jesus and the Powerful Blood that He shed for us.

We are still self-reliant. I felt the picture related a message from the heart of God that we turn our hearts back to reliance once again the power of Jesus blood to overcome the devil, blot out our sins and protect us. Is God telling us that it is time to get off the couch of psychology and into the truth of God's Word where she will live in victory?

God did not call us to powerless living and yet . . .

- ***So many*** Christians are ***not living*** in Victory!
- ***So many*** Christians are ***not secure*** in their faith!
- ***So many*** Christians are ***not free*** of besetting sins!

Sadly the death angel is ***not passing*** over some homes!

It's time the army of the Redeemed, blood bought; Spirit-filled saints of God learn the power of the Blood of Jesus Christ, the Son of the Living God!

We've been allowing too much! It's not just that we go to the enemy's camp and take back what he stole—the devil's come aboard to pirate away what is precious to us. He's pirated our loved ones and we've been tolerating way too much!

It's time to get violent!

He's looted our churches, stolen our children, pillaged our cities, states and nation, spoiled our dreams, plummeted our hope and stalled our faith! It's time to decree a matter and have it come to pass—not because of our voice, but because of that magnificent voice that said, "*It is finished,*" as the last drop of His blood was spilled.

When Jesus said, "It is finished," He said a mouthful to the devil and taught us the power of His sacrifice.

It's a promise kept—He destroyed the works of the devil by the power of the cross—Death, Hell and the Grave—Sickness . . . All the powers of darkness know the power of the Blood but the Church knows or hears or understands little of it!

This church, thought purchased by the blood of Jesus, has evolved away from the acknowledgement of it.

We've warred but many times we have forgotten our banner—the one that only the redeemed can carry into the battle of life and faith—Jesus and His shed Blood. We've forgotten our garments—the Robes of Christ's Righteousness.

> ***Revelation 19:13*** (Emphasis Added)—*And he was clothed with* ***a vesture dipped in blood****: and his name is called The Word of God.*

If this is the *Last Day attire* for Jesus, should not the saints of God find their garments washed in the blood of the Lamb?

There is no reason *on earth or in hell* for anyone to not live free of sin, live in victory, live in the light and walk in the Spirit. There is no reason *on earth or in hell* why anyone should live their life without Jesus Christ healing, saving, and delivering power. The price was paid for all you have need of today. If I desire to see people set free to walk as an overcomer, how much more does Jesus because of the price of His own blood He paid for your freedom?

- ***Some of you*** have suffered loss, pain, and sickness, going through some of the most difficult times personally or in your family, watching and wondering if there is victory in this time
- ***Some of you*** are desperate, maybe even feel this is your last ditch effort you will make before giving up
- ***Some of you*** know there is something standing between you and God
- ***Some of you*** know there is something between you and another
- ***Some of you*** are feeling the sting of spiritual death for your church and family
- ***Some of you*** are afraid of the future in light of all that is taking place
- ***Some of you*** have tried everything and still need something to remedy what you are going through

All of us know, if we're honest, that the church world of today is in trouble, failing to live up to the call God has for her, failing to thrive, failing to live in the Light of the Glorious Gospel of Jesus Christ, inviting disastrous plans of man to replace the eternal Lamb of God and His precious Blood. You and I know it is serious . . .

And maybe this is even you. Have you allowed religious movement and the newest emergent ideologies concerning faith issues to drain you of the rich heritage and spiritual life promised in Jesus?

Not everyone accesses the abundant life of Christ because . . .

- ***They don't understand*** the Blood of Christ
- ***They are in denial*** of the Blood of Christ
- ***They are offended*** by the Blood of Christ

. . . but, it is the only real and viable life line for the human race, for the church.

> ***Revelation 12:10-11***(Emphasis Added)
>
> *10 And I heard a loud voice saying in heaven, Now is come* ***salvation****, and* ***strength****, and the* ***kingdom of our God****, and*

> ***the power of his Christ:*** *for the accuser of our brethren is cast down, which accused them before our God day and night.*
>
> *11 And* ***they overcame him by the blood of the Lamb*** *and by the word of their testimony; and they loved not their lives unto the death.*

If any of you have ever watched as someone you loved slipped from this earth, you know the grief and sorrow of heart as you see life for them end.

I have a strong feeling in my heart for what God is going through right now as He sees multitudes of people He loves very much slipping from sight as life drains away.

The modern Church should be on life-support, receiving a blood transfusion, because of the kind of trauma she has suffered, sadly sometimes a self-inflicted wound. Much of the Church is sick unto death, dying or dead today, with its many members dead and lifeless. I can tell you why—***they have no blood***—they have drained from their own faith, the life of Christ's blood.

We are past the emergency state for what ails the church; we need a resurrection of the dead to take place though a transfusion of the Holy Blood of the Lamb of God.

The Church that is ***dead*** is for one reason—the blood, where the life of the body is housed, is gone—not because the fountain of blood that poured from Jesus' veins is deficient—but because the church has turned from the ***ONLY*** thing that keeps her alive—people have turned from the ***ONLY*** thing that keeps them abundantly alive—***The Blood of Jesus.***

> ***John 6:53***—*Then Jesus said unto them, Verily, verily, I say unto you, Except ye eat the flesh of the Son of man, and drink his blood, ye have no life in you.*

- **Translated:** Of a truth I say to you, unless you consume my body and receive into your soul the blood, the seat of life, that which nourishes it unto life eternal, you have no life in you, no absolute fullness, real or genuine, devoted to God.

  John 10:10 (Emphasis Added)—*The thief cometh not, but for to steal, and to kill, and to destroy: I am come that they might have life, and that they might have it* ***more abundantly.*** (Beyond measure)

We live in a day when everything possible is being done by the devil and men, including people who should know better, to remove every trace of the blood from our faith.

An all-out warfare has been released against the main element of our faith that works—without which we will spiritually die.

Years ago some parts of the church removed every song that had the word *blood* from its hymnals because they said it was *frightening* to the children. And now, even among the Evangelicals a thought has arisen in the mind of some to re-arrange the vocabulary of the faith to exclude the word, *blood,* because the unsaved are *offended* by *it.* ***As a result***, messages, denominations and lives are void of the Blood of Jesus.

Consider this: There are whole generations of children and youth that will never be taught about the power of the blood of Jesus. Do we know what we are doing to them by *taking it down a notch,* only bringing ***it*** up at Easter, one time a year?

- Sadly the devil has bathed our children and youth in blood through abortions, abuse and the media which revels in bloodshed.
- They can play bloody video games, watch movies that shows horrific murders and no one even blinks an eye at it, but just mention the blood of Jesus at church or in the city park and everyone cringes.

Can't we see the devil at work to take from the church the powerful, wonder-working blood of the Lamb?

If I asked you to remove every trace or remembrance of the blood from your natural body, you know you would be dead. Our common sense tells us ***we must have blood to have life.***

And to take the blood out of our faith, we might as well just slit our own throats and watch the life drain out—for that is exactly what is happening today.

God created mankind to live—from the time he breathed His own Breath of life into Adam and that breath infused the blood of man with life and for that cause alone he became a living soul.

God did not create us to be clumps of lifeless clay, shaped like a man or woman—and He did not create His church to be lifeless clumps of lay shaped like man and woman.

A child can sit down with clay and make things in the image of what is in their mind, you or I can do the same, but we cannot give life to it because the life is in the blood.

If there is no blood—there is no life.

We, *as the church*, stand today exactly where those of old stood when Jesus said something so offensive to them that many walked away . . . ***John 6:66***

- ***Eat*** my flesh
- ***Drink*** my blood

In a day when ***the Blood is out*** and ***bloodless religion is in***—we must embrace with all of our hearts, the Blood and Body of Jesus Christ! We are redeemed, bought back from the slave trader of bondage. Death doesn't own us anymore.

There's immunity in the Blood of Jesus.

- **Immunity**—Resistance to disease: Freedom from responsibility or punishment: exemption or protection from something unpleasant, to which others are subject;

Jesus has purchased us! He has redeemed us by His own blood and has given us immunity from the curse of sin and death. Jesus is at the Right Hand of God—Our Intercessor, our Mighty Warrior! He's not the little lamb being led to the slaughter anymore.

He's the King of kings and Lord of lords—soon to return for a glorious church washed in the Blood of the Lamb.

CHAPTER 11

NO OTHER NAME

Acts 4:12

Neither is there salvation in any other; for there is no other name under heaven given among men, whereby we must be saved.

We've tried it our way, folks—It's not working!!!

Galatians 1:6 (Emphasis Added)—*I marvel that ye are so soon removed from him that called you into the grace of Christ unto another gospel:*

"If anyone comes preaching any other gospel than Jesus Christ, crucified and resurrected—let him be accursed—even if it is an angel . . ."

We cannot outwit God on His Ways and Thoughts of doing things. God says, *"Do it this way"* and we say, *"but God, what about this way?"*

The Church has taken so many alternate routes to try to accomplish what Jesus already finished. We have turned to lesser powers—the power of the human mind and to the power of the arms of flesh—which have absolutely no salvation, healing and deliverance value.

God is calling the Church back to the only Name under heaven—whereby we can and must be saved.

The area mentioned, *"Under heaven,"* covers every territory that exists.

- Go to most remote star and ***Jesus is King.***
- Go to the distant lands and ***Jesus is King.***
- Go to the most difficult situation on the face of the earth and ***Jesus is King.***
- Go to the sickest and most infirmed and ***Jesus is King.***
- Go to the most lost person in all of eternity and ***Jesus is still King.***

There is nothing that we have faced, are facing or will face that cannot be covered by the Blood of the Lamb of God and come under subjection to that all inclusive and powerful name—Jesus Christ!

We live in a time when every solution and way and thought of man has risen higher than the King's head and exalted itself above that great and awesome powerful name!

The church is rampant with *"alternate routes."* She has created a path separate from *The Way, The Truth and The Life*—while still calling herself Christian.

Jesus Christ will not stand side by side with any other religion or thought or way or such—but He will stand alone as the only One who has the power to exact change in the human mind, heart and soul.

The cross was and is and will be enough for there is *no other way* or method or name that will ever match that priceless sacrifice and the wonderful words that Jesus uttered from the Cross—"It is finished."

Finished means finished.

There is nothing more that we have to do but believe in that name and the power that is behind that name. The Name of Jesus, preached as the One and only way to Salvation, is not very popular, even within the *"Christian churches."* So much has attached itself to the foundations of faith that Jesus has been pushed out the back door.

There is just *"no room"* for Him in *"that way."* He, as He presented Himself, has become an embarrassment to the Church.

This may sound extreme, but just stand within any group of *Christian*s from different denominational or experiential background and start talking about Jesus and watch the subject cause an uncomfortable wave to go through the group. Someone will change the subject as they shift their feet and lower their head.

Jesus knew that people would be ashamed of Him and forewarned of the consequences of that happening.

> *Mark 8:38—Whosoever therefore shall be ashamed of me and of my words in this adulterous and sinful generation; of him also shall the Son of man be ashamed, when he cometh in the glory of his Father with the holy angels.*

It will take a bold and faithful people to the Cause of Christ to persevere in this time and not care that your Jesus is an offense.

> *Romans 9:33—As it is written, Behold, I lay in Zion a stumbling stone and rock of offence: and whosoever believeth on him shall not be ashamed.*

We have been told in the Word of God what His coming would do and also what the response would be from the world as we took the message of Jesus to the world.

> *Isaiah 53:3—He is despised and rejected of men; a man of sorrows, and acquainted with grief: and we hid as it were our faces from him; he was despised, and we esteemed him not.*

He came into the world despised and is still despised. But, the Church of the Living God must not be ashamed of that Name.

- ***It is time*** that the church quits adding to Jesus, as if He's not quite enough or needs something added to His work of the cross to get the job done.
- ***It is time*** that we quit neutralizing the power of His name by being ashamed of it.

- ***It is time*** that we quit watering down the power of His Gospel and offering that diluted and polluted pabulum to a dying world.
- ***It is time*** that we became comfortable with His name on our lips outside the House of God as we take Him to the city streets.
- ***It is time*** that we no longer waltz around the Name of Jesus when we talk to people about "church."
- ***It is time*** that we remember that the Church is not the salvation of souls, but Jesus is Salvation.

People need Jesus—*not our version of Jesus.*

My son, Daniel Dummer, and I were talking one day about the subject of people's view of Jesus. He added this:—*"Do they have the Mind of Christ or the Christ of their Mind?"*

People have crafted for themselves a *custom-fit Jesus* and to go along with that, *a soft, padded cross* to carry.

Many times the people of God and His church attempts to size Jesus to their lives—to trim a little bit here, tuck him in; to clip a portion off to make Him fit. While it is true that Jesus is able to slip as a garment of righteousness over any sinner who is repentant, it is also true that He does not fit our models upon which we try to tailor him to fit us.

This mind of ours is capable of maneuvering just about anything that we don't agree with. The church has tailored Jesus to fit their denominations, their carnality, their mindsets, their religion, their doctrines—just about anything, you name it—Jesus has been trimmed to fit the mind-set, life-style that we have developed.

Jesus is not a person you can understand with or define with your mind and yet many do exactly that and it's not just the ungodly. Christians have let their minds define "their Jesus," in many ways.

We are to shape our lives to fit the Word and not the W ord to fit our lives.

That adage could be addressing the family, church, nations, as people everywhere are trying to find a gospel and a Jesus that fits their style of religion .

We have watched as formulas, techniques, and ideas have passed themselves off in the place of the Power of God. Workers for the church have spun their wheels in frustration as they have realized that no one is getting changed, healed, delivered, or saved—*really.* Oh a few come in and start attending church and yes, in some places, in some instances, there are true disciples made out of the converts, but that is not the norm.

We claim to be Holy Spirit filled and yet still rely upon our own thoughts and ways to *get the job done.* Committees are formed until we committee things to death and we still do not see the lost coming in record number—radically changed by the Power of God.

Many missionaries, as they face the foreign fields where the demonic powers are commonly understood and accepted by the populace, understand that "business as usual" is not going to get those in cultural and religious bondage free.

- ***They know*** that it going to take someone who knows the Name of Jesus Christ and the Jesus Christ of the name.
- ***They know*** that they have to have a name that is higher than the name of the demonic gods of the world. (Philippians 2:9-11)
- ***They know*** that they have to demonstrate that our God has power to set them free from the powerful forces that are at work in their lives.

When will we ever learn?

Our society is demon infested and the demons are not nice American or English demons that are civilized. They are killers and thieves of our destiny, our children, our churches, our finances, our peace, our cities, our nations, our families and so much more.

The enemy is out to kill, steal and destroy.

> ***John 10:10a****—The thief cometh not, but for to steal, and to kill, and to destroy . . .*

We will only be able to face the works of darkness with the powerful work of Jesus Christ and His shed blood and name—and we will only face the enemy with spiritual feet firmly planted in the Bedrock of our faith—Jesus Christ.

We can't go into this level of truth warfare with anything added to what Jesus did already.

- ***We cannot*** add a thing to the cross.
- ***We cannot*** add a thing to deliverance.
- ***We cannot*** add a thing to healing.
- ***We cannot*** add a thing to salvation.

> ***Isaiah 55:8-9***
>
> *8 For my thoughts are not your thoughts, neither are your ways my ways, saith the Lord.*
>
> *9 For as the heavens are higher than the earth, so are my ways higher than your ways, and my thoughts than your thoughts.*

We cannot add concepts, ideas or human thought to what God says.

We must not get caught up in the trap of trying to supply God's church and people with "our gifts and ideas," but rather, remember that God has supplied us with "His gifts, thoughts and ways." While He is creative in how He works through us within the gifts and movement of the Holy Spirit, we must use caution lest we impose our human spirit into the mix.

We have to know that this season is going to need a church that is full of the power of God and filled with faith in the Only Name under Heaven that has the power to Save, Heal and Deliver.

WE need Jesus—*NOW*—More than ever!!!

I believe that God is looking for people that will stand up—apart from the crowd—and be counted as one that will not compromise with any system or method that departs from the pure Gospel.

Not everyone has bowed our knees to *"other gods,"*—Not even to the *"Jesus of our mind."*

Now let's take this beyond salvation—into the realms beyond—those areas that move beyond time and eternity and have great value to them before the Throne of God.

There is *NO OTHER NAME!*

There are *'ways'* in which we take the seat of honor as we become *"bigger than Jesus,"* and present ourselves—overpowering His Voice, His Presence and His Glory. There are times when our presence is so large that no one can see Jesus!

It's time for us to sit down and quit blocking other's view of the Master.

Our ministry stinks without the anointing and when we stand, blocking other's access and view of Jesus because of our own slant on things—we are so wrong and so negligent of the great gift that would have desired to flow through us to others.

- ***There are hungry people*** and we are in the way of their approach to the only one who is called, *"The Bread of Heaven come down to you . . ."*
- ***There are thirsty people*** who need the Living Water and we are not it; we are just jugs, vessels, containers, but we are not the Water!
- ***There are people in bondage*** and they don't need someone all full of *self-help programs* coming along and thrusting that in front of the Lamb of God who came to deliver them.
- ***There are people who are blind*** and they don't need blind guides leading them into a ditch.

- ***There are spiritually, emotionally, mentally and cripple people*** who desire to walk and leap and praise the Lord who does not need a powerless church to just make people comfortable in their pain.
- ***There are people whose back has been bowed*** for "*these 18 years by a spirit of infirmity,*" and God help us to know that the key to release of that stiff spine to stand up and walk straight is Jesus Christ!

We live in precarious times when the Church has deviated far from Jesus—onto a path that embraces the many other ways—With people as the star attractions.

The church has married itself to a system that is spinning wildly towards the apostate church—and we sit here and wonder how this could have happened.

- ***When did*** we lose the power of God in our midst?
- ***When did*** we become impotent?
- ***When did*** we quit saying, *"Silver and Gold have I none but in the name of Jesus, rise up and walk?"*
- ***When did*** we go away from Jesus?

Or sadder yet, when did Jesus walk away and leave us to our own ways and thoughts because there was just no room for Him in our Inn? We need to realize that God does not allow mixtures—Jesus and little dab of this or that . . .

- ***God does not want*** the blood of the Lamb of God tainted with flesh and carnality.
- ***God does not want*** the Name of Jesus overshadowed by personalities, systems, and works.

God will have a church that has the name of Jesus on its lips and in its heart.

We must be a people that will honor the name of Jesus so much that to be without that name would be like a living death—that the separation of our lives from that name and the man of that name would be hell on earth.

How could we have lived so long just squandering the value of the Name of Jesus?

We have corrupted the simplicity of the Gospel! We need to realize that "There is a Name that is above every name!!!"

It is above the names of Sickness, Sin, Bondage, Death, Devils, Kingdoms and Thrones, and most of all above our own names and those things that we name as hopeless, incurable, lost and ruined—the things that we curse with death because we do not know that value of the Name of Jesus in all of our life's situations.

"If there was another way—another name, then Jesus would not have had to come."
Loren Dummer

But . . .

- ***He has*** come and He is here!!! *Thank you Jesus!*
- ***He has*** not changed. *Thank you God!*
- ***He has*** stayed exactly the same and remained faithful and constant. *Praise and Honor to that wonderful name!*

He is the anointed One of Heaven who came down and paid the price for us to say, whisper or shout His wonderful name and have it mean something to humanity.

His blood backs His Name and we simply cannot add anything to that.

We need to do what Jesus did—walk in holiness and in the anointing to see the blind see, the cripple walk, the infirmed loosed, the dead raise, the demoniac set free and the lost found!!!

There is no other Name!

CHAPTER 12

STAND

Galatians 5:1

Stand fast therefore in the liberty wherewith Christ hath made us free, and be not entangled again with the yoke of bondage.

While it's true we live in a world in which the voice of the compromised, religious church has been silenced by tolerance, there are many Christians who desire to stand bold for Truth.

The early disciples were just like us—they really wanted to live at peace with their world while following Jesus—but everyone of them had to come to terms with the truth—no one can live in peace with the world and Jesus at the same time.

> ***Matthew 26:7*** (Emphasis Added)—*And Peter remembered the word of Jesus, which said unto him, "Before the cock crow, thou shalt* ***deny*** [to affirm that one has no acquaintance or connection with someone] *me thrice." And he went out, and wept bitterly.*

Fear gripped his heart and because of it he failed to affirm his relationship with Jesus, but instead declared he was not connected to Him. While he spoke the words out loud, sometimes actions or lack of speaking yells to the world around us that we "are not connected all that well to Jesus."

Think of Peter pre-Pentecost—the denial of Jesus in a time when he should have boldly proclaimed his alliance with Jesus. Instead he drew back and distanced himself from Him—to preserve his own life.

Oh I believe we all want to be brave hearted in the face of danger, draw our sword and fight for our King . . . but when the heat is applied, many times God's people sit down and try to keep a low profile.

I like to call Peter *the Brave Coward.*

When there was no cost, he could declare he would die for Jesus. He, even with Jesus the miracle worker beside him, drew his sword and chopped off the ear of the offender. But, when Jesus was arrested and led away, when the trial came and he felt all alone and the crowd was trying to name names of those who followed Jesus—*he did not do so well.*

<u>But there was a transition in Peter</u>

> ***Acts 2:14*** (Emphasis Added)—*But Peter, **standing up** with the eleven, **lifted up his voice**, and said unto them, Ye men of Judea, and all ye that dwell at Jerusalem, be this known unto you, and hearken to my words:*

There came a time in his life when he stood up and told the truth—not only that he was ***fully aligned with Jesus*** but also addressed in one of the most powerful messages ever what the religious world had done to Jesus, rehearsing the crucifixion and those who had rejected Him. He, at this moment though invited earlier to follow Jesus, fully laid his life down to truly follow Jesus—all the way.

It was no longer a matter of *emotionally committing*, but was in fact *a total sell-out* to the cause of Christ.

We are going to take a close look at a few key scriptures in order to better understand the subject of standing up for Jesus when others hate Him or don't want to hear about Him or see you minister in his name.

The Truth is—we may be facing some days ahead of us that will greatly challenge the church—*if the Lord does not grant us some clemency.*

I think about the past freedoms we have had in openly sharing the gospel of Jesus Christ—but year after year He has become more and more unpopular in His exclusive claims. It is in this spiritual climate we are going to have to stand.

Hebrews 10:39 (Emphasis Added)—*But we are not of them who* ***draw back*** *unto perdition; but of them that believe to the saving of the soul.*

Draw Back

- To withdraw oneself; who with *timidity hesitate to avow what they believe;*
- To be unwilling to utter from fear;
- To shrink from declaring, to conceal.

I know people may be fearful and timid, finding it hard to speak at times, but our faith in Jesus should not be something we are afraid to share—no matter the circumstances. We all know the opposing message is loud and clear, demanding and offensive, and the believer needs to lift a testimony of faith and say what they believe about Jesus.

There will be times when all of us are faced with opportunity to speak up for the cause of Christ, to declare His name as the Only Name in a world of many ideas about God, heaven and religion.

In ***Acts 4:18-20*** we read the account of Peter and John being commanded to not speak. The strong essence of what was being commanded was that they ***not utter or proclaim, or hold a conversation with others in order to instruct them***, in the name of Jesus.

How did they respond to the pressure being applied? In verses *19-20* Peter and John said, "*Whether it be right in the sight of God to hearken unto you more than unto God, you judge, for we cannot help but speak* ***(to declare one's mind)*** *the things which we have seen and heard.*

We are witnesses and witnesses tell what they have seen and heard

When my husband stood up in a small meeting, after a leader of another religion had spoken, saying, *"We don't believe in your God or your Bible,"* my husband declared, ***"There is NO other name whereby man must be saved but Jesus."*** I'm pretty sure he was not the issue but the name He declared. As a result, the religious around the nation and yes, into other nations, went into a feeding frenzy. That would be a whole other book to write . . .

But, what they didn't know was this—God had spoken to my husband these words, ***"if you don't speak up for me, I am not obligated to you."*** So, he spoke up in the face of spiritual darkness and opened himself to public scrutiny and display.

The system that is intolerant to Jesus and the believers in Jesus in our society is already in place to silence or mock the man of God for taking a stand for Jesus.

They tried to silence him through intimidation and if that didn't work then tell lies to make a public spectacle of him through ridicule, slander and gossip—radio, television, emails, blogs, letters . . . threats to picket, lies and more lies . . .

This is the tactic used by those who surround us today—intimidation, fear—meant to silence you in your bold stand for Jesus Christ.

There comes a time when we know we have *crossed the line* from nominal faith to bold faith.

Everyone has to face this moment in their Christian faith—*a time when unbelievers, scoffers, haters of Jesus*—surround you and you feel the blood rush to your heart as the moment has come . . .

- ***On the fear side of this moment***, a decision has to be made—*are we going to speak or not?*
- ***On the faith side of this moment***, we have made a commitment that will cost us our reputation with man but decide our discipleship issue once and for all.

Once we speak—we know and they know that our message will be revolutionary.

I believe that God wants us to be prepared for taking a bold stand in a time when our faith in Christ is not going to be popular. We cannot just give consent with our hearts and minds, but we must also give consent with our mouths, ***in holy boldness***, to declare that Jesus Christ is our Lord, that He is the Only Door of Salvation.

> ***John 14:6*** (Emphasis Added)—*Jesus saith unto him,* (Thomas) ***I am*** *the way, the truth, and the life: no man cometh unto the Father, but by me.*

God does not want us to waver between two opinions in the face of persecution. He wants us to unashamedly declare Him to others. And folks, we are going to have ample opportunity to make declarations of our Faith in Jesus many times over in the days ahead of us.

> ***II Thessalonians 2:1-2*** (Emphasis Added)—*Now we beseech you, brethren, by the coming of our Lord Jesus Christ, and by our gathering together unto him,* ***That ye be not soon shaken in mind, or be troubled, neither by spirit, nor by word, nor by letter as from us****, as that the day of Christ is at hand.*

My husband had preached a powerful message on a recent Sunday, describing the condition of the world we live in and the need for the church to be the church in these darkening times we live in. A lady had attended and went away complaining, *"That was not very encouraging or uplifting."*

I get very concerned when I see the response of those who say they are Christians when the season demands a reply from the ministers of the gospel—not because of *my name or reputation*, but because of Jesus. I recall the messages of Peter on the day of Pentecost and Stephen's on the day of his death—both described the church world that had greatly declined from where God had brought them.

- ***I know people do not like*** to hear that persecution is going on and may yet come our way.
- ***I know people do not like*** the *doomsday messages as they would malign them,* but prefer words easy on the ears and heart.
- ***I know people do not like*** confrontation with the world around them, but prefer to not know or see.

But what are we going to do when the reality of the secular and apostate religious world closes in and demands that we quit teaching in His name because He's ***too offensive*** or ***too intolerant of other ways***, or ***too bloody*** or ***too Biblically narrow***?

The Word of God speaks of shakings that are coming, but we also see in this portion of scripture in *II Thessalonians 2:1-2* that the mind can be shaken.

- **Be Shaken**—The movement of winds, storms and waves that agitate the mind for the purpose of overthrowing our faith.

These winds, storms and waves spoken of here are not natural, but things that bring about mental stress. God wants our minds to be stable, unwavering in the face of adversity as the Day of the Lord draws near.

To have confidence is more than a person building themselves up in their personality to be more forthright. Look at this scripture and what it truly means for a believer to have confidence:

> ***Hebrews 10:35*** (Emphasis Added)—***Cast not away*** (don't throw away) *therefore your* ***confidence****, which hath great recompense of reward.*

How powerful it is to see that the definition of the word ***confidence*** in the scripture means:

- ***To have*** freedom in speaking without reservation or concealment.
- ***To have*** free and fearless confidence, cheerful courage, boldness and assurance.

Do you oftentimes find yourself praying for boldness? Do you oftentimes find yourself praying to be able to stand up for Jesus, regardless?

Holy boldness is what we all need!

> ***Mark 8:34*** (Emphasis Added)—*And when he had called the people unto him with his disciples also, he said unto them,* ***Whosoever will come after me, let him deny himself and take up his cross, and follow me.***

The defining moment in our faith in Christ is when we publically acknowledge Him while losing sight of ourselves and laying down our own interest for His. For us to, "Take up our cross," is to embrace a well-known instrument of death that was reserved for the guiltiest of all criminals. This was the crucifixion Jesus underwent.

Jesus further says to His disciples in *verse 35*, *"For whosoever will save his life shall lose it; but whosoever shall lose his life for my sake and the gospel's, the same shall save it."* He goes on to say in *verses 36-38*, *"For what shall it profit a man, if he shall gain the whole world, and lose his own soul? Or what shall a man give in exchange for his soul?* ***Whosoever therefore shall be ashamed of me and of my words in this adulterous and sinful generation****; of him also shall the Son of man be ashamed, when he cometh in the glory of his Father with the holy angels."* (Emphasis Added)

Part of the reward for *standing up for Jesus* is that He will stand up for you.

I believe the closer we get to the coming of the Lord, the more important it will be for us to be bold in our witness of Jesus. The disciples in Acts 4 and those they worshipped with, had to make a choice—speak or keep quiet, as ordered.

Their response was remarkable—The prayed and opened the heavens even more to release greater power and glory of Jesus on earth—and they didn't mind that the place where they gathered was shaken by God's Spirit.

I would pray that for all believers—that they would get hold of God in the face of adversity and declare even more the name of Jesus!

> ***1 Corinthians 1:18, 27-29****—For the preaching of the cross is to them that perish foolishness; but unto us which are saved it is the power of God . . . . But God hath chosen the foolish things of the world to confound the wise; and God hath chosen the weak things of the world to confound the things which are mighty; And base things of the world, and things which are despised, hath God chosen, yea, and things which are not, to bring to naught things that are: That no flesh should glory in his presence.*

When we come to the place that we make a determination to know nothing but Christ and the Cross . . . we have made a bold decision to move away from *church as usual.* We must hold fast to what God is teaching us about His Church and take it to another level of understanding and wisdom as the Holy Spirit reveals the truth about God's Church.

"I have determined"—is a crucial point in the life of a believer—a minister—it's a point where a decision is made—a life-altering decision—not just an emotional response—but one that will define the man/woman and the ministry of the Church.

What kind of determination—bending of your will, submitting to the ways of God, are you and I going to do this year—today, this week, and from here on out?

Pastors, Intercessors, People of the Church, we must continue to see Satan embarrassed by the Cross of Christ.

How? By setting in place 12 foundational stones of victory over death, hell and the grave!

1. ***By enforcing*** the Victory of the Cross of Christ.
2. ***By taking back*** everything Satan has stolen from us; our families, our churches, our nation and the uttermost parts of the world.

3. ***By modeling*** our lives after the likeness and image and nature of Christ, as revealed in the Word of God.
4. ***By using*** the keys that Jesus has placed into the hands of the Church.
5. ***By accepting*** nothing that Satan has to offer us, no matter how good it looks, or the promises (strings) attached to it.
6. ***By picking up*** our cross and following Jesus in obedience to His call upon our lives.
7. By being a people of faith, authority and integrity with a desire to spoil every scheme of the enemy who continues to entrap and snare hapless victims by his darkness and deceit.
8. ***By standing*** in the gap, interceding to see souls saved, healed and delivered.
9. ***By worshipping*** God with such intensity and sincerity that He will not even miss the beautiful voice of a once worshipping Lucifer.
10. ***By crying,*** *"Holy, Holy, Holy,"* with a multitude of voices that will ring with the sound of many waters around God, mingling our voices with the Great Cloud of Witnesses that have gone before us.
11. ***By yielding*** up the fruit of clean lips before a Holy and Righteous God, Who is Worthy of All Praise and Glory and Honor!
12. ***By honoring*** the Lamb Who was slain from the foundations of the Earth, for He is surely coming again in Clouds of great Glory at which time we will ride with Him to utterly destroy the enemy's camp, thereby winning the War of The Ages.

He has given everything we could possibly need to succeed at being His Church.

When we make a determination, in the fear and trembling of God and His Word, as to where we stand on the most important thing in the whole world—Jesus Christ and the Cross—it will impact every fiber of our being.

- ***I have determined***—to not access and add to my ministry anything that would detract from Jesus and what He did.

- ***I have determined***—that not even my personality and gifts will dominate the scene.
- ***I have determined***—that I will not go forth in oratory skill or seductive words, crafted to be used to draw people to me.
- ***I have determined***—that what I do will keep people's eyes on Jesus and build faith in Him alone.
- ***I have determined***—that I will not lean on or use the wisdom of the world or its prestigious people's wisdom of how to be the church.
- ***I have determined***—that those who receive of my hand will not lean on the wisdom of man but the power of God, realizing that if I give them anything else, it will come to nothing.

With this level of commitment
We will be as submitted to the Cross as Jesus was in His death.

Part II

Is what you're living for worth Jesus dying for?

"Though the cross of Christ has been beautified by the poet and the artist, the avid seeker after God is likely to find it the same savage implement of destruction it was in the days of old. The way of the cross is still the pain-wracked path to spiritual power and fruitfulness. So do not seek to hide from it. Do not accept an easy way. Do not allow yourself to be patted to sleep in a comfortable church, void of power and barren of fruit. Do not paint the cross nor deck it with flowers. Take it for what it is, as it is, and you will find it the rugged way to death and life. Let it slay you utterly."

A.W. Tozer

Unbroken

I was broken, lost, alone.
I wore scars as emblems of past mistakes.
I blocked others out, made my heart like stone.
I silenced myself, afraid to further break.

I pleaded for death to take me away
I pleaded for the Grim Reaper to steal my soul
For I had nothing further to say
I didn't think I could be whole

But One whose mercy was everlasting
Whose love was never-failing
Saw my pain and sorrow
And kept me from the passing

His hands reached out to me
His eyes bore into me
His grace uplifted me
His mercy redeemed me

He kissed my scars and told me,
"These aren't emblems of sorrow,
But of what I saved you from.
They're a promise of tomorrow."

Brian McBride April 23, 2012

Sand Castles

Recently I talked to my mother, Mary Seaton, on the phone. She had been meditating and wanted to share with me a golden nugget of inspiration. She had been mediating on the temporal things people spend their lives investing in. God brought to her ice and sand carvings as an example. Wow, did I ever get the picture—spiritually!

I live close to the Pacific Ocean and enjoy hearing and at times taking in activities that are related to the beach—with sculpting in sand being one of them. Many of you have either seen these artists or watched them on a television special and marveled at their work, for they truly do outstanding work.

You, along with others, have held your breath to see if what they were doing would hold together *long enough to be judged.*

These artists carve the spectacular, but fragile, sand castles on the ocean's shore, right in the face of danger of the coming tide. They know that all they will craft is going to soon be washed away, but they keep on putting their best work in sand. They spend countless hours on plans and then on carving, carefully crafting their masterpieces.

People watch as dozens of artisans all along the shoreline work to bring their brainstorm to fulfillment. They are then judged for their work, hopefully to win the reward of their labor. Sadly it is a temporal joy for in only hours; the tide turns and begins to erode the marvelous work of their hands.

At full tide nothing remains of what they have created.

A number of years ago I went to McCall, Idaho with my husband to see the ice carvings that had been finished in a winter contest of ice. I saw huge chunks of ice that had been chipped away at until a masterpiece of art was displayed on that winter day. Street after street of these carved beauties.

But then . . . the sun began to shine and they began to melt, a drip at a time, until nothing was left of them but a puddle.

A house of cards has the same feeling. Someone takes time to carefully place each card, hoping that the draft from a door or the brush of a sleeve does not topple it in its inception. But eventually, no matter how carefully one makes a house of cards; it is destroyed by those things feared because it is so unstable.

It is the same thing with dominoes . . . just one touch and they all fall down.

To live our lives close to the edge like the sand-carvers who build their masterpieces on the sand at water's edge, is to live with the risk of losing it all in a coming storm.

As we enter this section, let us all understand the simple truth Jesus spoke to us—*don't build on the sand* . . .

Chapter 13

Quicksand

Psalms 40:2

He brought me up also out of a horrible pit, out of the miry clay, and set my feet upon a rock, and established my goings.

We have all seen the movies where a person is running through brush and stumbles into a pit of quicksand. They quickly realize they are captured and sinking and will die unless someone extends something to them they can take hold of to pull their bodies out. They yell and struggle and soon, here comes someone just in time, to stretch out a long branch and help to pull them out. *If no one shows up*, they will struggle with the mire until it goes over their heads and totally sucks them under to their death.

The one whose feet are on solid ground can pull that person out, if they will take hold of what is being offered to them. The rescue is in the hands of the person who will receive the help—not only the one reaching out to help.

I have tried to help many people only to be rebuffed. I have had to stand helplessly by and watch people get so far in over their heads through ungodly choices that they eventually were taken into the depths of the mire of choice.

> ***Zechariah 6:12a*** (Emphasis Added)—*And speak unto him, saying, Thus speaketh the Lord of hosts, saying, Behold the man whose name is **The BRANCH** . . .*

Jesus is the BRANCH! He is the one who rescues—He's the one we stretch to the lost, dying, deceived—those trapped in the error of their own ways—and those trapped in the vanity of their minds.

- ***I pray*** that this section of Bedrock will be a Jesus Branch held out to those who are just about sinking in the quagmires their choices have brought them to.
- ***I pray*** for those who are on safe ground that they will extend the Branch and rescue through truth those that are in trouble.
- ***I pray*** this section will serve as a warning to *"take heed how you stand, lest you fall also."* ***(1 Corinthians 10:12)***

Quicksand is an interesting mixture of water and sand.

Look at this definition:

- **Quicksand**—A bed of soft or loose sand saturated with water and having considerable depth, yielding under ***weight*** and therefore tending to suck down any *object* resting on its surface.

  Hebrews 12:1b (Emphasis Added)—*let us lay aside every* ***weight,*** *and the sin which doth so easily beset us . . .*

The problem with quicksand is that it's *a mixture* of water and sand.

- ***When people believe*** they are saved *while* embracing and tolerating ungodly things—it is sand—not the Way, the Truth, the Life in Jesus Christ.
- ***When people believe*** they are saved by their church or religion—it is sand—not the Rock of our Salvation, Jesus Christ.

A person cannot be saved by . . . works, goodness, generosity, church membership or human effort.

It's not that those commendable things are bad *as long as they are connected* to and a part of our relationship with true faith in Christ; it's just that these attributes, standing alone and apart from obedient faith in Christ, are faulty quicksand. It is unstable and will not hold a life up when the storms beat upon the house.

We do not have enough goodness in us to substitute anything for what Jesus alone did to save, heal and deliver us.

Look at this truth:

The word, ***"quick"*** means, alive, denoting that quicksand is ***"alive sand."***

I know we know the Word of God is ***alive*** and that the Living water is ***alive*** and that Holy Spirit quickens ***(makes alive)*** and Jesus lives and even Jesus' blood is a continual ***living*** stream of salvation—but I am not sure many people really understand the ability of sand to move ***as if alive***, to take hold of the unstable soul that stands or builds their lives on its deceptive surface.

We all know that sand is not stable, ever shifting, changing shapes with the wind or tides. It also shifts with every step that is taken on it.

If you have ever stood at the ocean's edge in the wet sand and watched a wave come in, you have also experienced the feel of the wave pulling the sand under your feet when the wave goes back out to sea. Many of you have felt the spiritual ground you stand upon do that—move with every wave that rushes to your shore. Jesus used rock and sand as examples because of the truth they reveal in the natural is how it is in the spiritual.

In Cannon Beach, Oregon, there is a huge rock that juts up out of the sand called, *"Haystack Rock,"* which at low tide it is surrounded by sand and at high tide it is surrounded by ocean water.

What I have noticed is this—it never moves, changes or is threatened by the tides—*only the sand shifts.*

> ***Matthew 7:24-27*** (Emphasis Added)
>
> *24 Therefore* ***whosoever*** *heareth these sayings of mine, and doeth them, I will liken him unto a wise man, which built his house* (An abode, family, household) *upon* ***a rock****:*

25 And the rain descended, and the floods came, and the winds blew, and beat upon that house; and it fell not: for it was founded upon ***a rock****.*

26 And every one that heareth these sayings of mine, and doeth them not, shall be likened unto a foolish man, which built his house upon ***the sand****:*

27 And the rain descended, and the floods came, and the winds blew, and beat upon that house; and it fell: and great was the fall of it.

Jesus, in ***Matthew 7,*** clearly speaks of sand and rock, revealing how totally different they are, one from the other.

- ***If you are standing on the Rock***, you will never have to wonder if you are going to sink.
- ***If you are standing on sand***, not only is there a dangerous mixture of water and sand, but it is also the recipe for the total ruination of the whole house.

Every believer should take Jesus' warning about sand personally and every church should corporately heed this when setting their House in order.

The Apostle Paul in ***1 Corinthians 3:16*** asks this poignant question of the believer, *"Know ye not that ye are the temple of God, and that the Spirit of God dwells in you?* We personally are the house/temple Jesus refers to as *"whosoever,"* in ***Matthew 7:24.***

Oh, folks, Jesus made a way out of the pit! He Himself became the ***BRANCH*** who was stretched out to rescue us. Look at the scripture and see what He personally did for us. There's no reason why any of us should live trapped in the quagmires of life and its many propositions for failure.

We still have the power to choose to do right . . .

<u>Let's go back to our key scripture:</u>

Psalms 40:2 (Emphasis Added)—*He brought me up also out of a horrible pit, out of the miry clay, and set my feet* ***upon a rock,*** *and established my goings.*

- **Pit**—a pit hole (especially one used as a cistern or a prison):

Miry—swampy, boggy, marshy, mucky, muddy.

Ezekiel 47:9-11 tells us that everything that lives and moves wherever the river flows shall live, but the miry places, those places that are a swamp and boggy, wet marshes shall not be healed but they will be given to salt, meaning they are able to be ***easily crushed as salt is ground into powder.***

God has placed fences throughout His Word to secure us in a safe place on the Rock—fences around our free will—around our minds—to keep us from stepping into the miry pits of life.

The reason no one can get themselves out of the quicksand is because it offers nothing solid under their feet to stand on.

By the time someone gets in this far, they are both struggling and sinking.

Quicksand is a quagmire; a killing ground. Beneath the surface of the quicksand lays the bodies of many victims. The person that is now going under is surrounded by many silent witnesses to the fact that this is a death trap; a place of dead men's bones.

- **Quicksand is ground that *"sucks you into itself."***

It is filled with the dead and dying and offers nothing but a suffocating end of life. The way it destroys life is to remove the foundation, sinking the person, and then leaving only the five senses to realize the trap of death that they have entered into and an awareness that . . .

"Without outside help, I am a dead person."

The breath is getting ready to be cut off and life diminished by the overwhelming power of quicksand. This is so senseless because the good ground of the Word of God surrounds the pit.

The Lord took me to the scripture that declares . . .

> ***2 Peter 2:9-10*** (Emphasis Added)
>
> *9 The Lord knoweth how to deliver the godly out of temptations, and to reserve the unjust unto the Day of Judgment to be punished:*
>
> *10 But chiefly them that walk after the flesh in the lust of uncleanness, and despise government.* ***Presumptuous are they, self-willed,*** *they are not afraid to speak evil of dignities.*

Notice the word in *verse 10*—***self-willed.*** This is a big problem. We can readily see Lucifer was self-willed and presumptuous. What brought about the end of his anointed place in heaven was his own mind taking over his destiny. *Look how well that turned out . . .*

Believers have to know this—if Satan's free will could bring about his fall—*so can it ours.*

> ***2 Peter 2:20—22*** (Emphasis Added)
>
> *20 For if after they have escaped the pollutions of the world through the knowledge of the Lord and Savior Jesus Christ, they are* ***again entangled therein, and overcome****, the latter end is worse with them than the beginning.*
>
> *21 For it had been better for them not to have known the way of righteousness, than, after they have known it, to turn from the holy commandment delivered unto them.*

> *22 But it is happened unto them according to the true proverb, The dog is turned to his own vomit again; and the sow that was washed to her wallowing in the mire.*

Quicksand is about choice.

There is a big difference between the person who stumbles into a pit of quicksand and one who knowingly walks right back into the same pit that the Lord rescued them from. A person has to leave the everlasting arms of Jesus to be accepted by the arms of quicksand, which will gladly wrap itself around their body.

- I remember the story of two public servants who said they had to quit because they were *"getting sucked into some things, that if they didn't get out now, they may never get out."*

Back to ***Matthew 7***—Jesus tells us the sand was specifically made of ***the foolish man's*** disobedience. When there is any disobedience to the Word, then we shift our lives onto the unstable sand of mixtures—our opinion and God's Word.

Jesus said the foolish man is, by definition, "*heedless and negligent*" towards the things He taught.

This question in ***Hebrews 2:3a, "How shall we escape, if we neglect so great salvation,"*** *testifies* to the vastness of salvation ***(saving, deliverance, healing)*** for rescuing us *but also addressed* the issue of neglect as being a cut-off point to rescue. "*Neglect*" in this verse means *"to be careless of, make light of, to show no regard of."*

There are a few things we can be indifferent to, but our faith is not one of those things. Where and how we stand on pertinent subjects that relate directly to our faith have eternal dividends or consequences.

Quicksand is a pit of man's making—through careless, reckless choices—but a believer should be prudent and careful to nurture the right choices in regards to their faith. Even if the whole world of religion makes tolerant choices, we cannot. To do so will surely destabilize our whole house, family, church and yes, even our life.

By the time a person is in quicksand, they have no foundation left—*they are sinking.*

Phrases like, *"I'm all bogged down,"* are commonly used to mean, *"I can't do it right now—I'm not free."*

> ***Galatians 5:1b*** (Emphasis Added)—*Stand fast therefore in the liberty wherewith Christ hath made us free, and be not* ***entangled again*** *with the yoke of bondage.*

The church is made of people who are daily making choices.

Israel stood at a place of decision, no different than the multitudes of believers do today. What we are talking about is not whether we are going to be church members or not—it's about whether we will serve the Lord or not. Joshua stood before people to whom he gave the choice of who they would serve.

> ***Joshua 24:15*** (Emphasis Added)—*And if it seem evil unto you to serve the Lord,* ***choose you this day whom ye will serve;*** *whether the gods which* ***your fathers*** *served that were on the other side of the flood, or the gods of the Amorites, in whose land ye dwell:* ***but as for me and my house*** (abode, family, household) ***we will serve the Lord.***

It is evident from Biblical history that *their fathers*, though ***they said*** they served God, were actually serving gods and not a whole lot different that the Amorites. Everyone is going to serve something and maybe in some cases, several kinds of gods . . . ***but to serve the Lord He must be a solo choice—none other!***

> ***Exodus 20:3*** (Emphasis Added)—*Thou shalt have* ***no other gods*** *before me.*

God doesn't just *suggest* an exclusive relationship with us— He *commands* an exclusive relationship in which no other gods are served.

> ***Matthew 6:24***—*No man can serve two masters: for either he will hate the one, and love the other; or else he will hold to the one, and despise the other. Ye cannot serve God and mammon.*

Jesus exemplified a life of purity of thought, heart and spirit—living a life of daily choices to *"do all that His Father had sent Him to do."*

He was a role model of one who fully yielded and obeyed everything His Father said.

The convictions by which a person lives are their life-line of truth, integrity, morality, faith and such that keeps them from slipping into the ***moral morass***.

Morass—a tract of low, soft, wet ground; a marsh or bog; marshy ground; any confusing or troublesome situation, especially one from which it is difficult to free oneself; ***entanglement.***

In other words . . . *quicksand!*

- ***Convictions*** are what come to the rescue when temptations try to overtake us or when we hear the Word of the Lord and our heart says ***amen***.
- ***Conviction*** is what comes in like a rush of fresh water to our conscience when those beliefs are broken in any way.

If you have no convictions, then you cannot be convicted. You see this all the time in the prisoners who have committed a crime. The courts can say they are guilty, but even when guilty they will say they are innocent while sitting locked behind bars with all liberties taken away.

There is a stick that is being held out right now—a stick of rescue—***The BRANCH, Jesus Christ***, stretched to you in this message of liberty. If you will take hold of the only thing that can drag you out of the pit you are in—He will set your feet upon ***Bedrock*** and your spiritual house will stand in times of storm.

Isaiah 51:1

(Emphasis Added)

Hearken to me, ye that follow after righteousness, ye that seek the Lord: ***look unto the rock*** *whence ye are hewn, and to the hole of the pit whence ye are digged.*

"No matter how deep the pit is that you are in, God is yet deeper."
~Bessie to Corrie Ten Boom in Prison Camp~

He brought me out of the miry clay.
He set my feet on the Rock to stay.
He put a song in my soul today.
A song of praise, hallelujah!

Are you ready to reach?

CHAPTER 14

THE SPIRIT IS WILLING BUT THE FLESH IN WEAK

Mark 14:38b

The spirit truly is ready, but the flesh is weak.

Let's take the root language for this scripture and read it this way: "*The rational soul of man is forward in spirit, but the body with all its human nature and frailties, passions and carnal flesh is impotent, sick and without strength.*"

I have been teaching about a fresh outpouring of Holy Spirit for some time now and yes, even preparing our hearts, minds and lives for God to fill us. I have taught countless times on *crucifying the flesh*, but are we really doing it *daily?* How many times do we let *a little passion for something else* slip in, tolerating our fleshes excessive desire for *other things*?

> ***Galatians 5:24****—And they that are Christ's have crucified the flesh with the affections and lusts.*
>
> ***1 Peter 4:1-2***
>
> *1 Forasmuch then as Christ hath suffered for us in the flesh, arm yourselves likewise with the same mind: for he that hath suffered in the flesh hath ceased from sin;*

2 That he no longer should live the rest of his time in the flesh to the lusts of men, but to the will of God.

Jesus was born into a flesh body that had to be crucified daily in order to be that *once-and-for-all* spotless lamb to be put to death for our sins. He was not easy on His flesh, but rather beat it under to obey His Father's Will. The scripture setting where He states, *the spirit is willing, but the flesh is weak*, is at the Garden of Gethsemane where He fully submitted His will to His Father, which would mean He was to be crucified.

We see the Apostle Paul making the same decision in ***1 Corinthians 9:27*** saying, *"Like an athlete I punish my body, treating it roughly, training it to do what it should,* ***not what it wants to.*** *Otherwise I fear that after enlisting others for the race, I myself might be declared unfit and ordered to stand aside." TLB*

Jesus, in speaking to Peter in ***Matthew 26:40-41*** told him upon finding him asleep again right at the crossroads of life as he had known it, *"What, could ye not watch with me one hour? Watch and pray, that ye enter not into temptation* (solicitation, provocation, adversity) *the spirit indeed is willing, but the flesh is weak."*

Jesus—*while prepared to lay his flesh body down to be crucified*—knew that within a very short time Peter would try to save his flesh body from being associated with Him.

Jesus had come to terms with the temporary state of the flesh side of man. The whole purpose of God was to allow Jesus to take on the humanity of man to suffer in the flesh for fallen flesh.

No man can ever accuse Jesus of not understanding.

Hebrews 2:16-18

16 We also know that the Son did not come to help angels; he came to help the descendants of Abraham.

> *17 Therefore, it was necessary for him to be made in every respect like us, his brothers and sisters, so that he could be our merciful and faithful High Priest before God. Then he could offer a sacrifice that would take away the sins of the people.*
>
> *18 Since he himself has gone through suffering and testing, he is able to help us when we are being tested. NLT*

Jesus' physical body felt pain when He was beaten, crowned with the thorns, had the nails driven through His hands and feet and pierced in the side. ***(Matthew 27:29; Mark 15:17; John 19:2)***

He felt to the core of His heart the betrayal of Judas. Hear the heart-breaking words of Jesus as he asked His apostle this penetrating question, *"Judas, are you betraying the Son of Man with a kiss?"* ***Luke 22:48*** NKJV

His emotions were as real as ours are, feeling the rejection of those who called for His crucifixion.

> ***Isaiah 53:3*** (Emphasis Added)—*He is despised and* ***rejected*** *of men; a man of* ***sorrows,*** *and acquainted with* ***grief****: and we hid as it were our faces from him; he was* ***despised,*** *and we esteemed him not.*

His heart beat blood just like ours, and was pierced through with many sorrows.

His flesh body was what was crucified so He might redeem mankind's fallen flesh.

We all need to face it—*the flesh side of us doesn't want to suffer, sacrifice or die.*

- ***The flesh*** is where our human desires and weaknesses are contained.
- ***The flesh*** is carnal and lusty.

- ***The flesh*** is temporal and dying, but strives to live and dominate our spirit, our lives and our destiny.
- ***The flesh*** has a will and demand of its own.
- ***The flesh*** pays attention to the carnal things of life, feeding off those things that have no eternal value.
- ***The flesh*** will cause spiritual death if it is not put to death.

Flesh is an enemy of God.
Flesh cannot please God.

The flesh of man and Spirit of Christ cannot co-exist in our mortal bodies being as both are ruling monarchs in human life.

> ***Matthew 6:24a***—*No man can serve two masters: for either he will hate the one, and love the other; or else he will hold to the one, and despise the other . . .*

> ***Romans 8:5***—*For they that are after the flesh do mind the things of the flesh; but they that are after the Spirit the things of the Spirit.*

Peter has been with Jesus for three and one half years, being discipled by the Master. He had seen Jesus do many wonderful miracles. He had been caught in the middle of the controversy that surrounded Jesus. He had been in intensive preparation, chosen and had destiny, handpicked and prepared by Jesus.

Jesus told his disciple that all of them would be offended because of Him on this same night. He referred them to prophetic scripture saying, "I will smite the shepherd and all the sheep will be scattered." But Peter said to Him in his usual bluster of faith, "Even if everyone else is offended, I will never be offended by you."

Jesus said to Peter words that have made their way into countless Easter Plays, *"It is a truth, this day, even this night, before the cock crows three times, you will deny me."* Peter replied, without really hearing Jesus' heart, *"Even if they kill me, I will not deny you in any way, shape or form."* Then all the disciples joined with Peter in that vow. ***Mark 14:27-31***

But, there was still a part of Peter that lacked the preparation for burial. His flesh was a dominant factor in his life, *even though* he was an avid follower of Jesus, *even though* he was quick to speak and stand up for Jesus.

We can focus on preparing our spirits for habitation so much that we miss the low-lying issues of the flesh. Some of these issues don't show up in their weakness until a trial of our faith comes to bear on us.

A trial of our faith exposes flesh that is not dead.

In all the years of preparation, Peter had failed to deal with an area of his own life that was still speaking out of his own fleshly desires. When he told the Lord that he *wouldn't allow Him to be killed*, the Lord rebuked the enemy working through His flesh.

- ***When*** Jesus said that one of *them* was going to betray Him, ***Peter was the first*** to say that it could and would never happen.
- ***When*** the guards came, ***Peter was the first*** to draw his sword and attack one of them, cutting their ear off.

All of these actions and words came out of his zeal to be used of God, to stand for the Kingdom of God, to act on behalf of Jesus—but also out of fleshly actions and words that had not been tempered and trained to die to their cravings.

He was so busy speaking and acting that he missed the fact that he had an innate weakness in his flesh.

When we come to worship, we bring our hungry spirits but neglect to recognize the fact that the *flesh is not hungry for more of the Lord.* We may blame sleepiness or distraction for the reason behind why we have trouble focusing in worship or in the preaching or teaching of the Word, and that sometimes may be true, but most often is not.

The real reason why we cannot settle down and get our minds and hearts focused on Jesus is because our flesh is restless to get up and get moving onto greener pastures.

- ***Our flesh*** is always looking through the fence to see what is *more attractive elsewhere.*
- ***Our flesh*** does not want to *receive prayer*, but desires to get the service over so we can go home.

We miss the fact that our carnal appetites are still actively opposing our spirit in its quest to seek God with all our heart, mind and strength.

- ***Our spirit*** longs for God but our flesh recoils from Him for He is the sword at the neck of flesh.
- ***Our spirit*** is willing to *lay it all down for Jesus*, but our flesh holds onto *money, goods, time, position, attractions . . .*
- ***Our spirit*** is willing to follow Jesus but our flesh wants to *follow another path and another voice*—a pathway of ease for the flesh's sake, a pathway of comfort, for the flesh's sake, a pathway of plenty for the flesh's sake . . .
- ***Our spirit*** is ready to die for the cause of Christ, but our flesh wants to live for itself, offers no sacrifice or offering outside of what enriches itself.
- ***Our spirit*** kneels in humble love but our flesh stands proud.
- ***Our spirit*** is full of the Word, craving more, but our flesh wants *other food*, because the Word does not feed our flesh because its appetites are carnal, earthy.
- ***Our spirit*** believes the promises but our flesh has no faith.
- ***Our spirit*** is awake but our flesh wants to sleep.
- ***Our spirit*** needs only The Spirit of God, but our flesh wants to be entertained and stimulated. *(This is why the disciples were sleeping while Jesus prayed—no great miracles were happening—only a prayer meeting . . .)*
- ***Our spirit*** rises up to *higher ground*, but our flesh calls us back to earth, back to reality.
- ***Our spirit*** hears the sounds of heaven and sees beyond this earthly plain but our flesh desires the sounds of life below and does not want to *come up higher.*

The conflict is great because there is no power of agreement between flesh and spirit.

> ***Romans 7:18***—*For I know that in me (that is, in my flesh,) dwelleth no good thing: for to will is present with me; but how to perform that which is good I find not.*

The only solution to this dilemma is to do what the Word of God says to do—*"kill the flesh, daily!"*

You cannot redeem flesh—you kill flesh!

Sometimes the redemption of the spirit calls for extreme measures to be taken against the flesh, something that our society, much less the church, fails to understand.

The flesh never mourns its own failure but rather tolerates and excuses it.

You crucify it daily through *thousand's of little choices* with *big consequences.* This is the daily battle we all face—our own flesh. The Apostle Paul writes to the Corinthians, *"For though we walk in the flesh, we do not war after the flesh."* He said, *"For the weapons of our warfare are not carnal (flesh) but mighty through God to the pulling down of strongholds."* He was not speaking about the devil; he was speaking about the human mind (will). ***2 Corinthians 10:3-5***

The root cause of all spiritual failure rests in our flesh.

Example—We know that fasting kills the flesh, but that during a fast; the flesh screams at us to *take just one bite of the cookie on the cabinet, it won't hurt.*

Truth—The same desire for the cookie when fasting comes from the same source that lust comes from for an illicit affair.

> ***1 Corinthians 1:26-29***
>
> *26 For ye see your calling, brethren, how that not many wise men after the flesh, not many mighty, not many noble, are called:*

27 But God hath chosen the foolish things of the world to confound the wise; and God hath chosen the weak things of the world to confound the things which are mighty;

28 And base things of the world, and things which are despised, hath God chosen, yea, and things which are not, to bring to nought things that are:

29 That no flesh should glory in his presence.

The Glory that is coming is going to need dead men—*those dead to the flesh and all its lusts and alive to the Spirit*—to stand and minister, so that our flesh will not rise up to proudly take the glory for what God is about to do.

Only *dead* men can truly *see* God.

CHAPTER 15

BACKSLIDING FROM THE POWER OF THE SPIRIT

Galatians 2:18

For if I build again the things which I destroyed, I make myself a transgressor.

> ***Galatians 3:1-3***—*O foolish Galatians, who hath bewitched you, that ye should not obey the truth, before whose eyes Jesus Christ hath been evidently set forth, crucified among you? This only would I learn of you, Received ye the Spirit by the works of the law, or by the hearing of faith? Are ye so foolish? Having begun in the Spirit, are ye now made perfect by the flesh?*

When we first fell in love with Jesus there was a hunger and focus that captured us so much that our very lives were wrapped up in our pursuit of Jesus and His Holy Spirit's touching our lives.

- ***We were hungry*** seekers in the altars.
- ***We wanted*** those times of soaking and seeking and being refilled over and over again.
- ***We stayed*** on fire for God while searching for ***more***.
- ***We had*** an intense desire to fill our spirits with God's Word and His Spirit.

When we are not avid seekers of the presence of God, we will settle for a whole lot less. We will settle for hours of television, media, games or reading or some other *mind filler*, where before we could not get enough of the Word of God, Worship and Prayer.

Our heart's desire for God literally drove us to a place of hunger that became more acute with each encounter with Him.

I don't know about you, but I am not satisfied with *just having church*, and yet that is what we are so prone to do, if we do not provoke ourselves to keep moving into the unknown.

Some who were once consumed with a passion for a deeper place in God may be now more settled into just going to church than pursing God. It is an easy pitfall to settle into when the hunger to actively go after what God has promised is diluted by *other things*.

Entanglements

> ***Galatians 5:1***—*Stand fast therefore in the liberty wherewith Christ hath made us free, and be not entangled again with the yoke of bondage.*

- **Entangled**—to hold in or upon, i.e. ensnare; by implication, to keep a grudge: KJV—entangle with, have a quarrel against, urge.

These entanglements generally consist of many fleshly building blocks to wall us off from the presence of God, but no one is snared against their will. Entanglements are entered into by the appetite of the flesh man—the part of us that craves the carnal things.

Entanglements are made of *"stuff,"* that *"snuffs"* the fire of the Spirit in our hearts and lives.

It may also be things we would never tag as being a drain on our passion for Jesus—*Frustrations, attitudes, holidays, business, relationships, and difficulties—just stuff*

And . . . Distractions

All of these can result in the *"loss of hunger,"* which results in the *"loss of focus,"* which results in *"loss of anointing,"* which results in *"loss of power."*

If we are going to do what God has called us to do, we have to seek to be hungry and to develop a seeking heart that nothing else will satisfy. We have to realize that when there is a loss of the anointing and passion for God being nurtured and released in our lives, we have difficulty entering into the presence of God.

We cannot just enter into the House of God any way we want, ill-prepared, with little attention to the condition of our own hearts and lives and then expect that God will just *"show up,"* just because we did.

There is such a passion and thirst for the *flesh* to have its own way. We have to battle the flesh to release the Spirit. A slight compromise puts us in a *different room* than the one of God's purpose.

We need to *weed the garden.*

Weeds are crowding out the desired harvest of what God would like to produce in our lives. Sadly, there are things planted that are being watered in our vineyard that God didn't want planted. He didn't sow the seeds of discontentment, restlessness, carelessness, presumption, apathy and complacency—we did.

How did we sow such negative things that fight for space in our hearts and lives? We do it by tolerating our own attitudes that preempt God. We are going to have to fight for this with a really "sharp sword" against our own fleshly desires.

***Spiritually Tangible*—natural things growing spiritual fruit.**

We must understand this principle—what goes on in our natural life has a spiritual implication for us. You all have experienced it—been on the mountain top of God's glory one day and then slumped to the valley the next as some quarrel broke out in your heart or some trouble entered into your home.

These things do try to take preeminence over our lives.

Jesus wants to be the Lord of all the kingdoms of our hearts, but sometimes we allow things to spiritually entangle us in a yoke of bondage—arguments, attitudes over things that really should have no spiritual value.

I get the feeling that the enemy of our soul is fighting harder than what we think he is, but he's moving by *stealth,* in silence, tiptoeing—not roaring.

He's using our own problems, difficulties, disputes, and distractions against us.

Former days of glory, passion and love for Jesus were marked by diligence. We were in a *no-holds-barred* battle against the enemy on every front—at home, church and personally. That is what a true love and passion for God will do—set us on fire to not tolerate our flesh man to dominate our lives. We were so desperate to hang onto God with all we had, not wanting to lose His presence.

There have been times when we had absolutely no tolerance for any attack of the enemy and quickly took him to task should he dare to raise his ugly head in infirmity or attack on any member of our church, our city or our families.

Our prayer life must be on target and persistent in coming against the enemy with force.

We have a lot to think on as we face the future in pursuit of God in Revival Harvest Breakthrough. How are we going to enter into what God has for us to do and be?

I am reminded of the doors that God keeps showing.

A good number of years ago, a ministry friend of my husband and me, had a dream in which he was in a long hallway. As he walked down this very narrow and straight hallway he came to a door. He went through it, only to see the hallway narrower and in the distance another door smaller than the previous. As he went through each door along this hallway, the hallway grew more and more narrow and each door ahead of him became smaller and smaller, until he was on his knees crawling through the last door.

Jesus said, *"You can enter God's Kingdom only through the narrow gate. The highway to hell is broad, and its gate is wide for the many who choose that way. But the gateway to life is very narrow and the road is difficult, and only a few ever find it."* ***(Matthew 7:13-14)****—NLT*

The dream detailed a very clear picture of this truth—the first door represented our salvation in Jesus, with each door following representing a greater challenge—going from walking tall and straight to being on our knees in humble pursuit of God—having off-loaded all the weights and sins that had been holding us back from entering in to the fullness of God.

> ***Hebrews 12:1*** (Emphasis Added)—*Wherefore seeing we also are compassed about with so great a cloud of witnesses,* ***let us lay aside every weight, and the sin which doth so easily beset us****, and let us run with patience the race that is set before us,*

This is the only position that will take us where God wants us to go.

If we do not humble ourselves and begin to bend our wills to the walk of faith in Jesus with the way becoming more and more and more narrow to our flesh, we will not be able to enter into the depths of the Kingdom of God.

I know our spirits want to fully enter into the things of God's Kingdom and to live there—*but our flesh wars.* That is not an excuse or loophole for us; just a statement of the fact of the battlefield of our own mind that we have to win.

We need to be careful for in the time when we should be ***"laying aside every weight and the sin that does so easily beset us"*** that we do not pick up things that simply will not fit through the next door.

Who we *"think we are,"* in other words, *"our mantle of our pride,"* is not going to fit through the doorway of God's purpose.

We still have a job to do—God to worship, heaven's to open, demons to defeat, souls to be saved, rivers to release, ground to break, nations to cover in prayer, assignments and covenants, chains to break and people to be set free and *mediocre living is not going to do it.*

We are not called to just *have church,*—our call is much higher and our preparation is much more demanding to go where God has called us to go.

- ***I will NOT be satisfied*** with my life becoming *"status quo."*
- ***I will NOT be satisfied*** with my worship becoming *"status quo."*
- ***I will NOT be satisfied*** with my intercession becoming *"status quo."*
- ***I will NOT be satisfied*** with any of you becoming *"status quo."*

Where we are going will cost all of us something outside of ourselves—a kind of relentless sacrifice in excellence of spirit and heart—to be a vessel that God can use to His glory and honor.

There are things that are old and keep on being re-hashed; things in people's lives that need to permanently drop off and not be picked back up. It is time to deal with the old issues and *get over them* or we will never be more than a *status quo Christian.*

Though God is not about to cast us aside, He is also not willing that any of us stay where we are—there are doors of purpose, glory, revival, harvest, worship, intercession and passion for Jesus to enter through.

Chapter 16

Pour Out Your Heart to God

Psalms 62:8

Trust in him at all times; ye people, pour out your heart before him: God is a refuge for us. Selah.

This verse gripped my heart as I read it in personal devotions. Immediately I knew that God was speaking of something much deeper than just a surface-level encounter with Him. I believe that to, *pour out our hearts*, signify an emptying of the contents of our hearts, even down to the bitter dregs.

- **Bitter Dregs**—1) The grounds *(dregs)* in the bottom of a coffee pot that's been kept on the fire a long time, growing more and more bitter; 2) It also means to be left with the end of a situation with negative consequences.

I can remember when as a child my parents used a percolator coffee pot on the stove top to make their coffee. Invariably, before all these fine filters came to be, there were dregs in the bottom of the pot. I can remember seeing them also in the bottom of my parent's coffee cups. They did not drink that last sip of coffee but instead rinsed it out in the sink.

When Jesus was in the Garden of Gethsemane in prayer shortly before His crucifixion, He spoke of a cup that He was going to have to drink. He said it this way, *"Father, if thou be willing,* ***remove this cup from me****: nevertheless not my will, but thine, be done."* ***(Luke 22:42)*** (Emphasis Added)

Matthew Henry's Commentary says, *"He withdrew about a stone's cast further into the garden, which some reckon about fifty of sixty paces, and there he kneeled down upon the bare ground; he fell on his face, and there prayed that, if it were the will of God, this cup of suffering,* ***this bitter cup****, might be removed from him."*

If we are going to establish our faith life on the Rock of our Salvation, we are going to have to bend our will to His Word and His Ways—just like He did to His Father's. We too, will have to not pour out the last drop, but we will have to drink it, even though it is bitter to our taste.

I know with everything in me that Jesus died a cruel death that any one of us would have called, *bitter,* because He was not guilty. He was an innocent man being put to death, as a matter of fact, for all of our sins.

Sometimes the least injustice is enough to make us *lose our salvation* momentarily to do *justice on the wrongdoer*, but Jesus drank the cup of forgiveness—all of it!

It is easy for us to give the surface contents of our hearts, but buried much deeper are things that sometimes we just don't want to bring up—*not even to God.* To pray from the surface is to pray a shallow prayer. But to pray from the depths of our being we know that we must also reveal the depths of our hearts before our God.

This is really where most of us who have been in intercession for any length of time have found ourselves time and time again—on our faces, pouring out the things that God is continually dredging up from our hearts.

In those times we see that nothing is hidden from God's eyes.

> ***Psalms 51:17****—The sacrifices of God are a broken spirit: a broken and a contrite heart, O God, thou wilt not despise.*

He loves the prayer of the contrite and honest heart, but will despise the prayer that comes from the shadows that we hide in. We must come honestly and humbly before our God, willing to expose our weaknesses and struggles.

Adam, along with Eve, came to meet with God. God's eyes immediately found a foreign object between Himself and the subject of His love.

> ***Genesis 3:7****—And the eyes of them both were opened, and they knew that they were naked; and they sewed fig leaves together, and made themselves aprons.*

The foreign object, *a fig leaf*, represented man's own efforts to deal with his sin.

- ***How many*** other ways do we use to deal with the issues of our life?
- ***How many*** times do we excuse or rationalize our conduct, the attitudes of our hearts, bitterness and unforgiveness?
- ***How many*** times do we cover to keep from being exposed in the sight of man and ultimately God?

> ***Genesis 3:8****—And they heard the voice of the Lord God walking in the garden in the cool of the day: and Adam and his wife hid themselves from the presence of the Lord God amongst the trees of the garden.*

Now we all know it is no use to try to hide from God, so we just hide from man by not being transparent or honest with our own hearts and others.

I ask myself, *"Why would anyone try to hide from God?"* and then I know, because I have done it too.

There have been, in my life, times that I would have rather excused myself than to be honest with myself. I believe self-deception is the most difficult power to break because it is made of the lies we tell ourselves.

That is a fig leaf.

There have been times that I would have rather blamed another for my failures than to take personal responsibility. This is one of the greatest problems today—a failure to say, *"It's me who is responsible for my own heart—I cannot blame anyone else."*

That is a fig leaf.

There have been times that I was angry and felt justified for my feelings against another brother or sister or a loved one, saying, "*Well, I have a right . . .*" What if Jesus would have used *"His rights"* to call ten thousand angels and destroy the world instead of dying for the sins of mankind? We still, *if we are not honest with ourselves,* hold onto our rights to feel a certain way, act a certain way and speak a certain way.

That is a fig leaf.

There have been seasons when I struggled with unforgiveness, leading myself down a road of no return, attempting to be judge and jury, while still covered in my own self-righteousness. This kind of deep-seeded poison is carried in our emotions. It is baggage we hold onto as if it is our life-line. In fact, it is poison to our spirits, our whole life *and yet,* we nurture bitterness and drink our own bitter cup instead of accepting the fact Jesus drank if for us.

That is a fig leaf.

There have been unfortunate times, when I have gone before God and tried to justify my actions against another. Life sometimes is unfair and hurtful and we may try to find a way to deal with it that is not godly. At these times we are almost willing to sin in the flesh *to fulfill the lust of the flesh instead of walking in the Spirit.*

That is a fig leaf.

There have been times that I have knelt to pray, trying to have *sweet communion* with God, only to find that He was dealing with me on an issue that I had covered. Sometimes we struggle to be honest with ourselves, trying to act as if something is *not all that big of an issue.*

That is a fig leaf.

We see God entering his *once undefiled garden* to commune with his beloved creation—Adam and Eve—only to discover something wrong. Instead of finding the open, honest, pure relationship He desired with them, He had to search the garden for them. He called out, *(not for His sake because He already knew they had sinned,)* to them ***"Where are you?" Genesis 3:9***

Have there been times when God's people kneel that they hear the same voice that God spoke to Adam, *"Where are you, why are you hiding?"*

God wants us to drop our own self-righteous fig leaves and come clean with Him.

> ***Joel 2:13a****—And rend your heart, and not your garments, and turn unto the Lord your God . . .*

There are *not enough* man-made garments, *not enough* dust and ashes, *not enough* places to hide from God when He is searching for us.

> ***Psalms 139:7****—Whither shall I go from thy spirit? Or whither shall I flee from thy presence?*

He is after the heart of man.

> ***Psalms 139:23-24****—Search me, O God, and know my heart: try me, and know my thoughts: And see if there be any wicked way in me, and lead me in the way everlasting.*

We know about prayer, but do we know about coming to God with such deep rending of our own hearts that we allow the full revelation of all that is contained in our hearts?

God wants to do a deep work in His people today, to see them set free, not just from the most obvious sin, but from the fleshly, fatal flaws of our thinking. So how do we get free? That question is *the door knob* to a door of freedom to every heart desiring to walk in integrity before God and man. *Why not just reach out now and turn the knob and open the door of your heart?*

The Blood of Jesus is the antidote to everything that ails man's soul.

> ***Hebrews 9:20****—And almost all things are by the law purged with blood; and without shedding of blood is no remission.*

Fig leaves offend God.
They are not the Blood of Jesus.
They do not cover.
They do not wash as white as snow.

They only reveal that we have attempted to cover with a *do-it-yourself-program-of-self-righteous-works.* The Word says that Jesus drank the bitter cup—***all of it***. He did that for us. We should do no less for Him when He asks us to pour it ***all*** out before Him.

When Jesus hung on that cross of shame he did it in the public eye. He was revealed before all the gawking eyes of humanity.

And, yet, here we are, still trying to hide out, from each other and God, thinking that somehow, what's in the bottom of *our cup* really doesn't matter all that much. It does matter ***if we desire*** to have rivers of living water flow from our lives to a broken and sin-stained world.

> ***John 7:38****—He that believeth on me, as the scripture hath said, out of his belly shall flow rivers of living water.*

We could be a drink offering that is poured out to our God, one that is emptied of all the contents, the good, the bad and the ugly, so that He can fill us with an abundant portion of The Living Waters.

No one knows "*free*" like Jesus knows "*free!*"
Give it all to Him in humility and repentance and desire for more of Him in your life.
He can be trusted with the contents of your hearts and lives.

CHAPTER 17

BRANDED

1 Thessalonians 5:23

And the very God of peace sanctify you wholly; and I pray God your whole spirit and soul and body be preserved blameless unto the coming of our Lord Jesus Christ.

This scripture speaks of the whole man—not just the spirit of man. The errant teaching that it doesn't really matter what we do with our bodies as long as our spirit is focused on God has the power to reduce the heavenly value of holiness and excuse ungodly parts of our lives as insignificant to our salvation. This is simply not true.

Look at these definitions:

- **Sanctify**—purify or consecrate;
- **Wholly**—complete to the end, absolutely perfect:
- **Whole**—complete in every part
- **Blameless**—faultless, unblamable

Who we are—*completely*—should be presented blameless before our God.

Are we willing to go as far as is necessary to serve Jesus with our whole hearts, minds, spirits, and bodies? Yes, we have good intentions, good feelings at times that overwhelm us with passion to serve the Lord on this level of total sell-out. And yes, our passion can fizzle in the heat and difficulty of life and its choices if it is not established on more than an emotional response generated by being stirred.

The Lord Jesus was and is the Master at drawing the lines.

He was hated because He was so penetratingly direct that no one could escape the piercing of His proposals to mankind.

He drew the line between the outward and the inward from the very beginning.

> ***Matthew 5:27-28*** (Emphasis Added)
>
> *27 Ye have heard that it was said by them of old time, Thou shalt not commit adultery:*
>
> *28 **But I say unto you**, That whosoever looketh on a woman to lust after her hath committed adultery with her already in his heart.*
>
> ***Matthew 5:38-42*** (Emphasis Added)
>
> *38 Ye have heard that it hath been said, An eye for an eye, and a tooth for a tooth:*
>
> *39 **But I say unto you**, That ye resist not evil: but whosoever shall smite thee on thy right cheek, turn to him the other also.*

People had been religiously draping their old garments of the law around them in external self-righteousness and not allowing it to invade their own hearts. We see this in the story of the woman taken in adultery when she was dragged before Jesus by her accusers.

- While He was aware of her outward sin, He was equally aware of the accuser's heart in the matter.
- He challenged them to look deeper into their hearts and see if they were without sin . . .

> ***Matthew 5:48*** (Emphasis Added)—*Be ye therefore* ***perfect, even as*** *your Father which is in heaven is perfect.*

- **Perfect**—complete in mental and moral character, human integrity and virtue

We see in ***2 Peter 1:4-10*** a growth pattern that is a sure-fire antidote to failure and a recipe for receiving the great and precious promises. Look at the progression, "*. . . add to your faith virtue; and to virtue knowledge; and to knowledge temperance; and to temperance patience; and to patience godliness; and to godliness brotherly kindness; and to brotherly kindness charity,*"

Have we not read it many times over in the scripture and have we not seen it all too often in our time where the recipe failed and the promises were forfeited?

It is so futile to put so much effort into trying to live for and serve God when the whole man is separated by compromise, ideology and tolerance of things God will not wink at. Because in our time, when *the hidden things of dishonesty* and *handling the Word of God with craftiness* and *tolerating hidden sin* are being brought to light, it should be a huge ***S.O.S***. to us.

Such revelation should move us to yield our lives completely to God so He can make us blameless on all levels of living.

Here's a quote I heard years ago that goes something like this:

"Character is who you are when no one is looking."

Character: The aggregate of features and traits that form the individual nature of a person. Moral or ethical quality: qualities of honesty; integrity:

Looking again at ***2 Peter 1:4-10***, the features are *faith, virtue, knowledge, temperance, patience, godliness, brotherly kindness and charity.* Looking at ***Galatians 5:22-23***, we see the fruit of the Spirit is**,** *love, joy, peace,* *longsuffering, gentleness, goodness, faith, meekness, temperance.* This list of virtues end with the statement, *"against such, there is no law."*

The Spirit being spoken of is God's Spirit—which releases to us the divine nature of God into our fallen human nature.

The religious of Jesus' day (*and still today*) had been used to presenting an outward manifestation of holiness while living with secret, hidden sin, but Jesus probed into where the inner man really lived. We all know how to don our Pharisaical robes of self-righteousness at times and say, *"I'm glad I'm not like them,"* when we see the exposure of sinful things in another's life, but . . .

The Lord is going to put before all of us a choice.

The message of this chapter is to challenge all of us on a deeper level than ever before—to take our feet off the shore line of indecision and bring us into the deep waters of change. I believe the urgency of the hour is to become more and more fixed on the Rock of our Salvation through obedience to the things Jesus lived and taught.

We are living in a time when all kinds of new doctrines, emerging ideas and compromised, polluted twists of God's Word are being espoused by people who are not whole themselves. We must fix our lives in truth, *inside and out*, so everything about us matches Christ.

I know we are all thankful for the sinless sacrifice Jesus made for us so that our sins could be washed away—but have we ever thought about the fact that Jesus desires us to be that spotless living sacrifice before a world that needs their sins washed away?

> ***Romans 12:1-2*** (Emphasis Added)
>
> *1 I beseech you therefore, brethren, by the mercies of God, that ye present your bodies* ***a living sacrifice, holy, acceptable unto God, which is your reasonable service.***

> *2 And **be not conformed to this world**: but **be ye transformed** by the renewing of your mind, that ye may prove what is that good, and acceptable, and perfect, will of God.*

Do we not live in a time in history that is fast becoming like none other? How desperate God must be to truly have His church, His people, separated apart from the world, unto Himself. We will all make choices as to the ownership issues over our lives. We will be saying *yes or no* to a lot of the things that God is going to be speaking. Our answers will determine who our Master is.

The Lord walked up to many people and put them in a place of making a choice:

- ***The Rich Young Ruler***—He went away sorrowful—***Luke 18:18-23***
- ***His Disciples***—They put things down and picked up their cross and followed Jesus—***Matthew 16:24-26***
- ***His Disciples***—Most walked away until only the twelve remained—***John 6:56-66***
- ***King Agrippa***—*"Almost you have persuaded me"*—***Acts 26:27-28***

It is the same today—Jesus is still asking for a choice as to who we will follow.

God has been ***incessantly*** watching out for us—not in anger or in wrath, but with the Love of a Father who does not want to lose His kids to the devil. He's not willing that any perish, fail or fall away. ***2 Peter 3:7***

- ***Incessant*** describes the Lord—He has continued without interruption, ceaselessly reaching for mankind.

He is of a kingdom that has no end, constant, perpetual, eternal, and everlasting, with relentless love that goes on forever without stopping.

What a wonderful list of words to describe the Love of God towards us—but we must remember, love is also corrective and those same adjectives describe God's loving faithfulness to correct His children.

We have seen the results of tolerant parents who let *little Johnny or little Susie* do what they wanted to, without correction.

The title of this chapter is ***"Branded,"*** for a reason—to release a truth about the relentless and jealous love of God in wanting us to wholly belong to Him. We see at the end of Revelation the significance of the mark of God upon His servants.

> ***Revelation 22:4*** (Emphasis Added)—*And they shall see his face; and* ***his name shall be in their foreheads****.*

Those who brand their livestock do not like rustlers stealing their cattle or sheep and changing the brand. They do not appreciate someone backing up their truck in the middle of the night to their fields and robbing what belongs to him—that which they have purchased and branded as their own. Jesus is of the same heart.

> ***John 10:27-28*** (Emphasis Added)
>
> *27* ***My sheep*** *hear my voice, and I know them, and they follow me:*
>
> *28 And I give unto them eternal life; and they shall never perish,* ***neither shall any man pluck them out of my hand.***
>
> ***John 17:12a****—While I was with them in the world, I kept them in thy name: those that thou gavest me I have kept, and none of them is lost . . . .*

I cannot imagine any loving parent who would willingly sit neutral while drug pushers, pimps, rapist or any such person puts their mark on their kids. God is faithful to watch out for us. Sometimes it is tough love that is enacted to make sure the *"kids"* are safe in the fold where they belong.

God's Word and His Spirit are on constant watch for our souls. The Faithfulness of the Spirit of God, *the Absolute Truth of God's Word*, are relentless in speaking to us, bringing to us the desired place that God has for us in Him.

No slack is cut for anyone to live below the standard of God's holiness. Though *God understands* our weakness it does not excuse us. His expectations of us are *"higher* . . ."

It seems odd to be contemplating this after so many years of study, prayer and worship, but the battle of our inner self never ceases. We must learn to conquer the pull of our own mind, will and bodies.

<u>**There are pertinent questions it never hurts a believer to ask of themselves:**</u>

- ***What is it*** I struggle so with today, the thing that keeps pulling at me, drawing me to the same low place of living?
- ***What is it*** I have not fought very hard to overcome?
- ***What it is*** I have yielded to, on any level of thought or conduct, rather than keep fighting to remain fixed in Jesus?

Our failure to rise up is not always about blatant sin, but is more often about allowing something to slide that should be dealt a deathblow, corrected or given the axe to.

Sometimes it our attitudes, our speech, our behavior, our thoughts—the inward parts of who we are—that get us into trouble. It's the thing we coddle in ourselves, justify as righteous, when in actuality it is offensive to God's holiness and battles our daily sanctification.

We must learn to conquer the need to control our own destiny in order to stand where Jesus had told us to stand in faith and obedience.

He says, *"My sheep know my voice and another they will not follow,"* (***John 10:27)*** yet many who call themselves Christian are following other voices and ways—bearing no resemblance to the likeness of Christ.

Jesus was *totally obedient* to His Father, *never quibbled, or balked* at what His Father asked of Him. Jesus finished fully and without argument.

- **Quibble**—The use of irrelevant language or arguments to evade a point at issue.
- **Balk**—To stop short and refuse to go on; an unplowed strip of land

Luke 9:62*—No man, having put his hand to the plough, and looking back, is fit for the kingdom of God.*

Can we say that we are free of a *balking spirit?*
What is it that God has asked of us that we are putting off for a more convenient time?

Early on in revival many received what is called, ***Impartation***; an external visitation of God upon their life through someone who laid hands on them to release something to them.

But now, we are at a crossroad in church history where the movement of God is going to have to invade the depths of our hearts—***inward***—beyond impartation—***to Anointing***. There are things that you will pay a dear price for—to bear this level of anointing inside your vessel.

What is the Spirit of God speaking to you about?

- ***What*** has He asked of you?
- ***What*** pressure has He been applying to your heart to bring you to a place of yielding to Him?

I know God has required a lot of change already, but there is still a lot of "*me in me*," available to mess things up. Yes, this will cost a great deal and the branding time may be restrictive and painful to our flesh man, but in this season God wants us to rise to a higher level of encounter with the Living God!

God is invading our private space and demanding more of us because in many areas, He has had so little of us.

This is like the time when the Children of Israel approached Sinai and heard God call for them to *come up higher*, and they instead refused and made *a golden calf* to worship. To go up would have required a cleansing of their hearts.

- ***Change*** our patterns of worship?
- ***Change*** our mantles?
- ***Change*** our ways of doing things?
- ***Change*** our minds?

Yes, this would cost a great deal—this cleansing that would cause them to rise to a higher level of encounter with a Living God!

The old western movies depict it—*branding day.* All the little calves are gathered up into one place. A fire is built and the branding iron is placed into the hot flames. The calf is hog tied and then the hot branding iron is seared to his skin. The purpose? To register to all who see that brand that this one belongs to a particular ranch. Yes, it appears a very uncomfortable process for the calf to go through, *but after that day*, no one will ever have to guess whose it is.

> ***1 Corinthians 6:19-20*** (Emphasis Added)—*What? know ye not that your body is the temple of the Holy Ghost which is in you, which ye have of God, and* ***ye are not your own? For ye are bought*** (redeemed) ***with a price****: therefore glorify God in your body, and in your spirit, which are God's.*

Oh, to be that kind of Christian—to have what God has done in my life so deep, beyond my flesh, to my spirit man where my flesh is emblazoned with the brand of my Master.

There is a brand that goes deeper than the skin of an animal; it is that which goes to the depths of man's heart. Many in the church have the outer garment of their religion in place but if one was to look upon the heart it may not have ever touched that place God so desires of man.

<u>**God expressed it this way:**</u>

> ***Isaiah 29:13***—*Wherefore the Lord said, Forasmuch as this people draw near me with their mouth, and with their lips*

do honor me, but have removed their heart far from me, and their fear toward me is taught by the precept of men:

Jesus referred back to Isaiah as He spoke to people in ***Matthew 15:8*** saying, *"This people draws nigh unto me with their mouth, and honors me with their lips; but their heart is far from me."*

God is calling us to *an internal sanctification*—one that goes beyond the cleansing of the physical hands and clothes—to taking away our whining, our complaining, our moods and attitudes, our rights, our petty ways, our balking at His persistent voice. We, like Israel, forget we are getting ready to meet our Lord, who is holy!

- This means a character change—to be a different person than we have ever been before.

We have been hung up on our own patterns of life—not a whole lot different from Israel who had a hard time *letting go of Egypt.*

They were as addicted to the things of Egypt as people are today to their own patterns of life that have invaded minds and lives.

It was and still is time to "*Sell out to the King and the Kingdom*!" We are to bear the mark of the Lord in our inward man, ***clean through***, from the top of our head to the soles of our feet, from the mind to the emotions to the will and the passions of our heart. we are to be the Lord's fully and completely!

Anyone who wants to can walk away from the move of God towards man and the church, but the Move of God *(meaning, "He's moving and never stagnant*) will go forth—gathering disciples who are sold out—*lock, stock and barrel.* They will be those who will not look back.

"People will either sell out to follow Jesus"—*Or*—"They will sell Jesus out to follow their own ways." *(Judas)*

There are disciples, from the core outward, who are walking out from the crowd—no longer content to hide in the shadows—but bold and decisive in their stride.

God is looking for a people that will put things into Godly perspective. The day is now upon us in which we can no longer just choose out of our own minds what we want to do with our lives.

I love lists that challenge me. I can take a deep look at myself as I consider the things written for evaluation. I pray that the following list will encourage a deeper desire to allow God to deepen His work in your life.

- ***Branded People*** do not forget God and leave Him behind, neatly tucked away with the family Bible they left lying on the coffee table.
- ***Branded People*** do not compromise the Word of God and try to fit it in within their standards.
- ***Branded People*** have no problem taking an honest look at themselves in light of their Master's Word.
- ***Branded People*** live in integrity.
- ***Branded People*** will not cheat on God by having an affair with the world.
- ***Branded People*** will obey the Master Voice.
- ***Branded People*** are willing to lay down everything that the Master tells them to.
- ***Branded People*** are humble before God, realizing that they are not their own, but bought with a price.
- ***Branded People*** can be found in the place where God told them to be.
- ***Branded People*** realize that the weightier matters of life deserve the greater value and attention.
- ***Branded People*** have removed the word, *self* from their vocabulary, declaring, *"It's not about me Jesus—It's all about you."*
- ***Branded People*** watch the words of their mouths.
- ***Branded People*** watch and pray and do not leave their post unguarded.
- ***Branded People*** do not look back with desire for the old life's pleasures.
- ***Branded People*** make no excuses but live ready to give an answer concerning their stewardship all of all things that pertain to their life, ministry, family, church and city.

- ***Branded People*** take personal responsibility and do not blame others.
- ***Branded People*** are faithful and full of faith.
- ***Branded People*** have sold out for the King and the Kingdom, set apart for Him, living and walking wholly after the Lord, with their whole hearts, minds, bodies and souls.
- ***Branded People*** are yoked with the Lord and step as He steps and goes where He leads.
- ***Branded People*** are citizens of a different land and Kingdom.
- ***Branded People*** are submissive and no longer live their lives to please themselves.
- ***Branded People*** walk with awareness of the Holiness of God and of the Presence of their Master.
- ***Branded People*** are given the signet of the Master to do business on His behalf—with full power and authority.

> ***Psalms 17:15***—*". . . I shall be satisfied when I awaken with your likeness . . ."*

A wave of true holiness is coming to the church—*are you in?*

- ***No more*** compromise.
- ***No more*** hypocrisy.
- ***No more*** middle of the road.
- ***No more*** fence sitting.
- ***No more*** double mindedness.
- ***No more*** half n' half.

The brand is an internal brand. Don't just expect *outward manifestations* of this mark—it a deep internal work of Holy Spirit with eternal dividends.

John Wesley said it this way: *"What hinders the work of God? I believe we do. If we would just be holy, totally consecrated to God, we would be on fire and spread that fire across the nations."*

> ***John 17:17-19***—*". . . Sanctify them through Thy truth . . ."*

- **Sanctify**—to consecrate or set apart, to dedicate for holy service to God.

  2 Corinthians. 6:17-18—*". . . come out from among them and be separate . . ."*

Sanctification/consecration is a permanent, daily imperative for God's people and the greatest challenge that is set before us.

This is beyond the external anointing—*it is internal consecration*—a vessel that is fully yielded to Christ and His Kingdom. This is a supernatural manifestation of a holy, righteous God in the lives of those who are willing to fully yield their entire vessel to Him.

It is time for God's people to cry out, *"Sanctify us!"*

Part III

Lukewarm and Liking it

God has appointed a day in which He is going to judge the world.
The poor blind world doesn't know much about it—
and the poor blind church doesn't think much about it. "

Leonard Ravenhill

Chapter 18

Church—It's Me

Revelation 3:14

Laodiceans, *it is me, the Amen, the faithful and true witness, the beginning of the creation of God . . .*

Jesus, in opening His letters to each of the seven churches, gives an introduction vividly describing Himself. He uses particular attributes to define Himself to them—*and us*. And He signs off each letter with a parting thought to each church—*"He, who has an ear, let him hear what the Spirit says to the church."* The appeal from Jesus Christ in each case could not be clearer in helping us understand this Jesus we serve.

So, because He personally revealed the nature of the one speaking, it is important that He is in first place here before we say anything about the Laodicea church. There is no use in preaching or teaching or writing any message to the church in which Christ is not preeminent and chief. He speaks to John in ***Revelation 1:17-19*** making the declarations of who He is.

Jesus Christ is no longer in a flesh body on earth—He speaks from heaven by the Spirit saying,

"Don't be afraid! I am the First and the Last. I am the living one. I died, but look—I am alive forever and ever! And I hold the keys of death and the grave . . ." NLT

He is declaring He not only has the keys, *but is the key*, giving him authority over both death and the grave. When someone says they hold the keys it means they can unlock and lock the doors.

We see that thought strengthened to His letter to the church of Philadelphia:

> ***Revelation 3:7***—*These are the words of the Holy One, the True One, He Who has the key of David, Who opens and no one shall shut, Who shuts and no one shall open!*

The way Jesus performs His will is with absolute power and authority in His sovereignty.

I have heard recently a feeble attempt by some to put the Lord in a box by declaring "*He is not sovereign over everything because of all the wickedness taking place and troubles that come to people.*" The sovereign Lord has **never** relinquished the authority of being sovereign and made Himself dependent of man's attempt to control Him.

I love the word, "*Sovereign,*" because He is my Savior, Lord, Master and yes, King! Did He quit being King just because man refused to obey the rules of heaven? No! Man by his own desires refuses the Lordship and rule of Jesus Christ in their hearts. That does not mean Jesus has no sovereignty or is diminished in His power and authority.

The Kingdom of God is ruled by a King—King Jesus!

He is independent of the will of mankind and completely resists the power of men over Him. When He opened the door of Salvation and said, "*I am the way, the truth and the life; no man comes to the Father but by me,*" (John 14:6) He is revealing an absolute that cannot be changed by the will of man. He also revealed the devil has no power over Him either. The door, once opened can never be shut again. The only door mankind can shut is the door of their own heart.

- *If* anyone knows about defeating the devil, it is Jesus.
- *If* anyone knows what's best for His Church, it is Jesus.

As He is preparing to address the seven churches He is seeing clearly their need with eyes that miss nothing, as one who has true judgment. He also is the only one that can bring truth to them to set them free. He knows where they began and He knows where they were at that time, and He ultimately knows how each case ended in history.

Laodicea has gone down in Biblical history as the lukewarm church that made Jesus sick.

This is not a desired verdict but sadly, it is something that has repeated itself all down through church history.

I do not know any criminal that likes to be arrested for his or her crime against society, be hauled to the court and hear the charges against them. It appears that the whole objective of the defendant is to appear innocent, even if he is guilty, so rather than say, *"I did it,"* they plead, *"not guilty."*

Well, there is a judicial system called heaven's court and that judge and jury do not allow a plea of *"not guilty,"* if they say you are charged. But . . . thank God they offer something the human courts don't—grace, mercy and forgiveness. If a person will agree with their guilt and repent before the court, the slate is wiped clean.

The only way to restoration is via the cross of Jesus Christ. It may appear to be odd to place an altar call at the beginning of a chapter that is getting ready to dissect the problem but God can speak any time as He now is.

I believe those who are lukewarm already know they are and can simply say, *"guilty as charged,"* and repent. We don't have to labor through pages and pages of reading to know when we stand in need.

- He is ***The Amen***, the one who is not just saying, *"Amen,"* but is ***"The Amen—so be it,"*** Jesus who stands in the fixed, firm, unshakeable place of Truth, not just speaking truth, but is "Truth."
- He is ***The faithful and true witness***, whose testimony of men will be fully believed, a swift but true witness against all indifferent lukewarm professors of faith in Christ. Remember, the one who

is speaking has already been crucified, buried and resurrected and returned to heaven. This is the martyr witness, the one who judicially bears witness.

- He is ***the beginning of the creation of God***, The word, "*beginning*" means ***"chief"*** and ***"corner."*** It also means He, from whom all commences or begins, is built, created or ordained or put in place as an ordinance.

Did you see that?—The word, *"Beginning"* means, *"Chief corner."* When Jesus is speaking to John, He has already fulfilled the prophecy of ***Isaiah 28:16*** *which says, ". . . Behold, I lay in Zion for a foundation,* ***a stone, a tried stone, a precious corner stone****, a sure foundation . . ."*

- (Other references: ***Psalms 118:22; Matthew 21:42; Acts 4:10-12; Ephesians 2:19-22; 1 Peter 2:6-9***)

Jesus is the chief corner stone—not just any stone—but ***a tried stone*** (examined, proven); ***the elect*** (chosen by God) and ***precious stone*** (costly, excellent, clear and bright) who is set in first; the stone from which the whole house will be properly built!

In studying about the corner stone, I came across an interesting article. It said in modern Greece, when the new foundation of a building is being laid, the custom is to kill a cock, a ram, or a lamb. They then let its blood flow on the foundation-stone, under which the animal is then buried. The object of the sacrifice is to give strength and stability to the building.

- The Chief Corner Stone was not anointed with the blood of an animal, but He shed His own precious blood (***1 Peter 1:19)*** as the anointed of God.
- He was not buried *under* the corner stone of some man-made building, but buried in a borrowed tomb from which He resurrected.
- He did not come to bring a curse upon mankind but to break the curse of sin, death and the grave.

That is the power of the One who has the keys to death and the grave—to forgive and wash away all unrighteousness!

CHAPTER 19

UNCERTAIN RICHES

Proverbs 14:11-12

The house of the wicked will be overthrown,
But the tent of the upright will flourish.
There is a way that seems right to a man,
But its end is the way of death. NKJV

God's Spirit brings the gospel through a person sent to plant a church and a lighthouse rises up in the darkness to shine forth for the glory of God. It is planted in a city that has a personality, strongholds of religion, wealth, greed, witchcraft, bondages and without Jesus the citizens are in the dark, living in the dark and dying in the dark.

The church planted in a city, town or village or any viable area where the church is needed to shine, is a distinct group of believers banded together as harvesters for the Kingdom of God.

When the lights begin to go out there is a reason for that; with the most prevalent being, an adoption of the ways of the city, becoming like the city and even entering into the personality of the city and its strongholds through tolerance.

Laodicea is a church/believer pattern that still develops today—for exactly the same reason as it did then. Jesus, in speaking to this church also speaks to us about the church age we are now in and yes, even the churches and believers in the cities and town and regions that cover the world.

There are plenty of churches in the world—there are just not enough churches where Jesus has been welcomed as the Head.

I do not want to spend a lot of time on the history of Laodicea, but I believe a short review of whom and what they were as a city and region is necessary for us to understand some things.

We all live in cities or towns that came into existence, like this city. And sadly, many places around the world that once had a mighty revival move that swept souls into the Kingdom of God are now cold and indifferent to the gospel.

We need to know what the downfall of the church in Laodicea was. Her destiny was not to end up being what she became.

Laodicea was once (I say, *"Once"* because it is now no more) a great city founded near the river Lycus and enclosed by a great wall. There were a total of twenty-five cities beside itself. The city was on the crossroads of other important cities, creating a high volume of commercial activity in the region. Laodicea unique offering to the market was its raven-black wool from its sheep and the garments made from the wool and sandals.

It was a city of great wealth, had an extensive banking system because of its many wealthy citizens. It boasted of three marble theaters and, like Rome, was built on seven hills. It had a school of medicine and was the birthplace of two philosophers. Most of the people who lived in there held Zeus as higher than any other god. Its coins and inscriptions show evidence of the worship of gods and the emperors.

It was often hit hard by earthquakes but rebuilt by its wealthy citizens. History record they refused help when tragedy struck. It might seem commendable that they were able to get up and put it back the way it was, but that attitude represented the pride of their hearts to be independent of even Rome.

This self-sufficient and independent attitude marked a city that was self-sustained and needed no one else. It was at its pinnacle of pride, gaining wealth and reputation for everything money could buy.

It was in this city the church was planted.

The Apostle Paul appears to have been influential in bringing the gospel there and strengthened and encouraged the church of the city. Knowing Paul's epistles, the church had to have been founded and grounded in the truth, having the advantage being foundationally right with God. During the time of John, the church in Laodicea was one of seven churches important to Christianity in Asia Minor. The Laodicea church was the site of the council in A.D. 361 where the scripture canon was defined.

We have to ask a question so that we may learn from them . . .

"What happened to bring a thriving church in this city to the place that they made the Lord sick?"

There is no doubt that at one time, in its inception, the church in Laodicea had strong believers in it. But now, of the seven churches addressed by Jesus in Revelation, it was the worst. From the evidence Jesus brings as the true and faith witness, it is clear Laodicea is the opposite of the church of Philadelphia. Jesus has no commendation to the lukewarm, Laodiceans church, though He mentions them as being one of the seven golden candlesticks.

Jesus said to them, *"I know* ***thy works****, that thou art neither cold nor hot: I would thou wert cold or hot. So then because thou art lukewarm, and neither cold nor hot, I will spew thee out of my mouth."* ***Revelation 3:15*** *(*Emphasis Added)

- **Works**—toil (as an effort or occupation); by implication, an act: deed, doing, labor,

The history of the church, *from its inception,* reveals a lot has been done in the name of Jesus that did not reflect the craftsmanship of Jesus as the builder. He, as the Chief Corner Stone, upon whose placement the whole house is aligned and built, has not been put in place in the modern church. Therefore, the whole house is not *"square with God."*

So much of what bears Jesus' name is flawed and sometimes, *as in the case of Laodicea*, fatally flawed. Jesus desired a well-laid foundation (His doctrines and teachings) to support a house to the Glory of God.

He desires to be able to say, "*Well done.*"

But, when all is not well, He is the one who can say with eyes that see everything, "*I know your works.*"

The Apostle Paul makes reference to the fiery judgment of works: *For* (no) *other foundation can* (a) *man lay than that is laid, which is Jesus Christ. Now if any man build upon this foundation* (Jesus Christ) *gold, silver, precious stones, wood, hay, stubble;* ***Every man's work shall be made manifest:*** *for the day shall declare it, because it shall be revealed by fire; and the fire shall try every man's work of what sort it is. If any man's work abide which he hath built thereupon, he shall receive a reward. If any man's work shall be burned, he shall suffer loss: but he himself shall be saved; yet so as by fire.* ***1 Corinthians 3:11-15*** (Emphasis Added)

Manifest in this scripture means "*our works—good or bad—will be made apparent publically, externally.*" Nothing is hid from the probing eyes of Jesus Christ who is Truth. When He tells us He knows our works, oh my, we must sit up and take notice of what He reveals to our hearts. The time to hear is now—not to wait until we stand before Him in all "our glory . . ."

> ***Luke 8:17****—For nothing is secret, that shall not be made manifest; neither anything hid, that shall not be known and come abroad.*

Jesus knew the Laodicea church/believers better than they knew themselves. He could see what they could not see and as a true witness He spoke a word to them that still speaks to the lukewarm church of today.

> ***Revelation 3:17-18****—Because thou sayest, I am rich, and increased with goods, and have need of nothing; and knowest not that thou art wretched, and miserable, and poor, and blind, and naked:*

They said, "*I am* . . ."

- ***Rich***—money, possessions,
- ***Increased with Goods***—wax) rich.
- ***Have need of Nothing***—not even one man, woman or thing; i.e. none, nobody, nothing:

Jesus said, "*You are* . . ."

- ***Wretched***—miserable:
- ***Miserable***—pitiable:
- ***Poor***—pauper
- ***Blind***—blind (physically or mentally):
- ***Naked***—nude

It's always best to search the Word of God for the council of God on any matter. In this case, Jesus greatest concern with this church is that they had become just like the city and region they lived in—self-contained, self-sustained, self-satisfied—rich and needing nothing from anyone, ***including Him.***

<u>What does Jesus, the Living Word, say about riches?</u>

> ***Matthew 13:22*** (Emphasis Added)—*He also that received seed among the thorns is he that heareth the word; and the care of this world, and* ***the deceitfulness of riches****, choke the word, and he becometh unfruitful.*

Jesus said riches will cheat you and choke out the word through deception, leaving you fruitless.

> ***Mark 10:24-25*** (Emphasis Added)—*But Jesus answereth again, and saith unto them, Children, how hard is it for them that* ***trust in riches*** *to enter into the kingdom of God! It is easier for a camel to go through the eye of a needle, than for a rich man to enter into the kingdom of God.*

Jesus said of those who trust in riches, they will find it hard to enter into the Kingdom of God.

He uses the example of a camel going through the eye of a needle. This draws an interesting picture of a big old camel trying to get through the eye of a sewing needle. Well sometimes our attachments to things are pretty significant in size.

In studying the commentaries on this analogy, a few suppositions are made as to what it means, but all we need to do is look at the context of where this is being said to understand the heart of Jesus.

Back up a few verses to ***Mark 10:17-22*** where Jesus tells us of the rich young man who went away sorrowful after Jesus had told him to *sell all he had and give it to the poor.* His religion was intact in every commandment ***until*** Jesus reached the core of his heart's attachment. Jesus always sees past our piety and can find the strongholds of our hearts that hold us back from fully serving Him, unencumbered.

To follow Jesus this rich man would have to give up everything—and he had a lot of riches to give.

> ***1 Timothy 6:17*** (Emphasis Added)—*Charge them that are* ***rich in this world****, that they be not high-minded, nor trust in* ***uncertain riches****, but in the living God, who gives us richly all things to enjoy;*

Did we hear Paul's charge to Timothy? He told him to not trust in ***uncertain*** riches. One of the definitions for *"uncertain"* means *"subject to change, variable, unstable."* We can already see in our time the truth behind the uncertainty of riches as turmoil has erupted in the streets over the failure of banks, governments and industry to keep churning out the money.

So where is the true riches to be found on *"the day the dollar dies?"* Paul emphasized that we should trust in the Living God who gives us richly all things to enjoy. Riches, *if not understood as the temporal thing it* is, can overtake a person, a church, a city, a nation.

When everything we establish to sustain life and pleasure rests on riches and riches fail, the whole house falls because the foundation is temporal, shaky, and uncertain.

Riches are not Bedrock—they are Sand.

This is what Jesus is trying to warn Laodicea believers about. Their lukewarm state is directly connected to the charges He brings against them.

If the church of today would understand the riches in Christ Jesus far outweigh the riches of this world. So much of what we put our trust in is perishable. The money system of today is handing by a thread in many nations.

> ***Revelation 3:18***—*I counsel thee to buy of me gold tried in the fire, that thou mayest be rich; and white raiment, that thou mayest be clothed, and that the shame of thy nakedness do not appear; and anoint thine eyes with eyesalve, that thou mayest see.*

When Jesus says, *"I council you . . ."* it's head's-up time.

It is easy to mistake the *"blessings"* as we would perceive them as being in good standing with the Lord. It is also easy to mistake education, gifts, wit and charm, wealth and prosperity, charitable giving and church influence as being in God's good graces. And, it is possible for the human soul to starve in the midst of abundance.

It is possible *to think we see* when we are actually blind to Jesus Christ and all His provisions found in the realm of the Spirit.

Oh, but what a wake-up call that Jesus Christ sends to His church in any and every city where a lukewarm state has entered into the heart of His people . . . and what mercy and grace to allow time for repentance. Thankfully, when the Lord is bringing judgment he always brings a remedy to restore, *if there is repentance.*

> ***Revelation 3:19****—As many as I love, I rebuke and chasten: be zealous therefore, and repent.*

Jesus is saying to them *(and to us as needed), "I am the lover of your soul who cares enough to rebuke and correct you so that you may repent."* If in rebuking them He is declaring His love for them, He would have been declaring His indifference or hatred for them if He would have left them to their own ruin of their souls.

- ***Thank you Jesus*** that you did not leave me to my ruin, but that you loved me enough to rebuke and correct me.
- ***Thank you Jesus*** for those in my life who love me enough to speak a loving word of correction to me to try to spare me ruin.

It's very difficult today to give godly council and have it received and a hundred times more difficult to rebuke or correct someone and have them receive it with humility and repentance.

Sadly, Laodicea's church is no more, with the city long since demolished. A terrible earthquake eventually destroyed the city and it could not be revived again. It is now a heap of ruins, called by the conquering Turks *"old castle."* The ruins that remain are a witness against its condition to this day. It speaks clearly that, though Jesus sent a message of judgment and hope to them, calling for repentance from the lukewarm state they had fallen into, they did not repent. There was no revival, reformation, restoration . . .

We must take a lesson from this very real church in a very real church age with very real people who lived their life in spiritual delusion and self-satisfaction.

1Timothy 6:7

For we brought nothing into this world, and it is certain we can carry nothing out.

CHAPTER 20

SHADES OF GRAY

Revelation 3:16

. . . So then because you are lukewarm . . .

***Laodiceans*—Who are those people anyway?**

They are us, if we don't keep the fiery heat of passionate love for God burning in our lives, keeping Him first in everything.

We have to learn how to hate lukewarm to the same degree God does. We have to feel sickened by it.

What if Jesus lived His life the way the nominal church world does or even as we do—lukewarm, mediocre, half-hearted, faithless, fireless, waffling, without vision or purpose, struggling with sinful habits or practices, lacking devotional and prayer time with God—what impact would He have made on our society?

The story would be totally different today.

What if we lived our life like Jesus, totally sold-out to God's Kingdom, making all our choices, how we spend our time, how we walked our walk and talked our talk, just like Jesus—what impact would we have on our society?

What if we stand idly by, what impact will that have on our society?

Here is a portion of the October 17, 2004 word from the Lord to our church:

"*. . . And it must be upon your head and shoulder and under My anointing and leading that those things* (strongholds in people's lives) *shall be broken. But they shall not be broken any longer* ***by casual praying****. They shall not be broken any longer* ***by mediocre living****. I'm calling you to a higher level. I'm calling you into a deeper place in me . . .*"

Consider this outline for Lukewarm and On Fire for God:

I. **Lukewarm**—Neutral, Fireless, Safe Ground, Comfortable Ground.

Truth: Lukewarm Living is not ever, under any circumstance acceptable to God.

> ***Revelation 3:15*** (Emphasis Added)—*I know thy works, that thou art neither* ***cold*** *nor* ***hot*** *I would thou wert cold or hot.*

When we hear the word, "*cold*" we might think of winter or a refreshing drink on a hot day. I there are people that look forward to the snow, skiing, and snowboarding who not only look forward to but love the cold weather. Some call them "*Snow Birds.*" Having lived in the Mojave Desert for several years, I learned to love the hot weather. There are many who thrive in that kind of terrain. Some call them "*Desert Rats.*"

I love iced tea. I love hot tea. But in my partaking of them I am not revolted by the lack of intense cold or intense heat. I am not moved very much by either extreme.

That is not the language Jesus is using to describe the Laodiceans church.

To fully grasp the language Jesus used to John, we have to understand it *in His terms*. Look at the following definitions and see the strength of the words used:

- **Cold**—one destitute of warm Christian faith and the desire for holiness:
- **Hot**—of fervor of mind and zeal)

Revelation 3:16 (Emphasis Added)—*So then because thou art **lukewarm** . . .*

Ah, this is what Jesus called them—***Lukewarm***. They are not Desert Rats and they are not Snow Birds; they are living on some *Paradise Island of Pleasure* where they don't have to feel the chill cold or the sweat of the heat of anything, just enjoy the tepid island breezes.

Jesus did not come to the world to take a vacation from the extreme elements of this world. He came and fully invested in extreme living and extreme sacrifice.

Jesus is stating their condition as being a soul that is fluctuating somewhere in the middle between cold love and hot love. And He is also moved to reject with vehemence that which is making Him sick—their condition. He says, *"Because you are neither hot nor cold, I will spew you out of my mouth."*

- **Spew**—vomit, the utter rejection of what has been tasted.
- **Mouth**—the mouth, since thoughts of a man's soul find verbal utterance by his mouth, the heart or soul and the mouth are distinguished 2) *the edge of a sword*

They are like the soldiers in the midst of a battle that have laid down their sword and are living a life of ease while others around them are sold out to a cause. The world and the church are either dying in their sin ***or*** dying for the cause of Christ—choosing a side to live on. With people around them invested in a kingdom—*an either or choice*—they call themselves *"Christian"* while investing nothing into the Kingdom of God.

We have heard pet or key scriptures all of our Christian life, so much that they have become a catch all phrase that we can quote to match a sermon or discussion. But, ***"I will spew you out of my mouth"*** said by God, to any of us in the church, is no small matter; it is a verdict with an eternal sentence attached to it—a divine casting away as one who vomits.

None of us even like to think about vomiting. The first thing we feel is that wretched sense of our body preparing to cast off something that has made us so sick. It is so miserable to feel the throat tighten and the mouth begin to water and then finally heaving with such force from our bodies the sickening thing which has fouled our system.

When Jesus says something is sickening to Him, it would do us all good to find what it is.

This is more than just a mild stomach ache our Lord is suffering. He is sickened by the condition of His church.

He said to them, *"Because you say, I am rich, and increased with goods, and have need of nothing; don't you know that you are wretched, miserable and poor and blind and naked*

- You say, *"I am rich."*
- You say, *"I am increased in goods."*
- You say, *"I have need of nothing."*

The *"I am"* statements have been a big problem for God from antiquity. This is the vivid description of *"Lukewarm,"* a condition of the whole man that makes Jesus sick.

He cannot bear it as a part of His sacred and holy body, as a part of His Church so He spews it out.

How does "Lukewarm" manifest in our lives and what should I be looking for in me?

1. ***Lukewarm*** is indifferent to God.
2. ***Lukewarm*** is self-satisfied.
3. ***Lukewarm*** doesn't take sides.
    a. It is easy to look like an *either-or* and with just a little step get close to one or the other side, the Hot or The cold.

   b. It's being a fence-rider stuck in *the limbo of neither.*
4. ***Lukewarm*** is compromising.
5. ***Lukewarm*** sells out God's best and settles for mediocre.
6. ***Lukewarm*** is neither black nor white, but is a blending of both colors, so it embraces no absolutes.
7. ***Lukewarm*** is unrepentant because it simply has no need.
8. ***Lukewarm*** has religion but not Jesus.
   a. He's outside the house, locked out, calling as if he were a visitor, being forced to knock. The house is no longer His.
9. ***Lukewarm*** answers no altar calls.
10. ***Lukewarm*** feels nothing for anything or anyone other than themselves.
11. ***Lukewarm*** has no zeal or passion and is basically fireless.

There is nothing wrong with bowing your head right now and seeking the Lord in these particular areas, to see if He might lay His hand on something.

I am aware that the majority of people reading here are sincere and really desire God to work in their lives, to mold and shape them to be like Jesus *in every way possible.* I know so many of you want your love for Jesus to burn passionately in your hearts.

It is about us laying aside everything that drains our passionate devotion to God and embracing and being constantly aware of the presence of Jesus. ***"Emmanuel, God with Us."*** This is more than a Christmas saying; it is God's presence being counted as a valuable part of everything we will ever do that will have eternal value.

Wherever the Presence of the Lord is there will *never* be a lack of Fire.

II. **On Fire for God**—Full of Passion and Full of Faith!

The word, ***"FIRE,"*** draws up a picture of many things to us—*all natural.*

- ***A warm fire*** in the fireplace on a cold winter night
- ***A Bon Fire*** around which we are roasting hot dogs and marshmallows

- ***A Pile of trash*** or leaves being burned in a back yard
- ***A house*** on fire destroying everything
- ***A forest*** fire moving and consuming everything in sight

But these all pale in light of God's Fire.

If you have truly *seen* (as in experienced) even a flame of God's Fire, it will make a believer out of you. The church has barely caught a glimpse of God's Fire that is yet to be manifested. When we are calling upon the Lord for His Fire, we are seeking something that is far above our earthly reality—We are seeking the Fire of God that comes from His throne.

Earthly fire and heavenly fire are not the same.

- ***His Fire*** is not passive
- ***His Fire*** is invasive
- ***His Fire*** purifies
- ***His Fire*** judges
- ***His Fire*** loves

Truth: Being on Fire for God reveals there is an altar laid with a sacrifice that has been found acceptable to God. This is where we are to be.

> ***Leviticus 6:13***—*The fire shall ever be burning upon the altar; it shall never go out.*

It was Leonard Ravenhill who said, *"The fire never falls on the altar, the fire falls on the sacrifice."* There are a million altars of all kinds all around the world upon which God will not send fire, *for one reason alone*; there is no living sacrifice upon them. God requires a people who will lay their lives down for His cause, to be consumed by what consumes Him.

And that sacrifice must be, according to His standard—holy and acceptable to God.

> ***Romans 12:1***—*I beseech you therefore, brethren, by the mercies of God, that ye present your bodies a living sacrifice, holy, acceptable unto God, which is your reasonable service.*

As I was leading prayer quite recently, I called on the people to present their lives before the Lord as a living sacrifice to be consumed by His Holy Fire. As they came together in the altar and sought God's Spirit to fill them fresh and anew, I realized a truth:

- What we were asking for could be considered by God to be an intense encounter with Him, but to the people, it appeared to be more or less short-lived—*like a prayer-meeting experience.* Within a brief time everyone had moved onto another thing and I felt very little had been accomplished in our hearts.

As I waited before the Lord, He spoke into my heart.

He said this: *"I want more than kindling. Kindling burns fast, consumed in an instant, leaving behind only ashes of the past experience. I want the timber of the people's lives to continue to be fed to the altar of my Fire, so that what I do will be sustained—not just for the duration of a prayer conference or a service, but until I come."*

Finney, a man of prayer was preparing to go in to pray one day when a minister asked to join him for prayer. It is said that they both went into Finney's prayer room and about two hours later this minister came out. He said, *"It is too much God for me."*

The true cry of a hungry heart is still an insatiable thirst and hunger for *"more of God."* If we drank and ate at His table for the next thousand years, we would never tap in the fullness of this Great and Awesome God we serve.

My daughter, Debra McBride, had the Holy Spirit show her a picture of a huge bonfire in which people were gathered very close to the fire, which she knew to be the presence of God's holiness. But there was another a group of people standing afar off with their hands extended out like they were warming themselves by the fire, but they could not draw close. It was simply too hot for them. They kept shielding their faces and trying to keep up the front as if they were enjoying the fire.

Sometimes the greatest darkness is right in the cold church—a place where the Fire of God should be hot but has died down to less than an ember. We are so used to going to church, feeling fed and good about what God did in a particular service. We may even go away declaring *how great the visitation of the Lord was.*

We go to church as if that is where He is and go home as if we will see Him again pretty soon.

I oftentimes have wondered how God feels about things when it's all over and everyone goes home . . .

Yes, there have been some great and powerful moments, but we still haven't seen what His heart's desire.

- ***Why haven't*** our houses of prayer shaken yet?
- ***Why haven't*** we seen tongues of fire on our heads and our churches on fire for the Glory of God?
- ***Why haven't*** we seen the fresh outpouring of Pentecostal Fire that we all so greatly desire?

It was the white-hot fire of the love of God that pushed His heart over the edge of extreme to offer up His only Son for our sins. For us to return our hearts and lives in lukewarm condition back to Him, in exchange for all He's given us, is an insult to His Grace.

For us to settle for anything less than God consuming our lives with Holy Fire is *"mediocrity ready to slip into a fireless, lukewarm state."*

David Wilkerson, not too long before his death, said this in a message titled, ***"The Last Day Church:"*** *"The Lord is preparing a powerful yet humble army of shepherds after His own heart and also a remnant congregation of hungry sheep who have turned away from the deadness and sin of the modern church. The scene is being set for that church which will be hot, not lukewarm-and it will rock the very foundations of hell. No power on earth will be able to ignore or despise it!"*

> ***Luke 3:16*** (Emphasis Added)—*John answered, saying unto them all, I indeed baptize you with water; but one mightier than I cometh, the latchet of whose shoes I am not worthy*

to unloose: ***he shall baptize you with the Holy Ghost and with fire:***

The fire we need comes from outside of ourselves—a supernatural blaze that lights a properly laid sacrifice.

We need God's fire in our intercession.
We need God's fire in our worship.
We need God's fire in our Word.
We need God's fire in our witness.

We need God's fire in our lives, day and night

Oh God of burning, cleansing flames; Send the Fire!
William Booth/Salvation Army

CHAPTER 21

UNCOMFORTABLE REPENTANCE!

Revelation 3:19

As many as I love, I rebuke and chasten: be zealous therefore, and repent.

The letters to the churches in Revelation is a call to repentance—an attempt on the part of Jesus Christ to wake up, stir up and sound the alarm to His church to revive them and draw them back to Himself through repentance.

God spoke to the Laodicea church to repent. John the Baptist came with a message of repentance. ***(Matthew 3:2)*** Jesus followed after John the Baptist with the cry for repentance. ***(Matthew 4:17)***

He still comes to His church today and cries with the same urgency, "*Repent.*"

I recall a number of years ago when the move of God began to sweep through our church, *as it was all around the world*, it was a revival of repentance—getting right with God. After God had dealt with deep-seated issues in the lives of many people, a complaint began to form in the heart of and from the lips of some people, saying, *"How much repenting are we going to have to do anyway?"*

By the very nature of the complaint it was evident that God was still working some things out in people's lives. When the Word of God speaks of *"daily sanctifying ourselves,"* I am sure repentance is involved in keeping our hearts right with God. Our flesh is too demanding of us to allow us to live a single day without it raising its ugly head—so we beat our body under and bring it into obedience to Jesus Christ. We simply don't have enough goodness in us to purify our hearts before a Holy God.

As we try our best to
"Make ourselves better,"
"Mend our ways,"
"Clean up our act,"

God is waiting for us to recognize our helplessness to *"do it ourselves."*

Repentance has key things that mark it as genuine when it happens. It is also easy to see when it hasn't happened because there is evidence.

I love forensics as the specialized men and women search for clues that a crime has been committed. It is a fine-tooth comb that picks up the least things, unseen by the human eye. When those items are run through a series of test to see where each has come from, they eventually point a finger of accusation at a person. This evidence will hold up in a court of law as the crime is prosecuted. The guilty person is soon found out and sent to jail, based upon the evidence gathered at the scene of the crime.

I wonder how much evidence could be found at the scene, the altars of our churches, pointing to true repentance or the lack thereof.

- Would we find evidence of lives restored as a result of forgiveness flowing as lives are healed from the wounds of gossip and other such things, ***or*** would we find that there is still evidence that no healing has taken place because no true repentance has taken place?
- Would we find evidence of families and churches enjoying the sweetness of relationship ***or*** would there still be a root of bitterness because there was no deep work of forgiveness and repentance releasing the healing in those situations?
- Would we be able to see our enemies with a clear conscious ***or*** would we side step to another aisle when they come our way?
- Would we feel the hurt of our wounds ***or*** would we enjoy the healing that is ours?

Would we find restoration or further erosion?
Would we find resolution or more pollution?
Would we find renewal or deeper stagnation?
Would we find freedom or more bondage?

Repentance is something that we must understand, from God's viewpoint and how it works in our lives. It works in the deep things of our heart; the surface things of our lives; the recesses of our minds; the eternal things of the spirit—It works, *if it is actually done*, according to the specifications of the Word of God.

People want to say they are sorry to God but avoid, as if it were the plague, saying they are sorry to others—their pastors, husbands, wives, children, friends and enemies.

Some feel that as long as they have repented to God that *"everything else"* is okay, but that is not what the Word of God says. We know the way and yet we don't always walk in it.

> ***Deuteronomy 30:19*** (Emphasis Added)—*I call heaven and earth to record this day against you, that I have set before you life and death, blessing and cursing:* ***therefore choose life*** *that both thou and thy seed may live:*

The Word lights a path, showing us the way, and some still want to take a detour around the obvious things right before the eyes. God's Word is the best road map we have to follow the way of the Lord into all He has for us. A lot of people do not follow the path of repentance but instead cut their own path of *"dropping it,"* and moving on. This is not God's way.

The thing about this is that if we do this long enough, we can convince ourselves that we are fine, ***"as long as God understands our hearts."*** But the evidence is still there. A crime has been committed and there is a forensic specialist, called Holy Spirit, which is always sweeping the area of the deeds that we do and the words that we say.

As the *Master of Truth,* Holy Spirit always presents an open and shut case before the Father.

We have only one thing to do, plead guilty and ask for His grace and mercy, otherwise known as godly sorrow for those words and deeds.

We repent and He forgives.
We cover and He uncovers.

We talk of holiness and righteousness, but do not realize that the price tag on such treasures is our lives, sold out to the Word of God working in each and every part of our lives—our minds, our emotions, our relationships, our wills, our marriages, our churches, our families, our desires.

There is a cleansing that takes places when we open up all the secret places of our hearts to be cleansed through the means that the Word of God commands—not requests—but commands.

We really don't like anyone telling us what we have to do, so we relegate the commandments of the Word to meaning something other than what they do mean. It is the job of an escape artist that wiggles out of the responsibility to the Word; by avoiding its searching probe.

One of these days there will be a trumpet blast signifying that the Bridegroom has arrived and we will be either ready or caught without the proper oil for our lamps. You see, no matter how much we pretend to be okay, if our oil has diminished to a seriously low supply, we are not okay.

Oil is always a sign of the Holy Spirit throughout the Word of God. There is one thing I know about the Holy Spirit—He can be resisted, quenched and grieved.

We can tell Him, *"No."*
We can put out the fire of His burning in our lives.
We can cause Him to feel great sorrow.

He reflects perfectly the face of our Father God.

***If Holy Spirit is grieved*, then so is God.**
***If Holy Spirit is resisted*, then so is God.**
***If Holy Spirit is quenched*, then so is God.**

The work of the Holy Spirit is recorded in the Word of God and is expressed as God in our human spirit as we make place for Him to work. Where does Jesus fit in to this? Holy Spirit is the One who leads us to Jesus and lifts Him up in our lives. We have to have the Holy Spirit to Worship, to pray, to Love, to live in peace, to have joy, to have compassion, to feel the heartbeat of the Father.

When we don't listen to Him about our own conditions, then we put His light out and we become dull and lackluster. He is our fuel for our light.

It is time for a national church of multiple-denominations to fall on their faces and cry out to God for mercy upon their own souls. That level of repentance will exact an immediate change of lifestyle, message, faith and practice of the faith before our communities.

One by one our world will see a real church rising up to love them to Jesus.

<u>Repentance</u>

- ***Repentance is*** the only thing that will turn a person around, stop the stagnation of a church and set it to marching.
- ***Repentance is*** the only thing that will stop the downward spiral of degradation that many a soul is trapped in.
- ***Repentance is*** the only thing that will move a soul from lukewarm living and set them on fire for God.
- ***Repentance is*** the only thing that will turn a proud heart from its haughty ways and bring in a spirit of humility.
- ***Repentance is*** the only thing that will take a stiff neck and make it pliable.
- ***Repentance is*** the only thing that will turn a perverted soul to purity.
- ***Repentance is*** the only thing that will change the bitter waters of our lives to sweet water.
- ***Repentance is*** the only thing that will take a heart of stone and make it flesh, beating with the heartbeat of the Father.
- ***Repentance is*** the only thing that will take a rebellious person and turn their life around to a life of submission.

- ***Repentance is*** the only thing that will take the stubborn in heart and mind and bring them to a place of yieldedness.
- ***Repentance is*** the only thing that will remove the spot and blemishes and iron the wrinkles of our lives and make us white as snow.

Repentance is not a minor adjustment or tune up—
It is a total change of faulty parts.

Well, the wake-up call is being sounded even now. It is time to take off our rose-colored glasses that we look at ourselves through and look hard and long in the reflective mirror of the Word of God and see if we really look like Jesus.

My mother, Mary Seaton, made this statement: *"Unless our altars on earth are connected in purity to the altar of heaven, God will not receive that sweet offering."*

There's nothing as sweet to God's ears as repentance that cries out,
"Father Forgive me."

CHAPTER 22

IT'S TIME TO GO DEEP!

Ecclesiastes 7:24-25

That which is far off and exceeding deep, who can find it out? I applied mine heart to know, and to search, and to seek out wisdom, and the reason of things, and to know the wickedness of folly, even of foolishness and madness:

Everything here may not apply to you at this time, but no doubt some of it will. It is always better to paint sin and error and negligence in the worst possible light so we will not go too easy on ourselves in the light of God's Holiness. So, don't cringe at the words or the weight of the questions, but just lean into them and see what God might say to you through them. You never know but what there is freedom right here on these next few pages . . .

I call this, ***"It's Time,"*** to indicate the urgency of the hour and the need to be awakened from any level of slumber concerning our own hearts.

- ***It is time*** to make ourselves accountable to do it God's way.
- ***It is time*** to get under the protective covering of the things that God has placed over us.
- ***It is time*** to rid ourselves of error and deception.

***It is time* to realize that there are no private interpretations of the Word of God and that no matter how hard we try; we cannot make the Word match the lifestyle that we are presently living.**

- ***It is time*** to realize that we must pour ourselves into the mold of God's Word instead of trying to mold the Word of God into our philosophies and ideas about life, ministry, revival, family and the things of this life.
- ***It is time*** to understand that Truth remains a constant source of safety and peace for those who abide in it.
- ***It is time*** to know the *joy* that comes in being totally saturated with truth, even if it means the end of our *"happiness."*

***It is time* to realize that to shift truth from its center to make it fit our needs to be right is to toy with the very nature of God the Father, God the Son, God the Holy Spirit and the Written Word of God.**

- ***It is time*** to understand that the only thing that shifts is us.
- ***It is time*** to destroy the pride in our life that has caused us to walk our own path so many times.
- ***It is time*** to know the God who made us instead of knowing the God we have made.

***It is time* to realize that when our thoughts and ways are no higher than the thoughts and ways of man, that we are living way beneath the level that God would have us live.**

- ***It is time*** to realize that our perceptive and logical mind is capable of being held captive to our own thoughts and ideas, corrupting our spirit with their wanderings and alternate paths that they are sure to take if unchallenged.
- ***It is time*** to understand that our journey of self-realization is a path of man's making and holds nothing in common with God's will and call upon our life.
- ***It is time*** to realize that today's morality is not truly morality but corrupt and has slowly conditioned us to accept things that God would never allow.

***It is time* to understand that Jesus is not tolerant of sin but rather, because of the sacrifice of his own life, would never condone that which he suffered and died to erase from mankind.**

- ***It is time*** to realize that salvation, the sheepfold, does not have a swinging door but rather only one door. For the man who thinks that he can come and go as he pleases, he has to go past Jesus to do it.
- ***It is time*** to allow a faithful heart to develop in our spirit to match the faithfulness of God to us.
- ***It is time*** to realize that any message that is easy on the flesh is a gospel that Jesus would never preach. All flesh must die in the presence of Jesus and His holiness.
- ***It is time*** to allow the Sword of Truth, which is the Word of God, to pierce our heart to the very depth of our soulish nature, so that the spirit man can arise to glorify our God and Creator.
- ***It is time*** to open the door to our interior and let Jesus in.

***It is time* to give our mind to Jesus so that He can wash it and renew it through His Word, which is truth.**

- ***It is time*** to quit drawing back into our old reservoirs to strengthen ourselves in our resolve that we are right.
- ***It is time*** to understand that God's Word has a system of Check and Balances that help keep them centered on God's unshakable foundation.
- ***It is time*** to understand that when God says, *"Be Holy, even as I am Holy,"* that this means me and you.

***It is time* to realize that God is getting ready to entrust to the prepared church with the greatest harvest that has ever come in.**

- ***It is time*** to realize that there is a harvest out there that needs a place, safe and truthful, that they can come into and not be contaminated by man's perversions of thought, ideas and lifestyles and religion.
- ***It is time*** to understand that the *message of our* life is overriding the message of the cross.
- ***It is time*** to hold ourselves personally accountable and responsible for the harvest that is waiting to come in.
- ***It is time*** to realize that they are sick of hypocrisy and flimsy living, called Christianity, and are looking for clean water that

has not been fouled by the selfish feet of God's servants and a pasture that has not been trampled by our walk.

- ***It is time*** to realize that they have had their fill of living here like the world and that they need Jesus, The Word and Truth—His Way, like He lived it and delivered it when He walked upon the earth.
- ***It is time*** to discover that they don't need to come into the House of God and find people with their feet in two worlds, practicing worldly living and claiming to be like Jesus.
- ***It is time*** that we realize that they will not listen to a message from one who looks like the world, walks like the world, lives like the world and talks like the world.

It is time **to realize that a person who is submitted to God and man could never approach ministry without repentance, so that they can flow out as clean vessels.**

- ***It is time*** to understand that to move in any level of compromise or error will cause us to be prone to justify ourselves in our own eyes but be visible to the eyes of others.
- ***It is time*** to realize that the road from submission to rebellion against God and His directives in His Word is paved with Stones of Compromise, Crooked places of Deception, Acts of Disobedience and Ignored warnings.
- ***It's time*** to rise up with our feet planted firmly in obedience to the Word of God in every area of our life, so that when the storms come, we will not be washed away

***It is time* to realize that if our heart and flesh yearned after the things of God with the same passion that we go after the temporal things of this life, we would have an outpouring, such as we could not contain.**

It's Time!!!

CHAPTER 23

THE VOICE OF ONE

Mark 1:3

The voice of one crying in the wilderness, Prepare ye the way of the Lord, make his paths straight.

There must be a voice for every generation—one that will cry out—*"Prepare the Way of the Lord"* and one that will cry out for repentance and return to God.

And for some reason, this true and pure voice directing earth's attention to Jesus, birthed in heaven prophetically centuries ago, is dismissed yet today. Oftentimes it is said of those who approach the times soberly, *"You guys are always negative and looking for the bad things—we want a positive message."*

But, in spite of what others say or do, there has always been a voice that stands out as making some people uncomfortable. But folks, sometimes we need to be made uncomfortable to be awakened to the facts that all is not well in the world.

While we have our motivating conferences, the nation's children are still dying in the streets, families are falling apart and churches are growing cold in their love for Jesus. And beyond our own nation, to the uttermost parts of the earth, the turmoil increases all over the world as mankind that has trusted their own minds are having the props pulled out from under them.

And that truth is not just found in the secular world—but also in the church world as sin has taken its toll inside the doors of the ministry.

When there are complexities such as surround our world, they gives vent to a multitude of voices—all prophesying, as it were, of what was, what is and what is to come. You can hear these voices on street corners, shopping malls, bars, foyers, pulpits and pews, lodges, senates and congresses, school yards, colleges, Wall Street, banks, television and across the fence in the back yard. These voices rise from the least to the greatest, the prominent to the obscure, the private to the public, the poorest to the richest, the government to the church and the secular to the religious.

Even if someone's word is spoken in a small setting of peers or on a grand stage of democracy—a waterfall of words tumble over the precipice of history as speculation is made as to what is going on in our world.

Words of fear and words of faith—words of doom and words of hope—words of lies and words of truth—words of promise and words of hopelessness—words of anger and words of love—are continually filling the air we breathe with foretelling or foreboding—prophecy of some kind.

The words are a mixed salad of ideas and opinions for the most part as people wrestle with a world without answers.

Even in religion, as we are facing the most difficult days of earth's life, the churches voices are not giving a clear sound. The message is as mixed here as on the street.

Early in 2011, a preacher released his voice and many people followed him, believing he was telling the truth. His message was a direct violation of scripture and yet he did what so many have done over and over—*set a date Jesus was coming back*. The result was a devastation of a multitude of people's faith all over the world.

There were some tragedies connected with this false prophet's words as people's lives were left in ruin. Chaos filled with disillusionment, fear and embarrassment in some Christian communities erupted as the day came and went.

While he spoke his message, others kept debating about when Jesus would come—pre-tribulation, mid-tribulation or post-tribulation, and whether there is a rapture or not and how the kingdom is going to be set up and whether the church is relevant or not to the post-post modern world we live in.

Others within religious circles debated as to the inerrancy of the scriptures and elevated their brain power above that of the creator by deciding for themselves the things pertaining to spiritual matters apart from God's Word. Many others infused erroneous doctrine into the church while others debated over worship styles, politics and elections.

***And outside the church doors,* heart-wrenching scenes of hopelessness, pain and despair are playing out in the hearts and lives of throngs of lost people as close as the neighbor next door.**

Multitudes of lives are hapless victims of sin; souls caught in the web of lies spun by the thoughts and ways of fallen man in conflict with His creator.

- America and other industrialized nations are caught in the clutch of hedonism (pursuit of happiness as the ultimate goal in life) greed.
- Many other nations are sadly wrapped in the grave clothes of poverty and death.
- Human trafficking takes place on every continent, catching away children and youth into the whirlpool of perversion as dark souls who are more devil than man buy and sell them to the highest bidder.
- Drought and famine have decimated whole populations with disease, with loss and pain being the pallbearer to the dying and dead.

Little skeleton babies latched onto skeleton breasts and search for the phantom milk from a dying mother who with hollow eyes grieves for her child futile struggle to survive.

- Rapes, murder, prostitution—from the back alleys to the higher echelons of the governments of the world are a rampant part of the chaos that has the world in its grip.
- People are scurrying to try to fix it, while they themselves are a part of the problem within the chambers of their own hearts.
- The spirit of tolerance for things just as horrific, whitewash the truth while abortions and child abuse mark homes and the lives of those trapped in the web of deception that didn't even have answers for their own problems.

Things are where they are because of the schoolrooms, board rooms, senates, congresses, judge's benches and pulpits of the world. The voices have been expressed and the world has become drunk on the proverbial *Kool-aid*. Gross spiritual darkness has covered nations and governments, school houses and colleges and pulpit and pew—as mankind has thought his thoughts and had his way.

And . . . when a voice of truth speaks into the darkness—the voices of dissent escalate to crucifixion level once again.

> ***Acts 5:40b***— *. . . and when they had called the apostles, and beaten them, they commanded that they should not speak in the name of Jesus, and let them go.*

I have sadly watched, *as many of you have*, as the trendy world-view has arrested the voices of those considered strong in faith by their followers. Even some people who know truth and have spoken it have vacillated under pressure and duress to be quiet and not speak.

An opposing voice will demand you not speak in the name of Jesus.

Events like ***9/11*** come to pass and public Christian leaders are compelled to answer the problem so they speak and the world listens. Immediately they are lined up before a firing squad of demand and told to recant what they said. And sure enough, many times, there is a recanting of the thing spoken. No one is really twisting their arm, but they feel the heat of displeasure by those who scream in rage against their voice. And then another kind of attack takes place as bullets of contempt are fired and their life message is hindered because they recanted their positional statements.

A Christian cannot recant enough to get on the good side of the devil and the enemies of the cross!
The world has distain for those who have a message but they dislike even more those who vacillate in their message.

Our world today needs Jeremiah's, Ezekiel's and John the Baptists, Stephen's and Peter's—people who will not change their message when faith is under fire. Truth is not alterable, does not fluctuate, and cannot be tampered with to fit any idea because truth is not the words you speak but a person called Truth—Jesus Christ the Son of the Living God.

You and I can say, *"I'm telling you the truth,"* but if we do not know and accept the truth in and through Jesus Christ, we have no truth at all.

We may have *the chaff of truth* and even live on that surface-level of shallow-belief but never get past our ideology to really *"know Truth"* as a person—Jesus Christ. Then when the first wind of adversity comes blowing against our lives our level of truth is not enough to keep us established.

We must know when these storms come and our faith is under fire whether our faith is chaff easily blown away or is it a corn of wheat prepared to die? ***John 12:24***

I am not afraid of being a voice—I am concerned about being another voice added to the cacophony of noise on the earth.

When John the Baptist came crying out the message of repentance in the wilderness shortly before Jesus came on the scene, he came as a voice of one.

> ***Mark 1:3***—*The voice of one crying in the wilderness, Prepare ye the way of the Lord, make his paths straight.*

The voice sounded like John but the message was the message of One.

If there is no eternal value to what you or I say, we would do everyone a favor by shutting our mouths and stop adding to the religious and secular madness of words that are being released. But if our message is that of our Master, Jesus Christ, still finding sound and vent in one more life and voice dedicated to declare Him truth to a dying world, then we should not shut our mouths, even if it's hated or silenced.

No drama here folks—just a determination to not falter in yours and my steps of faith on the most difficult point of all—Jesus Christ is Truth and we each are the voice of one.

Do you really know Jesus Christ is *"The Truth,"*—not—*"a truth?"*
Do you know He is *"The Word,"*—not—*"a word?"*

In the mass confusion and mixed messages the world needs "The Word—The Truth" and God needs a voice.

Will you be that un-erring voice of Truth to a world steeped in deception and error?

Will you . . . ?

Part IV
Two Breads

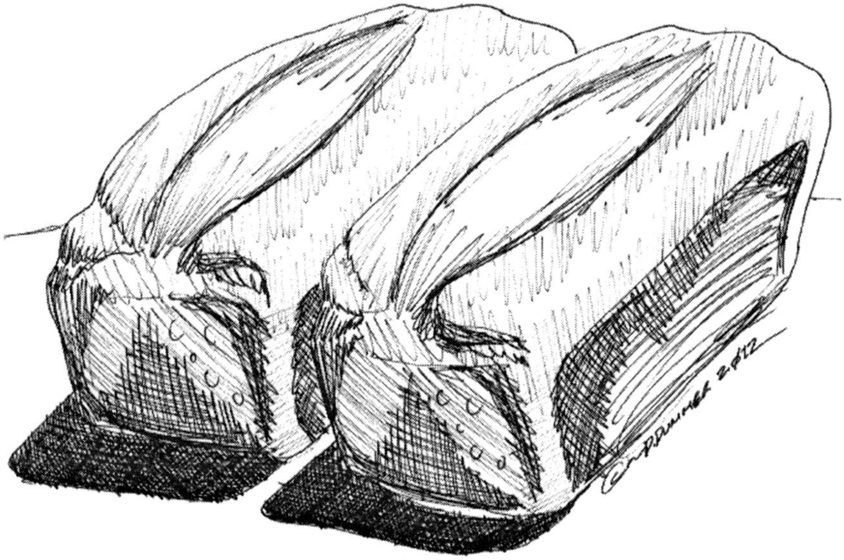

John 6:35

And Jesus said unto them, I am the bread of life: he that cometh to me shall never hunger; and he that believeth on me shall never thirst.

CHAPTER 24

NO ORDINARY DREAM

Acts 2:17-18

And it shall come to pass in the last days, saith God, I will pour out of my Spirit upon all flesh: and your sons and your daughters shall prophesy, and your young men shall see visions, and your old men shall dream dreams: And on my servants and on my handmaidens I will pour out in those days of my Spirit; and they shall prophesy:

It was one of great magnitude and has had a lasting impact on me.

It was in early April, 2008, while vacationing in Victoria, B.C., Canada, when the LORD gave me this very troubling dream. It had a very specific message in it, most of which I understood upon waking up. I knew that it pertained to the move of God many have been experiencing in their churches and personal lives.

I felt the dream to be a warning of something that was coming to the church.

In the dream my husband and I were in a house with a group of revivalists. There was a knock at the door and two men, both dressed in white robes stood there with easel and charts in hand. They were asked to come in by the leadership. They entered into the place where the saints of God were gathered. I was on immediate alert as I felt a clash in my spirit with these two. I spoke to the leadership and asked if he knew them and to check out the two men before allowing them to have access to the believers. He appeared to be unwilling to *rock the boat*, or *offend them*.

I was truly alarmed that these two *false prophets* had been invited in and were now being allowed to bring their teaching inside.

Now, in this dream, those gathered in the house were believers, those who had committed themselves to years of prayer, preparation and study—a wilderness people, if you will—well into their journey into the promises of God. I knew the house represented the household of faith, the church of the Lord Jesus Christ, which He had purchased with His own precious blood.

They were hungry people, a people who desired to be used of God in a deeper way.

These two men came in and sat up their easel and began to teach about the *health of the church*. I knew they were teaching on healing and the miraculous, something all was interested in. They delivered their *message* with great skill, gaining the immediate attention of those gathered there.

What do the two men represent?

- They are false teachers who with a spirit of error and deception are craftily diluting and polluting two elements that are essential to truth—The Word and the Spirit.

I noticed they had given a green drink to a gifted intercessor, one used in prophetic worship. She was dressed in a beautiful flowing dress and appeared to be totally dedicated to her Lord and Savior, Jesus Christ. But as they were imparting this cup to her, she was drawn in and drank without question.

- I know the devil is after the intercessors—and that those who have been strong in the area of discernment have been targeted by a specific impartation of error—to destroy the power of their intercession, to shut their eyes and silence their mouths.

    2 Peter 2:20 (Emphasis Added)—*For if after they have escaped the pollutions of the world through the knowledge of the Lord and Savior Jesus Christ,* ***they are again entangled***

> ***therein, and overcome,*** *the latter end is worse with them than the beginning.*

As they continued to teach their doctrine to the group, a very troubling manifestation began to occur, which I could see plainly. These grounded Christians began to become restless, which then gave way to frivolous activity. They were giddy with what they were hearing.

- Instead of behaving wisely, they began to act immaturely.
- It was similar to a group of kids on a playground having fun.

Then a deeper manifestation of the teachings they were receiving began to move them from stability to instability. These students of the Word got up and began to become disassembled and disjointed. Some who were still sitting on a sofa were suddenly being nuzzled and loved by black and white cats. They began to stroke and pet them, believing them to be domestic cats . . . but they were spirits of compromise released by the teachings of the two false prophets.

- What had been so clearly understood now was being drawn into question as these spirits worked to take their eyes off truth.

Chaos began to take over . . . the cohesiveness was gone.

I was amazed at how quickly it happened at how just this one teaching could wreak such havoc to the unity of the Body of Christ. It was frightening to watch as these people lost their mooring and began to chase after these two men's teaching.

I then saw these two men take a plate of what appeared to be beautifully baked bread.

It looked like bread *until it was broken open.* It was crawling with worms that were the same color as the bread, as if they had blended in with their background like a chameleon. I cautioned people to not eat it, but they did anyway, oblivious to the worms, big grub worms about the size of a human thumb. If someone had eyes to see, they could have easily seen them—***but***

it was as if everyone was blinded by their hunger for whatever these men offered them.

> ***Jude 1:18-19*** (Emphasis Added)
>
> *18 How that they told you there should be mockers in the last time, who should walk after their own ungodly lusts.*
>
> *19 These be they who separate themselves,* ***sensual,*** (the sensuous nature subjected to appetite and passion) having not the Spirit.

I began to try and call the people to stop and hear me.

I was calling for them to *"run to sanctuary."*

No one was listening.

I then saw the gifted intercessor, who had partaken of the cup offered to her, move into a sensual dance. She had received a perverse spirit, one that moved her to lasciviousness and error. As she danced, she was suddenly sick and began to vomit this green substance.

She had fallen to her knees and being soiled by the vomit of her own soul.

Where formerly the Living Water of the Spirit of God had flowed from her, now this perversity began to come forth. I knew she was dying. To me this meant that what God had desired to do in her life was being forfeited because of an unholy impartation by false teaching. There was a feeling of helplessness. I remember trying to clean up after her and trying to help her out of the mess she was now laying in.

Then there appeared in the room an old man, a prophet of Biblical proportion, dressed in a white garment, long beard, aged with wisdom—infused with godliness, one like unto *Jeremiah, Ezekiel, Isaiah.*

He stood there with an ancient scroll in his hand and began to unroll it as he prepared to speak. It was soon fully opened as he began to speak above the clamor and into the people gathered there. I knew he was speaking the true Word of God but the chaos in the lives of those gathered had darkened their eyes of understanding and closed their ears.

No one was listening to him.

I saw him sadly roll the scroll up and prepare to leave the room. The sense of urgency at the loss of the Word of God was intense. I cried out to the people to stop and ***"Hear the Word of the LORD!"*** No one was hearing him. No one paid any attention to my cry of warning that the Word was leaving the House.

I asked this old man of God to please not go, but he looked at me sadly and began to withdraw from the room.

Before he left he turned and held out a plate of beautiful bread, warm and smelling so wonderful, fresh baked. I noticed the bread the two false teachers had offered and the prophet's bread looked alike, except this bread was fresh and good. He was offering it to anyone who would eat, but no one in the room was even seeing it.

> ***John 6:35***—*And Jesus said unto them, I am the bread of life: he that cometh to me shall never hunger; and he that believeth on me shall never thirst.*

Then suddenly I was on a corner lot, a place I have been in other dreams, *a place of decision for people.* With me were a handful of those who had left the house with me. They were stunned, wiping at their clothing, trying to get the remnant of what they had just involved themselves in off their garments. They appeared to be dazed, like, how did that happen?

I then looked off to my left and saw a very large concrete block totem altar. I noticed it was quickly and sloppily made, tilting somewhat in a skewed way. It was way over my head, and was crowned with three blocks across the top, like cap stones. It was very poorly mortared.

I was angry against that false altar which was elevated far above man's head. I went over to it and kicked it three times. It fell crumbling at my feet and turned into small pieces of gravel. (Deuteronomy 9:21)

I was shocked at how easy it was taken down.

I then looked up and saw in the empty lot across the street, a vehicle, without a top, slowly driving by. It contained twenty-four men from the waist up, who were all dressed in black suits, which I knew to be preachers of the gospel. All the men were sitting straight in their seats, but their heads were turned my way like a sightseeing group. They had no expression on their faces, just a blank stare.

I cried out to the LORD that He would open their eyes to see the coming deception.

~End of Dream~

Questions and Answers:

What is in the hand of the two men? It is the bread of the false prophets who enter in the House of God in Sheep's clothing. The two men of this dream were dressed in white robes, which made them *appear to be holy.*

I went to the Word of God to look at the bread that had worms. Here is what I found:

> ***Exodus 16:19-20; 23-24*** (Emphasis Added)—*And Moses said, Let no man leave of it* (don't keep any left-over's) *till the morning. Notwithstanding they hearkened not unto Moses; but some of them left of it until the morning, and **it*** (the manna) ***bred worms*** (maggots), ***and stank**: and Moses was wroth with them. And they laid it* (the manna) *up till the morning, as Moses bade**: and it did not stink, neither was there any worm therein.***

The Holy Spirit has spoken some things to me about this scripture. The Manna is an act of God, from His hands to His people. The people did nothing to bring about the Manna. They had no formula or power to *rain Manna from heaven.* It was totally God!

***If* you put your hands on what comes from God, what belongs to God and try to manage or control it and practice disobedience and pride, the Manna will breed worms and stink.**

- ***When*** something moves from the administration of God to the administration of man—*it stinks.*
- ***When*** something that God is doing is taken over in greed, control and lust—*it stinks.*

There is a parallel drawn but also a distinction between the Manna of the Old Testament and the Bread of Heaven come down to earth in Jesus. How? God sent Him and now man is trying to control and define the Bread of Heaven, every way but God's way.

Anything and everything but God's Word is eminent and anything and everything but God's Spirit is leading when man is in charge.

Things that die spiritually have the stench of death comes up in the face of God. We can see death all around us as nations are dying, churches are dying, people are dying. The decline of a nation, a church or a person is a very sad thing to watch—as all that was alive and beautiful fades to black.

When a move of God is infiltrated with flesh, pride and immorality and error—it begins to die and stink and, like the manna of the wilderness, gets wormy.

- **Stink**—to emit a strong smell, highly offensive or abhorrent.

- ***If*** God's commands were followed, the manna was sweet and wholesome, emitting no foul odor or crawling with worms.
- ***If*** God's commands were not followed, the manna bred worms and stank.

Only that which was sought for and gathered to oneself in obedience was kept free of worms and the stench of death

God's commands are not given just so God can be saying something—He has a purpose for why He commands His people to do or not do a thing. God knows the heart of mankind and its propensity for greed and hoarding—and for presumption upon the grace of God as if he would overlook *minor infractions* of His law.

It is possible that what God sends down from heaven to man, pure, sweet and healthy, can be defiled by man taking hold of it in disobedience and greed.

With this dream came a great warning of the coming deception that was to enter right into the ranks of those hungry for God to move and to be used of Him. I don't know why we who seek God would think that the devil would not try to bring deception in *the form of light*—but he has and he does—It's his job title, *"the father of lies."*

> ***2 Corinthians 11:13-14*** (Emphasis Added)
>
> *13 For such are **false apostles, deceitful workers, transforming themselves** into the apostles of Christ.*
>
> *14 And no marvel; for Satan himself is **transformed into an angel of light**.*

Once again—***the uncomfortable truth***—*these are people the Word is talking about*—evidently backed up by the devil in a satanic transformation to shield the darkness with what appears to be light.

These false apostles, deceitful workers, had transformed themselves, by arriving looking like apostles of Christ. They entered into the place where the saints of God were gathered.

In ***Jude 1:4*** (Emphasis Added) we are forewarned, *"There would be certain men who would **creep in*** (wormed their way in) *unnoticed, ungodly men who would turn the grace of our God into lasciviousness, and deny the only Lord God, and our Lord Jesus Christ."*

The way they *worm their way in*, as one translation says it, is to come in sheep's clothing—to come dressed in white. Many pastors are accused of being too much of a watchman, but I say for the sake of those who stand firm against such things, they are discerning of the hearts of men.

Jesus regularly looked into the heart of man and saw *(knew)* their thoughts being played out mentally in order to entrap and snare Him.

It is incumbent upon the gatekeepers of ministries, when someone knocks on the door of your church or ministry seeking entrance to know the intents of their heart and the contents of their lives. It also gives caution to believers to take note of and know by the Spirit of God who enters into their personal space as well. We are all gatekeepers of our own hearts, opening and shutting doors.

The disturbing part of the dream was the fact ***these were believers***, those who had committed themselves to years of prayer, preparation and study—a wilderness people, if you will—well into their journey into the promises of God.

> ***1 Corinthians 10:12****—Wherefore let him that thinketh he standeth take heed lest he fall.*

Overconfidence in *not being able to be deceived* is already an open door for deception.

The people in my dream were a hungry people, those who desired to be used of God in a deeper way.

God was about to teach me a much-needed lesson for the Body of Christ on not being led solely by our hunger . . . and "***to know those who minister among you.***"

1 Peter 2:1-2 read in modern language might sound like this: "*There were false prophets, teachers and apostles who came into our midst acting like they were divinely inspired prophets and began to utter falsehoods under the name of the Divine. They came in among the people and fraudulently introduced destroying, diverse opinions and aims, not associating their teachings with*

Jesus Christ, but of their own set of belief taught. Anyone who imitates their filthy ways, entering into lascivious behavior with them, will also follow the path of blasphemy of the Way of Truth."

The false teachers in my dream did what I have witnessed in real life—they delivered *their message* with great skill, grabbing the attention of those who gathered there. We need to remember that talented speakers with charm and charisma are not the same as those who are anointed by God's Spirit.

It is a good time to ask ourselves a question—Is our heart able to be played by the words that offer our flesh some relief—whether in monetary gain or healing needs that we may have?

We must arm our hearts in this hour to not cater to the flesh demands that sound a lot like spiritual needs.

Notice here in the following scripture once again, it is a person that is being used to bait the hook to draw us out of the rivers of living water.

> ***2 Peter 2:18*** (Emphasis Added)—*For when they speak* ***great swelling words of vanity****, they* ***allure through the lusts of the flesh****, through much wantonness,* ***those that were clean*** *escaped from them who live in error.*

Once again, remember this—the false comes ***as light***, so we must keep a guard on our flesh that it not make demands that mislead us.

> ***I John 2:16*** (Emphasis Added)—*For all that is in the world,* ***the lust of the flesh****, and* ***the lust of the eyes****, and* ***the pride of life****, is not of the Father, but is of the world.*

- The Lust of the Flesh—***I want it***
- The Lust of the Eyes—***I need it***
- The Pride of Life—***I deserve it***

Sometimes the biggest deception in the church today is a sense of entitlement—which is simply put—PRIDE.

> ***James 1:14-17*** (Emphasis Added)—*But every man is tempted,* ***when he is drawn away*** *of his own* ***lust*** *and* ***enticed.***

I was interested in the phrase, "*when he is drawn away of his own lust and enticed,*" and it's meaning—***To lure forth as game is lured from its hiding place by its cravings who then is caught with the bait laid out to lure.***

> **2 Peter 2:14a** (Emphasis Added)—*Having eyes full of adultery and that cannot cease from sin;* ***beguiling*** *(to catch with bait; to allure, to entice, to deceive)* ***unstable*** *(vacillating; unfixed)* **souls** . . .

It is amazing how quickly just one teaching partaken of by an eager soul, can wreak havoc on the unity of the Body of Christ, not excluding the individual soul that becomes ensnared by false words passed off as light.

I remember hearing of intercessors who said, as they entered into a particular movement, "*It didn't feel right, but I went on in and then the worship started and I felt okay about it.*" I know there were many, many others who embraced some things that, even though the Word of God was elevated to a place of truth, it was abandoned with the statement . . .

"Everything doesn't have to be in the Bible."

I realized that sometimes you can call and you can warn but many will simply not hear the alarm because they want what they want. My call for people to "run to a sanctuary, a place of safety in God's Word, was not heeded. I know some harm was done to some wonderful people who got their eyes off God and onto man.

Oh how we need ears to hear what the Spirit of the Lord is saying to His church!

I believe for me the worst part of this dream was the disregard for the Word of God in exchange for the false bread. When I saw that old man dressed in a white garment, aged with wisdom—infused with godliness, and saw the complete contempt for what he held in his hands, my heart was so grieved.

As he stood there with the eternal Word of God in his hand and made an attempt to open it to the people, and no one would give heed, I was gripped with desperation for people to open their ears to hear.

I then remembered the truth—we are all called to speak the Word, *whether we are heard or not.*

This picture is not about a man being rejected but the Word of God being rejected.

> ***Ezekiel 2:5***— *. . . And they, whether they will hear, or whether they will forbear, (for they are a rebellious house,) yet shall know that there hath been a prophet among them.*

When I saw him roll the scroll he looked at me sadly and began to withdraw from the room. As he held out that wonderful bread and I compared it to the wormy bread of the false teachers, I wondered how anyone could miss the truth of the bread.

I believe this is a very big concern for God today—that people are gobbling up the words of men's mouths, while ignoring the Word of God.

The church all around the world has come to a place of choice. Not only is the church as a whole being challenged to choose the Bread of Life, but also the ministers are being brought to a place of choice—to preach the Bread of Life.

If we get it right in our hearts and turn to others who are snared by false teachers, then just possibly we can save them from their own end.

We must pray for an alarm and awakening to resound in the ears of those who "drank the cup of devils," at the hands of false teachers. As in Jude 1:22-23, *we can show compassion and make a difference and save them from destruction and yes, even pull them out of the fire, though their garments are defiled by the sensuous nature of man.*

- ***Is it not time*** to dash to pieces the idols of our own hearts?

- ***Is it not time*** to get our eyes off man and back on God?
- ***Is it not time*** to remove the false altars erected by false teachers and break our covenant with them?
- ***Is it not time*** that we become righteously angry at the perversion of the truth?

Wherever there's ***perversion of doctrine*** *and* ***immorality,*** there will be a false altar erected by man. All idolatry consists of these two facets, as shown time and again in the Word of God. Jude and 2 Peter expresses it in very clear terms that lasciviousness and false teachers go hand in hand with each other.

When the lifestyle is perverse, the doctrine will be perverse.

When the doctrine is perverse, the lifestyle will move into perversion of some kind—ethically and morally.

Where perverse doctrine and perverse lifestyles exists, you can find a foundation of lies to support it ***and*** you can find man's altar fashioned by his hands, shaped, chiseled and placed as *an altar to which others are invited to worship.*

> ***Ezekiel 13:10*** (Emphasis Added)—*Because, even because they have seduced my people, saying, Peace; and there was no peace; and one built up a wall, and, lo, others daubed it with untempered* (foolish, insipid; tasteless, unseasoned; whitewashed) *mortar:*

What was the issue with saying, *"Peace and there was no peace?"*

It was because it was the wrong message, one that did not come from God. Though the prophets spoke it as in His name, it was not what God said. God said they had seduced the people with lies. Yes, it was what everyone wanted to hear, but it was not the truth. In a word, *"they whitewashed the truth."*

False teachers and prophets use flattery and false hope to gain people's attention and trust. They tell them what they want to hear.

We all need to increase our desire for the Bedrock of Truth found in obedience to Jesus teachings, so we will not settle for a lie through the mouth of men or devil.

I love the way ***2 Chronicles 34:4*** breaks an idol—a way we should all practice. ***He*** broke down the altars, he cut down the images and the groves that were elevated high, and the carved images, and the molten images, ***and he broke in pieces, and made dust of them,*** and threw the dust on the graves of them that had sacrificed unto them. And Moses also took the calf which had been made and burnt it with fire, stamped on it and ground it very small, ***until it was small as dust*** and then cast the dust into the brook.

Everyone needs a deeper level of discernment, but those who lead the church really need eyes and ear open.

Leaders, we are leading God's church, so we must go beyond just watching it all go by, to taking a stand against all deception, error, immorality, false doctrine in those who teach and touch lives.

I believe we sometimes forget the impact we have on the LORD with what we do or don't do.

We don't think about how we affect Him in what we offer in His name. We want the sweet incense of our worship rising up to fill His nostrils with the beauty of purity. But . . . many times He gets a lot less than He deserves from us.

God is worthy of the best, free of mixtures, free of any offensive odors brought about by man's greed and disobedience.

Jesus Christ is the Living Bread—*the Bedrock of our Faith.*

It is time for God's people to anchor themselves to truth in obedience to that powerful, never-failing Rock of our Salvation.

John 6:51

I am the living bread which came down from heaven: if any man eats of this bread, he shall live forever: and the bread that I will give is my flesh, which I will give for the life of the world.

Chapter 25

Tampering with the Word of God

Hebrews 4:12
(Emphasis Added)

*For the word of God is **quick,** and **powerful,** and **sharper** than any two-edged sword, **piercing** even to the dividing asunder of soul and spirit, and of the joints and marrow, and is **a discerner** of the thoughts and intents of the heart.*

Quick, having vital power in itself
Powerful, Effectual, Operative
Sharper, Decisive, as if by a single stroke
Piercing, Penetrating
A Discerner, Discriminative, Decisive, Judging

This sword is not flexible, soft, revised, dull, small, or impotent
It does not pull back once thrust forward
It is rigid, hard and unchanging

God's Word is an invasive power, one that intrudes upon the thoughts and deeds of mankind.

Romans 1:16*—For I am not ashamed of the gospel of Christ: for it is the power of God unto salvation to everyone that believeth; to the Jew first, and also to the Greek.*

<u>What is the gospel?</u>

Strong's states, *"It is the glad tidings of the Kingdom of God soon to be set up and subsequently also of Jesus the Messiah, the founder of this Kingdom. After the death of Jesus, the term included also the preaching concerning Jesus Christ as having suffered death on the cross to bring eternal salvation for the people of the Kingdom of God, with Him resurrected and exalted to the right hand of God in heaven, one day to return to consummate the Kingdom of God."*

Much of what is being passed off as the gospel today would not pass muster if the Rod of the Lord crossed over it.

It is evidenced by Paul's proclamation in ***Romans 1:16***, in which he states *he was not ashamed of the gospel of Christ* that he was speaking in the face of certain persecution. To preach in his day was to insure beatings, imprisonment and even death.

I never thought I would see this day—the day when the church is slipping into the quagmire of the one-world-church system—where relevancy has for many, neutered the Word of God to them.

The message of being relevant to the culture we live in has invaded the world of faith. Every good missionary, regardless of the nation and ground they stand on, must know their culture—but to mold the gospel to the culture? God forbid!

I have heard it all my life,
"Don't shape the word to fit your life; shape your life to fit the Word."

Today many people are interpreting scripture in some very perverse ways, molding it to fit their particular life-styles. This mindset is responsible for many falling away from the gospel of Jesus Christ into deception and error concerning their faith. Many have made shipwreck of their faith as they have sunk in the seas of relativity.

Yes, it has been prophesied for years—that a day would come when the church, as we had known it, would eventually fall away from the gospel of Jesus Christ and embrace a one-world religious system. Unbelievable to me—because all I knew was the gospel in its fullness was being preached.

Many years ago, my father made the statement, *"There was a day you could enter into any evangelistic church and hear the same thing being preached—it's not so today."* He was deeply concerned for what he saw as ministers and churches were falling away from the pure gospel of Jesus Christ being preached.

In 1983 God visited him in vision and showed him some things about the Last Days' church—literally seeing the *great falling away*, in vivid descriptive vision. He saw the division that split the Evangelical/Pentecostal churches *(those who have made the claim of preaching the full council of God's Word)* right down the middle. So much has happened since then to prove the truth—man by man, church by church, denomination by denomination; choices are being made about the gospel and even Jesus Christ.

When I was a little girl, growing up as a preacher's daughter, the coming of Jesus was preached, hell was preached, salvation through Christ was preached, the Holy Spirit was preached, and the things that were to come sometime far in the future was preached.

I never thought I would see in my lifetime the things I have witnessed to date, as spiritual erosion has entered into the lives of believers and churches—enough in number to be deeply concerning.

II Thessalonians 2:1-3 (Emphasis Added)

1 Now we beseech you, brethren, by the coming of our Lord Jesus Christ, and by our gathering together unto him,

2 That ye be not soon shaken in mind, or be troubled, neither by spirit, nor by word, nor by letter as from us, as the day of Christ at hand.

3 Let no man deceive you by any means: ***for that day shall not come, except there come a falling away first****, and that man of sin be revealed, the son of perdition;*

There must be a strong warning for the Saints of God who are *tampering* with the Holy Spirit's voice and the Word of God and their Salvation that has come to them through the suffering of Jesus Christ on the Cross of Calvary.

While no one likes to hear hard messages, *(as people like to call them)* they are necessary to awaken us out of our stupor that our own stiff-necked ways and hardness of heart has placed us in from the many times of rejecting the Word of the Lord and the Voice of the Spirit of God.

I recently heard of a comment after my husband preached on the signs of the times in America and the need for a return to God. The visiting guest remarked to someone, *"That was not very uplifting."*

Soft sermons to soft Christians sitting on soft pews have kept people immature and unable to endure sound doctrine and the truth.

> ***Genesis 3:1b*** (Emphasis Added)—*And he [the serpent] said unto the woman, "Yea, hath God said, ye shall not eat of* ***every*** *tree of the garden?"*

The serpent is asking a misquoted question, indicating that God forbid them to eat of ***any*** of the fruit of the garden. See that sneaky little word he slipped into his question? Eve is then engaged in a conversation in which she tells the devil exactly what God said—***"Eat of every fruit, except . . . and death will come if we do."*** The serpent then makes a frontal attack on God's Word by saying, ***"You will not die."*** The subtlety here was to get Eve talking to him so that somewhere in the conversation he could insert the lie against God's Word.

When dialogue is established and the door is open for doubt to enter in, God's Word comes under fire—not *"out there"*—but in your mind—*up close and personal.*

The devil knows exactly what to say in order to get us to doubt God's Word. He didn't abolish God's Word; he's too smart for that, for the Word is the mask he wears. He rearranged the order of things in such a way as to seduce Eve, leading her to discover ***a new-found freedom to interpret God's Word for herself.***

> ***2 Peter 1:20***—*Knowing this first, that no prophecy of the scripture is of any private interpretation.*

When Jesus gave the prophecy to John in ***Revelation 22:18-20*** He said, *"For I testify unto every man that hears the words of the prophecy of this book, If any man shall add unto these things, God shall add unto him the plagues that are written in this book. And if any man shall take away from the words of the book of this prophecy, God shall take away his part out of the book of life and out of the holy city, and from the things that are written in this book. He who testifies these things says, 'Surely I come quickly.' Amen. Even so, come Lord Jesus."*

Jesus commanded, *"Don't change or remove a single word of it."*

This command at the end of the Bible is a very thought-provoking scripture but is also one of the scariest scriptures of the Bible. We are told that if we change, remove or tamper with a single word of Revelation that we will have the plagues of the book added to us.

While I realize that this is in reference to the specific and prophetic book of Revelation, it is also a clear truth that God does not like His Words or His prophecies altered—in reference to ***any*** of the Word of God.

Religious people have watered down their concept about the Word until they have made the stories read like they want them to and rewritten key things to impact things the way they want.

- **Example:** No one wants to go to hell, but then no one wants to give up sin either, *so just do away with hell*—and yes, what about just doing away with the idea that a little fun, sowing a few wild oats, will cost you your salvation.

We live in a church world in which people are tampering with the Word of God by living like they desire and finding just enough Word to excuse their choices ***and*** alter the impact on the modern world as if God is as flexible as their time and space, date and age.

If we say, *"God is Love"* enough and never say, *"God Judges,"* at all, then our balance and light is gone and we move into error and deception.

We make God in our image—one that allows us to do what we want to do and still get to go to heaven. We say things like, *"God would never send anyone to hell . . ."* and totally ignore the places in the Word that speaks of the inevitable end of those who are unrighteous or unfaithful or deceitful or wicked. Words like, *"Depart from me, I never knew you,"* are not in some Christians vocabulary.

Religious people who do not *know* Jesus avoid an explanation of what it means to truly follow Him.

This is the world—*the religious world*—that we live in—a world of compromise, easy living, and plenty of money and plenty of time to spend our life in pleasure and ease.

Let us hear and understand ***Amos 6:1a***—*"Woe to them that are at ease in Zion."* Woe is a dreadful word, one that no one really wants to hear, especially if you are at ease.

- ***It is a judgment word*** that has the strength of God's voice behind it.
- ***It is an indictment word*** revealing that God has found a cause to pass sentence on something or somebody.

It should send a chill through the Body of Christ and urge one towards repentance for slothful and careless living—for making God a *tolerating, easy going, flexible God.*

The phrase, *"at ease"* is the charge. It is not a case of being tired or depressed, but it is a phrase that denotes a personal focus on one's own pleasure and comfort.

***"Eat, Drink and be Merry for tomorrow we die"* (Luke 12:19) should not be the motto of the church of today for tomorrow may come sooner than we think.**

Read a little further down in ***Amos 1 to verses 4-7*** (Emphasis Added) and see the conduct that was bringing a charge from God's throne: *"That lie upon beds of ivory and stretch themselves upon their couches . . . that chant to the sounds of the viol, and invent to themselves instruments of music, like David, that drink wine in bowls and anoint themselves with the chief ointments, but they are **not grieved** for the affliction of Joseph . . . the banquet of them that stretched themselves shall be removed."*

> ***Isaiah 28:15*** (Emphasis Added) also states the obvious sin of God's people and God viewpoint on it: ***"Because you have said,*** *We have made a covenant with death and with hell are we at agreement . . . for we have made lies our refuge, and under falsehood have we hid ourselves: Therefore, thus saith the Lord God, Behold, **I lay in Zion for a foundation a stone, a tried stone, a precious corner stone, a sure foundation:** he that believeth shall not be forced to flee. Judgment will I also lay to the line, and righteousness to the plummet, and the hail shall sweep away the refuge of lies and the water shall overflow the hiding place, and your covenant with death shall be disannulled and your agreement with hell shall not stand . . . . for the bed is shorter than that a man can stretch himself on and the covering is narrower than he can wrap himself in it."*

In order to get cross-wise to God's Word, we have to move into deception and error. That is a gross rearranging of the Word of God to make ourselves at ease with what we are doing.

- ***Taking it easy*** has never been the way of the righteous people of God.
- ***Living for personal enjoyment*** is not advisable, according to God.
- ***Eating the best, drinking the best*** and ***using the best*** anointing oils is self-centered.

- ***Singing and even making new instruments*** of music is not worship in the ears of the Lord.

We have been told in the Word of God, *Old and New Testament*, that one was coming who would prepare the Way of the Lord in the Wilderness. It was John the Baptist who came preaching repentance and clearing a pathway fit for a King to walk in upon—his words very demanding of the church of his day. The Holy Spirit has not changed His mind on how we are to prepare the Way of the Lord as we are called to do the same thing today.

- The coming that John prepared was for Jesus' appearance on the earth as the Messiah.
- The coming that we prepare for is Jesus appearance on the earth as the Messiah.
- We are called to Prepare!

We have not been called to Prepare the way of the antichrist, but the way of the LORD.

So many people today have made the survivors of the rapture, *(i.e. they didn't make it because they were not prepared and lived their lives void of a personal relationship with Jesus, even though they had every opportunity to prepare their heart before Him)* heroes of the last days, who outsmarts the devil at his own game.

God does not call these reckless and ill-prepared people heroes of the faith.

Once again we need to check out ***Hebrews 11*** and see those who stood the test even to their death as they *"lived for Jesus—sold out for Jesus—stood firm for Jesus—paid the price for living for Jesus."* Jesus' word to the man who was going to build bigger barns for himself because he was so prosperous was, *"thou fool, today your soul shall be required of you."* ***Luke 12:16-21***

The Word of God is clear—I don't see a redemption plan for the foolish.

Folks, the heroes of the last days will be the two prophet witnesses who stand in Jerusalem at the command of God, to show Israel the way of the Messiah and speak the Truth into the very midst of a hellish kingdom rule that will have taken over that city.

> ***Revelation 11:3****—And I will give power unto my two witnesses, and they shall prophesy a thousand two hundred and threescore days, clothed in sackcloth.*

They will denounce the anti-Christ and prophesy truth and will die for that, and many of God's chosen people will listen and believe. The main thrust of that day's redemption is going to take place in Israel to bring them to the Messiah and to set up the Throne of David in Jerusalem upon which Christ, not the anti-Christ will rule the world.

The Church will be with Jesus—not here running around making disciples of people!
We are to be doing that right now!!!

Yes, there will be some who realize too late that they have missed the most important date, due to a lack of preparation and failure to embrace truth. I believe many of these who were deceived or careless will understand the magnitude of what they have neglected and will choose to take a stand unto death, but . . .

How can we be great soul winners in that horrible day if we are careless and idle and still not right in the sight of God?

> ***Ephesians 5:14-17*** (Emphasis Added)
>
> *14 Therefore He says, Awake, O sleeper, and arise from the dead, and Christ shall shine* (make day dawn) *upon you and give you light. (**Isaiah 26:19; 60:1,2**)*
>
> *15 Look carefully then how you walk! Live purposefully and worthily and accurately, not as the unwise and witless, but as wise* (sensible, intelligent people),

16 Making the very most of the time (buying up each opportunity), *because the days are evil.*

17 Therefore do not be vague and thoughtless and foolish, but understanding and firmly grasping what the will of the Lord is. AMP

The days ahead of us are going to cost a great deal to those who are going to go all the way with the LORD.

There will be many challenges to get things in our lives right with God—not just the easy things but the glaringly obvious things for which the Lord is calling us to account. God is talking to people in this season, even today, and people need to really hear the Word of the Lord! God is dealing with His Church to Prepare the Way of the Lord in their own lives and Prepare the Way of the Lord for others.

- ***Oh, if only*** the Church of today could capture the real truth about Christian living and not the watered down version that is popular today.
- ***Oh, if only*** the movies would have captured the real truth and not the Christian Hollywood version of the end days.

No one can capture that time unless you go back to the throne of heaven and understand that this Lucifer deceived one third of the angels of heaven. They were right there in the midst of the most holy and beautiful city of God, seen the face of God, served God and ministered to Him for eons and now were taken out by the deception of Lucifer.

This angelic being was a master at smooth words that called them from their focus on God. He has had over six thousand years in deception of mankind, starting with Eve at the Garden of Eden. He is skilled, crafty and much smarter than any of us as far as strategy goes.

The only way that we can even do warfare against him is if we are covered with Robes of Righteousness and hold the Sword in our hands and speak it from our mouth, and have Holy Spirit's insight into what to do.

This is the power of the last days that is currently escalating and will be deceiving men and women who refuse to grip the full truth of God's Word NOW!!!

No one will be able to take their *devalued spiritual currency* and cash it in on that day when the church has been taken out. Few will be able to stand against the master of deception in the Last Days without the discernment of the Holy Spirit. Too many glamorize strength and wit and brilliance, actually believing that somehow they are invincible and can make it.

If there are any that do not make it after sitting in a fellowship of believers where the Word of Truth is being preached, the day of the Lord will be a day of sorrow and loss. *So much Word and so little response . . .*

We had better get our bellies filled with the Word of God now, *while there is still time* and get our minds changed from our own thoughts and ways, *while there is still time.*

Error begins to be enthroned in our lives when we are deceived *(and self-deception is the worst kind)* and do nothing about it, even though Holy Spirit is relentless in speaking Truth to us.

- ***We can*** have visions, revelation, gifts *and still be in deception.*
- ***We can*** attend church, move in warfare, praise the Lord will all our strength *and still be in deception.*
- ***We can*** be faithful in our tithes and to the church that we attend *and still be in deception.*

Think about an octopus and how he works to get his victims—he wraps his many tentacles around his victim until he can suck him under, dragging him to his death and then pulls him to his mouth and devours him. If you don't get loose from the tentacles, you are in peril of being taken in by deceit.

Our deceptive thoughts are like that—if we don't break loose from them and allow God to have HIS WAY (Jesus said, "*I am the WAY . . .*") in our hearts and minds—we are taken by captive by our self-speaking, thinking and doing.

Judas sat at the feet of Jesus, *the Word of God*, and heard, first hand, what the Kingdom of God was all about. He heard it and he heard it . . . . but ***HIS MIND*** overruled the truth! How did that happen? How could one who sat in the middle of the most powerful revival to ever hit planet earth, one in which Jesus was the speaker, fall to the wayside of his own thoughts and ways, in spite of the fact that he heard the same words everyone else did?

The Word of God says in ***Jeremiah 17:9-10***, *"The heart is deceitful above all things, and desperately wicked: who can know it? I the Lord search the heart, I try the reins, even to give every man according to his ways, and according to the fruit of his doings."*

Wickedness is not new to our culture and era—it is as old as the anarchy within heaven's gates when Lucifer's mind led him away from the Ways and Thoughts of God, his Creator.

How many things can we think up to make *our religion* work the way we want it to?

Deception comes in many packages and all of them look pretty and are very acceptable—because Deception always tells us what *we want to hear.* It makes us feel good about ourselves and makes all of that *bad conviction* go away.

***"I have decided to follow Jesus,"* is a mental decision that has to go into the heart and become an invasive decision.**

If our decision to follow and serve Jesus Christ is just a mental assent, then we can change our minds with the shifting of the winds *(every wind of doctrine)* or the seasons of our life move us into something we did not expect *(depression hits our nation or we strike it rich or we suffer loss or we lose in some other way).*

- Our mind is the seat of the greatest stronghold and greatest enemy.
- Doesn't the devil always want to take the highest seat?

The enemy and the carnal world would like for us to believe that our mind is the greatest gift that God gave us when actually the greatest gift God has given is Jesus. The mind is a powerful force for God as long we submit that faculty in obedience to Jesus Christ ***(2 Corinthians 10:5).***

We see God's concern for the power of the human mind when it was used for human power in ***Genesis 11:6,*** (Emphasis Added) *"And the Lord said, Behold, the people is one, and they have all one language; and this they begin to do: and now nothing will be restrained from them, which they have* ***imagined*** *to do."*

If people tamper long enough with truth, it will soon be what will take them into the deepest deception of the last days—a deception that will be embraced as truth and lead them straight into the arms of the antichrist.

"Who gave man the right to tamper with the Word of God?"

> ***Hebrews 4:12****—For the word of God is quick, and powerful, and sharper than any two-edged sword, piercing even to the dividing asunder of soul and spirit, and of the joints and marrow, and is a discerner of the thoughts and intents of the heart.*

It's not our Word.
It's not our preacher's Word.
It's not a denominations Word.
It's not your Word.

It belongs to God—eternally! He spoke it from His own mouth—uttered it forth in creation of everything, including the written Word of God. It's His Word!

It is the ONLY place in our shaking world that is Solid Rock!

CHAPTER 26

THE TWO LENS OF REVELATION

1 John 5:6-8

(Emphasis Added)

This is he that came by water and blood, ***even Jesus Christ****; not by water only, but by water and blood. And it is the Spirit that beareth witness, because the Spirit is truth.*
For there are three that bear record in heaven, the Father, the Word, and the Holy Ghost: ***and these three are one.***
And there are three that bear witness in earth, the spirit, and the water, and the blood: ***and these three agree in one.***

While the church has been seeking Holy Spirit, there has been another spirit at work—one that is prophesied by Jesus Christ and detailed in the Word of God—the spirit of anti-Christ. There is only one reason we are deceived—we do not know the Word well enough nor listen at key times to the voice of the Holy Spirit when He speaks Truth to us.

The Word and the Spirit agree.
I call these the two lens of revelation.

Don't underestimate the power of the Word and the Spirit in agreement; these two are at work all the time to keep us grounded on the Rock. But if we don't access ourselves of them in proper balance of truth—It's not that *we might be deceived . . .* it's that ***we will be deceived***!

Jesus said, as recorded in ***Matthew 24:4-5,*** *"Take heed that no man deceives you. For many shall come in my name, saying, I am Christ; and shall deceive many."*

This verse could read this way: *"Weigh very carefully and be careful that no one causes you to stray or leads you from the right way, far from truth, into error. For* ***many will come*** *to make their appearance in the public as if on a stage. They will use my name to arouse your mind to think they are my messengers, saying of themselves,* ***"I am the anointed one."*** *They will lead many astray from truth and into error because they are deceivers".*

There is a very real power with any anti-Christ pre-dating the second coming of Jesus Christ, the true Anointed One! The anti-Christ personalities are many and by the nature of their name, are ***against the anointing,*** coming with great presence, emitting an aura of presence, power and status that will *wow people* by just being around them.

They will cause others to stand in awe of them, drawing as many to themselves as they can.

Who are they? They are men, women; human beings who hold power over others by their charisma and presence.

The *lying signs and wonders of the anti-Christ's ministry* looks more *real* than the *real* to the undiscerning eye.

You will ***see*** these lies, signs and wonders—they will be the demonic calling card, right in the middle of the move of God, especially as the time for the appearing of the last anti-Christ comes.

The devil has and will yet attempt to infiltrate the church with people who will be moved to challenge the truth by these lying signs.

The function of Error is to specifically lead away from Truth. While Error is the work of demonic darkness, the fact is revealed that ***the vehicle used is man*** as termed by Jesus: ***He*** called them false Christ's and false prophets. The Word of God tells us many of these men will rise on the stage of the world, and escalating more than ever, as related by Jesus to His disciples in ***Matthew 24***, as a sign that the end of the age is coming.

The fuel for their vehicle is a light show of signs and wonders—things that will stun the crowd and cause them to believe a lie.

He warns His disciples to not believe the reports that come concerning some powerful anointed teacher or prophet showing up *over here or over there*, ***(Mark 13:21)*** even so much more as the day of Christ' coming approaches.

Ok, Jesus warned us so why are we so slow in understanding this particular sign of the end of the age?

We believe the signs of earthquakes, famine, floods, wars, etc . . . ***but fail*** to imprint the Word on our hearts about deception and that *"evil men are advancing, becoming more and more evil, as that day approaches."*

> ***2 Timothy 3:13*** (Emphasis Added)—*But evil men and* ***seducers*** (enchanter; a deceiver, an imposter) *shall* ***wax*** (go forward, advance, make progress) *worse and worse, deceiving and being deceived.*

Leaders in the church have a responsibility to prepare believers to not be deceived—to teach those that will hear what the Word of God teaches on this subject.

- ***Few want to admit*** that *"not everyone who is with us is actually of us,"* ***(Acts 20:29-30)*** but imbedded in the body of Christ are those who will attempt to lead believers from truth into error.
- ***Few want to admit*** that they are somewhat gullible when it comes to those who dwell within the framework of the House of God.
- ***Few want to even reckon*** with the idea that they may be deceived by such people and yet Biblical history reveals a real problem in this area.

> ***I John 2:18-19*** (Emphasis Added)—*Little children, it is the last time: and as **ye have heard*** (to be endowed with the faculty of hearing, not be deaf; *to* comprehend) *that **antichrist*** (the adversary of the Messiah) *shall come, even now are there many **antichrists**; whereby we know that it is the last time. They went out from us, but they were not of us; for if they had been of us, they would no doubt have **continued with us*** (remained, abided, not departed)*: but they went out, that they might **be made manifest*** (to visible or known what has been hidden so as to thoroughly understand who and what one is) *that they were not all of us.*

There ***are*** those who are deceptive in their faith and are positioned in their heart to lead as many as possible astray, not by blatant, *in-your-face heresy*, but by things mocking so close to the real that you will have to see or be deceived.

But the Word teaches that they can plainly be seen, recognized, and thoroughly understood for who or what one is—***if we look, through the two lens of the Word and the Spirit*** and understand what Jesus taught about these who filter in and out of the church, to gain access to the Body of Christ.

Paul tells Timothy, *"For the time will come when they will not endure sound doctrine; but after their own lusts shall they heap to themselves teachers, having itching ears; and they shall turn away their ears from the truth, and shall be turned unto fables."* ***2 Timothy. 4:3-4***

This verse simply means *"the time will come when people will not put up with sound teaching but instead follow after their own desires and accumulate to themselves teacher who will turn them from truth, which is easy, because they desire to hear something pleasant to the ears rather than truth; accepting falsehoods and fiction, rather than truth."*

It is interesting that the phrase, *"They shall turn their ears away,"* translates from the original language . . .

"Putting the sword back in the sheath and deserting."

Now that definition deserves some pondering and giving strong attention to the implications of turning our ears away from truth; deserting.

We must stop and ask, *"What is the sword?"* Of course we know the answer is declared in

Ephesians 6:17b, *"the sword of the Spirit, which is the word of God"*

This is very serious . . .

We don't have to ***wonder*** if Jesus is *in something* today. ***He told*** is *"when he, the Spirit of truth, is come, he will guide you into all truth: for he shall not speak of himself; but whatsoever he shall hear, that shall he speak: and he will show you things to come."* ***John 16:13***

Holy Spirit is not some act on a stage like people are trying to make Him—He is the Power and Glory of God on earth and in the hearts of men and women who are seeking God in humility and repentance and holiness today.

- People who do not have their eyes on the manifestations, the signs and wonders will see Jesus.
- Those who have their eyes on the manifestations will see them and possibly miss Jesus.

My greatest concern for the Christian/Church today is its ***failing eyesight***. In order to navigate the days ahead of us, we must have sharp eyesight, be able to see clearly, to discern, to rightly divide the Word of Truth . . .

I am not expert on anything, but I am a student of the Word and the Spirit, which is the only way to fully see anything. I refer you back to the ***two lens of discernment—The Word and the Spirit***—the only way for a believer to see clearly.

I get deeply concerned when I see people plunging headlong into the spirit realm without the Word of God in hand. I get very concerned that we are entering the most dangerous time for the Church/Christian—the Eve of the Return of Jesus Christ.

There can be *God signs* that are handled wrongly by people who are immature and quickly led by their earthly sight. In this case, it is the job of mature leaders/believers to help focus the spiritual eyes and ears to the things of the Spirit so that ***Bedrock truth*** will stabilize the flesh during times of the supernatural. We must train the people to listen to the voice of Jesus, our Great Shepherd and the lover of our souls.

I have discovered that people or the devil can pervert anything that God does—*if left to their own ways and imaginations.*

We have to be willing to prepare the hearts of the people through truth and to be discerning and not afraid to *test the spirits.*

It will take a person who is clear in their focus and not easily swayed—one who has planted their lives deep into the safety of the ***Rock,*** entrenched in the Word of God, led by the Spirit of God—one who is discerning enough to know the spirit (whether it be of God or not) behind the sign or manifestation or the person who is *moving in some kind of power anointing.*

Question: What would it take to get you off course from where you know God started with you?

Of course it wouldn't be something you could readily recognize as wrong or seductive. Most would never fall if the devil sent someone to personally seduce them away from all relationships that are holy and true—but what about the devil sending a teacher or movement your way that is so close to the real, so flattering, *so meets your personal needs* . . . are you prepared?

If the devil came to you looking like himself, you would not be fooled *so* he comes to you looking like God, like Jesus, like Holy Spirit.

The air waves are filled with voices today, of all kinds, with many propagating *what is right in their own eyes.* The church must enter the days ahead prepared to deal with deception. It will not come in the garments you think it will. It will not look blatantly like a devil. It will not even sound devilish.

Deception sounds like truth.
Deception looks like the real deal.
That is what makes it so dangerous.

And when there is a display of power mingled with deception the danger increases. The church and the world today are becoming increasingly fascinated with the supernatural that so many are becoming more and more open to entering into this realm. There are true believers who are desperate to know God on a supernatural level and will go to any lengths to get there.

While Jesus didn't downplay the fact the signs of the times would be very prevalent in the Last Days, he placed as a priority His message to His disciples—*Take heed that no man deceive you.*

We live in a very spiritually dangerous and complex time in which we face very real issues of faith, practice and such—where without the Word of God wielded by the Spirit of God, we would be literally drifting in a sea of human thought—*caught in the quicksand we have been talking about.*

The Church is not called to sink or drift, led by every Wind of Doctrine that is blowing.
We are called to "hold the course," to remain steadfast, unmovable and unshakable.

Question: How can you stay true to the journey you have been taking so as to see the fulfillment of all He's said?

> ***1 Corinthians 15:58****—Therefore, my beloved brethren, be ye steadfast, unmovable, always abounding in the work of the Lord, forasmuch as ye know that your labor is not in vain in the Lord.*

Many people in the church are unprotected against deception 1) *because they don't think much about it*; 2) *because they don't think they can be deceived.*

We are years into a very serious move of God towards mankind upon the earth but we are also closer to the age in which the devil is increasing in his rage against the saints of God and God's plan for mankind.

The enemy of everything right, holy and true is unleashing evil, *masked in spiritual garments,* on every hand, with great darkness unfolding and enveloping great segments of the earth *and yes, the church.* We must not ever think that all of our enemy's tactics are obvious enough that we would never fall for them.

While we are saved by the blood we must realize that we are kept by the blood.

The works of deception are hidden, except to the eyes of God. For us to survive in days such as this, we must be endued with the eyes of the Spirit of God. Discernment is a powerful and must have piece of the *Last Days Survival Gear.*

Pray for deeper spiritual discernment *(a quickening of the Spirit)* and delve deeper into the Word of God like never before!

On Jesus Christ the Rock I stand—All other ground is sinking sand.

CHAPTER 27

HUNGER IS NOT ENOUGH

1 Corinthians 10:3-6
(Emphasis Added)

And did all eat the same spiritual meat;
And did all drink the same spiritual drink: for they drank of ***that spiritual Rock*** *that followed them: and* ***that Rock was Christ.***
But with many of them God was not well pleased: for they were overthrown in the wilderness.
Now these things were our examples, to the intent we should not lust after evil things, as they also lusted.

No one who has known me for any period of time could ever accuse me of not being hungry or not *"going hard after all that God has for me."*

I'm as hungry today as I have ever been—*but* not enough to dine on everything people set before me.

In today's culture, the word, '*discrimination*' has a negative connotation, even in the church. People don't like, *"Judgment,"* feeling it's unfair to people. While prejudicial discrimination is wrong and hurtful, and God does not condone prejudice of any kind based on the differences He created in people—race and color and cultural differences—God does call for us to *"put a difference"* between things that are offensive to Him and the holy.

- **Discriminate** (long ***'a'***)—to note or observe a difference; to distinguish accurately.

We don't have to look very far into the Word of God to discover what offends God. He plainly states what is holy, right and true and that which is unholy, vile and false. He lists sins against Him by name, detailed within His word in shocking detail. He even goes so far as to give us examples from real life, real people; those who did what was right in His eyes and those who did evil in His eyes.

Every sin is offensive to God. Immorality, False prophets and Teachers, Greedy and self-centered ministers, Rebellion and Stubbornness, Pride, Strife and Division . . . etc—are all offensive to God.

Ultimately, these all come under very specific headings, distinguishing the things that are Holy and Unholy, Clean and Unclean, Pure and vile.

> ***Leviticus 10:10****—And that ye may put difference between holy and unholy, and between unclean and clean;*

This means we are to be discerning enough to divide the sacred, holy things from the profane, common things (***sand as opposed to rock***) to be able to discern between the ethically and religiously unclean things and the morally, ethically and physically clean things.

I am a discriminate eater—one that likes to know, not only what is on my plate but *who the cook is, how clean his kitchen is* and *how clean he is*—naturally and spiritually.

For Example: Some time back we went to a very popular restaurant on the South Coast of Oregon that served Chinese food. As I had my stir fry sat down in front of me, I noticed something moving on my plate. At a closer look I realized my vegetables were crawling with heated potato bugs. Other customers began to complain of the same thing. It seems the kitchen was not clean and bugs had contaminated all the fresh vegetables. And somehow, the cook failed to notice that for every handful of veggies, he took a half a hand-full of bugs. And we had to wonder, *"If there are bugs in there, what else is there . . . ?"*

- I pushed my plate back and called for the waiter to take it away.

The problem was not with my hunger ***(I was very hungry),*** but the problem was that I sat at a table where I was served something from an unclean kitchen, serving unclean food—but it was my hunger that had taken me to that table to eat. I was the one who had to refuse the food, get up and leave because the food was crawling with vermin.

How many times have God's people gone ahead and sat through a spiritual meal, taking tiny bites, pretending to eat, knowing the plate was crawling with vermin, afraid to get up and leave because *it might offend someone*?

In the same way I refused the unclean food in the natural, we should also refuse unclean food in the spiritual.

I must be more concerned about offending the Holy Spirit and what I am dining upon than I am the one who prepared and served the spiritual food to me at their altar. There is nothing wrong with and a lot right about leaving such a place.

> ***2 Corinthians 6:17****—Wherefore come out* [to go out of an assembly, that is to forsake it] *from among* [the middle of] *them, and be ye separate,* [to mark off from others by boundaries] *saith the Lord,*[owner] *and touch not* [to fasten oneself to, to adhere to, to cling to] *the unclean thing;* [impure ceremonially, morally lewd, in a moral sense: unclean in thought and life; demonic] *and I will receive you . . .*

Another Example: Years ago, at Thanksgiving, when my children and I all had the flu, my husband was invited to go to a home of one the parishioners for dinner. The invitation was sincere and well-meaning . . . Upon arriving, my husband discovered that the home was very dirty, filled with goats, chickens and stuff that comes from such co-habitation, from one end to the other. He also discovered the *food.* It was three roasted turkeys lined up on a counter, carved and spread out all over. This lady had invited many, many people to come eat but all the food was crawling with flies. He knew he would have to be *very discriminating* about what he ate or he would become sick from the food. After he picked his way through that meal, he was "loaded up with food" by his very gracious hostess for him to bring home to me and my children. Yes, it looked like a Thanksgiving dinner, but it was defiled . . . so . . .

- We threw the food away.

An invitation and a take home bag of food to meet the hunger of my family was not enough to cause us to eat the dirty food.

Another Example: We were eating in a restaurant a number of years ago. My husband had ordered a chef's salad, which he loves. It arrived at the table, looking wonderfully made. He applied his dressing and took a big bite of the salad. In that bite was a piece of boiled egg. The egg was rotten.

- He shuddered and spit the whole bite out into a napkin.

All eggs are not equal! He got what he asked for, and to all appearances, the egg looked edible—but was in fact rotten to the core! Even though the bite had been taken, it had to be spit out due to that rottenness. After that experience he was revolted by it and it almost ruined eating boiled eggs, which he had previously loved.

That rottenness can be found imbedded in spiritual food as well. When spiritual food is served in a mixed salad, watch out!

Another Example: Years ago a lady offered to give our family a turkey that was "too big" for just her and her husband. We accepted her *gift.* What we didn't know was that the neighbor's pig had killed the turkey and it had died of fright. Its poor legs were rigidly sticking straight up in the air frozen in place. The turkey was sitting in a pool of blood. When we turned it over, we discovered massive bite marks all over its back, punctured deeply into its flesh. We could not eat the turkey . . . because of the way it died and the blood that saturated its flesh.

- We buried it.

This *gift* was one that had to be rejected and buried. Sometimes what another person gives us, even when well-intentioned—prophetic words, impartations, council—may need to be rejected and buried, so as to not have our lives contaminated by the unclean way it was rendered for our consumption.

Another Example: While traveling to Tulsa, Oklahoma, we stopped in Oklahoma City for lunch. I ordered a turkey sandwich. I wasn't very hungry so I shared my second half with others, offering different ones a bite. Thankfully they each only took a bite, because the food was contaminated with food poisoning. About a half an hour out of Tulsa, I began to get seriously ill. By the time I reached the place we were staying I was running into the restroom with a major rejection wracking my body. I began to throw up, seriously ill. Others with whom I had shared my food were sickened as well by the small portion they had eaten.

- For three days I purged my body of that poison, regretting ever eating the sandwich.

I was amazed that such a small portion could tear my body up so severely. I had dined on contaminated food and I had offered it to others, believing it to be good food. It didn't just hurt me; it hurt my family. What I received at the hands of another, I passed onto to people I love, and inadvertently poisoned them.

We must be careful, not only of what we eat, but also what we give others of the portion we received. This experience weakened me for days and almost sent me to the hospital.

Food is a kind of impartation.
It is prepared by another's hand and sat before us for our consumption.

Whatever is in that food goes into our bodies—*good or bad*. Our natural bodies tell us very quickly when food is poisoned, contaminated, unclean—but there is a great ***resistance*** today in the body of Christ of warnings about spiritual food. There is a ***resistance*** to anyone declaring it unclean, impure and harmful to the Body of Christ—***resistance*** to rejecting such tables and food, ***resistance*** to rejecting the teachings of the one who prepares that which is harmful to the soul.

In each of our personal examples we had to be *discriminating*, making a judgment call about the food, refusing that which was unclean and contaminated—or suffer the consequences for taking it into our body.

Everyone has had to do that at one time or another, but why not apply the same standard and diligence in regard to spiritual food that is served on the tables of a questionable ministry? The church and even revival, by virtue of the many personalities and tastes of people, offers a literal smorgasbord of food to satisfy the appetite of indiscriminate eaters.

- **Smorgasbord**: an extensive array or variety:

There is a time in every move of God—as people get their appetites whetted for different things—it becomes sadly apparent in some cases that *"Jesus is not enough"* for some who crave a whole lot more than *"just Bread."*

I know that is a bold statement, but bear with me as we take this journey.

This season is going to take more than just hunger to survive. It's going to take discernment on a level such as never before, for what is coming is not just one thing, but a multitude of things that will move in like a fog to encase the land in deception, *if it were possible.*

The last days are going to be marked by what the Word of God says is, "*a great falling away.*" While there has always been deception, there is a time in prophetic history when it will escalate to usher in the anti-Christ.

> ***II Thessalonians 2:3*** (Emphasis Added)—*Let no man deceive you by any means: for that day shall not come, except* ***there come a falling away first,*** *and that man of sin be revealed, the son of perdition;*

- **Discernment**: the faculty of discerning; discrimination; acuteness of judgment and understanding

Discernment is NOT attached to hunger—it's a work of Holy Spirit in us!

This is why it is so easy for people to be misled at the hunger level—because discernment is not attached to your mind, emotions or your body. Discernment is a Holy Spirit work of a complete marriage of the Word of God and the Spirit of God.

When anyone *attempts* to separate the Word from the Spirit in order to accept a thing, deception has a door. This is a very spiritually, dangerous precedent to set for one's life. Spiritual hunger is a compelling drive that, if not schooled by the Word and the Spirit, will take us to places we should not go.

It is easier for a person to say, "*I was led of the Spirit,*" than to say, "*I was led of the Word.*"

> ***John 6:35*** *And Jesus said unto them, I am the bread of life: he that cometh to me shall never hunger; and he that believeth on me shall never thirst.*

This message is not meant to be critical of anyone, but to challenge all of us to draw closer to Jesus than ever before. The time is upon us when we must be the Church Jesus set in motion—not veering off course to any "other Jesus or gospel."

The Holy Spirit spoke to me, starting in December 2007 and escalating 2008 this word through various means:

"My Church is not prepared for the Last Days Deception."

Following that He continued to deal with my heart about, not the apostate church, but the one that is *"seeking God."* He forewarned that the devil was going to strike with vengeance against the revival church right at the place of their hunger.

Think about it—right before Jesus was released into His earthly ministry, He was led up by the Spirit to the wilderness. It was there He was tempted by the devil that was doing everything in his power to knock Jesus off course.

Where did he first hit Jesus?

Matthew 4:3-4

3 And when the tempter came to him, he said, if thou be the Son of God, command that these stones be made bread.

4 But he answered and said, it is written, Man shall not live by bread alone, but by every word that proceeds out of the mouth of God.

He hit him at the point of His natural hunger, tempting Him to turn the stone into bread.

Wilderness Walking does something to a person—it moves you either directly in line with God or moves you into your own venue, leading ultimately to failure. What started as something that sounded reasonable to a hungry person would have devastated Jesus spiritually and brought about a failure to finish the work His Father had sent Him to do.

The Wilderness is rough on the flesh; it is a place where there is no middle of the road between God's Manna ***or*** the Flesh Pots of Egypt. This is where we still get into trouble. We can dress a flesh pot up any way we want to, but when it's all said and done, it is still a flesh pot.

Man's appetites for the supernatural, angels, manifestations, gifts and power . . . *though in their right place are wonderful* . . . have become the flesh pots for many who overinvested in the supernatural without the Word in place. It is true that many times these glorious things that appear and become a reality when God moves are not flesh—but man's inner appetite can be fleshly in its desires.

A lot of people are just a breath away from turning their hunger for God into hunger for power—and some have stepped far over the boundary that requires everything to be in proper alignment with God.

The early days of revival were started in the hearts of *hungry people* who began to cry out to God for a fresh touch on their lives. They were as tired of 'nominal church' as Israel was of Egypt. The routines of Christian life had become a bondage to these hungry souls—*there had to be more to life than this . . .* That is a good cry that gets God's attention.

***There were not enough flesh pots in Egypt* to satisfy these people who wanted to be free.**

It was their hunger to be free from bondage that began to release a cry from deep within.

> ***Exodus 2:23-25*** (Emphasis Added)
>
> *23 And it came to pass in process of time that the king of Egypt died: and the children of Israel* ***sighed*** *by reason of the bondage, and they* ***cried,*** *and* ***their cry came up*** *unto God by reason of the bondage.*
>
> *24 And* ***God heard*** *their groaning, and* ***God remembered*** *his covenant with Abraham, with Isaac, and with Jacob.*
>
> *25 And* ***God looked upon*** *the children of Israel, and* ***God had respect*** *unto them.*

<u>We can learn from this scriptural pattern:</u>

- ***They*** sighed
- ***They*** cried
- ***Their cry*** came up to God
- ***God*** heard their groaning
- ***God*** remembered His Covenant
- ***God*** looked upon the children of Israel
- ***God*** had respect unto them

This same pattern has brought about movement from heaven all down through the generations of mankind.

This is what brought about two Great Awakenings and revival all down through the church age—the outpourings of God's Spirit in to people everywhere all over the world.

Israel had cried out so loud for Divine Intervention that God responded by sending them a deliverer in Moses. But along the journey something happened—the *flesh pots* became the desire of their hearts, *even as manna was raining upon them* from heaven.

Now there was not enough 'manna in the wilderness' to satisfy these people who wanted to be fed.

<u>**Think on this—There's a world of difference between *wanting to be* free and *wanting to be fed* . . .**</u>

> ***Exodus 16:1-3***
>
> *1 And they took their journey from Elim, and all the congregation of the children of Israel came unto the wilderness of Sin, which is between Elim and Sinai, on the fifteenth day of the second month after their departing out of the land of Egypt.*
>
> *2 And the whole congregation of the children of Israel murmured against Moses and Aaron in the wilderness:*
>
> *3 And the children of Israel said unto them, Would to God we had died by the hand of the LORD in the land of Egypt, when we sat by the flesh pots, and when we did eat bread to the full; for ye have brought us forth into this wilderness, to kill this whole assembly with hunger.*

It is always interesting how quickly people go from rejoicing in the new-found freedom God gives them and how quickly they move to murmuring because "*they are not getting fed.*"

This has been an attitude prevalent in the church for years—a people who have developed a crutch-mentality of being led and fed.

This is when hunger becomes a dangerous symptom of a *peevish heart* that is ready to eat anything, as long as the belly is filled.

There is a moment in time when the cry towards heaven turns God attention from bestowing favor to testing the hearts of his people.

> ***Exodus 16:4***—*Then said the LORD unto Moses, Behold, I will rain bread from heaven for you; and the people shall go out and gather a certain rate every day, that I may prove them, whether they will walk in my law, or no.*

To them, the taste of manna no longer satisfied them—*there had to be more.* Jesus warned of this manifestation of *hunger gone wrong*—a hunger that develops a taste for the flesh pots, as it were, to fill the desires of man's lusty and undiscerning heart. He warned His disciples to not run hither and yon, but to keep their eyes on the eastern sky and look for lightning.

> ***Mark 13:21-22***
>
> *21 And then if any man shall say to you, Lo, here is Christ; or, lo, he is there; believe him not:*
>
> *22 For false Christ's and false prophets shall rise, and shall show signs and wonders, to seduce, if it were possible, even the elect.*

People all over the world are setting up stages that are very alluring in this time of God's testing His churches hunger. There is a cry for ***"More"*** that, if not grounded and rooted in the Word and the Spirit, is deceptive and misleading in a time of hunger.

It sounds just like a people still crying out to God, but the heart behind it is far from God because of the complaint and discontent of the heart.

A certain kind of complaint began to formulate in the hearts of people in the wilderness as their old desires to be fed rose up again. They were used to being fed by another's hand, a hand that would give them what they wanted. When God did not come through with enough of what they wanted, they complained against Him and began to lust backwards for what they used to have.

We human beings have appetites for a lot of things—but the natural law of eating tells us that not everything we crave is good for us. It is also human nature to not necessarily have an appetite for that which is good to eat . . . i.e. babies prefers the sweet, creamy custard to spinach.

Bottom line—we like the table spread with what *we like* to eat . . .

Let's ask a few questions and probe for some answers to what ails the modern revival movements of today—and might I say us?

Question: What was the real issue with the children of Israel and their hunger; what was behind it all?

- Was it that they had not dealt with their old appetites and just embraced something else in addition? This proved to be true as their history with God reveals—He was not enough . . .

Question: Did they find that in leaving Egypt, their excitement had led them right into a wilderness where there was nothing but just them and God? ***Nehemiah 9:19-21***

- People can get upset when it doesn't work out the way they had expected it! Many opportunities for false teachings appear in this interim—prosperity—golden calf worship.

Question: What is *our golden calf?*

- It's a concept that develops into something we call ***god.*** "*This is the real move of God here—after all, look at all the worship, power, healings, manifestation, angels, hungry people, etc . . .*"

Question: Was Israel angry with God because He had not met their expectations of Him—"*after all they had left everything behind for Him* *and for what?* Are we also somewhat bent that way when the journey is long and things get rough?

- This is the breeding ground for murmuring and complaints.

Question: Why were they angry with God's leaders, Moses and Aaron?

You could put hundreds of other leadership names in this slot and find that they too were accused when the wilderness became the biggest reality in the lives of those who went hard after God. "*Well, the pastor prophesied revival and a harvest coming in and all I have seen is people leaving the church . . .*" It is common for people to blame human leaders for God not performing all they thought He would do.

As we answer these questions *about them*, we answer the same, problematic questions that have risen in *our hearts* because the ground is ripe for complaints when we have "*left it all behind*" to journey with God . . .

Someone has to take the blame when it is not working out the way we thought it would—"*It certainly couldn't be me, could it?*"

I think that we sometimes think that somehow God owes us something for so faithfully obeying him in laying it all down to follow Him . . . Is this the crux of the matter—we feel God owes us more than we got for our investment?

God help us if we are holding him captive to any mentality that demands He performs to our satisfaction because of anything we have done for Him!

Once again, there's a difference between hungry people and *power-hungry people.*

. . . And it is sad when truly hungry people clutter around a power hungry move and call it God when in fact, it doesn't even resemble Him. But once again, I say what I hear God say to me,

"Hunger is not enough."

We need to check what we are hungry for.

> ***Matthew 5:6***—*Blessed are they which do hunger and thirst after righteousness: for they shall be filled.*

That's the hunger that gets God's attention.

- We can't be hungry *for worship.*
- We can't be hungry *for power.*
- We can't be hungry *for manifestations.*
- We can't be hungry *for gifts.*
- We can't be hungry *for impartations.*
- We can't be hungry *for angels.*
- We can't be hungry *for the glory.*
- We can't be hungry *for healings.*

Please understand what I am saying—I am talking about *what drives our hunger; what motivates our hunger.* We have so much wisdom and understanding in raising our children—even we know better than to facilitate their hunger for everything they want.

What we want from them more than anything is a relationship with them that is based on honor, respect and obedience to what we know it right and good.

We don't want our children playing both ends against the middle to get what they want. We don't want them sweet-talking, whining or stamping their feet to get what they want from us.

And when they do, we say, *"Okay for you; go to your room if that's the way you're going to act."* We send them into *a personal wilderness* for a season to see if some of their spots can be removed and if their wrinkles can be ironed out.

So what am I saying—don't be hungry because you might get something bad to eat?

NO! I am saying, *"If you go after the LORD and His Righteousness you don't have to strive about the journey, revival, gifts, power, ministry, who's who and who's in charge . . . You will find that everything is in Him."*

If you have Jesus, the Word and the Sweet Spirit of God on earth . . . you have it all.
God Spirit will always direct you to Jesus where all you need can be found in Him.

I am convinced that God already had all the provisions all planned out on how He was going to take care of the hunger and thirst of the children of Israel—but they jumped the gun with Him and began to complain about Moses taking them out so they would *die of hunger.*

Their hunger was a very big thing with them—it consumed them so much that they failed to see God in anything He was doing.

Might that also be a problem with the current move of God? Have we seen the barrenness around us and do we also have a tendency to get ahead of God's plan of provision?

Fleshly hunger masking as hunger for God can be very blinding to the truth.

Our Flesh demands flesh!

There is a subtle message in this "*manna*" message that one can miss if not careful; People have Jesus, dine and feast at His table but still look beyond Him to fill ***something*** He will not give them—***something*** that will consistently fill the fleshly hunger for things they crave to fill their idea of God.

Yes, we can dress it up all we want . . . but it is still our own hunger generated from something that God cannot and will not fill or give—***a flesh pot.***

- We can call it "*hunger.*"
- We can call it "*seeking more of God.*"
- We can call it "*more of your glory, more of your power.*"

But, not *every cry* of our heart is pure in God's eyes.

This is the nature of man—to have what his heart desires. But God speaks of man's heart telling us it is wicked. Even David knew to ask God to *search his heart and know him and see if there was any wicked way in him . . .* ***Psalms 129:23***

God loves hungry people, as long as they are hungering and thirsting for Him! Once again, look at the words spoken by Jesus in His Sermon on the Mount in ***Matthew 5:6***, *"Blessed are they which do hunger and thirst after righteousness: for they shall be filled."*

The greater Glory comes to those who hunger and thirst after righteousness.

Get a longing—a craving to see God fill you with His righteousness and to see God then rain righteousness down upon your city and region through your lives and intercession and witness.

Get Hungry—Stay Hungry for which God is hungry for—souls!

- ***Give us*** the Harvest
- ***Give us*** the Prodigals
- ***Give us*** the Backsliders
- ***Give us*** the Children
- ***Give us*** the Youth
- ***Give us*** the Aged
- ***Give us*** the Infirmed
- ***Give us*** the Bound
- ***Give us*** the Demon Possessed
- ***Give us*** the Desperate
- ***Give us*** the Broken
- ***Give us*** the Lonely
- ***Give us*** the Wounded
- ***Give us*** the Hopeless.

It's time to fill God's House with True Worshippers, as defined by Jesus . . . with Hungry People who are willing to cry out for the Living God—and as surely as His Glory fills the House, everything we need will be found in His presence!

Part V

The Emerging Disaster

"I resolved, never to do anything which I would be afraid to do if it were the last hour of my life."

Jonathan Edwards

Prophetic Word

Pastor Mark McBride—December 10, 2006

Let the trumpet sound!

I will no longer allow My hands to be tied by My Church. I will no longer allow My hands to be shackled by My Church. My Church has shackled Me with their unbelief, with their doubt, with their religious tradition. I will no longer allow it.

The trumpet has sounded. The alarm has been sounded in My Church says the Lord. The day is coming very quickly that I will not strive with My Church much longer. I will not continue to have My hands bound by those that call upon My name. I will break free of the religious church. I will break free and I will do what I said I will do. My promise shall come to pass. Every word that I have spoken shall come to pass. It shall be just as I have spoken it. Every detail shall come to pass.

I will no longer allow My Church to shackle Me with their unbelief. I will no longer allow My Church to shackle Me with their religious tradition. I will enter My Church. I will enter in upon the altars of My Church. Behold I stand at the door and knock. Open the door and let Me in. Open the door and let My Spirit move. Unshackle My Spirit. It has not been the enemy in many cases, it has been My Church that has restricted My Spirit and I will not have it any longer. I will not be shackled by My Church any more.

Marks remarks:

I believe there is a season that has opened for the Church. With the sound of the trumpet, there is a season that has opened for the Church where the Spirit of God is going to test hearts. He is going to come to every heart, every church. He is going to ask, ***"Will you open the door?"*** Every heart is going to have an opportunity, every person that sits in the church. There is going to be an opportunity for people, for those that call themselves the people of God; to respond to God in truth, in reality, in repentance.

There is a season that is coming to the church. The trumpet has sounded, it is a mark of the beginning of a season that God has sent to the church where He will flow in power, and He will flow in revelation. Many will be confronted, not just spoken to in that still small voice, but God will confront them. They will sit in pews, adulterers, those in sexual sins will be sitting in pews and they will be confronted by Jesus Christ, by the Holy Spirit himself.

There is a season that has been marked and it is our job and God's intention for us to pray and intercede that that season will bring forth fruit, that that season will be effective, that the people of God will respond in repentance and in obedience to God in faith.

CHAPTER 28

A HOLE IN THE WALL— EAT ALL OF IT

1 Peter 4:17

For the time is come that judgment must begin at the house of God: and if it first begin at us, what shall the end be of them that obey not the gospel of God?

Ezekiel was a great prophetic intercessor. He was one whom God used greatly as a sign and wonder to Israel through more recorded prophetic acts than any other place in the Bible. He walked a very lonesome and difficult path prophetically, in absolute obedience to God

He was also allowed a deep and horrifying look into *the church* of his day and preached to the people of his day—a people who would not hear him.

A search into the Old and New Testament will reveal that God as always had a man or woman whom He raised up at key times to battle, prophesy, intercede and act as an agent of truth, as an instrument of God. These people had divine mantles and accomplished some remarkable things in and for God's Holy name.

Common people—*Moses, Jeremiah, Ezekiel, John the Baptist, Isaiah, David, Deborah, Esther, Mary, the Apostle Paul, Stephen, Peter, and many others*—hand-picked by God to do something for Him.

What we don't see is the preparation that was accomplished through hard times, trials, abuse and rejection that brought them forth into God's plan.

Within the first chapter of Ezekiel, we find him in captivity. We find him repenting and acknowledging the sins of his people.

Intercessors have no problem with repenting, especially when in captivity. It is really the only approach that gets God's attention, if the captivity has occurred because of sin, *as in Israel's case.*

- ***Some*** in captivity spent their time in idolatry.
- ***Some*** complained while other wept and cried out in pain.
- ***Some*** destroyed their children, they got in so deep.
- ***Some*** became complacent, feeling that there was no use.

But Ezekiel was in a place of preparation, for the Lord was about to use him. It was thirteen years into captivity, a time when it appeared as if nothing was going to change.

Let's take an introspective moment here and consider ourselves.

The modern church has not experienced ***true*** spiritual freedom for a long time. A lot of responses have developed, just as it did for Israel.

- ***Some*** in the modern church have gone deeper into bondage.
- ***Some*** have adapted to other gods.
- ***Some*** are enveloped in complacency.
- ***Some*** of the children of the church have been sacrificed to the gods of this world.

A deepening spirit of toleration and compromise has contaminated the standards of holiness.

They were human beings that went into the deepest of degradation as they were totally intertwined into the society they were captive in while some just sat down and moaned and groaned. But one man repented and took a long hard look at some things.

It takes courage and honesty and humility to admit the failures and compromises of the church.

Ezekiel upon identifying the sins of God's people began to repent. He understood why *his church* was in captivity and knew that sin was the cause—and was actually deeper than anyone could have imagined.

Sometimes we get so used to seeing things as they are because they just developed that way over a period of time. But when God opens our eyes to really see from His viewpoint the things that grieve Him and are due His judgment, it is a vision that can shake our world.

There are Ezekiel's alive today in God's church—those gathered around the river with others.

Nineteen years ago we came to our church. It was a nice church, but it was not free. If you could see with your physical eyes, you would see our crutches, chains and shackles in the altars and hanging off the ends of pews and from the pulpit and in the classrooms. No matter which way we turned, we were in captivity to religion and for many compromise and sin had captured their hearts and lives. We cried out aloud in our captivity, *as some of you have*, and God set us free.

There are evidences of captivity in the modern-day church and the Christians of today.

So many are not free.

Thank God that He has come to us in our captivity—a people who were still aware of God—a people who had not forgotten Him—a people who were hungry for something real. In these people is a holy dissatisfaction with captivity. Once you are free, you never want to knowingly go back.

It is to sincere people, the ones from every walk of life, that God comes—early on, forerunners, hopeful, prayerful people with dreams of the old days of Glory when there was freedom in the House of God and in His people—it is to these that He comes and opens the heavens and releases the vision.

**While the heavens are still closed over the heads of many others sitting by the river in captivity, Ezekiel is awakened—
He sees visions of God.**

Ezekiel 1:1-4 (Emphasis Added)

*1 Now it came to pass in the thirtieth year, in the fourth month, in the fifth day of the month, as I was among the captives by the river of Chebar, that the heavens were opened, and **I saw visions of God**.*

2 In the fifth day of the month, which was the fifth year of king Jehoiachin's captivity,

*3 **The word of the LORD came expressly unto Ezekiel the priest,** the son of Buzi, in the land of the Chaldeans by the river Chebar; and **the hand of the LORD was there upon him.***

It was in this open heaven time that the Word of God came *expressly* to Him and He looked and saw—with his eyes wide open—with discernment awakened in his heart.

- **Expressly—**to exist, always emphatic, and not a mere ***copula***: KJV beacon, accomplished, committed, come to pass
    - o **Copula**—something that connects or links together.

God's Word connects to nothing else—it stands alone.

The word, *"expressly,"* is not used to simply link the word, *"came"* with the word, *"unto;"* it is used to create the emphatic, existent word of the LORD, coming as a beacon of light, with intent from God Himself. The New Testament use of the word *"expressly"* in ***1 Timothy 4:1*** means, *"out-spoken, i.e. distinctly."* It adds impetus to the urgency of what God is saying and takes it to a whole new level, exponentially.

Our God is an outspoken God—emphatic, distinct, and direct.

What Ezekiel saw and heard was to change his perspective—lift him up—take him up higher—into the heavenlies above. He saw the whirlwind, fire flashing, four living creatures, burning coals of fire, wheels, strength, power, movement, sounds of wings, like the noise of great waters, as the voice of the Almighty. But then he saw the throne. I don't know anyone who has had such a vision.

How long has it been since the church has truly had a discerning look at the One who sits upon the Throne?

Oh how we want to humanize Him, reduce Him, and bring Him down to our level—but if you see, comprehend and understand Him—you will know He is nothing like us. John, in ***Revelation 4:1,*** seven hundred years later on the isle of Patmos, saw the same vision of the throne and it was still occupied.

> ***Ezekiel 1:25-27*** (Emphasis Added)
>
> *25 And there was a voice from the firmament that was over their heads, when they stood, and had let down their wings.*
>
> *26 And above the firmament that was over their heads was the likeness of a throne, as the appearance of a sapphire stone: and upon* ***the likeness of the throne was the likeness as the appearance of a man above upon it.***
>
> *27 And I saw as the color of amber, as the appearance of fire round about within it, from the appearance* ***of his loins*** *even upward, and from the appearance* ***of his loins*** *even downward, I saw as it were the appearance of fire, and it had brightness round about.*

Ephesians 6:14 tells us to "***stand having our loins bound with the belt of truth.***" ***Verse 27*** tells us from around about His loins fire rose and from the loins fire fell. This verse reveals the Glory of God is a baptism of truth!

From above them came fiery truth, the rainbow and the appearance of the glory of the Lord!

Ezekiel saw it and fell on his face and heard the voice speak to him. He had this great and fearful vision and then the assignment came:

> ***Ezekiel 2:1-8*** (Emphasis Added)
>
> *1 And he said unto me, Son of man, stand upon thy feet, and I will speak unto thee.*
>
> ***2 And the spirit entered into me when he spake unto me, and set me upon my feet,*** *that I heard him that spake unto me.*

We can only sit so long. If we are of a heart to serve God, the apathy and complacency must be broken from our hearts and minds. God told Ezekiel to stand on his feet and then He would speak to him. It goes on to say that the Spirit entered into him when He spoke to him and set him upon his feet. God got his attention. Not only will God take us by the locks of our spiritual hair and put us in a place to see, but He will also stand us up, readying us for action. We can only sit by the river for so long before God calls us out of our reclined state.

A lot of the church knows things are not right but are still reclining around the river with the other brothers and sisters.

I believe God is saying *"it's time to get up."*

> ***Ephesians 5:14-16***—*Wherefore he saith, "Awake thou that sleepest, and arise from the dead, and Christ shall give thee light. See then that ye walk circumspectly, not as fools, but as wise, redeeming the time, because the days are evil."*

God's Word is telling us to break off the lethargy, the sleepiness, the apathy, the complacency and use the time we have because the days we live in are evil.

Ezekiel 2:3-8 (Emphasis Added)

3 And he said unto me, Son of man, I send thee to the children of Israel, to a rebellious nation that hath rebelled against me: they and their fathers have transgressed against me, even unto this very day.

4 For ***they are impudent children and stiff hearted.*** *I do send thee unto them; and thou shalt say unto them, Thus saith the Lord GOD.*

5 And they, whether they will hear, or whether they will forbear, (for they are a rebellious house,) yet shall know that there hath been a prophet among them.

6 And thou, son of man, ***be not afraid of them, neither be afraid of their words,*** *though briers and thorns be with thee, and thou dost dwell among scorpions: be not afraid of their words, nor be dismayed at their looks, though they be a rebellious house.*

7 And thou shalt speak my words unto them, whether they will hear, or whether they will forbear: for they are most rebellious.

8 But thou, son of man, hear what I say unto thee; Be not thou rebellious like that rebellious house: open thy mouth, and ***eat that I give thee****.*

In complex religious worlds like ours where everyone is accepting things once thought of as wrong, where the church is lowering its standards to an agreeable level . . . who really wants to go to speak to such a house? For the one, *like Ezekiel*, who is asked to look at the truth and then speak to those who do not want to listen—this is a tough assignment.

- ***Who wants*** to have a ministry that is hated and despised?
- ***Who wants*** to be persecuted for telling the truth?
- ***Who wants*** to be rejected?

- ***Who wants*** to speak to those who stop their ears against your words?

It is not just enough to believe on Him, we must associate our lives with Him, opening, in spite of what others think or say.

John 12:42-43

42 Nevertheless among the chief rulers also many believed on him; but because of the Pharisees they did not confess him, lest they should be put out of the synagogue:

43 For they loved the praise of men more than the praise of God.

This scripture says they believed on Jesus ***but*** because of those around them that were opposed to Jesus, they were afraid they would be put out of the synagogue. They wanted to be well-thought-of.

- Facing those who are offended and prickle at your words and those who strike back like a scorpion is not very inviting.
- So to be told to take an unpopular message to the church is not the most glorious commission.

Wouldn't we all rather be liked and accepted? I know we would, but that is a dangerous sink-hole that will neuter our message to please the masses.

A lot of people would love *the vision* but not *the assignment.*

It was not going to be popular with anyone and no one was going to listen to a word he said. But the Spirit of the Lord entered into Ezekiel at the sound of *the voice.* He was lifted to his feet, told his assignment and told "*just speak my words.*" He was further warned to not be rebellious *like them*, to just open his mouth and He would fill it.

Ezekiel then saw the book!

It was filled with lamentations on both sides. *(Lament: the act of expressing grief)* The fact both sides were filled with lamentations tells us there was nothing good to say, nothing to bring joy to the heart of God.

Sadly, all that was written in that book released grief.

Surely we understand the heart of the Father in this, being earthly dads, moms, children who are part of a family that is built on trust, obedience and love and faith. Once in a while a child totally rebels against their parents and then the law gets involved and the charges begin to be layered. Unless there is repentance and change on the part of the son or daughter of the family, they could end up on the wrong side of the law for the rest of their life.

I was sitting with an assistant district attorney talking to her about the future of a young girl who was out of her home. The woman lifted a large stack of papers and told me, "*This is the rap sheets on this man,* (the girl's father)." It was at least an inch or so thick. She showed me nothing good when she held them up. For the family it was lamentations—things that brought grief to the whole family.

Was Ezekiel a super-saint, some kind of man who was made of steel and simply deflected the bullets of hatred, criticism and anger and blew off the volley of angry words, hardly feeling anything? No! He was flesh and blood just like you and me. He may have quaked in his shoes just like you and I do when God asks us to step out with truth in the face of the emerging ideology of the deceptive and religious world about us.

And the task hits closer to heart when it's our own brothers and sisters in the faith who are falling away from the truth that was handed down to all through Jesus Christ.

Jesus said it this way in ***Matthew 10:22***, "*And ye shall be hated of all men for my name's sake: but he that endures to the end shall be saved.*"

No true messenger of the Lord is out to win a popularity contest, but to obey the Lord in word, life and deed requires an uncommon commitment to "not being liked or accepted by everyone.

What kind of person willingly opens their mouth to devour the Word of God, taking it deep into their bellies so they are prepared to deliver the message of the hour?

Is this me?
Is this you?

> ***Ezekiel 3:1-3*** (Emphasis Added)
>
> *1 Moreover he said unto me, Son of man, eat that thou findest; **eat this roll, and go speak**_unto the house of Israel.*
>
> *2 **So I opened my mouth,** and he caused me to eat that roll.*
>
> *3 And he said unto me, Son of man, **cause thy belly to eat, and fill thy bowels*** (abdomen) *with this roll that I give thee. Then did I eat it; and it was in my mouth as honey for sweetness.*

This is where churches and many Christians have lost the deeper work of Holy Spirit in their midst. People love to ***see the visions***, they loved to ***hear the word***, but they don't ***open their mouths to eat the Word***—to chew it ***(meditate on it)*** and swallow it.

- Many fail to fill their bellies with the Word and allow it to come back out as a word of truth to others.

We have become so good at passively giving mental assent to what we read and hear of the Word, but in times like these, times of deepening deception and the encroaching world entering into the House of God, that will never do.

This is the ultimate test of obedience—will we eat the Word, regardless of what God puts in our mouth?

> ***John 7:38*** (Emphasis Added)—*He that believeth on me, as the scripture hath said, **out of his belly** shall flow rivers of living water.*

While this scripture speaks of being filled with the Holy Ghost, it also speaks of the belly as being a place from which a river flows. If we have filled our bellies with the Word of God and the Spirit of God dwells to bring forth a living river, then that is what the world around us will receive. We have seen the devastation when a person releases an evil river from their heart. That is not God's will towards us—He wants us filled with His Word.

How many spit it back out the moment the bitterness of that Word hits their belly?

Oh yes, the belly, the place from which Living Water is meant to flow forth, must be able to eat it all and drink the bitter cup, just like Jesus. If we rebel, we will not be used by God but become like others who refused the Word of God. God told Ezekiel to eat it and not be rebellious like the others.

We can't tell others what we have heard—we have to tell them what we've eaten!

It is easy to teach from the Word in Sunday school classes, conferences, in the city and in churches, but have "they/we eaten it?"

- ***If*** anyone teaches you, have they partaken of what they serve?
- ***If*** they teach, warn, rebuke or prophesy—have they eaten it?
- ***If*** not, then nothing is working out of the *"inner most belly as rivers of living water."*

God tells Ezekiel to *give* to others what he has eaten—but there is a catch to it—he will be facing his own people. This is where it gets really difficult for the modern Christian—to open our mouth to those of our own language—the familiar ones.

- ***Your*** church
- ***Your*** family
- ***Your*** denomination

- ***Those*** you hold something in common with.

God then told him, *"Don't fear them."* I believe that the spirit of intimidation is the most formidable foe we have when facing our own house, family, church, denomination and city. This, most of the time, is the hardest ground to plow with a word of truth.

We have to fight the spirit of fear and intimidation and push past to obey God in stepping into this familiar, yet risky territory.

> ***Ezekiel 3:10*** (Emphasis Added)—*Moreover he said unto me, Son of man, all my words that I shall speak unto thee* ***receive in thine heart, and hear with thine ears.***

- ***God knows*** that we don't want to hear some things.
- ***God knows*** that we would rather not see some things.
- ***God knows*** that we would rather not speak or do some things, but He presses us to obedience.

> ***Ezekiel 3:14*** (Emphasis Added)—*So the spirit lifted me up, and took me away, and* ***I went in bitterness, in the heat of my spirit;*** *but the hand of the LORD was strong upon me.*

There are times, even though the Spirit of the Lord has lifted you up, even though you've had an open heaven and visions, even though you heard from God, even though you have received and eaten the Word of God, there is a bitter taste in your mouth for what the Lord is asking of you.

Ezekiel's spirit was agitated but the hand of the Lord was compellingly strong. Have you ever been there—wishing you could just stand in the shadows but God is compelling you to the forefront to speak up for Him?

- ***What*** is it that you really don't want to do?
- ***What*** has God shown you that you would have rather not seen?
- ***What*** has God said that you wish you wouldn't have heard?

It's not that you're rebellious or even disobedient or void of the presence of the Lord—it's just that you are now accountable for what you've seen, know and heard and that you have received God's directives.

We all want to be used of God, *but this?*

There's a lot of digesting the vision and the Word of God in this hour.

God is asking some to do something more difficult than seems fair. To obey means a loss of friends, reputation, status, placement—*it's hard!*

Then God's voice comes again and this time . . . He appoints ministry. He establishes the call and places the mantle and the mandate.

> ***Ezekiel 3:16-17*** (Emphasis Added)
>
> *16 And it came to pass* ***at the end of seven days,*** *that the word of the LORD came unto me, saying,*
>
> *17 Son of man, I have made thee a watchman unto the house of Israel:* ***therefore hear the word at my mouth, and give them warning from me.***

At my mouth—*this proximity*—draw close and pay attention to what I tell you—*"warn them!"*

It's a fact—we will not be able to convince anyone that we are *sent by God* when we are warning them. We will never be able to make our voice sound like God's—it will always sound like *just me.* But the crux is—a watchman looks, hears and warns. To do what God is calling us to do, we have to leave our comfort zones and step into what sometimes is a war zone.

> ***Ezekiel 3:22-23*** (Emphasis Added)
>
> *22 And the hand of the LORD was there upon me; and he said unto me, Arise,* ***go forth into the plain,*** *and I will there talk with thee.*

23 ***Then I arose, and went forth into the plain****: and,* ***behold, the glory of the LORD stood there,*** *as the glory which I saw by the river of Chebar: and I fell on my face.*

Wherever God sends us, his glory will be there.

If we are in our place of obedience, his glory will be there. If Ezekiel would have stayed at the river Chebar, the glory would not have been there. The move required by God was accompanied by his glory.

Don't we just believe that God's glory is a wonderful place, a special encounter that simply thrills us?

This was not Ezekiel's experience.

Verses 25-26 shows us that he was told to go shut himself in his house where he was arrested and bound and God actually took his ability to speak. He was unable to even defend himself. In ***Verse 27*** we see that God spoke to him, telling him that when he is able to speak again, he will be saying what God gives him to speak to the rebellious. From that point on, ***chapter four through seven,*** Ezekiel was used as a living sign and a messenger of God to the House of Israel, performing the prophetic acts as God told Him and speaking what God told him to speak.

He must have looked like the crazy man of the city.

Prophetic people today want to stand before kings, accepted and honored—but what kind of appointment is this given to Ezekiel?

- ***Lay siege*** with the tile upon which is etched the city, put a skillet in front of your face and pretend it's a wall, make miniature battering rams, mound some dirt up, make a little camp, and lay in the street for 390 days and then again for 40 days.
- ***Shave your head and beard***, weigh it, divide it (now we have a bald man) burn part of it, smite part of it and scatter part of it, but don't forget to keep a small part to bind into your robes for later casting into the fire . . . *and this is only part of what God told him to do.*

There's a lot of obedience going on here and a lot of preparation for what God will show him.

God takes a common person, empowers them with His Word and Spirit and sends them forth to take a bold stand in a warped and twisted church world. The voice of a messenger now is far better to hear than when the thunder and lightning of heaven is released in the wrath of the Final Days.

Someone on earth has to speak *for* God before He speaks *for* Himself.

2 Chronicles 7:14

If my people, which are called by my name, shall humble themselves, and pray, and seek my face, and turn from their wicked ways; then will I hear from heaven, and will forgive their sin, and will heal their land.

CHAPTER 29

A HOLE IN THE WALL— AN ENCOUNTER WITH TRUTH

Ezekiel 7:25

Destruction cometh; and they shall seek peace, and there shall be none.

Ezekiel knew that judgment was upon the land as recorded in ***chapter 7***, knew of the sword, famine and pestilence *(this sounds strangely familiar—somewhat like Jesus in Matthew 24)* that was coming in judgment, but he had not really taken a deeper look at ***why*** it was coming. What he was to see was to shock him . . .

> ***Ezekiel 8:1*** (Emphasis Added)—*And it came to pass in the sixth year, in the sixth month, in the fifth day of the month, as I sat in mine house, and the elders of Judah sat before me, that* ***the hand of the Lord GOD fell there upon me.***

One day we were sitting in our homes, in our church when the hand of the Lord GOD fell upon us. We were awakened to our own condition. The Spirit of God let everyone know that He had arrived to deal with us. We felt the strength of His power as His hand fell upon us. Some survived and others did not.

But God has melded the hearts of many together to remain faithful to the call and the vision that God had given His people.

The Lord has a people that He has awakened today to the things that the Spirit of God wants to reveal concerning why our city, state and nation are in trouble. But there is a level of revelation that God is getting ready to release but only to those whom He can trust with the gates of the church, the city, the nation in intercession for the sin of the church and the people of God.

God wants us to know that *all is not well* in the church, if we will just take a closer look with the eyes of God and see what it is that is breaking His heart and stirring Him to jealousy.

> ***Ezekiel 8:2*** (Emphasis Added)—***Then I beheld, and lo a likeness as the appearance of fire: from the appearance of his loins even downward, fire;*** *and from his loins even upward, as the appearance of brightness, as the colour of amber.*

For us, as in Ezekiel's day, this encounter comes with a great big dose of truth—and a demand that *our loins be grit about with truth* as an essential part of our armor. God's truth comes as fire when He enters our Churches and purges the sin. He knows nothing but truth and will never speak *a part truth* to us when cleansing His temple.

Remember the truth that hit the doors of the temple in His day as He angrily drove the money changers out and declared the prophetic purpose of the Temple—a House of Prayer!

> ***Matt 21:12-13*** (Emphasis Added)
>
> *12 And Jesus went into the temple of God, and* ***cast out all them that sold and bought in the temple****, and* ***overthrew the tables*** *of the moneychangers, and the seats of them that sold doves,*
>
> *13 And said unto them, It is written,* ***My house shall be called the house of prayer****; but ye have made it a den of thieves.*

I have heard people refer to the anger of Jesus Christ in this instance and try to make as if He had a problem with anger and didn't handle things very well with the issues in the Temple. That is so dismissive of the truth—***that Jesus is God in the flesh*** and He's coming in upon the doors of ***His House,*** polluted with the flesh of greedy men who got rich on the back of the worshippers coming to make sacrifice.

Anger—Jealousy? Yes, and righteously so.

<u>If it was your home, you might do and say something like this:</u>

"I went home and found thieves in my house, as if they had a right to be there. They had acted as if it was theirs and came in without regard for the fact this was private property. I found them sitting there having a garage sale in my front yard, selling my stuff, things I had use of in my house. It made me so angry and I felt so defiled that I drove them from my home and told them it was my house, to never come back and to take their tables with them."

I believe certain emotions would rise up in your heart at the audacity if you were to find such things going on at *your* home.

- ***Why wouldn't Jesus*** feel anger at such atrocities in regards to His House?
- ***Why wouldn't God*** be righteously jealous upon seeing things in His Temple that were defiling?

> ***Ezekiel 8:3*** (Emphasis Added)—*And he put forth the form of an hand, and took me by a lock of mine head; and the spirit lifted me up between the earth and the heaven, and brought me in the visions of God to Jerusalem, to the door of the inner gate that looketh toward the north; where was the seat of the image of jealousy,* ***which provoketh to jealousy.***

> ***Deuteronomy 32:16*** (Emphasis Added)—*They* ***provoked him to jealousy*** (Jealous for cause) *with strange gods, with abominations* ***provoked they him to anger.*** (Grieved, sorrowful, vexed)

I cannot imagine any person who loves another with all their heart not being jealous if that one upon whom they set their affections cheated on them with someone else. To be *jealous for cause* is not the same thing as having a jealous, envious spirit.

What is the cause for God's jealousy?

> ***Deuteronomy 32:17-18*** (Emphasis Added)
>
> *17* ***They sacrificed unto devils****, not to God;* ***to gods*** *whom they knew not,* ***to new gods*** *that* ***came newly up****, whom your fathers feared not.*
>
> *18* ***Of the Rock*** *that begat thee thou art unmindful, and hast forgotten God that formed thee.*

A question is asked in ***1 Corinthians 10:21-22, "Do we provoke the Lord to jealousy?*** *Are we stronger than he?"* What had provoked the Lord's jealousy? His people had their feet under two tables—***His and that of devils.***

The word ***"Provoke"*** means to anger, enrage, exasperate, or vex. The answer to the cause for God's jealousy is extremely clear—*they cheated on God* without any thought as to how that would make Him feel. They gave no thought to what He had done, what He had sacrificed for them and the love He had shown them.

- They acted in their own interest rather than remembering the Rock that begat them.
- They had got so involved in their pursuits of other loves, they forgot God.

It is similar to what a husband or wife would feel if they found that the one they are married to is keeping company with someone other than them. Oh yes, jealousy would be an issue for the faithful mate.

There is something in all of us that feels the weight of betrayal and the sorrow and grief and feeling of being vexed in our emotions when someone we love turns aside from us to another—whether it's a husband or wife, a friend—someone we entrusted with our love, affections, someone to whom we invested our lives.

God is not being overbearingly jealous here—He's grieved and sorrowful, and with just cause.

He had completely invested in the children of Israel, to bring a people to Himself and they simply could not totally commit to Him alone.

They had unfaithful hearts that broke God's heart.

> ***Ezekiel 8:4-6*** (Emphasis Added)
>
> *4 And, behold, the glory of the God of Israel was there, according to the vision that I saw in the plain.*
>
> *5 Then said he unto me, Son of man, lift up thine eyes now the way toward the north. So I lifted up mine eyes the way toward the north, and **behold northward at the gate of the altar this image of jealousy in the entry.*** (Just like Jesus found the money changers at the entry of His House)
>
> *6 He said furthermore unto me, **Son of man, seest thou what they do?** even the great abominations that the house of Israel committeth here, that I should go far off from my sanctuary? But turn thee yet again, and **thou shalt see greater abominations.***

This is a strong question that we need to answer today—*do we really see and know the church the way God knows it?*

We must take note of what is being said here and the impact of those things that stir God to jealousy over His House. The things that enter into the House of God still push Him out the door. His Glory was upon His House and then because of abominations, His Glory left the House. Would we be okay with sharing our home with another who was stealing the heart of our loved one? Of course not! Only someone with a perverted heart would take any delight in such abominations.

***And as for God*—why should He share His Glory with another?**

In taking a look at the base root for the word ***"abominations,"*** it means something morally disgusting, i.e. abhorrence; especially idolatry or an idol: Even relating to a custom or thing that is abominable. It could be that people today may not like such a descriptive word being used for what goes on in the Church, but if we distance ourselves from God on this subject, we will never see the error that has invaded the thinking of those called by His name.

God wants a holy people—those who are committed to Him and anything that gets in the way of that exclusive relationship is abominable.

Ezekiel 8:7-9 (Emphasis Added)

7 And he brought me to the door of the court; and when I looked, ***behold a hole in the wall.***

8 Then said he unto me, Son of man, dig now in the wall: and when I had digged in the wall, behold a door.

9 And he said unto me, ***Go in, and behold*** *the wicked abominations that they do here.*

The first thing Ezekiel sees is a hole in the wall. But when he is told to dig deeper he discovered a door. This indicates to me that God was not satisfied with Ezekiel looking at the surface condition.

God wanted to show him the depth of depravity that was on the inside.

We can present a very nice outward appearance to those around us, not only as a person but also as a church where people collectively gather. But, as we know from the Word of God, He is not so interested on the outward appearance (***1 Samuel 16:7***) but looks much deeper to the heart of the matter.

Those who have felt the urgency of prayer for the church and the people of the church have been asked by God to pray deep, because for the most part, many of our prayers for and over the church have not even scratched the surface.

Once you make a determination to pray, only the discerning, honest prayers are going to suffice.

We cannot pray all around the problems that have entered in to God's House, from the pulpit to the pew, and expect them to move the hand of God. God already knows the truth about His people, His church, so we may as well get our vision cleared and see through the eyes of the Holy Spirit and the Word of God.

God's view is so much higher than what even the most revived, reformed, renewed church could ever imagine.

First and foremost—The greatest desire of God is that His church would wash her garments, inwardly, and become that chaste bride for His Son. God loves the church but He does not love the churches sin—He never has and never will. Furthermore, God cannot help but judge the church for her sin ***if*** she will not repent *(a soul at a time, if necessary).*

God must judge sin and according to the Word of God, *judgment begins in the House of God.*

> ***1 Peter 4:17****—For the time is come that judgment must begin at the house of God: and if it first begin at us, what shall the end be of them that obey not the gospel of God?*

Solomon built a physical House of God, putting in place the natural elements, carefully, according to plan, and then the Glory of God filled the House. Unfortunately for Israel, they did not keep the Glory of God in the House because they allowed sin to enter into their own hearts and ultimately the house of worship and sacrifice were polluted.

Evangelist Ormel Chapin received this word from the Lord on January 8, 2008, called, "*Give Me back My Church.*"

You model the church after earthly models that are not Mine. You model after the big church across town and many other so called churches of many nations but you have forsaken **THE** *model I have given you and that can only be found in the Book of Acts.*

When I walked into Jerusalem 2000 years ago I found My Temple had become a den of thieves led by personalities, laws and ideas that had nothing or little to do with Me. From that day till now, I am still searching for a church that is a House of Prayer where I am the only One receiving the honor of perfected praise by humble people who have been fully washed in My blood, truly filled with My Holy Spirit and are in full pursuit of holy and righteous living according to My Word.

I am still searching for My church where the glory of My Presence is evidenced by supernatural miracles, where genuine Holy Spirit Power and Gifts are daily in operation that produce an atmosphere and conviction of sin in believers and unbelievers to fully reap the great harvest of souls that I died for. I want My church back.

I am sickened by what I am seeing in My church, it's priesthood, ministers, leadership, deacons and many followers a **FORM OF GODLINESS** *that I warned you to run from as it was a sign of a dead last days church. Open your spiritual eyes and your heart and hear what the Spirit is saying to the church: Give Me back the control of My church: there is only One Lord of My church, One Holy Spirit to lead and One Holy Bible to follow.*

The divisive spirit in My church is evidence that man is large and in charge.

I call you to humble yourselves, surrender your right of control and your right of fleshly opinions, then passionately, with all your heart pursue My Presence and My perfect will for My church for if I do not build My church, all your labor will be in vain and have no eternal results.

I want My church back.

.Give Me back My ministry: My calling upon people for ministry in scripture was for the express purpose of doing what I was doing with the same purpose, passion and power anointing.

Mark My Word, I have not changed, My Holy Spirit has not changed, but ministry today has changed. The spirit of religion has blinded many of My ministers and altered the purpose, motivation and the results of ministry. Personality and personal giftings have replaced the Gifts of the Holy Spirit and My anointing. So called sermons, thoughts for the day, and "Let me help you How To's" have replaced the "Word of the Lord".

Puny, short, silent, passionless conversations called prayer have replaced genuine intercession, prayer and fasting. Whatever happened to "praying through" till My Spirit shows up and you find the answer? Can't you see the evidence of decreasing spiritual hunger in My people and My priesthood where few seek Me passionately at the altars?

Where songs are sung but there is no true worship in Spirit and in Truth? Where a few minutes on Sunday mornings are endured so folks can get back to their real desires and priorities?

Doesn't it bother you that in many areas few are discovering genuine salvation by My grace through faith? Are you not troubled when so many of My people are weak, fruitless and not pursuing the Power, Anointing and Gifts of the Holy Spirit?

If your pursuit of success in ministry is based on a priority where most of your time and effort is spent on education, knowledge, talents, programs, searching the web, modern trends and patterns, where there is little or no hunger to "know Him and the Power of His resurrection" and no evidence of Holy Spirit anointing for supernatural miracles of deliverance of bondages, healings of bodies and broken relationships, Godly conviction and sorrow for sin with genuine repentance and God confirming

His Word with signs and wonders, you are missing it. O if my priesthood could see ministry and My church as I see it, surely they would humble themselves, weep bitterly in the sanctuary and repent for who and what they have become.

I want My church back.
I want My ministry back.
Jesus

~End of Word~

God's people must realize that *you either sell out to your world*—or *you sell out to God.*

There comes a time when church, the people who are called by His name, must make a choice—when the rationalization of their faith comes ***face-to-face with a Living God*** who has come to judge His Church.

We are entering such a time as this. God is drawing lines in *the sand of the human heart* that claims Jesus name and for the churches that cover the surface of the world. Choices will be made as God deals with the sin in the church. God tells us that He does nothing but first He warns His prophets. I thank God for those who are willing to raise their voices in times like these and declare a word of the Lord that strikes like a sword at the heart of the Church.

All it takes is a discerning look by those who care to see and declare something is not right.

We may think we have seen into the problem in the church, but folks, we have seen nothing compared to what God sees and knows to be true.

Many have lived in a beautiful sequestered environment where the Spirit of God is among them, and repentance is a way of life, with worship deep and sincere in Spirit and in Truth; a place where faith is real, the vision is sure. ***But the wider truth is this***—while churches are still splitting up over the same old church issues that always divide God's people and His church—dumb things like elections and color of carpet or use of the building—there is the graver issue of sin in the camp.

Revelation 3:1-3

1 And unto the angel of the church in Sardis write; These things saith he that hath the seven Spirits of God, and the seven stars; I know thy works, that thou hast a name that thou livest, and art dead.

2 Be watchful, and strengthen the things which remain, that are ready to die: for I have not found thy works perfect before God.

3 Remember therefore how thou hast received and heard, and hold fast, and repent. If therefore thou shalt not watch, I will come on thee as a thief, and thou shalt not know what hour I will come upon thee.

He has to deal with this because this House bears His name but does not reflect His Glory.

God will draw a line where the choices man will make will divide His church because of the sin behind closed doors. He will separate between the vile and pure, the holy and profane. He will split His house wide open and eradicate what is wrong—either through repentance or through judgment.

Are we ready to dig in the wall and see the door and take a deeper look at what grieves the heart of God?

2 Chronicles 7:14

If my people, which are called by my name, shall humble themselves, and pray, and seek my face, and turn from their wicked ways; then will I hear from heaven, and will forgive their sin, and will heal their land.

Chapter 30

A Hole in the Wall—Do you see what I see?

Ezekiel 8:7-9

And he brought me to the door of the court; and when I looked, behold a hole in the wall. Then said he unto me, Son of man, dig now in the wall: and when I had digged in the wall, behold a door.

I found it curious that Ezekiel was taken to the door of the court yard. It was the obvious passage way to go in and out. And yet, Ezekiel, with Lord's direction sees a hole in the wall.

Sometimes we are so focused on one thing, the obvious, that we fail to see that which is hiding in plain sight.

Remember this is a spiritual vision of the condition of the House of God. God is revealing to Ezekiel things that other were passing by and accepting as *normal church life*. Ezekiel sees the hole in the wall and once his spiritual eyes are set on that place, God gives him the instruction to dig in the wall. Why not just go through the door?

Because **. . . to see what God wanted to reveal, Ezekiel had to approach it from God's perspective.**

I heard many years ago a minister speak to the subject of the natural appearance of the church. He said, *"We get used to the spots on our carpets and the smell of our own church, but when a visitor comes in they see and smell all."* He went on to say, *"Look at your church from the viewpoint of a guest and get rid of all those spots and smells that offend them."* So, I began to view our physical structure from that perspective from that day to now. It was true—those who are regular attendees can walk past a lot of stuff they no longer see.

When God makes a move upon the doors of His church, visiting them, be sure of this—He sees the spots and blemishes, sees the wrinkles and smells the things that foul the air—spiritually.

Look at the definitions of the key words of this verse:

- ***A Hole***—a cavity, socket, den: cave
- ***I Had Digged***—to force a passage, dig (through)
- ***Door***—an opening (literally), i.e. door (gate) or entrance way

He saw a cavity, a breach in the wall, and began to dig there to force a passage way through the wall. When he had dug there he found an entrance way that took him into the belly of the temple.

God has shown this to me as a breach in the wall with Ezekiel in a prophetic intercessory position—a place God has brought him to by His Spirit to see what God sees and now wants Ezekiel to see.

A lot of people can describe the *hole in the wall,* meaning many understand the church is *open to some things* she once rejected. They are concerned with the declining state of things, but have yet to take that next step and begin to dig to see inside the depth of degradation that has entered in through doors that have been opened by those in the house.

> ***Lamentations 2:13-15*** (Emphasis Added)
>
> *13 What thing shall I take to witness for thee? What thing shall I liken to thee, O daughter of Jerusalem? What shall I equal to thee, that I may comfort thee, O virgin daughter of Zion? For* ***thy breach is great like the sea: who can heal thee?***

> *14 Thy prophets have seen vain and foolish things for thee: and* ***they have not discovered thine iniquity,*** *to turn away thy captivity; but have seen for thee false burdens and causes of banishment.*
>
> *15 All that pass by clap their hands at thee; they hiss and wag their head at the daughter of Jerusalem, saying,* ***Is this the city that men call The perfection of beauty, The joy of the whole earth?***

When there is a breach and things of the world find entrance into the heart of believers and the church, unless that opening is discovered, sorrowed over, repented of and the house cleaned of all abominations, the breach becomes greater and greater. It will never get better on its own.

The world sees the decline; knows the church has compromised their standard of holiness and polluted the gospel of Jesus Christ and merged into the developing apostate church of the last days. Because of this, those thought to be friends, things we tolerated and accepted in order to be tolerated and accepted have become the very stones of mockery that are thrown at the church.

People of the world know when sin is in the camp of *those called by His name*, but rarely do those who are compromised see their own sin.

The indictment by the world of, "*Is this the city that men call the perfection of beauty, the joy of the whole earth*" can be heard today ***if we want to hear truth***. Besides God, the greatest judge of the church is the enemies of the church because, even though they declare their indictment through mocking lips, they also speak truth many times.

"You're a hypocrite."
"And you call yourself a Christian?"

Ah, but sometimes it is true folks; they see the double standard of those who say they are Christians.

__2 Corinthians 7:10__—For godly sorrow worketh repentance to salvation not to be repented of: but the sorrow of the world worketh death.

When things reach a crisis point, it is time for Divine Intervention. God is moving a man into place to see and what Ezekiel sees is startling. It is truth slapping him in the face.

Ezekiel 8:8-9 (Emphasis Added)

*8 And he said unto me, **Go in, and behold** the wicked abominations that they do here.*

*9 **So I went in and saw**; and behold every form of creeping things, and abominable beasts, and all the idols of the house of Israel, portrayed upon the wall round about.*

God's house was totally polluted with wicked abominations and every form of creeping things, idols and engraved images.

- ***Form Of***—structure; a model, resemblance: figure, likeness, pattern, similitude.
- ***Creeping Things***—a reptile or any other rapidly moving animal that creeps, creeping (moving) thing.
- ***Portrayed***—to carve; to entrench: carved work.

This condition *then and now* is at an emergency status when God sends His word of revelation through ministers of the gospel, through intercessors to pull out all the stops and probe to the depths of the condition that is grieving God. I sometimes wonder if anyone truly cares how God feels about His people/His church today. Do we believe He has an opinion on what we do, say and adore?

We may say that this is not a picture of the church *in general*, but we have to see the truth if we are going to pray for the church.

Now is not the time for denial or whitewash.
Only truth is going to set us free to return to God with our whole heart.

It's interesting to see the use of words—*wicked and abominations*—spoken by God. I believe that those who were in the house of God had long ago become blind to the condition of all that was around them. They no longer had spiritual discernment about such matters.

- Once a person starts to practice the ways of the world, the *defense mechanisms of the mind and heart* begin to click into place.
- And the error of the ways of man becomes *their truth.*
- What we have tolerated in past generations *has now become the standards* for those who live today.

The only way to break that pattern of decline is to repent of wickedness and yes, in many more cases than we would think, those things that are an abomination to God.

There are things that have entered into the church that are an abomination to God. Every sin that the sinners are committing, those called by God's name are also doing—at an almost equal rate as the world. Sadly, this has also become a problem in the ministry as well. In ***Luke 6:38*** Jesus poses this question: *"Can the blind lead the blind? Shall they not both fall into the ditch?"*

The spiral of degradation has sucked the church into an ever-deepening whirlpool of sin and excuses for sin.

2 Chronicles 7:14

If my people, which are called by my name, shall humble themselves, and pray, and seek my face, and turn from their wicked ways; then will I hear from heaven, and will forgive their sin, and will heal their land.

CHAPTER 31

HOLE IN THE WALL—THE SPIRAL OF THE IMAGINATION

Romans 1:21

Because that, when they knew God, they glorified him not as God, neither were thankful; but became vain in their imaginations, and their foolish heart was darkened.

Revivalists Leonard Ravenhill said this: *"I believe if we were as spiritual as we think we are we would have gone to church yesterday in sackcloth and a handful of ashes to put on our heads and mourn that the Glory has departed."* As we continue into this journey of seeing from God's perspective, let us keep ready the sackcloth and handful of ashes for our own hearts, to rend them before our God.

He is worthy of a people who will come before Him with a broken and contrite heart.

> ***Ezekiel 8:11-12*** (Emphasis Added)
>
> *11 And **there** stood before them seventy men of the ancients **of the house of Israel,** and in the midst of them stood Jaazaniah the son of Shaphan, with every man his **censer in his hand**; and **a thick cloud of incense went up**.*

Remember the incense as we go further into this chapter . . .

> *12 Then said he unto me, Son of man,* ***hast thou seen what the ancients of the house of Israel do in the dark, every man in the chambers of his imagery*** *for they say, The LORD seeth us not; the LORD hath forsaken the earth.*

- ***In the Dark***—literally darkness; obscurity.
- ***Imagery***—imagination:
- ***In the Chambers***—innermost part,

This describes a place in the innermost part, a place of obscurity where man's imaginations arise to think a certain thing through to reach a conclusion that removes them from God's path. It is a place of thought where mankind devises so many ill-thought plans and ideas and excuses the things that are done against the truth of God's Word.

> ***Jeremiah 7:24****—But they hearkened not, nor inclined their ear, but walked in the counsels and in the imagination of their evil heart, and went backward, and not forward.*

I have heard people say, *"I am just following my heart,"* as if that is the place from which decisions about life, relationship and faith are made. Nothing could be further from the truth.

- God's Word, His precepts, laws, statutes and commandments were given for that purpose.
    - o Man's imagination tells him/her that such things pertain to the law and we are now free from such bondage of laws.
- God also has given us Holy Spirit to guide us into all truth—
    - o . . . and yet when God speaks to us, we may find ourselves following our ideas and desires instead.

> ***2 Corinthians 10:5*** (Emphasis Added)—*Casting down imaginations, and every high thing that exalteth itself against the knowledge of God, and bringing into captivity* ***every thought*** *to the obedience of Christ;*

Oh, the scripture is full of warnings of following our imaginations and thoughts; to bring them into obedience to Christ, who is the ***Bedrock of our***

Faith. Without Him in place in our hearts, established by our obedience to His Word, we stand on *the shifting sand of imaginations.*

> ***Ezekiel 8:13-14*** (Emphasis Added)
>
> *13 He said also unto me, Turn thee yet again, and thou shalt see greater abominations that they do.*
>
> *14 Then he brought me to the door of the gate of the LORD's house which was toward the north; and,* ***behold, there sat women weeping for Tammuz.***

Various commentaries tells us, "The god, Tammuz, can be traced back to a culture of idolatry where the god dies before winter. Mourning for the god was followed by a celebration of resurrection. Human sacrifice and obscene cult rituals were performed to celebrate the resurrection."

Can we see the perversion of the death and resurrection of the Son of God, Jesus Christ, in prophetic type? It is not just the worship of Tammuz in ancient times that replaced the worship of the One True God, but what is still being practiced today.

We may say, *"Oh, I would never worship an idol such as that,"* and yet perversion *(moral or spiritual),* mixed with worship has truly entered into the House of God!

If we do not get a picture of this, we will totally miss the importance of what God is trying to show us. The seventy men in this scripture are representative of the whole nation of Israel. In prophetic typology they represent the church as a whole, not individual denominations or church bodies. The top leaders of Israel, those who stood in responsibility and leadership over Israel, were the ones holding the censor with the thick smoke of incense pouring forth.

The picture seen here is of the church and what has happened to worship.

I can hear the arguments: *"How can this possibly have anything to do with us today? This is nothing more than the Old Testament priesthood . . ."*

Look at the original language of the incense in their censors. It isn't just smoke—***it is worship!***

These seventy elders of Israel ***(verse 11)*** were standing in a place of worship but God was taking strong issue with it. The reason was something that we may tend to overlook—the condition of the heart and soul of the one who stands to worship before a holy God.

Psalms 24:3-4 tells us of the purity that is needed to enter into the presence of the Lord. It is a question that is immediately answered:

- **Question:** *"Who shall ascend into the hill of the Lord? Or who shall stand in his holy place?"*
- **Answer:** *"He that hath clean hands, and a pure heart; who hath not lifted up his soul unto vanity, nor sworn deceitfully."*

***They could* fill a million censors with incense and wave them before God but it would never be acceptable to Him.**

- ***They could*** stand before the altar and lift their hands and say the right words, but it was not acceptable to God.
- ***They could*** have all the right garments on, perfectly placed according to the law but not be acceptable to God.
- ***They could*** open just the right book of prayers and psalms and say the right words with just the right intonation and not be acceptable to God.

Oh yes, while God was specific about the garments of the priesthood in the Old Testament, He was also very specific about the condition of the heart of the one who stood before Him.

> ***Proverbs 30:****10—There is a generation that are pure in their own eyes, and yet is not healed from their filthiness.*

And we also see the New Testament teaching of Jesus that the outer garments were not especially important in qualifying a person as clean, but that He looked upon the heart—from which flows the issues of life and even our speech.

I am amazed at the growing problem amongst Christian leaders who have dirty mouths. Many sound like the world around them. I know some may say I am being legalistic, but I did not lay down the law for holiness—God did.

Some see the filth of the world staining the garments of the modern church leaders and flowing into the main stream of the churches culture . . . and if it's not right in the sight of God it cannot be right in the sight of the godly.

Oh how we need a fresh outpouring from on High in a convicting stream of holiness.

2 Chronicles 7:14

If my people, which are called by my name, shall humble themselves, and pray, and seek my face, and turn from their wicked ways; then will I hear from heaven, and will forgive their sin, and will heal their land.

CHAPTER 32

HOLE IN THE WALL—BETWEEN THE PORCH AND THE ALTAR

Ezekiel 22:30
(Emphasis Added)

And I sought for a man among them that should make up the hedge, and ***stand in the gap before me*** *for the land, that I should not destroy it: but I found none.*

- ***Gap***—a break, breach
- ***Hedge***—enclosure: fence, wall.
- ***That Should Make Up***—to wall in or around: repairer.

Here in ***Ezekiel 22:30,*** we see a problem—a gap or breach in the wall that has formerly enclosed a place for security. Something, someone, has allowed this hole to develop in ***the security system of holiness*** and God is searching for anyone who will stand in the gap and close the wall by standing there.

- To stand there is the same as taking a stand for and against—for God's purposes; against the enemy's purposes.
- Sin was in the camp and no one was praying.

That is a terrible plight to find God's people in—sinning and unprotected by prayer that will lead to repentance.

Ezekiel 8:15-16 (Emphasis Added)

> *15 Then said he unto me, Hast thou seen this, O son of man? turn thee yet again, and thou shalt see greater abominations than these.*
>
> *16 And he brought me into the inner court of the LORD's house, and, behold,* ***at the door of the temple of the LORD, between the porch and the altar,*** *were about five and twenty men, with their backs toward the temple of the LORD, and their faces toward the east; and they worshipped the sun toward the east.*

Between the Porch and the Altar—a Place of Intercession—the most sacred spot in the inner court—an area the priests alone were permitted to walk.

Look at the priests in Joel and what they were doing . . . they were crying out to God in intercession for the people, that they would be spared.

> ***Joel 2:17***(Emphasis Added)—*Let the priests, the ministers of the Lord,* ***weep between the porch and the altar,*** *and let them say,* ***Spare thy people, O Lord,*** *and give not thine heritage to reproach, that the heathen should rule over them: wherefore should they say among the people, Where is their God?*

Now, in this holy place Ezekiel sees twenty-five men with their backs toward the temple who were worshipping the sun in the east, with the high priest at the head. This action was apostasy because they turned their backs on the Temple and therefore upon Jehovah who was enthroned in the temple. These twenty-five leaders, representing the entire priesthood, had sunk into idolatry, doing exactly what Moses had warned the people about.

> ***Deuteronomy 4:19*** (Emphasis Added)—*And lest thou lift up thine eyes unto heaven, and* ***when thou seest the sun, and the moon, and the stars, even all the host of heaven, shouldest be driven to worship them, and serve them,*** *which the Lord thy God hath divided unto all nations under the whole heaven.*

In ***Joel 2:12-13*** we see the heart of God when He says to His backslidden people, ***"Turn ye even to me with all your heart****, and with* ***fasting****, and with* ***weeping****, and with* ***mourning****: And* ***rend your heart****, and not your garments, and* ***turn unto the Lord your God****: for he is gracious and merciful, slow to anger, and of great kindness, and repenteth him of the evil."* (Emphasis Added)

Is there that kind of sorrow, the kind God calls for, anywhere in the world today?

I believe so, but should there not be a river of tears and an ocean of godly sorrow rise to meet God's plea to us today?

> ***Ezekiel 8:17*** (Emphasis Added)—*Then he said unto me, Hast thou seen this, O son of man?* ***Is it a light thing*** *to the house of Judah that they commit* ***the abominations*** *which they commit here? for they have* ***filled the land with violence,*** *and have returned to* ***provoke me to anger****: and, lo, they put the branch to their nose.*

Is it a light thing? What a question to ask in light of the abomination that is being described. This phrase, "***light thing***" meaning, "***trifling or vile thing,***" denotes one holding something in contempt. This describes the attitude of those who were committing abominations in the sight of God—and yet diminishing it as "*no big thing.*"

The human mind is incredible force in that it can make a defense for us on just about anything we want to do or have done.

The problem with sin that is diminished is it easily becomes something that is not only practiced but defended as well. And given time, that thing becomes the standard practice of a person or group who now commit abominations *without thought to God.*

There should be a holy urgency in the heart of every believer, in light of the secular world spiraling out of control, to search their hearts diligently in this day of great deception.

We should cry out with David *(Psalms 139:23-24)*, in all honesty, "*Search me, O God, and know my heart: try me, and know my thoughts: And see if there be any wicked way in me, and lead me in the way everlasting.*"

This level of invitation for God to search us is not like you see today when the police come hitting the door with one of the heavy duty instrument used to bust down a door. It is not like when they rush inside and yell at the top of their lungs, "*Police—Hands in the air!*"

It is nothing like that.

- ***It is*** us opening the door of our heart and asking God to examine us in the most penetrating way possible, leaving nothing unsearched.
- ***It is*** to open every closet, every hiding place, of our own free will and invite Him to look.
- ***It is*** to go even further and allow Him to see if there's any place beyond our sight that He may desire to search, to seek, to examine intimately.

And then, it is to take it an honest step further and ask Him to go deep and ***try us.*** This is a judicial invitation allowing him to test, examine and prove by trial to see the caliber of person we are—i.e. test our metal.

Have you ever considered asking God to *"put you on trial,"* so that which is guilty in your heart can be judged by One who is Holy; One who is Worthy?

> ***Ezekiel 8:18***—*Therefore will I also deal in fury: mine eye shall not spare, neither will I have pity: and though they cry in mine ears with a loud voice, yet will I not hear them.*

- Something was horribly wrong in God's house and God was being bluntly honest with Ezekiel.

The leaders of the church had adopted and put into practice the things taken from the world around them . . . pagan, witchcraft, astrology, and such ungodly things that in times past they would have shunned. Their worship had shifted from glorifying and obeying God to the corruption of the inside of the temple.

It still looked like a church; the robes were still being worn by the ministry; the laity was still weeping—but the purpose of and the cause for which the house was built had long since been forgotten for the more favorable and rewarding worship of the world.

We live in a nation today that had lost its blush, but worse yet the blush is gone from the House of God.

> ***Jeremiah 6:15*** (Emphasis Added)—***Were they ashamed*** *when they had committed abomination? Nay, they were not at all ashamed, neither* ***could they blush****: therefore they shall fall among them that fall: at the time that I visit them they shall be cast down, saith the LORD.*

When the people and the ministry are polluted, the blush goes and repentance is no longer even thought about as the Babylonian way of life takes over where religion is popular in a secular sort of way.

We need a trip into the center of the church via the Holy Spirit of God.

He must lift us up by the hair of our head and show us the hole in the wall and tell us to dig in the wall until we find the door to look inside and see the truth. It might shock some of us to realize that God is seriously close to judging the church all around the world for what's inside her doors.

This is why we pray!
This why we seek God for a revival in the church so there will be an awakening in the land.

The nations are in trouble, but graver still, the church is in trouble. We need national revivals. If we are indifferent about the nations and stick our head in our church patterns don't awaken to the fact that we must pray, we will feel not only shakings, but persecutions.

Look at the gut-level, honest cry recorded in ***Lamentations 3:40-44:***

- *Let us search and try our ways, and turn again to the LORD.*
- *Let us lift up our heart with our hands unto God in the heavens.*
- *We have transgressed and have rebelled: thou hast not pardoned.*
- *Thou hast covered with anger, and persecuted us: thou hast slain, thou hast not pitied.*
- *Thou hast covered thyself with a cloud that our prayer should not pass through.*

The Prophet Jeremiah said in Lamentations 3:40-41, *"Let us search and try our ways and turn again to the Lord. Let us lift our heart with our hands unto God in heaven."* Then he goes on to confess the sin of rebellion against God, so deep that even seasons of shakings are not jarring them awake. He is acutely aware that even the prayers are being resisted by God.

Many nations are already feeling the shakings that have brought the mighty down low and seen the nations rumble—but there is still not an awakening. We must still stand in the gap and intercede, and cry out to God for the people of the church—for the people of the world. And let it be prayers that will be heard in heaven from the purified lips of a people wholly set apart for God. We can be that people whose prayers God will hear, but there is a price to pay for that passage.

We have yet to see an awakening to the core condition of rebellion so that repentance flows and heals the land.
And the church has yet to admit there's sin in the camp.

The church is in trouble—a fact many are not willing to face. We are busier than ever and emptier than ever. The power is gone from the midst; the presence of the Lord has departed; the Glory of God has crossed back over and out of the threshold of the church and no one even knows that He's gone.

Dr. Billy Graham made a statement some time ago that really rang true in my spirit: *"The church could go on and do what she is currently doing and not even know that the Holy Spirit has left."*

So much of what is currently going on in the name of the Lord bears no mark of holiness or humility. The *user friendly—seeker friendly* church has cost us the power of God. God is not user friendly.

God does not market Himself to the world on any of our levels of low-living *but rather* forces us to humble ourselves to His Son's level of sacrifice.

I have been giving quite a bit of consideration for the season that we are in, mostly in regards to intercession. Prayer is at times a roller-coaster ride that not only goes up and down but is also at times like a train with many changes of scenery.

In the last number of years I have witnessed the starts and stops of intercession and yet have watched as *the revival movement* has continued even though *deep intercession took a back seat.*

- ***I am more convinced than ever*** it is possible to move on earth and move nothing in heaven.
- ***I am more convinced than ever*** the church can do just about anything that it puts its mind to without prayer.
- ***I am also convinced than ever*** the church can even "*have a revival*" and yet not pray.

These are statements that are backed up by a history of church movement that kept going after God stopped.

I have to say that we are in the most demanding times spiritually-speaking as God is drawing lines for the Church and making a demand on her to choose a side. We can actually fool ourselves at a time like this and believe that *all is well*, when *all is the same as it has always been.* There has been a loss of "*from glory to glory He's changing me . . .*"

To stop praying during the move of God is to cut the life-line that keeps us on track.

Have we moved into a new season in which the intercession of days gone by was only for that time and now we have moved onto bigger and better and brighter days?

<u>**This could not equate with the statistics that I see all around us.**</u>

- ***The world*** still is at war.
- ***The souls*** still fall headlong into eternity where the sun never shines.
- ***The churches*** are still squabbling over rights and the color of paint and doctrine.

"Rend your heart, and not your garments" *(**Joel 2:12**-13)* speaks of a deeper work than has been going on in God's people. He has not been impressed with all their outward movement and is calling for internal sanctification. ***2 Chronicles 7:14*** tells us that it is we, *those called by His name,* that are the responsible parties.

- I love my nation, ***but*** I love God more!
- I love the church, ***but*** I love God more.

If our nation is not healed—then none of us are healed—for a healed nation reveals there is a healed people who dwell in that land.

If the church does not repent, then the nations of the world and the church will face the continued downward spiral that will soon dump into the developing cesspool into which all nations will end.

Let us not be fooled into a passive stance about
our nation or the church.
We are responsible for its condition.

Wake up!
The day is far spent and the night is upon us!

We see that God's spirit is continually with Ezekiel, wherever he is taken. What he has been prepared for is not what revival was supposed to look like. The glory of God was supposed to be in the temple, but what is revealed is that God is not there.

There are intercessors that God has raised up over many things, nations, people groups, governments, judges, entertainment, cities . . . but there are those that God has raised up as intercessors for the church—***His Church***.

His heart is broken for what is going on behind the closed doors of His church.

Some of you are going to see things that God must judge if there is no repentance.

What you see will have been buried deep behind closed doors.
It is so gross that it will astonish you.
These things are an abomination to God.

There's no point in hiding from the truth or watering it down because God sees and God reveals.

- ***God will*** show you things *because you fear Him*
- ***God will*** show you things *because you can still be astonished.*
- ***God will*** show you things *because you can still blush.*
- ***God will*** show you things *because you still weep.*
- ***God will*** show you things *because you will keep looking, even though you want to turn and run from what you see.*
- ***God will*** show you things *because you still repent, pleading for mercy.*
- ***God will*** show you things *because you still stand in the gap and pray.*

You will be thrust face-to-face with the breach.

When you are told to dig into the hole, you will dig. You will not draw back because it is dirty. You will dig into a place of negligence, a place where watchmen used to be, a dirty place, a difficult place, a place, though hard, will not prepare you for what lies ahead.

Your eyes are looking at the same spot God's eyes have looked.
He's already been there and He's come after you.
He wants you to see what He sees.

You know it's significant. You know it's important, or God's Spirit would not have brought you here by His hand to this wall and let you see the *Hole in the Wall*—the opening—and said, ***"Dig."***

As you dig, you come upon a door.
God's spirit has placed you now face-to-face with a closed door.
Do you dare open it?
What is behind the door—past the wall?

The sense of urgency with which you have been brought here holds your heart and then the Spirit of the Lord speak to you, ***"Open the Door."*** You have been engulfed by the size of the ***Hole in the Wall*** but you now fill the hole in the wall. From this position, you reach for the door.

God has always had a person whom He raised up to see what is *behind the door.* They will never be popular. Some are martyred for their position. Some are greatly persecuted for what God calls them to do. Others are misunderstood and accused.

Remember Jesus? He was one who looked deep into the temple. He was hated for it.

When Jesus cleansed the temple he called it for what it was—
"a den of thieves."
He knew it was to be a house of prayer but it had degraded to a den—
a grotto.

No fear, no blush, no tears, no astonishment, no shame—this is the condition that is behind the walls of the churches who have embraced their culture and turned from God.

> ***Ezra 9:6****—And said, O my God, I am ashamed and blush to lift up my face to thee, my God: for our iniquities are increased over our head, and our trespass is grown up unto the heavens.*

It takes an intercessor to stand in the gap and make up the breach and do it for those who do not. Someone has to call for repentance.

Someone has to see the truth and intercede before the Throne of Mercy for ***"Judgment must first begin at the House of God."***

- ***Recognize***—the problem as it really exists
- ***Remember***—what it was like in the former days of glory
- ***Repent***—for the actions of the past
- ***Return***—to the place from whence you have fallen
- ***Rebuild***—that which is broken down
- ***Restore***—that which is removed
- ***Resist***—the enemy who tries to stop you
- ***Reinstitute***—the Word and Worship

Anything that bears His name will be judged by His righteousness.

2 Chronicles 7:14

If my people, which are called by my name, shall humble themselves, and pray, and seek my face, and turn from their wicked ways; then will I hear from heaven, and will forgive their sin, and will heal their land.

Chapter 33

A Hole in the Wall—Where has the Conviction Gone?

2 Chronicles 16:9

For the eyes of the LORD range throughout the earth to strengthen those whose hearts are fully committed to Him.

We have thoroughly examined the Temple where Ezekiel was taken by the Spirit of God and was shown the condition that was on the inside of, not only the Temple but the people who served and worshipped there. Let's now take a much deeper look at our hearts, individually . . . in these modern times, where we live and worship.

We must ALL be diligent to keep a guard over our own lives that we *hear what the Spirit is saying to the Church.*

There is a lack of conviction in God's House today. There are people that commit sin and walk away from church services unmoved and unchanged by the Glory of God. It appears that anything can go on right in the face of God, while the Spirit of God is moving mightily in the preaching, worship, teaching, prophecy and even rebuke and have people still sit unmoved.

The walls of complacency and indifference to the Holy things of God abound in the church.

The Word goes out over the air waves, over the television, in churches all over our nations and still the lukewarm church is immune to the majority of the Word of God today.

Many of those who fill the church pews have inoculated themselves so thoroughly that they now can resist it all.

Most nations are saturated with the gospel and the churches are more than saturated and yet people are not being changed into the likeness and image of the Lord Jesus Christ. Everywhere we look there is an invading force right into the house of God—worldliness and sinfulness, tolerance and self-justification for all kinds of things that *defy the holiness of God.*

It is as in Ezekiel's day when he was taken to the ***Hole in the Wall*** of the temple and saw the images that were engraved on the walls—*idolatry was not only practiced but posted.* The elders of the temple were committing all kinds of abominations inside the dwelling place of God.

This is the same arrogance of sin that we see today.
Everything is *out of the closet* and *blatant* as Christians practice the same things the world does.

Our own opinions are engraved in our own mind's image—falling far short of the mark of God's glory. We have to fight idolatry all the time. Our thoughts can chisel out all kinds of ways to get to do what we want to the exclusion of what God wants.

Even in the revival movement in a church, ***the shrine to man's opinion is erected for all to bow down to.*** This control is very much idolatry because it is stubbornness in holding onto ideas, even those that oppose God's Word. How can those called by His name sin and seemingly not even feel any quickening of the Spirit of God?" Where is the Conviction that we have been praying for? The Lord answered me this way . . .

"It is lost on a people who have no convictions."

No standards
Not principles

No firm beliefs
No absolutes
No pure doctrine

The lawless nature of our age has crept into the House of God and has eroded the foundations of our convictions.

The church has grown so calloused from sinning without repenting.

Look just within the walls of our own lives and yes, our churches—see the stony, crooked, hard ground of religion.

- ***It is full of weeds*** of man's imaginations and doctrines.
- ***It is full of the compromise*** with the fallen values of the world.
- ***It is full of many choices*** like a shopping mall, filled with many tastes, styles, diversities, all under one roof.
- ***It is full of leaders and people*** who are all now incorporated into a business

The word, ***Corporation*** comes from the root word, ***Corpulent*** which means ***"to have a fat, distended belly."*** This is far from the "***rivers of living water that are supposed to flow out of our bellies."***

We find churches of man's pride and man's throne but void of God's presence and power, filled with people void of understanding of God's higher ways and thoughts, indiscriminately meandering their way through the maze of beliefs and concepts that now fill the bellies of the churches people.

Where is the Spirit of God?
Where is the Conviction?

He is still powerful and totally capable of storming our bank, but He would like for the Church to let Him in because they are listening to His cry to *"come to Jesus, to repent, to prepare . . ."*

Many have allowed God to go deep and cleanse so much and are still willing, *if necessary*, to have God go deeper still.

Oh, yes, the cry for a heaven-sent revival in the church and lives still comes from many who have been gripped with the urgency of the hour. Many have laid their lives out before the Lord in deep repentance and now try with all their heart to live right before their God.

And, many, like Ezekiel, know the hardness of the ground of the church world and its people and wonder if godly sorrow and repentance will enter in upon the people of the House.

- ***You are wondering***, possibly if there is ever going to be a time when God shakes the house with His Holy Spirit's presence.
- ***You are wondering*** when the fire is really going to fall.
- ***You are wondering*** when the river will flood the banks of your shores and wash away the slime and mire of shore living.

Revival is God expressing His deepest desire to take His church back from the hands of man, get Jesus in the door, past all the stuff, to the deep places and cleanse the house.

God has been moving towards His Church now for years, working to repair the damage that the years of neglect and waywardness has done to His Son's Bride.

2 Chronicles 7:14

If my people, which are called by my name, shall humble themselves, and pray, and seek my face, and turn from their wicked ways; then will I hear from heaven, and will forgive their sin, and will heal their land.

Chapter 34

Broken Cisterns

Jeremiah 2:13

For my people have committed two evils; they have forsaken me the fountain of living waters, and hewed them out cisterns, broken cisterns, that can hold no water.

The first mention of a door in the Bible is with a warning to Cain who was harboring jealousy and murder in his heart against his brother's sacrifice. God spoke to him saying, "*If you will do well Cain, would you not be accepted? And if you do not do well, sin is laying at the threshold of the door of your life.*" *(Gen 4:7)*

Strong's describes ***door*** as an opening, a gate or entrance way. We all have doors for entrance into our lives. God, in Revelation 3, is telling the church at Philadelphia that He had set before them a door that no man can shut.

What an opportunity for a person or a church to hear this from God—to know that He has opened a door, a point of access into His Will for them.

But we all know that, even if a door is open, we have to choose to go through the opening God has made for us. It does no good to hear of an open door, identify where the door is and then just sit there and observe the door.

A God-Door is for entering into.

Many times that door is an open door for the opportunity to intercede into a situation. And there is a door of opportunity for a visitation of God in our lives, churches and nations. But, it is all entered into by prayer.

We have entered *The Season of the Door,* in which there is *The Opportunity of the Door,* in which people would choose to either let God Spirit in to move or to shut Him out and stay unyielding and unchanged.

I have oftentimes wondered how long God is going to contend with His people, His church, to see them return to Him, rending their hearts before Him in humility and repentance. I know, according to God's written Word that a season can end with God shutting the door of opportunity.

- ***Queen Esther*** had only a short door of opportunity to do what God told her to do.
- ***Gideon*** has a time frame in which he was to do what God has commanded of him.
- ***The demise of Jericho*** was timed to the minute in what was to happen.
- ***The Children of Israel*** lost their door of opportunity.
- ***Lot and his family*** had only a very small door in which to get out of Sodom and Gomorrah.
- ***The world in Noah's day*** had only a certain time to get on board with God's Plan of escape.
- ***And we***, as the denominational church of today have only our generation in which to get on board with God's plan for the Church.

While many do not wish to consider that God will judge His church, we must believe the word of the Lord in His Holy Scriptures.

> ***1 Peter 4:17****—For the time is come that judgment must begin at the house of God: and if it first begin at us, what shall the end be of them that obey not the gospel of God?*

I know God's heart and faithfulness has been to allow time for response from His church and from individuals within the church. This is really scary because many have whiled away their days of God's grace in this matter.

In many cases, it is not as if most Christians don't know, but it is a truth that many have rejected it.

We must keep going through the door of opportunity to keep praying the heart and will of God and that we pour out of the depths of our hearts in intercession into the right places of the church, our city, nation and the nations of the world.

Generic Prayers simply won't do when there are issues hanging on the closing curtain of time.

We must put our prayers where and how God wants them. I believe it is going to take a lot of discernment in the season ahead to know where and how to target our prayers. Only Holy Spirit will know how to conduct the prayer meetings of this very important season.

So much is hinging upon our being able to hear and obey to use the time allotted us to the Glory of God and for His purpose, that all He desires to be done will be accomplished in our seasons of intercession.

The River of God has flowed with a great abundance into our season of renewal all over the world, but, tragically, much of the secularized church world has either turned a deaf ear or flat out refused entrance.

What an impact this has had on the entire world.

The seasoning of the church, the influence, the salt, the light that is shed upon the nation through righteousness has an incredible influence.

Here's the disconcerting part:

The nominal, religious church that has grown cold in their passion for truth, having become tolerant of "other ways," the gatekeeper to the nations, have abandoned the responsibility to stand guard over the spiritual values of the nations.

Look at this soul-searching scripture:

> ***Jeremiah 2:11-13*** (Emphasis Added)
>
> *11 Hath a nation* ***changed*** (alter, barter, dispose of) *their gods, which are yet no gods? But my people have changed their glory for that which* ***doth not profit*** *(can do no good, no benefit).*
>
> *12* ***Be astonished,*** (stunned, stupefied, devastated) *O ye heavens, at this, and* ***be horribly afraid,*** (shiver in fear) ***be ye very desolate,*** (parched through drought, laid waste*) saith the LORD.*
>
> *13 For my people have committed two evils; they have forsaken me the fountain of living waters, and* ***hewed them out*** (dug) ***cisterns*** (a pit; well*),* ***broken*** *(*crushed, shattered, crippled, wrecked) ***cisterns, that can hold no water.***

We need to really look closely at what this portion of scripture contains: God says man has changed his glory for that which does not profit. The cry is for the heavens to be astonished and horribly afraid and very desolate because God's people, *those called by His name*, have committed two evils. They have . . .

1. ***Forsaken the fountain*** of living waters
2. ***Dug for themselves pits*** that are so broken they can hold no water.

Even if God wanted to send an outpouring of His Holy Spirit, where would it be stewarded and not lost? This would be like asking God to send the fire when no altar has been built and no sacrifice has been prepared.

It will never happen.
God simply does not put the Living Water into any old man-made pit.

The typology of ***"Digging their cistern,"*** and ***"Swamp Land for Jesus,"*** is offensive to God. There are places that are not prepared to hold what God is doing.

- ***These cisterns*** are described in the Bible as unable to hold water because they are broken.
    - o They represent "*man's efforts,*" by use of the word, "*hewn out.*"
- ***The Marshes***, because they are nothing but pits filled with stagnant water in which serpents and other such creatures live, are not fit for the river of God.
    - o They represent sin.

The tragedy of the home-made, home-dug cisterns is that they will never hold what God wants to do in His church, His ministers and the lives of His people.

2 Timothy 3:1-5 (Emphasis Added)

1 This know also, that in the last days perilous times shall come.

2 For men shall be lovers of their own selves, covetous, boasters, proud, blasphemers, disobedient to parents, unthankful, unholy,

3 Without natural affection, trucebreakers, false accusers, incontinent, fierce, despisers of those that are good,

4 Traitors, heady, high-minded, lovers of pleasures more than lovers of God;

5 ***Having a form of godliness****, but* ***denying the power thereof****: from such turn away.*

- **Form**—appearance; formula

The natural consequence of creating ***a formula*** void of true godliness is the loss of power to live in true godliness. Man cannot turn to his own ***formulas*** and have the power to make any change that can please God.

Man's ways please man but sicken the LORD.

> ***Exodus 20:25*** (Emphasis Added)—*And if thou wilt make me an altar of stone, thou* ***shalt not build it of hewn stone:*** *for if thou lift up thy tool upon it, thou hast polluted it.*

Oh we really do see the heart of God in this verse—He is so opposed to our own tools shaping anything about His altar. He plainly reveals His heart in this matter, that if a tool is used to shape a stone for the altar, it will be considered polluted.

> ***Ezekiel 47:11*** (Emphasis Added)—*But the* ***miry places*** (Swamp; Marsh) *thereof and* ***the marshes*** (Pit, Cistern) *thereof shall not be healed; they shall be given to salt.*

God wants to heal our broken lives and fill us to overflowing with the Holy Spirit. He wants to be able to flow out of our lives, but we have to let God dig the well; prepare our hearts to contain what He wants to pour in.

It was the day of the water libation. Jesus stood among those who had gathered to see the water poured out. Scripture tells us that onn the last day of that great feast day Jesus stood and cried, saying, ***"If any man thirst, let him come unto me, and drink. He that believeth on me, as the scripture hath said, out of his belly shall flow rivers of living water."*** (John 7:37-38)

Jesus stood there that day offering living water to everyone who heard—and still, yet, His voice echoes down through the ages from the pages of scripture. And still, yet, today, many walk away to their own cisterns filled with the stagnant water of living life in a pit.

Some heard Jesus call out years ago as He began to visit His Church around the nations of the world. What a great outpouring of the River of God for those who drank deep of the things of the Spirit. So many do not believe in the River and yet . . .

The Word of God speaks clearly that The River of God flows from the Throne of God into the Temple and over the Threshold to the City.

- ***The River*** did not come from someone's broken cistern—it came from the fount everlasting.
- ***The River*** did not flow from someone's pit dug from a miry place—It came from the Father.
- ***The River*** was not muddy, stagnant water—it was Living Water.
- ***The River is the Holy Ghost—John 7:39***

Are we not the Temple of the Holy Ghost?

Should not the River of God, the Holy Ghost, flow from the Throne of God into our Spirits and over the threshold of our lives into the city?

My husband, Loren Dummer said this: *"A church can desire revival and have a pastor who does not* ***and*** *a pastor can desire revival and a church who does not, but* ***until*** *both pastor and church desires revival—****until*** *the two are joined together in hunger;* ***until*** *the two are joined together in repentance;* ***until*** *the two are joined together in prayer;* ***until*** *the two are agreed to* ***'Give God back His Church;'*** ***until*** *the two are joined together in unity of purpose;* ***there can be no revival in <u>that</u> church.***

<u>What is the Lord finding in His Church today?</u>

The broken wells are the broken church and broken ministry and broken people who are so busy digging their own cisterns that God is left out of the picture.

It's not that there has been no outpouring of God's Spirit, or that He hasn't contended with His Church to open the door and let Him inside to move and work—*Oh He's tried.*

But to God the condition of the church is unacceptable to Him to place His Spirit to co-exist with compromise, worldliness and sin.

We all remember the early days of revival in which the altars were filled with as many repenting ministers of the gospel as there were congregants. Repentance must once again *sweep* the house. This is the quality of God's double-edged sword in revival—it strikes at the heart of both the ministry and the congregation.

If God is to get His Church back, He must target both.

Some say, "*Isn't this too harsh a word, not very loving—would Jesus actually come on strong like this?*" I've said it before and will say it again, "*we must paint sin in the worst possible light, because that is how it appears to God.*"

God is speaking of the sign of the dead, last days church,

> ***Revelation 3:1***— . . . *I know thy works, that thou hast a name that thou livest, and art dead.*

Some may say, "*God loves His church and all is well,*" but do we really understand the grief we cause Him.

- ***Men,*** suppose you has purchased with hard-earned money, a brand new, much desired vehicle. Now suppose you saw someone come up to your vehicle and start taking the motor apart, rewiring the dashboard, removing some of the finer details you loved and changed the tires from special wheels and hubcaps and special ordered tread—how would you feel?
- ***Women***, suppose you had just got a new home, the dream house you had waited and saved for until you could purchase it. Now suppose someone came in and started ripping up the carpets, plugging the plumbing, spray painting the walls and removing your furnishings—how would you feel?
- ***Youth/children***, how would you feel if the special thing you had worked and saved to purchase was suddenly taken over by someone and crushed under foot or beaten with a baseball bat in front of you—how would you feel?

I imagine a good number of responses are developing in your minds and hearts as you consider how you would feel: Angry, sickened, shocked, sad . . . and yet we think God is okay with what we have done to His House—Our bodies, His Church?

Oh how God must feel grief and nausea when that which was purchased with His Son's own blood has been taken apart, rearranged, defiled and broken . . . and we can say, *"He doesn't feel sickened at heart by what He sees?"*

We must open our spiritual eyes, our heart and ears and listen to what the Spirit of God is saying. He is not saying anything this time that He has not already said before. In the Revelation of Jesus Christ, He speaks this phrase ***7 times***—*"He that hath an ear, let him hear what the Spirit saith unto the churches,"* plus in the book of Matthew, ***3 times,*** echoed in Mark and Luke. Matt 11:15; Matt 13:9; Matt 13:43

Does Jesus Christ have a valid claim to cry out,
"Give Me back *My* church?"
Yes! He owns the House!

2 Chronicles 7:14

If my people, which are called by my name, shall humble themselves, and pray, and seek my face, and turn from their wicked ways; then will I hear from heaven, and will forgive their sin, and will heal their land.

CHAPTER 35

IT'S HIS HOUSE

Matthew 5:14-16

Ye are the light of the world. A city that is set on a hill cannot be hid. Neither do men light a candle, and put it under a bushel, but on a candlestick; and it giveth light unto all that are in the house. Let your light so shine before men, that they may see your good works, and glorify your Father which is in heaven.

My husband and I have had so much going on in our spirits concerning the church—our church—all churches.

- ***Ours*** because of what God has placed on our shoulders and our deepening responsibility to see our mandate through to the fulfillment of the destiny that God designed for us and the harvest of souls that are at stake.
- ***Others*** because of the burden of our heart and our deepening concern for the condition of the churches and the lost destiny and the lost harvest.

I know that many know a lot about the condition of the church world of our cities and beyond but have not fully taken hold of God's heart and vision for His Church.

We still see through the lens of our own ideas, religion and experience so much—and even our revival patterns.

We have called the people of our church and prayer gatherings together many times to pray for the churches, leadership and congregations worldwide. We do not pray in a sense of *having arrived* at some elevated place above others, but we have prayed from the position of recognizing our own need as well. I know we are not alone for I hear a sound that has risen to the heavenlies. Great intercession is going up from all over the nations—that God will awaken our hearts and the heart of the church in this hour—for great darkness is rising to put her lights out.

I had a dream Saturday, February 7, 2009, about 5:30 a.m. With this dream, I gained some understanding as to what God was speaking to me.

- ***I know*** God was speaking about intercession for the ministry and the church.
- ***I know*** God is speaking about individual and corporate purity and preparation for the season we are in.

I also felt that God is strongly impressing upon us to take our mandate and the time we have to prepare very seriously . . . In spite of the storm clouds that are gathering and rolling in over nation of the world, we are still too much at ease.

In this dream, my husband and I were in a house *(church)* **that was not ours** . . .

I knew that it represented the church and I also knew that whatever went on in the house represented what goes on in the church. I knew the house was unclean, not as in untidy, but as in sinful. I saw a man in the house down a hallway, facing the wall and bent forward as if peering into the wall, like in travail. This man was obese and balding. He was seeking a vision of what is coming to the United States of America. I then see through his eyes that everything he sees has a blood wash over it, turning everything red. He then prophesies that in one year *all will be well*, that *the crisis will be over.*

> ***Jeremiah 6: 14***—*You can't heal a wound by saying it's not there! Yet the priests and prophets give assurances of peace when all is war. TLB* [4]

He seemed to be oblivious to the obvious—the blood representing the crisis of the people involved in this nation.

While he is declaring his vision, I hear a siren and a phone ring. I then hear an airplane flying overhead. The voice on the telephone tells me that the USA is under attack and that a nuclear bomb is going to be dropped.

I then rush to a room down that hall into which I look. It goes down about three to four steps, as if it is a shallow basement. I see the whole room is made of concrete, like a bomb shelter . . . but I see a regular bedroom window on the wall, in essence opening anyone taking shelter to nuclear fallout. There is absolutely nothing in this shelter. I see shelves and closets but all are empty I am suddenly overwhelmed by the facts that *there has been no preparation for this moment.* I hear the drone of the plane overhead, emphasizing it is too late.

The feeling of not being ready is intensifying because I realize there is no time left for them to prepare. I inventory all that would be needed to get the place ready and no one knows where anything is, nothing has been purchased to put in place, there has been no thought for the reality of this moment ever coming.

Time has run out.

The *feeling* of this dream woke me up. I then tried in my waking time to furnish the room and realized that every turn I made there was something else that was needed.

As I pondered this dream, my mind went to the man who prophesied falsely, though it was clear to him that there was going to be great bloodshed, I asked God, who is this man?

Instantly I heard the LORD say, *"Eli."*

I knew this man in my dream was the ministry of the church. I knew that though he saw the right picture, he did not declare the truth. I told my husband the dream and what I felt the LORD impressed on me about the man being ***"Eli."*** He spoke into that saying, ***"Eli is the ministry that does***

not want to deal with the sin in the church because if he does he will lose his paycheck and position."

Years ago when God began to move upon His church, bringing a revival of repentance and return, there were those that desired to be a part of what God was doing, but drew back because of the cost. Many churches that embraced the move of God were battled from the inside by people leaving the church and withdrawing support. This brought about almost overnight a reduction of membership and loss of support for the church.

Many weathered through those rough days of deep sacrifice and others said, "*This ship is just too big to turn around.*" That was the attitude of those who met Jesus at the door of the Temple when He desired entrance and change and consequently many "*woes*" were pronounced on them ***(Matthew 23).***

Eli was negligent of his call to rule his house well and sadly, it overlapped into the ministry. His sons were left to their vices and judgment came upon the whole house.

So what was the cause of the failure of Eli that resulted in the removal of the Glory of God?

We just need to look back a bit and see. Eli had been warned by God not only by Samuel, but by a prophetic voice before and had given no heed to the seriousness of the word. He sat on it, doing nothing to make the needed changes in order to comply with God's desire for His House. We read in ***1 Samuel 3:11-1,*** God telling Eli that God was going to judge his household for the iniquity which he knew about, *because his sons had made themselves vile and he had not restrained them.*

Eli was in leadership.
On his watch, sin had become a way of life for his sons.

From that point forward we can see the sequential things that began to unfold as God dealt with the disobedience and tolerance of Eli. We see in ***1 Samuel 4:11-15*** the beginning of sorrows upon Eli's house.

1. The Ark of God was taken, *(meaning the presence of the Lord was removed);*
2. Eli's heart began to tremble because of the Ark being taken *(meaning the full measure of awareness had come to Eli as he realized he had blown it)*;
3. And now that he was old, his eyes were dim and he could not see.

    a. When we read the word, ***"blind"*** in Jesus' letter to the Laodicea church in Revelation 3, we see it means, ***"Morally blind."***
    b. When you ***"choose not to see,"*** eventually you no longer can see.
    c. This results in self-deception.

Moral blindness no longer sees the compromise that has entered the House of God.

In a time when Eli's family should be welcoming new life into their family, it was sadly the end of Eli and his two sons and a daughter-in-law's life. Phinehas' wife was with child ***(1 Samuel 4:19-22)*** and ready to be delivered when she heard the Ark of God was taken. She bowed herself and travailed and delivered a son. She, in recognizing the Glory was departed from Israel, named her son, Ichabod and then she died.

What a sad story indeed but folks, it's more than that; it's a picture beyond Israel's history during the time of the Eli priesthood. Looking at this for our time, being as we are kings and priests unto God ***(Revelation 5:10)*** and being as Jesus is the Ark of His Presence in the church, we can see a danger. Jesus is seen in Revelation ***standing outside the Laodiceans door***, knocking to get back in so He can fellowship with His church.

> ***Revelation 3:20****—Behold, I stand at the door, and knock: if any man hear my voice, and open the door, I will come in to him, and will sup with him, and he with me.*

This has always been seen as a nice little picture of a gentle Jesus standing patiently outside the door of our hearts, asking to come in and have tea with us. But that is not the picture depicted in the scripture. Jesus is addressing the Laodicea church, the Lukewarm Church—one that was at one time on fire for Him.

What is He doing outside?
It's His House!

My husband, Pastor Loren Dummer, gave a prophetic word concerning Judgment and the Church on May 5, 2006. I believe it is still a timely word for the church, in keeping with the heart of God.

I heard the Lord say a moment ago prophetically to the churches, ***"His knocking is soon to cease, and it shall change to judgment, and then if they don't respond to his judgment that Ichabod*** (meaning, The Glory has departed) ***will be written over their door and He will move to the next place."*** *That is not to the churches that haven't heard. It is to those places that God has tried to move in and break upon, that have resisted and resisted and hold to their own ways.*

I felt this very strongly—people think judgment doesn't come till after the rapture. No, judgment is a part of grace. That's scary to me. That's scary to me. But God is not willing that any should perish, and He will do everything it takes. But when man says ***"I'm going to do it my way,"*** *when he says that, and resists and does it his way, that's the same thing as saying no to God. That's exactly the same thing as saying no to God. You know what that is, it is the same thing as flagrant open rebellion.*

So it's a serious time. God isn't going to continue on this way with His church. There comes a time when a change comes.

We're entering a season of change, a season of transition in the Church—A season of change of the manifest presence of God.

There's going to be something's that's significant that's going to happen that's going to mark those that have been faithful.

As it was in the book of Ezekiel, the Lord is sending His angels to mark those that sigh and cry for His people.

He has been watching;
He has been taking notes as it were.
He has been very aware of everything that has been taking place, and who has been faithful.

Even though they have struggled, even though at times they have fallen, even though at times they have felt like giving up, He has watched them and watched them, and watched them, as they got up and got up and got up and continued moving and continued going forward. He has not been oblivious of those things.

- *It has been His Spirit that has picked you up when you have fallen.*
- *It has been His breath that has blown into you when you felt you had no breath left.*
- *It has been His water that has washed you, when you felt you were overloaded with the dust of this world.*

It has been MY Spirit says the Lord that has led you onward and you have been diligent; You have been faithful. You have been yielded. You have been pliable.

I have been shaking you. I have been making you. I have been leading you. And yes, I have been calling you. And you have heard my voice. And you have yielded to my call.

But I say to you, I say to My church, I say to you all: Things are about to change. They shall not always be like they were. Transition is about to take place. It's about time for the sickle that I thrust into the harvest field. The time of playing games is coming to an end.

I am serious about this hour.
I am serious about My Church.
I am serious about those I will use.
And I am serious about those who have rejected Me and My ways.

My time is coming at hand. Harvest is coming upon you. The season that you have been in: the season of dancing in the rain, the season of playing in My presence is coming to an end, and it's a season of work. A season of hard labor, a season of fruitfulness, a season of My joy that you have not known or xperienced before. It shall be as the one that found the lamb and gave a party and rejoiced over one sinner that was saved.

There shall be joy in the camp once again.
There shall be joy in My house once again.

Not the natural joy of the flesh, but the joy of the Spirit when they see people set free, and the power of God is unleashed and burdens are broken, and the sick are healed. Those things shall begin to come forth in My church, in those faithful places, through those faithful people saith the Lord.

The hour of transition is soon to be upon my church, and things are about to change.

~End of Prophecy~

There comes a time when the House of God goes dark as the heart of leaders and God's people goes dark with sin. This condition is a serious issue in the day and time as surely as it was in days gone by.

God has called to us to pray for the church because time is running out. Oh, I know, to some this sounds so "*doomsday* . . ." I do is what is mine to do—release the Word and allow people to respond in the same way generations before us have had opportunity. It is my prayer that many will receive the *wake-up call* and stir their hearts to the ***S.O.S. of the Lord*** who is so gracious and merciful to give us forewarnings.

The dream, which I have no doubt was spiritual, left me with the feeling that ***we had better knuckle down*** and take things we are coming into ***very seriously.***

The spiritual emergency is that few realize there is an emergency.

I know that we believe we know a lot about the condition of the church of our city and beyond but have we truly got hold of and embraced God's heart and vision for His Church? Do we really see it the way He sees it?

The greatest desire of God, the lover of our soul, is that His people would wash their garments, inwardly, and become that chaste bride, without spot or wrinkle or any such thing.

~2 Corinthians 11:2; Eph 5:26-27~

God loves the church but He does not love her sin.

God cannot help but judge the church for her sin *(meaning those who are called by His name)* if she will not repent—because He is Holy, Just and True.

> ***1 Peter 4:17-18***
>
> *17 For the time is come that judgment must begin at the house of God: and if it first begin at us, what shall the end be of them that obey not the gospel of God?*
>
> *18 And if the righteous scarcely be saved, where shall the ungodly and the sinner appear?*

A spirit of toleration for just about everything has invaded the Church to the detriment of Truth.

The church today has made the word, "*Judge*" sound harsh and unloving, *judgmental*—but when God says this to us, He is saying He will personally measure, test and judge what is contained within His House. ***Matthew 21:12-13*** It is His House and He has the right to enter in upon the threshold of His House and take inventory.

We have the choice of fierce judgment in the end *or* sweet judgment today as we obey.

When a business or church has someone serve as steward over the finances, they have expectations that this person will not treat that money as if it is their own. They have the right to ask for an accountant to come in and run the books to discover the handling and integrity of the funds. They have the right to bring to justice anyone who embezzles the funds, and even turn them over to the law as a criminal. There is no toleration for such conduct because they used and abused their position as steward of what did not belong to them.

God says He is coming to His House to judge her *first* . . . why? Because it's *HIS HOUSE* and it must be in order!

Solomon built a physical House of God, putting in place the natural elements, carefully, according to plan, and then the Glory of God filled the House. Unfortunately for Israel, *(those who worshipped in the House of God),* they allowed sin to enter into their own hearts and ultimately their worship of God was deeply and adversely impacted. They failed to keep themselves separate from the world, allowed intermarriage into the heathen world, and adopted the gods of the heathen, keeping pace with the evolution of their society.

The morality of their nation slipped into debauchery with the practice of the world's religions and gods, as *their tolerance* for the ***other gospels and other ways and other gods*** became ***an enlightened way of life for them.***

The rationalization the church world today is using to adopt the *world-view of religion* is the same as it has ever been.

- ***Lot*** and his family in Sodom learned to mesh in with the degraded and corrupt community they lived in—to their own hurt and spiritual decline.
- ***Lot*** had gained *a sort of mocked acceptance*, which was short-lived when he would not send the angels out to the town's people.
- ***Lot*** began to realize that *you* either sell out to the faithless generation that you live in—or *you* sell out to God.

There comes a time the Church has to make a choice—when the ***human rationalization*** of our faith ***comes face to face with a Living God.*** We are entering such a time as this.

Isaiah 55:7-9

7 Let the wicked forsake his way, and the unrighteous man his thoughts: and let him return unto the LORD, and he

> *will have mercy upon him; and to our God, for he will abundantly pardon.*
>
> *8 For my thoughts are not your thoughts, neither are your ways my ways, saith the LORD.*
>
> *9 For as the heavens are higher than the earth, so are my ways higher than your ways, and my thoughts than your thoughts.*

God has drawn a line *in the sand of our lives and churches*, so to speak. Choices will be made as God deals with the mixtures integrated into His church. God always sends forth a call for humility and repentance. I believe that call is presently going forth. Are we listening?

Once again, this is the spiritual emergency of the hour—people are adjusting, but not repenting.

This is the grossest of errors because it ***circumvents the Cross*** and helps to ***keep us justified by our own actions.***

- ***I believe*** the alarm has sounded in the heart and soul of ***individuals*** and many are hearing what the Spirit of God is saying.
- ***I believe*** the alarm has been sounded to ***collective body of believers***_where things have not been right in the church. God has raised a voice to declare truth and righteousness, calling His church to repentance.
- ***I believe*** God has spoken to many ***churches*** to open their doors to His Holy Spirit ***(Zechariah 4:6b)*** and let Him move upon the hearts of the Church, touching a people with Truth and the Power of God on earth.

***I believe* that God has spoken to His Church—and that He has come to *cleanse His Temple*—even at a time when everyone is looking for God's Glory to *fill His Temple* once again.**

God's Glory responds to what goes on inside the doors of our hearts and yes, inside the doors of the church and ministry—by ***drawing close*** or ***drawing back***.

God is dealing with people—one on one—and individuals know, in their heart of hearts, that they are not right with God. The Holy Spirit of God is faithful to speak, to bring people to the place of repentance for their personal and hidden sins.

- ***I believe*** that the warnings, the urgings, the call to repentance must and will increase as time goes on, if the church does not respond appropriately.

Many calls to repentance, calls to humility, calls to separation, calls to return to God—have sounded into the ears of multitudes of believers.

- ***I believe*** God has spoken to some that "something is coming that will shake the church world, pastors and people" if there is no repentance for the sin in the church.

We think we have seen into the problem in the church, but folks, we haven't seen anything yet as to what is readily visible to God. He sees things that would shock us all. And He is not pleased with what He sees.

We must always look into our own hearts, churches, lives and homes as we look at the world to assess their shameful conduct. Oh how we can talk about the sins of our nation while ignoring the sins of the church! Things in our nation are in a decline of a caliber that many can never recall a day such as this—nationally and in the churches condition. Other nations have fallen into oblivion for sins similar to what is going on behind closed doors.

My husband shared an illustration to show a point he was trying to make. He drew a line representing the world and inches above that he drew another line representing the church.

He spoke of how in the past the church always carried a standard that was significantly above the worlds so everyone knew the difference that existed.

He then re-drew the world's line in a down-hill decline and asked where the church was now. He then demonstrated a startling point by drawing the churches line exactly above the world's line, in other words, also on a down-hill slope, but *still* above the world. The error of being just slightly above a declining world standard is misleading and can bring us into deception.

We make the world our standard instead of Jesus Christ who *is never* in a decline.

> ***Hebrews 13:8***—*Jesus Christ, the same yesterday and today and forever.*
>
> ***Malachi 3:6a***—*For I am the Lord, I change not . . .*

As I stood there and listened to these people, they were already, that many years ago, talking about the church which was beginning to accept so much of the world's philosophy and make some drastic changes in her structure to accommodate *a more modern society.*

I had even heard from *Christians* at that time say *"this is the '90's now and things have changed,"* thereby excusing themselves in their new-found freedoms that they were experiencing. I don't believe that kind of statement is relegated to any time particular in history; I believe people have had a tendency to *update their faith* to match the year's culture and values in which they live.

We must search for truth from within the House of God as to how this level of decline in the churches of the nations could have happened under the watchful eyes of the church.

I am 64 years old and have spent my whole life in church. I spent the first 21 years as a preacher's daughter; the next 7 years as a deacon's wife and the last 36 years in full-time ministry with my husband. I have seen some things in the church and it has not all been lovely or kind.

Yes, I know there are good things in the church—its benefits to the community, its faith, its foundation, the fact that it preaches the Word of God, the people in it who love the Lord, and more, ***but that is not what an inspection is for***. We must search for the deeper things—the hidden stuff in the closet and sometimes that which is laying right in plain view for anyone who cares to see.

There comes a time when we tolerate or excuse something for so long there is no more shame attached to it.

We have to realize that we have possibly accepted things that are no okay with God and even worse are blatant sin being openly practiced amongst those who say they are Christians. It is like the videos of the past—people would rent some they knew they should not rent and keep it secret what they had begun to watch in the privacy of their homes. It wasn't long though until those same movies were displayed for anyone to see in the entertainment centers of our homes.

When shame has ceased, there is a sin that has become normal and accepted with all stigma removed.

> ***Jeremiah 6:15-17***
>
> *15 Were they ashamed when they had committed abomination? nay, they were not at all ashamed, neither could they blush: therefore they shall fall among them that fall: at the time that I visit them they shall be cast down, saith the Lord.*
>
> *16 Thus saith the Lord, Stand ye in the ways, and see, and ask for the old paths, where is the good way, and walk therein, and ye shall find rest for your souls. But they said, We will not walk therein.*
>
> *17 Also I set watchmen over you, saying, Hearken to the sound of the trumpet. But they said, We will not hearken.*

Can we just stop right here and make a fresh commitment to listen to the Lord, to give heed to His Word?

The greatest cry of Jesus at the end of each of His letters to the seven churches in Revelation was, *"He who has an ear, let him hear what the Spirit says to the churches."* Jesus spoke the same word to his disciples.

I am willing to look long and hard at what is wrong within the House of God and remove all the make-up so we can see things as they truly have become. How we need to be transparent before our God! And may we embrace a cloak of humility as we open our hearts to become real before our God!

Here are some of the things I have seen *(and I know you have too . . .)*:

- ***I have seen*** cancers of pride of place and position, rank and money;
- ***I have seen*** pastors abuse the people, manipulating and controlling them;
- ***I have seen*** the dark days of church splits and division;
- ***I have seen*** false prophets come in dressed in sheep's clothing, bringing in deception;
- ***I have watched*** as the fire of God has gone out of the life of His people and they have settled into mediocre living;
- ***I have watched*** as worship died and words from people's lips but not their hearts replaced the sounds of praise;
- ***I have watched*** as the congregations dwindled due to lack of interest if there was something else that was more exciting;
- ***I have watched*** as the Word of God was preached hitting the resistant hearts of people who no longer wanted truth;
- ***I have watched*** as the altars have been removed from the House of God, no longer used as everything was shuffled to a closed place out of sight;
- ***I have watched*** as programs were passed off for the power and Spirit of God;
- ***I have watched*** as the things of the world have entered into the homes of God's people until you cannot tell the difference between the worldly and the godly;

The years of history tells you a lot about the church.

There is a little story of a couple of people who decided to play a joke on a friend. They snuck some Limburger cheese *(stinky cheese)* into the pocket of their friend's jacket. When he got ready to leave and slipped his coat on, he sniffed the air and said, *"Something stinks in here."* He walked to the door and said, *"Something stinks here too."* He then went outside and sniffed the air and said, *"The whole world stinks."* Friends, he had failed to notice it was he who stunk. Sometimes it is we who stink and blame other things around us for the fouled air we breathe.

Something is very wrong when there is no admission, much less recognition, that it is the Limburger cheese in our own pockets that stinks.

- ***Maybe it's time*** we quit telling each other the church is in beautiful shape, beautifully dressed.
- ***Maybe it's time*** we quit going on with life as usual, without the garment of the righteousness, naked, as the Lord spoke to Laodicea in ***Revelation 3:17-18.***

Her message cannot be heard by the city because of her shamelessness.

I know a lot of people will say that this is not true about *their church*, but it is true about *the church*, as it has been spiritually neutered by the worldliness and carnality that has moved like a tidal wave of unrighteousness.

And folks, it never hurts to ask God to search us for what we may be blind to . . .

Where is Jesus in all that is going on in His name? Ask God, He will tell you the truth! The church of today looks nothing like the bright, pure, and spotless and unwrinkled bride that Jesus is coming back for. The garments are soiled with the world's filth and this is what we are expecting Jesus to accept at His return?

We are in a spiritual decline, yes, even in the midst of a visitation of God's Holy Spirit—and if there is not a proper response to Holy Spirit and obedience to the Word, God will increase the weight of His hand pressing upon His church, just before He truly presses the nations by the weight of His hand.

The Church cannot hide from God, nor can she *have it her way.*

- He sees behind every closed door, into every heart and mind of the ministry and the believers that regularly attend church, those who claim to be called by His name.

He knows things we don't yet know that must be dealt with according to Truth. I just don't think we know how grievous sin is to God. Yes, the alarms have been going off, but greater alarms and warnings are yet to sound because God is going to reveal the heart of His Church in days ahead if she doesn't humble herself and repent.

All it would take is a healthy dose of Godly Fear, Humility and a Righteous wave of Conviction and Repentance to turn things around and see God's Spirit consuming the nations with His Righteousness.

The House could be instantly cleansed if only God's people feared Him!

> ***Malichi 1:6a***—*A son honors his father and a servant his master: if then I be a father, where is mine honor? And if I be a master, where is my fear, saith the LORD of hosts unto you . . . ?*

God will draw a line of choice which will divide His church—because of sin. No one will be able to escape the scrutiny of God's eyes. He will separate between the vile and pure, the holy and profane.

> ***Ezekiel 44:23***—*And they shall teach my people the difference between the holy and profane, and cause them to discern between the unclean and the clean.*

He will split His house wide open and eradicate what is wrong—either through repentance or through judgment. Those who have ears to hear and eyes to see and hearts to pray—it is time to intercede on an emergency level. But know this—***to those who still blush and cry out to God for His people***—He will reveal things on a deeper level yet.

Repentance of the Church/believers is the prerequisite of Revival and national change in any society, in any time or era comes as a result of that.

The key to open the door to Jesus is *still, yet and always* in the hands of the church.

> ***Revelation 3:7-8*** (Emphasis Added)—*And to the angel of the church in Philadelphia write; These things saith he that is holy, he that is true, he that hath the key of David, he that opens, and no man shuts; and shuts, and no man opens; I know thy works: behold,* ***I have set before thee an open door, and no man can shut it:*** *for thou hast a little strength, and hast kept my word, and hast not denied my name.*

2 Chronicles 7:14

If my people, which are called by my name, shall humble themselves, and pray, and seek my face, and turn from their wicked ways; then will I hear from heaven, and will forgive their sin, and will heal their land.

CHAPTER 36

GOD WATCHES

Proverbs 15:3

The eyes of the Lord are in every place, beholding the evil and the good.

When God looks upon the earth, mankind and the church—what does He see?

Oh, He sees it all and He misses nothing. He sees the depth of the heart in everyone and everything. God has always seen into the heart of mankind, much deeper than man can conceive. He sees every nuance, thought, plan and device that is being conceived in the mind of humanity. He sees. Nothing is hid from Him. He sees the decaying hearts of humanity bent on self-destruction, on every level. He has looked upon societies like ours before.

Is He shocked?

No, nothing shocks God, but deeply grieves His heart and moved Him long ago to make a way of escape from the inevitable traps and deceptions that became a part of mankind's DNA.

No, He's not shocked as if He were human, but I believe He is amazed that people still don't and won't take the way of escape He's offered them. He's made a way of escape from every place of decline and death, if only . . .

The whirlpool of darkness that engulfs this world, the darkness that the god of this age has cocooned the world in, is sucking people under from all quadrants of life. But, folks the hand stretched down inside of it has been mostly ignored and in many cases hated and despised as man has clamored to have his own way. The drowning masses will grasp at everything but the rescuing hand of Jesus Christ.

That hand is easily reached and yet . . .
People still mock,
Still reject
And
Still die.

No, He's not shocked because He's used to seeing human nature play out before His eyes. He has seen humanity's desire for,

The pleasure of sin,
The immediate,
The temporary
The broad way that leads to destruction . . .

Societies like Noah's and Lot's, Abraham's, Moses' and Jesus' were religious, but idolatrous and evil, espousing every kind of sin as acceptable and tolerated. Nothing is new under the sun, but in these Last Days the level of evil and deception is going to increase until it tries to drown out the Son.

This same poison that invaded the cultures and people groups of times past is still running rampant and unchecked. No nation has escaped. And sadly, the church has not escaped either. Much compromise has entered into the House of God, into the believer's lives, effectively eroding the foundation of faith that once appeared to be in place. But there is an antidote for the poison, the creeping flesh that has overpowered the spirit man.

Thankfully God is in the redemption business.
Thankfully, God not only sees but He also reaches!

There is a powerful, building and continuing move of God right now that is snatching many who are dying, right off the church pews; religiously sincere people who have been sitting in complacency and religious wraps. His hand is also reaching for and pulling those who have never heard that there is a way of escape. He is rescuing those who are steeped in their own brand of superstition and self-worship.

People, by the masses, are entering into the outstretched arms of Jesus.

But, still, the many social indicators of the nations indicate that things are getting worse, rather than better. Even God-mindedness has not brought an end to the national sins that have gripped the nations of the world, because everyone is talking about God but few are embracing Jesus' redeeming power. Your nation, my nation, city by city, is headed for destruction, unless we have an awakening brought about by a work of Holy Spirit, the power of God on earth. People everywhere are praying for revival in the church and an awakening of the lost.

A move of God will come through one of two ways.

Either we repent because we recognize the need to do so, or we will repent the same way Israel did, when crisis and captivity came. The need to repent, while there is time, must be emphasized. If your nation, your country, your city, your village is to escape a crisis, we need as never before, church leaders who will decry the sins and call people to repentance, God's way, with great humility before Him.

On October 14, 2006, Pastor Mark McBride, while leading worship, delivered this message from the heart of God:

"Let out a roar over your people Jesus. Let out a roar over your church oh God. Let out a roar over your pastors Lord. Let out a roar over your people oh God. Let out a Holy Roar oh God. A Holy Roar oh God, for you are the Lion of Judah. You're the Captain of the Hosts; You're the leader of the church. You're the holy and anointed one. You're the sent one Lord. You are the one and only God. Let out a roar oh Lord. Come Lord! Come Lord! Awaken your Church Lord. Breathe the breath again Lord. Come to your Church Lord.

My day is coming says the Lord. My day is coming Church, say the Lord. Make yourself ready. I've told you time and time again, Get ready, get ready. And the day is soon approaching,

My day, it won't' be anybody else's day. It will be My day.

- *It won't be your preacher's day,*
- *It won't be your board member's day,*
- *It won't' be your Sunday school teacher's day,*
- *It won't' be your day,*
- *It will be My day says the Lord.*

My day is coming. Make yourselves ready church. Shake yourself of the things of this world. Shake yourselves of dead, dry religion. Shake yourselves of the world. Shake yourselves of everything that holds you back.

Make yourselves ready, for My day is coming, says the Lord. I will not put up with the junk that I have been putting up with in that day. I will not put up with those that play and pretend and fake it in that day. I will not put up with it.

My day when it comes, you will know it. It will come in both glory and it will come in judgment. It will come in the glorious presence of the Lord, but for many it will be judgment. Make yourselves ready. I will warn you this day, My day is coming. I have prophesied it in my scripture through holy men of God. Believe the Word. Live the Word. Act the Word. Do the Word. And make yourself ready says the Lord. I will no longer put up with the impurity of heart, with the impurity of motive. My day is coming and it shall be My day, says the Lord.

Remarks by Pastor Loren Dummer

*This will be glorious and this will be serious and we need to ask God, **"Give me Your heart, Your burden in this season for the church, that we do not gloat over the glorious things we experience, but that we rejoice in that He passed over us, His judgment did."** Take this as a prayer burden. Set a pattern for purity in the house of God and set a pattern for purity in your home and your space.*

Here are some areas that breakthrough prayer must reach and prevail at the Throne of God:

- **There must be Pastors**—Who will open godly truth to the congregations of believers about repentance, without fear of losing attendance and support.
- **There must be Prophets**—Who will speak a word of truth about a Holy God who is grieved with the weight of the sins of the nations and the arrogance with which they continue to go their own way.
- **There must be Teachers**—Who will, uncompromisingly, share the truth of the Word, in its completeness, raising up a generation of disciples who truly follow Christ.
- **There must be Evangelist**—Who will travel from city to city and enter into the churches that will let them in, to share about the dying masses of humanity, stirring the hearts of the Church to equip for the harvest.
- **There must be Apostles**—Who will enter into the uncharted territories, physically and spiritually, to establish the ground for the church to be raised up in power and authority.
- **There must be Believers**—Who will follow Jesus unashamedly, with passion for Him to the end of the age.

And with all that in place we will see a *Bold Church* rise up *full of the Holy Ghost and Fire,* yielded to God in this hour to work in their cities and regions, harvesting the fields, while there is still time.

The kind of revival that is needed must begin with the obedience of the Body of Christ. It may take a major shaking to stir us to repentance and prayer, or perhaps, we shall simply obey the Spirit's pleading the cause of God before His Church.

The underpinnings of societies are collapsing.

God is talking.

Are we listening?

The earth is heaving and moaning. It is in the pains of labor. Travail is being heard from all quarters of the earth. The cry, "How long Oh God?" pierces the darkness as injustices and martyrdom take their toll.

Parts of the earth are bathed in the blood of the murdered masses. The innocent blood cries out for justice from the soil upon which it has been shed.

We may say that we are civilized, not like the *barbarians* that are slaughtering the innocent citizens of *other* nations, but we have not yet looked into our own heart, past the garments of pride, to see the blood that has been shed in our own nation. The blood of millions of aborted babies cries out for justice.

The calloused, hard-hearted attitude is, *"Am I my brother's keeper?"*

It rings in the ears of God as He watches us turn from our own responsibility for these deaths. He sees and He knows every child that has been destroyed. He holds the nations accountable.

He has seen the altars of Baal before and this is nothing new to Him.

From God's throne, He watches. What does He see? He sees earth's timeline, from its beginning to the present. And humanity has yet to understand a great truth, that in spite of the fact that they feel that they *fly by their own wings*, that God holds the stop watch in His hand.

How long before He says, "Enough?"

How long before He stops humanity in their tracks with one of His alarms?

God watches as evil gets worse, heading full speed into the arms of the Anti-Christ. Idolatry, witchcraft, Satanism, corrupt governments, secret orders that play their games behind closed doors, and, a Cold Church sitting in the middle of it all Marks the end of a society that has gone its own way.

So is there any good news?
"What is with all the dooms-day type of book?" you ask.

Remember? God Watches; He sees other things too, not just the injustice and wicked . . . He sees towers in the middle of the field of harvest. They have been built and positioned carefully to guard this golden grain that is ripe. Upon them sits watchmen.

A closer look reveals that they have been asleep.
God cries, "Awake, Oh Watchman."
There is a thief and a devourer in the fields.
"Awaken!!"

When exactly it happened to each who have heard this call in the past years or just yesterday varies, but the call has been heard. We heard the sound of alarm in the voice of God. There was such urgency with what He was saying to us that we rose up from our sleep and shook the slumber off. Like a sleeping giant the church begin to wake up, stretch her atrophied muscles and flex her muscles. Somewhere, one day, many watchmen all over the world began to stir from their slumber.

Some who were AWOL returned to their post.
New ones, hearing the commissioning cry for the first time, are taking a position.

God's cry for His watchmen to wake up has been heard by a multitude. All around the world, hearts have been stirred with a passion to awaken and fill the gap, get on the wall and upon their face in repentance before their God.

But is it too late?
Have we waited too long?
Look at all the damage that has been done to our society, to our churches, while we were asleep.

But, wait,
We now see.

All around us, *now that we're watching*, we see our families, churches, cities, villages, states, countries—the nations of the world; have been taken by an insidious enemy that has moved systematically stealing, killing and destroying everything in his path.

- ***We see*** a generation of young people who have all but lost their way. We've even told them, repeatedly, how lost, how mixed up and how hopeless they are. Most of them believed us.
- ***We see*** the rampant perversion of every kind that has invaded on every block of our cities.
- ***We see*** the family fragmented, with children being tossed to the new mind set of "*a family can be many things.*"
- ***We see*** rebellion, anger, and filth jump from the screen, the CD's, the games, books and toys into the minds our children, destroying their innocence.
- ***We see*** that *Christian homes* have adopted a more tolerant view of these things, helping their *little Johnny and Susie* to fit into the New Age of open-mindedness.
- ***We see*** God's House, fallen into ruin or built upon faulty foundations, full of people who sit in them, without a clue that "*all is not well with their soul.*"
- ***Yes, we see*** and our hearts are grieved as we take on God's burden for our fallen nation. The scales of spiritual blindness have fallen off of our eyes and we are now wide-awake.

We now see,
We now watch,
And,
We're all but overwhelmed with the magnitude of the job ahead of us.

Our churches are, Religious, but not spiritual—Busy, but not alive in Christ. Pews fill, Pews empty, depending on the mood swings of the people.

Praying for a sovereign move of God in the churches that surround us is so overwhelming. We *feel* like the Red Sea is before us and the enemy is on our tail, closing in.

God Watches

He sees our wavering, our double-mindedness, as we look back and then look to the other side, remembering that the old way was easier and that the path ahead of us is uncertain. Do we really even know where we are going?

We are at a place where,
Discipleship,
Following the leader,
Has a cost.
Are we willing to pay the price?

It is time for us to overthrow the kingdom of darkness through repentance. We must turn and plead with God for revival. We really have no other options open to us. We must! It is time for Christian citizens to join hands across the nations, in holy dissatisfaction and refuse to continue watching the destruction by demonic forces and evil hearts go unchecked. God's people must rise in the power of intercession and move with spiritual authority in the heavenlies.

Surely such evil demands a response by the Godly.
God watches.

In the middle of many places all over the nations, some little town like yours or mine or your big cities or the wide spots in the road that people call home, sits a little church . . . . a big church . . . Nobody is giving it a glance.

People for years may have
Distained you,
Mocked you,
Ignored you
And
Expected absolutely nothing of you,
Except to
Keep quiet
And
To know your place.

You do know your place. It is on your knees in repentance, intercession and then at last, on your feet marching to a different sound than you have ever marched to before. You hear the sound of the battle. Like the war horses of old, those pioneer prayer warriors, you run to the battle. You can hear the roar of your King! You are declaring that Jesus Christ is Lord and is exalted above the Nations of this World.

Yes, you know your place now. It is one of being seated with Christ, in heavenly places, *far above all princes and powers of this world*, far above every kind of spiritual wickedness. You have decided to listen to the call to awaken and rise out of your sleep, to arise a Church triumphant.

The world around you doesn't especially like it, but it's too late.

You have got a taste of freedom and honey from the new land and you will never live under enemy rule again or eat of the flesh pots of the world.

God watches.
A rumbling has begun in the heavens.

God sees
A people
A church

He has stood at their tombs and called to them to,
"Come Forth!!"
He has breathed the breath of life into their dry bones.
The Spirit has empowered them
And
They are on the move.

<u>That "No Place Town" and that "No Name Church," is ready to:</u>

- ***"Prepare the Way of the Lord,"*** like a John the Baptist!
- ***"Birth the Messiah into a region,"*** like a Mary!
- ***"Prophesy,"*** like an Isaiah!
- ***"Fight,"*** like a Gideon!
- ***"March around the Enemy's Walls until they fall,"*** like a Joshua!

- ***"Lead,"*** like a Moses!
- ***"Dance, because the Ark is coming up the road,"*** like King David!
- ***"Cry Holy, Holy, Holy,"*** like the angels and the four and twenty elders!
- ***"Intercede,"*** like Moses and Abraham!
- ***"Be in One Accord,"*** like those in the Upper Room on the Day of Pentecost!
- ***"Build up the broken down walls,"*** like Hezekiah!
- ***"Seek Jesus,"*** like the Wise Men and Shepherds!
- ***"Receive a Double Portion,"*** like Elisha!
- ***"Ready with Oil in Your Lamps,"*** like the Five Wise Virgins!
- ***"Create no small stir,"*** like the Acts 2 church!
- ***"Preach that the Kingdom of God is at hand, heal the sick, raise the dead and cleanse the lepers,"*** like the early disciples!
- ***"Say, Here I am, Send Me,"*** like Isaiah!
- ***"Bring all that we have to Jesus,"*** like the lad with the loaves and fishes!
- ***"Press in and touch the hem of His garment,"*** like the woman with the issue of blood!
- ***"Lay our lives down for the sake of the gospel,"*** like the early martyrs!
- ***"March forth into the battle,"*** like Deborah and Barak!
- ***"Discern the Times and Seasons,"*** like the Issachar people!
- ***"Fling the stone at Goliath's head and watch him fall,"*** like the shepherd boy, David!

The Church of the Living God is rising and living holy in the sight of God!!!

Our world is not without an intercessor standing in the gap between Almighty God and the gross sins of people, government and judges.

God has seen!
God had heard!
God has listened!

God's voice is now preparing to thunder louder than the profanity of the nations, over this earth! He is ready to shake this old world to its core!

Nobody has ever seen the Hand of God like He is preparing to move it in the day and hour that we live!
Satan!
World!
America!
Watch Out!
Here comes the Hand of God!

- ***He comes*** in the midst of an army, a people who have got out of the boat and are walking upon the waves of humanity.
- ***He comes*** in the cries of intercessors that are praying until the very core of the earth is being shaken.
- ***He comes*** in the faithful church that is persevering through the tough times, with a spirit that allows for no compromise.
- ***He comes*** in the midst of the disciples who have gripped the Word of God with all of their hearts, embracing its life-giving words, no longer tossed about by every wind of doctrine.
- ***He comes*** in a people that have their spiritual eyes and ears alert to the voice of Jesus, those who know His voice and follow no one else.
- ***He comes*** through Houses of Prayer, praise and worship, those declaring with clean hands and pure hearts the greatness of God in this earth.

***He comes* in the voice of the Church.**
***He comes* in the cries of Intercession and Repentance!**
***He comes* in Truth!**
***He comes* in Righteousness!**
***He comes* in Word!**
***He comes* in Deed!**
He comes!

Can your nation be saved?
I don't know, but this one thing I do know,
It can and will be saved by the multitudes.

PRAYER POINTS

Pray that the Shackles of Religious Control will be broken.
Pray that the Spiritual Blinders will fall off.
Pray for the Ears of the Church to "Hear What the Spirit is Saying" to them.
Pray for Stony Hearts to be made Flesh.
Pray that the Church will open its doors so that Jesus may come in.
Pray that the "Dry Bones" will rise with the Breath of God in them and live.
Pray for Conviction to flood the churches
Pray that Repentance will flow as tears.
Pray for a Holy Righteous Fear to come upon the Church.
Pray for the Floodgates of Heaven to open.
Pray that Revival Churches will find each other and join together in heart and spirit.
Pray for a Breakthrough in the Harvest.

Part VI

It's Time

"The neglected heart will soon be a heart overrun with worldly thoughts; the neglected life will soon become a moral chaos; the church that is not jealously protected by mighty intercession and sacrificial labors will before long become the abode of every evil bird and the hiding place for unsuspected corruption. The creeping wilderness will soon take over that church that trusts in its own strength and forgets to watch and pray."

A. W. Tozer

CHAPTER 37

THE WALL

Matt 21:12-14
(Emphasis Added)

And Jesus went into the temple of God, and cast out all them that sold and bought in the temple, and overthrew the tables of the moneychangers, and the seats of them that sold doves, And said unto them, It is written, ***My house shall be called the house of prayer****; but ye have made it a den of thieves. And the blind and the lame came to him in the temple; and he healed them.*

Jesus Christ will challenge everything that is in the way of having His Church to be the House of Prayer.

To grieve the Spirit of God on any personal level would be so disabling to us as believers—but to grieve the Spirit of God concerning His church would be unthinkable! Jesus paid it all, invested all He had to give design to and build His church His way.

If we fail to make the house of God a House of Prayer, something precious is lost—the purpose for which the house exists.

Every one of us has to take personal responsibility for the condition of God's House—for this thing we've invested years of our life for—to take down the mountain of resistance and obstruction, to see the House of God become the place of prayer for which it was created. Every place a church has been built should reflect this purpose. Can we even imagine what would happen to our world if every table of man own agenda were turned over and prayer once again filled the House of God?

What would happen to our harvest fields, our families, the nations of the world if the people who are called by His name had a massive turning to God in prayer?

There is an expectation of the Spirit that we win every victory in intercession. He never said it would be easy or fast—but He said "it would be, "just as the Lord has spoken it."

Everything the Church will become will be directly linked to the prayer found in her. Prayer has been the pulsing force behind everything we do and will yet do in the name of the Lord. If we slack off or allow other things to crowd out this spiritual discipline, we risk a whole lot more than we really understand.

Prayer sustains; holds together, like glue, the elements that bring revival to a people—and Prayer prepares a house for salvation, healing and deliverance to flow forth to needy people.

A little over fourteen years ago, God began to move in our church here in Oregon, USA to dedicate ourselves to a life of prayer. From the very beginning, once we made that commitment, God began to entrust some things to us.

- ***He*** placed us on the *Wall of Intercession* over people, places, churches, pastors, revivals, islands of the sea, nations, America and Israel; enlarging our vision quite rapidly.
- ***He*** placed in our hearts a burden for families, people groups, age groups and congregations.
- ***He*** positioned us over our city and everything that pertains to it—its streets, highways, schools, businesses, churches, waterways, souls—our harvest field.
- **He** positioned us to call in the harvest and take down the strongholds of the enemy in intercession.
- ***He*** positioned us to pray and seek God.

He has not made a single ministry we do independent of intercession.

Prayer is so interwoven into the fabric of our church, so much so that we simply would not exist in the spiritual place God has brought us to.

There is not a single thing we do in this church that is not bathed in prayer. Are we unique? I don't think so—I believe there are multitudes in prayer today around the world—but folks; there is always, not only room for more, but a need for more Houses of Prayer.

<u>**Here are some things we have learned as we have opened our hearts wider and wider to value the power of prayer:**</u>

- ***Preaching*** without intercession is *just words.*
- ***Worship*** without intercession is *just noise.*
- ***Teaching*** without intercession is *just ideas.*
- ***Warfare*** without intercession is *just movement.*
- ***Giving*** without intercession is *just religious duty.*
- ***Missions*** without intercession are *just a nice story.*
- ***Listening*** to the world news without intercession is *just religion and politics.*
- ***A vision*** without intercession is *just a goal.*
- ***Witnessing*** without intercession is *just leg work.*
- ***Revival*** without intercession is *just dead.*

A casual approach to prayer is death to intercession. Intercession dies when we return to *saying prayers about things, people, places and things.*

Adding a couple more ingredients to a healthy church is faithfulness and unity—two elements that bring major strength to what God desires to do through us. These two have to work hand in hand because if one is missing the other doesn't work.

- ***If*** there is unfaithfulness, then unity suffers.
- ***If*** there is a loss of unity, it doesn't matter how much church we attend together.

One of the things that we have to take very serious about intercession is that *it is very serious*—and *our part in it is serious.* We have to understand that all of us together release something in the heavens that cannot be fully accomplished if we are not all together. I cannot stress enough the need for us to find our place on the *wall of intercession* and face the fact that no one but us can fill it—meaning, I cannot take your place. If you are not here, the prayer gap is not filled by another.

If the Lord wants to form a group of believers, the church in any given place in our world, on any given day, into an intercessory sword to thrust forth into the strongholds of the enemy, He needs a church who is faithful and in unity to do it.

When He reaches for us—we need to be there.

CHAPTER 38

A PROPER RESPONSE

Nehemiah 1:3

And they said unto me, "The remnant that are left of the captivity there in the province are in great affliction and reproach: the wall of Jerusalem also is broken down, and the gates thereof are burned with fire."

As Prayer Warriors there has never been a better or more serious time to know that we are responding correctly to all that we see, hear and know. The reports are not always good and sometimes very disturbing in regards to our world. And because they are disturbing, we may *react* rather than *respond.*

Most of the time there is one of two reactions from people—apathy or overreaction.

- ***Apathy is*** a non-reaction, non-response, immobilizing heart condition.
- ***Overreaction*** is a quick, ill-thought-out knee-jerk reaction to something we have an opinion on or prejudice about.

But there is proper response to the things that take place.

We are bent towards reacting from our soulish nature a lot of the time, *allowing our mind* to run away with the issues, *allowing our prejudices* to flavor our attitudes, *allowing our emotional makeup* to rule the day, and yes, even reacting to something in a way that is not godly. We really are *a fix-it kind of people.* Rather than really getting down to the heart of the matter and finally and ultimately praying into things, whether it's a family issue, a church or national issue, whether it's a son or daughter or some world leader, we oftentimes find ourselves reacting rather than responding.

The Prophets of old were of those who understood the deeper matters of the events that surrounded their lives. So much of the time, we lean towards sensationalism, ***discussing*** the outward appearances at length, ***detailing*** everything, but ***not really looking deeper*** into the reason things are the way they are.

I have found several places where servants of God have come to grips with the reality of a situation and moved into a proper, godly response.

Nehemiah is an example of godly response, when he heard the report that some of his kinsmen were in affliction and reproach, and that Jerusalem's wall was broken down and the gates burned. ***Nehemiah 1:3***

Nehemiah is in captivity in Babylon, a slave to a foreign king, having been taken in the overthrow of Jerusalem. His brother from Judah has come to see him where he is serving in the palace as the king's cup bearer.

What happens next, as he asks the question that is on his mind defines the heart of true intercession.

> ***Nehemiah 1:4****—And it came to pass, when I heard these words, that I sat down and wept, and mourned certain days, and fasted, and prayed before the God of heaven.*

I noticed something here when meditating on this verse—there's sense of a building response—from the time Nehemiah heard it, ***until*** he sat down, ***until*** he wept, ***until*** he mourned, ***until*** he fasted and after that, he finally prayed. There is *a real heart-connection* with this man and the condition of the city and people that has just been described to him.

Is it possible that we pray before we sit down, weep, mourn and fast?

There are some cases where immediate prayer is warranted, but there are some conditions that we need to assimilate into our hearts, respond to and prepare for prayer. Prayer is the response of a heart in right relationship with the facts, events and conditions and God who answers our prayers.

We can pray and pray and pray, talking to God about the conditions, mentally and verbally discussing it with God, while never weeping or mourning the situation.

Maybe it's time, considering the gravity of the situations that surround us, to . . .

- ***Sit down***—stop—let it sink in!
    - Take stock of the situation!
    - Understand the thing
    - you have heard, seen, had happen.
- ***Weep***—let it sink in further until it hits your heart.
    - Feel the emotion of those involved—be empathetic with them for what is happening.
- ***Mourn***—let it grip your heart and create a groan.
    - Allow yourself to enter into the pain,
    - the loss, the travesty . . .
- ***Fast***—let it stop your body from its quest as you are overcome with the greater need.
    - Become hungry for an answer, for intervention from on high.
- ***Pray***—let your prayers come from that deep realization that what we have seen, felt,
- heard and know.
    - This prayer for this condition is worthy of our response from a deep place.

CHAPTER 39

WHAT ABOUT PRAYER?

Ephesians 6:18

Praying always with all prayer and supplication in the Spirit, and watching thereunto with all perseverance and supplication for all saints;

What if the Church really got hold of God and asked Him what He wanted to have happen when we come together to Worship? What would happen if we heard God speak and we stepped into the path of obedience for the things that we gather for?

- ***We spend*** more time talking about the evil of the nations and decrying the actions of sinners, ***but what about prayer?***
- ***We meet*** for church and sing our songs, ***but what about prayer?***
- ***We hear*** the Word of God, Sunday after Sunday, ***but what about prayer?***
- ***We hold*** our annual business meetings to set the house in order for the next year, ***but what about prayer?***
- ***We have*** youth meetings, women's meetings, men's meetings, children's church, Bible Studies, ***but what about prayer?***
- ***We vote***, sing, preach, pray and teach, ***but what about prayer?***

With the level of evil that is being released on our earth, I ask again, *what about prayer?*

Andrew Bonar, now gone on to his reward said, *"Oh brother pray, in spite of Satan, pray; spend hours in prayer, rather neglect friends than not pray, rather fast and lose breakfast, dinner, supper and sleep too, than not pray.*

And we must not talk about prayer—we must pray in right earnest. The Lord is near. He comes softly while the virgins sleep."

I am not talking about the kind of prayer that dribbles off our lips, but the kind of prayer that erupts from our hearts and flows like a river from our lips.

- ***I am talking about the kind of prayer*** that keeps on pushing through.
- ***I am talking about the kind of prayer*** that does not sleep nor grow weary.
- ***I am talking about the kind of prayer*** that does not need to feel great to pray, but prays because it does not feel great.
- ***I am talking about the kind of prayer*** that moves heaven's hand and shakes hells gates.
- ***I am talking about the kind of prayer*** that took place in the Garden of Gethsemane that prayed when the cost was so great.
- ***I am talking about the kind of prayer*** that makes no deals or compromises but states the Word of God as it is.
- ***I am talking about the kind of prayer*** that stands between the living and the dead and intercedes for those that are almost dead.
- ***I am talking about the kind of prayer*** that will not let go of the horns of the altar.
- ***I am talking about the kind of prayer*** that does not have to be seen to be done or heard by man to be answered.

I am talking about prayer that stretches its hands to the heavens and cries out, "God, come down and visit us!"

- ***How we love*** to dissect the issues.
- ***How we love*** to point out the failures, flaws and sins of others.
- ***How we love*** to stand clean in our own sight, while the greatest sin of the church is that they are not praying, they are not repenting, they are not seeking God, they are not crying out for mercy . . . .

It is sinful to speak of such degradation and sin and never lift a voice to heaven to beseech God to intervene and show His power.

Someone has to stand in the gap where the gates of hell have opened.

- ***Are we not*** the church?
- ***Are we not*** the blood-washed?
- ***Are we not*** the ones with garments of salvation?

The moment you place your feet on the floor in the morning, the fact that you are awake and have risen should shake the corridors of hell with fear—not because you are so great or mighty, but because the blood of Jesus and His name in, on and through you is so great.

You should shake hell because you are obedient, committed, repentant, submitted, yielded, humble servants of God.

What about prayer? *"My house shall be called a House of Prayer,"* Jesus said. That statement was made by Jesus when he encountered those who had set their seats up at the doorway of the Temple and were profiteering on the holy things that were to be dedicated to the Worship of God. He is still driving out our profiteering mentality that acts as if the Church is about us and what we can get out of it. Jesus stated what ***He*** wanted of ***Hi***s Temple—to have a House of Prayer.

> ***1 Corinthians 6:20****—For ye are bought with a price: therefore glorify God in your body, and in your spirit, which are God's.*

The Church has her story as well, from long ago to now. Those of us who have accepted Jesus still have daily decisions to make in regards to how we will live our lives.

We live in a time when the church is statistically no better than the world. We do have some tough decisions to make as to how we are going to live our lives, in light of the cross of Jesus Christ and His claims upon us.

Jesus comes in with great love but Holy confrontation for what is wrong in God's House. When He entered the temple He was direct and to the point in dealing with the religion of the people and it greatly angered many of them. They did not like the challenge to change, so they fought back by trying to discredit the move Jesus made into His Father's House. Ultimately they called for His death!

> ***Matthew 21:12a-13***
>
> *12 And Jesus went into the temple of God, and cast out all them . . .*
>
> *13 And said unto them, It is written, My house shall be called the house of prayer; but ye have made it a den of thieves.*

Jesus spoke this truth so long ago but He could come into our modern churches and decree the same thing.

What He really did was call the church to her knees.
Should Jesus not call the church—your church—to her knees?

Is there anything different He is doing today in this current church age, current revival? Jesus calls the sins of the church, the prayerlessness of the church, the compromise of the church, the worldliness of the church for what it is—sin.

The truth is—the religious church does not bend her knees easily. She has grown used to standing up, proud and in control.

Humility and Repentance is a door that opens for God to have His way!

- ***Why do we keep on singing*** when Jesus is calling us to repentance?
- ***Why do we keep on building*** when Jesus is calling us to repentance?

Why don't we stop everything and quit doing and moving until we have recognized our intense need of Jesus Christ?

Why don't we stop the merry-go-round until we can get up changed?

There were a lot of issues in people's hearts that brought them to the place of calling for the execution of Jesus and we can readily see how horrible what they did was. But, do we see the church world of today as capable of crucifixion if anyone messes with *"our church?"*

The truth is—Jesus wants His church back—from you and me.

We didn't die for it—*He did.*
It is not our church—*it is His!*
We did not save the people—*He did!*

- ***He has every right*** to walk into any church, in any time in history and challenge its condition.
- ***He has every right*** to turn our tables over and call for a prayer meeting.

The question is—will we bend our knees in humility to Him or will we cry, *"Away with Him?"*

Churches and Christians all over the world are making this decision. We have to do more than attend pageants, hold special services, have plays and sing special songs at Easter. We have to make decisions as a church as to whether we will give Jesus the liberty to deal with us and make us *"A House of Prayer."*

> ***Romans 8:34b*** . . . *It is Christ that died, yea rather, that is risen again, who is even at the right hand of God, who also makes intercession for us.*

Think of it!
Jesus making intercession for the churches around the world, and in your city!

That's you and me, folks!
If the King of Glory is bending His heart, then why don't we?

From the cross to the grave to heaven—His life was and is one of total involvement with mankind. He stepped into people's lives and performed miracles of intervention in their sickness, brokenness, lameness and blindness. Think of what His prayer might be for you, for your church.

This Great Intercessor is still stepping between you and that which would afflict you, cripple you or blind you.

CHAPTER 40

THE RESTRAINING FORCE

James 5:16b

The effectual fervent prayer of a righteous man avails much.

"Prayer can do anything that God can do."
-E.M. Bounds.

***I don't know* if we understand how powerful prayer is.**
***I don't know* if we understand how much is held back or released by our intercession.**

I saw a little picture as I meditated on this subject of *restraint,*—a leg with one of those tracking devices bolted on so that if the one wearing it crossed the restricted boundaries, an alarm would go off.

I felt two things are represented with this

- ***God restraining*** the devil by our intercession
- ***God restraining*** our loved ones, nations, people by our intercession.

Any movement that goes on from the darkness that surrounds us, or any movement that goes on from those that we love and are deeply concerned about—is registered in heaven and transmitted to earth by God's Spirit to a praying people.

I had been awakened in the night to pray for my brother, Paul, and his wife, Ona, and their two children, Shaun and Rochelle, when they were traveling through Mexico some years ago. I had not seen them in a long time, had no idea they were on the road after dark or in an area where it could be dangerous to travel. I did not know they were about to have a very serious accident that might take their life if played out to the full extent of what was happening. I began to have a real burden on my heart to pray for them and I did so until I felt it lift off my heart. I made a point of recording the event so that I might ask them about it when I saw them again. Months later they were in the States and I asked them about that date and what might have happened on that day. They were able to tell me the story of the wreck that rolled their vehicle in a very serious accident, leaving them upside down alongside the road, along a road where banditos frequented. He spoke of how someone stopped and helped them, giving them safe haven from the night and the danger along the highway. He recounted how God had not only spared them, but sent them a man to give them refuge.

Does this stuff just happen?

No, my story can be retold over and over of how God stepped in through the prayers of an alert prayer warrior who prayed when the urgency of the hour hit them and history in progress was forever changed—something that is rarely noticed when it happens . . .

If we could somehow see how our world, *minus the years, decades, centuries, millenniums of prayer,* would appear today, we would be shocked at a world left unrestrained by God's great power on earth through our prayers.

While God is sovereign and does many things just because He is God, there are some things He does through a praying people.

I know we can magnify the terrible things going on and they surely are, but there would be an onslaught of evil force such as we could not imagine released upon the lives of those we love and our land and nations of the world—if no one prayed.

- ***If you thought*** the World Wars were bad, if you thought Hiroshima was bad, or the World Trade Center tragedy was bad,

If you thought the hurricanes, tornadoes, tsunamis and cyclones and floods and fires were bad, then you would not want to see what they would have been like if no one prayed.

- ***If you thought*** genocide, abortion, murder, rape, atrocities of all kind were bad, then you would not want to see what would have happened if no one prayed.

My sense with what I am feeling is; I am glad for prayer warriors who stand upon the wall to guard a family, a church, a city, a state, a nation who see, know and pray. I am glad for the intercessors that have stood upon the banks of rivers, seas, and boundaries around towns to stand in prayer against the raging storms, flood and fire.

Oh yes, you can see what happened and question and blame God . . . but

- ***Did you ever see*** what didn't happen when a people prayed?
- ***Did you ever see*** what was spared because a people prayed?
- ***Did you ever see*** lives and property spared as if by a miracle because someone prayed?

Let the world around us miss the intricate place prayer has on planet earth, but never let a Christian miss the picture others may not see—the things that didn't happen because someone prayed.

<u>And then there are the things that happened because someone prayed.</u>

- ***Did you ever see*** the times when your loved one changed their mind on an activity and their lives were spared because someone prayed?
- ***Did you ever see*** God release His angels to protect and guard someone from tragedy, because someone prayed?
- ***Did you ever see*** the moment in time when God's Spirit began to deal with a person about yielding their lives to Jesus, and the subtle shift in their heart in leaning towards God, because someone prayed for them?
- ***Did you ever*** see the miracle rescue or the miracle salvation from something horrible, because someone prayed?

You see there is a restraining force on the earth that works in concert with God Almighty—the intercessory prayers of the common man who does one thing that many underestimate—Pray.

- ***Just let*** the devil know that the thing that holds him back much of the time is a praying people.
- ***Just let*** the nations know that those who interceded for them actually have more power before the Throne of God than they do in their nuclear bombs and their threats against others.
- ***Just let*** those who think they are working in darkness behind closed doors to do evil, there is a people who know, see and pray.

For all they have been able to do, have they ever wondered how much they have failed at because someone prayed?

I believe it's time for God's people everywhere to step up to the plate and knock the ball out of the park. Intercede like you have never prayed before, because a lot is hinging on your prayers.

You have power before God when you pray and He listens to those whose hearts are pure before Him.

CHAPTER 41

DIVINE REVERSAL

Galatians 3:13

Christ hath redeemed us from the curse of the law, being made a curse for us: for it is written, "Cursed is every one that hangs on a tree."

- **Divine:** relating to, or proceeding directly from God
- **Reversal:** an act or the process of reversing

One look at people in bondage, families in trouble and the church in need of revival and restoration will tell the story—we need a reversal of what has been set in motion to destroy the promised life in Christ through His Salvation.

Sometime ago I began to pray for *"Divine Intervention,"* as a statement of fact that without God's Intervention, absolutely nothing will or can change. Not a soul can be saved without God's Spirit drawing them.

- ***Intervene / Intervention*** means to become a third party to a legal proceeding begun by others for the protection of an alleged interest.

I know of a reality show on television in which concerned family and friends set up their loved one, who is in bondage to drugs or alcohol, for intervention. They have secretly arranged for a trained councilor to step in the gap and then bring their loved one in on it, laying down an ultimatum to *"get help or else"* Because of pressure applied by those who love them, they eventually concede to go and get help. Sadly a good number of them relapse—because truly there is only One who can do intervention with totally deliverance.

Without God's intervention, the world would have destroyed itself long ago.

There are examples where God's mercy intercepted the deserved judgment on mankind and rescued them from the death traps in which they were living. God did this for Israel several times in their journey from Egypt to Mt. Sinai, sending intervention to spare them from the end results of their sin.

1. One of the greatest Old Testament stories of intervention was in regard to an uprising brought about by Korah, sided with by Dathan and Abiram. We see God dealing with these men for the sake of everyone, including their own families, but they would not hear or obey. In ***Numbers 16:2***, Moses sent for Dathan and Abiram to which they replied, *"We will not come up."*

Even with God, through Moses, attempting to turn the rebellion around, showing the grace of God and the willingness of Moses to intervene, we seen in ***Numbers 16:19*** that Korah gathered all the congregation against them at the door of the tabernacle. They were determined to take a stand against Moses and by doing so, they stood against God's spoken will for them.

Then, the glory of the Lord appeared to the entire congregation. You would think that with such a profound presence of God in their midst, they would all immediately yield to that glory in the fear of God. And yet, I have seen it too . . . God's Spirit is present in such measure that a response is going to be given. In these times no one can remain neutral; they will make a choice as to where they stand in relationship with God and man.

- God's Spirit is relentless in trying to get man out of the sinful condition they find themselves in and if they will just yield to Him, He will intervene in their lives and deliver them.

And the Lord spoke unto Moses, saying, *"Speak unto the congregation, saying, 'Get you up from about the tabernacle of Korah, Dathan, and*

Abiram.'" Moses went to Dathan, Abiram with all the elders of Israel following him. And he spoke to the congregation there imploring them to get away from the tents of the wicked men and to not even touch anything of theirs, lest they too were consumed in their sins. So, the congregation got away from Korah, Dathan and Abiram. Then the three men came out and stood in the door or their tents with their wives and their little children. ***Numbers 16:23-27***

Numbers 16:32-33 reveals the rest of the story as the earth opened up and swallowed them up, their houses, and their entire house. And then a fire came from the Lord and consumed two hundred and fifty men who were offering incense. ***Numbers 16:35***

- ***One would think*** that God's response was unwarranted, but the men who offered the incense were offensive to God. They were not authorized to approach Him but had recklessly ignored His law becoming not only disobedient but irreverent in His sight.
- ***But one would also think*** the witnesses of such a magnificent display of God's judgment would establish the fear of the Lord in people's hearts, but no . . .

Scripture reveals *"all the congregation of the children of Israel murmured against Moses and against Aaron, saying, Ye have killed the people of the Lord."* ***Numbers 16:41***

What happened next was an act of God that struck fear and intercession in the heart of Moses. God said, *"Get you up from among this congregation, that I may consume them as in a moment. And they fell upon their faces."* And Moses said unto Aaron, *"Take a censer and put fire in it from off the altar, and put on incense, and go quickly unto the congregation, and make an atonement for them: for there is wrath gone out from the Lord; the plague is begun."* ***Numbers 16:45-46***

- ***Ezekiel 22:30-31***—*And I sought for a man among them that should make up the hedge, and stand in the gap before me for the land, that I should not destroy it: but I found none.*

I believe Israel, as many we pray for today, were unaware that God found a man. Aaron did as Moses had commanded and ran into the midst of the congregation and saw the plague had begun among the people: and he put on incense, and made atonement for the people. And he stood between the dead and the living; and the plague was held back and stopped. ***Numbers 16:47-48***

This was an instance of Divine Reversal, a time when God was justified in destroying but because a man stood in the gap, He did not destroy them. Moses and Aaron held back the continuation of the plague that would have run unhindered throughout the whole congregation until there was no one left alive.

2. Another example of Divine Reversal was at the Red Sea when certain failure loomed for the Children of Israel as God stepped into the plans of Egypt and brought them down under the sea.

And, as in the case of Moses and Aaron, many are still unaware there is an intercessor that stood in the gap between life and death for them, taking their place so they would not be destroyed. But Jesus did . . .

3. The greatest example of *Divine Intervention* was to touch the whole world, generation after generation through the life, death and resurrection of Jesus Christ. He became the third party intercessor between fallen man and a Holy God—one who would step in between in intervention.

The Cross is one, non-stop, continuous decree of Divine Reversal—a plan to turn man back to God and destroy the impact of sin in the world.

<u>The Cross of Christ reversed the curse of sin.</u>

- ***By it*** Jesus turned defeat into victory
- ***By it*** Jesus turned death to life
- ***By it*** Jesus broke the bondage and brought deliverance
- ***By it*** Jesus took sickness upon His own body and brought healing
- ***By it*** Jesus took man from lost to found

- ***By it*** Jesus gave man a straight path to God.

Divine Reversal is when God steps into a situation and totally turns it around.

Some of you have been on a prayer journey, asking God for something beyond yourself. This prayer vision depicts the kind of intervention where Jesus steps down into your *"prayed over territory,"* whether it is your city or your family or some social area in need of change.

Jesus enters into covenant with such prayer warriors who lay claim to a region, to a city, to souls, to a deeply entrenched area of sin . . . and transitions a church and a people from being introverted to Holy Ghost extroverts, spiritual travelling a region in prayer.

- ***Intercession can turn*** the hand of God on behalf of mankind when man is bent towards hell on a broad path.
- ***Intercession can intercept*** the devil's missiles, his lies and attacks and breaks up his plans for those things that pertain to our assignment.
- ***Intercession decrees*** a divine intercept of the devil's progress into a territory—whether it's a family, city, state or nation—and reverses the devil right in his tracks, forbidding him to advance any further.

God is positioned to step down into the *"prayed for places and prayed for people."* In a moment's time—everything changes. Not only have multitudes prayed but God has moved and when God moves—things renew and transition, shift and reverse and even stop permanently.

There have been a lot of *"suddenlies"* in life where it was *this way* and in a moment's time it was reversed.
God doesn't just *alter* something—He changes it.

I don't know how God is going to save our loved ones, revive the churches, transform our city, awaken a nation, but I know that He can turn anything to do His bidding.

Any demonic or human movement can be disrupted by the move of God, by an awakening or a shaking.
Man can make plans, the devil can make plans, but when God says the plan will not prosper—it is over.

- ***We've all seen*** the impact of salvation and how the blood of Jesus washed sin away and reversed the death sentence of a person.
- ***We've all seen*** the years of loss and pain erased as *"all things were made new."*

"All I know is, once I was blind, but now I see."

Awakenings are seasons of Divine Intervention that results in Divine Reversals.

It may all look impossible—*but in a moment's time*—everything can change! If ***911*** could change America and the world the way it has, transitioning everything from the way it used to be to how it is now—think what can happen when God moves and says *"everything's changing now."*

Imagine the *Hordes of Hell* going one way and God says,
"No, you're not allowed to traffic there anymore; that's prayed for and under the blood."

If God says, *"Because of my people's faithfulness to me, I am going to crush the head of the serpent and destroy the devil's stronghold in the lives of their loved ones, their city and region,"* then the serpent will feel ***a Foot of Divine Reversal*** come down on his head and hear God say, ***"No more!"***

I believe that God, simply because of His great love for souls and because of His great mercy and grace, is about to give a wake-up call ***(Divine Intervention)*** to do for mankind what they refuse or do not know to do for themselves. This will bring people face to face with the Living God resulting in feeling the weight of their sin ***(Divine Conviction)*** in order to bring them to their knees ***(Divine Reversal,)*** crying out for mercy and freedom from their sins.

Every major revival has resulted in an awakening where heaven met earth plummeting towards hell on its broad road of destruction.

This is why ***Divine Reversals*** are needed or else wicked mankind would utterly be destroyed and then even the backslidden church would collapse into a moral decline that would totally destroy them.

What and who have you been praying for?

I am certain that your intercession has gained the attention of God Almighty who is poised even now to bring heaven's kind of answers to your situations. He will step onto that territory that is bathed in prayers and move to save, deliver and heal in a mighty wave of revival. This river will then be so powerful it will break it boundaries and impact places that surround this *taken and held ground* of souls in our region.

Every **soul,** ***every*** **loved one,** ***every*** **prodigal,** ***every*** **city, state, nation . . . God has people positioned to pray for** ***every*** **concerns of His heart.**

We don't understand how powerful this prayer movement really is. There are people who are carrying burdens for all kinds of things as their primary prayer focus.

How He intends to reverse the ***"March of Death"*** by these unfortunate souls who have been taken as prisoners of war by the devil, I do not know . . . but I believe that even the faithful intercessors will be amazed to see the purposes of God come to pass.

His mind is already made up to totally fulfill His promises to us. You have been faithful to what He has given you to do—prayer—now . . . watch God move!

Prayer Points

1. ***Pray for*** a fresh outpouring of the Holy Spirit to anoint you with boldness to preach the gospel.
2. ***Pray that*** the Holy Spirit will use you powerfully to see people set free, healed and delivered.
3. ***Pray for*** the Holy Spirit to open doors of opportunity to enter into the world of darkness and turn the light on so people can find their way out into freedom.

Chapter 42

God is not ashamed

Hebrews 11:16

But now they desire a better country, that is, an heavenly: wherefore God is not ashamed to be called their God: for he hath prepared for them a city.

If there's any one thing I desire, it is to be able to stand before God and not have Him be ashamed to call me His own.

- I want to hear Him say, *"Well done, good and faithful Servant."*
- I want to hear Him say, *"My Child."*
- I want to hear Him say, *"Friend of God!"*

I never want to hear Him say, *"I am ashamed of you!"*

Many parents, friends and relatives today are ashamed of the conduct and speech of people they know—who have embarrassed or disgraced them in some way.

- ***I wonder*** how God feels about His family, those who say they are His friends and servants.
- ***I wonder*** how proud God is of His church and the things He has had to endure as she has brought shamed upon His name and Kingdom.
- ***I wonder*** how God feels when He views those who are *called by His name* engaging in sinful practices, attitudes and speech.
- ***I wonder*** how surprised many people are going to be when they stand before God and an account is given of their lives and they

realize that they have embarrassed God by acting shamefully and by being ashamed of Jesus Christ.

Mark 8:38 (Emphasis Added)—*Whosoever therefore shall be ashamed of (**feel shame for; disgrace**) me and of my words in this adulterous and sinful generation; of him also shall the Son of man be ashamed, when he cometh in the glory of his Father with the holy angels.*

A look at the scripture setting in *Hebrews 11—the Hall of Faith*, reveals the kind of people that God is not ashamed of—*people who stood out as common folks serving their God in uncommon faithfulness.* **Hebrews 12:1**

The use of the terms, *people of faith*, and *faith community*, have little to do with the kind of faith these people lived. These words are tossed around in reference to anyone who believes anything, people of all religious persuasions.

- The term, ***"people of faith"*** is about those who go to church, any church or temple, mosque or hall.
- The term, ***"faith community"*** is the sum total of everyone in any region, from a city, to a state, to a nation, who hold some sort of religious belief.

We live in a time of *easy believism*—a kind of religion that was foreign to many of the faithful witnesses who have gone on before us . . .

- ***Who knew*** God was faithful!
- ***Who embraced*** the promises of God,
- ***Who lived*** on the cutting edge of God's Word,
- ***Who took*** each challenging step of their faith in confidence

There are times that I wonder how God really feels about His People. There are times I wonder how God feels about me, our church, our faith, our prayer life, our obedience, etc . . .

Is He proud of me, you, and us or is He *ashamed* to be called our God?

I believe that God takes pleasure in His church, the dedication to prayer, but I also believe, according to what the Word of God says—there are areas of concern to God.

I know that we all understand the cost of discipleship but as time goes on some things pertaining to our faith do erode as the world's flood of filth and corruption wash against us—as we open up old doors once shut in honor of the Lord's ownership over our lives.

- ***The fight is to*** hold our integrity.
- ***The fight is to*** stay pure before God.
- ***The fight is to*** live a life above reproach.
- ***The fight is to*** keep our minds stayed on Him.
- ***The fight is to*** check our mind and heart motives.
- ***The fight is to*** keep our love for Him hot, above all other things.
- ***The fight is to*** keep walking in the Spirit, and avoiding the fleshly living.
- ***The fight is to*** keep our mouths, hearts and spirits holy and true before God and man.

We live in the last days for certain, and as Jesus prophesied in ***Matthew 24:12***—*"And because iniquity shall abound, the love of many shall wax cold.* (To be made (grow) cool or cold by blowing; used of waning love)"

We are watching even now what the Apostle Paul wrote in ***2 Thessalonians 2:3***—*"Let no man deceive you by any means: for that day shall not come, except there come a falling away first, and that man of sin be revealed, the son of perdition;* (A falling away, a defection from truth, an apostasy)"

We live in a time when people who are still sitting on the pews of churches have grown cold in their hearts, having received the kingdom of man as the way they live.

Compromise, Sin and Coldness of Heart has taken a great toll on the church.

Many churches and believers that have devoted themselves to prayer, intercession and warfare, have embraced a life of holiness and separation, a life of repentance.

It has taken an uncommon kind of faith to keep going, keep knocking, keep seeking, even when nothing has appeared in answer to those prayers.

The scripture records a parable that Jesus told his disciples, about a persistent woman

Luke 18:1-5 (Emphasis Added)

1 And he spoke a parable unto them to this end, that ***men ought always to pray,*** *and not to faint;*

2 Saying, There was in a city a judge, which feared not God, neither regarded man:

3 And there was a widow in that city; and she came unto him, saying, Avenge me of mine adversary.

4 And he would not for a while: but afterward he said within himself, Though I fear not God, nor regard man;

5 Yet because this widow troubles me, I will avenge her, ***lest by her continual coming she weary me.***

This lady found a key that we sometimes fail to use—***persistence, importunity!*** She kept entreating the carnal judge to answer her request. Jesus ends this parable with a question for us, in *verse 7* saying,

"And shall not God avenge his own elect, which cry day and night unto him, though he bears long with them?

Isaiah 62:6-7

> *6 I have set watchmen upon thy walls, O Jerusalem,* ***which shall never hold their peace day nor night:*** *ye that make mention of the Lord,* ***keep not silence,***
>
> *7 And* ***give him no rest,*** *till he establish, and till he make Jerusalem a praise in the earth.*

There were in ages past and yet today, watchmen and watchwomen who stand upon the wall of Jerusalem to intercede. And some day . . . the eastern sky will split wide open and Jesus will return to that city to ***"make Jerusalem a praise in the earth."***

Every intercessor that is praying for Jerusalem is praying a prophetic prayer from the Word of God.

Intercessors have always captured the moment in time in which they lived and by the Holy Spirit have been assigned to pray truth—*the way God sees things.* These are fierce prayer warriors, men and women, youth, boys and girls of all ages, who stand in the gap over churches, nations, schools, governments . . .

As an American I can clearly see, with the natural eye the things that are wrong naturally and spiritually—but it takes the heart of God capturing my heart to truly turn my prayers in his direction—or I will just pray political prayers over my nation and religious prayers over the church.

God needs intercessors *who sigh and cry, weep and pray, entreat and declare* the heart of God over the earth—from the north to the south; from the east to the west—with the sound of travail reaching the Father's heart and invading the darkness of this world.

Yes, sound travels, wave after wave, rippling outward from the place it was released.

Every move of God on earth has been preceded by a cry from earth—people in need of God. Every revival started with prayer warriors, intercessors, some who prayed for years for God to come down.

The story is told of the intercessors of the Hebrides Revival—just one among many . . .

They were two elderly women named, Peggy and Christine Smith—eighty-two and eighty-four years old. Peggy was blind and her sister had severe arthritis in her back. They had not been able to attend church services, so they turned their cottage into a sanctuary and began to meet with God to pray. They prayed the promise of, *"I will pour water upon him that is thirsty and floods upon the dry ground."* They began to intercede, pleading night and day in prayer.

One night Peggy was given a revelation that revival was coming to the church. She was shown the first wave of revival would be the young people of the land. She sent for her minister and told him what God had shown her, asking for all the leaders of the church to come together for special times of waiting upon God.

At that same time, in the same region, there was another prayer movement in which a group of men were praying in a barn and began to experience an outpouring of God's Spirit. As these men gathered, a young man read a part of ***Psalms 24,*** *"Who shall ascend into the hills of the Lord? Or who shall stand in His holy place? He that is of clean hands and a pure heart, who has not lifted up his soul to vanity nor sworn deceitfully, he shall receive the blessing from the Lord."*

Then he turned to the others who were gathered there in the barn and said, *"Brothers, it seems to me just so much humbug to be waiting and praying as we are, if we ourselves are not rightly related to God."* Then he lifted his hands towards heaven and cried out, *"Oh God, are my hands clean; is my heart pure . . . ?"* He got no further than those words and fell prostrate to the floor. A deep awareness of the presence of God filled the barn as the power of God fell on each of them. They entered into a wave of God's Glory and believed *without doubt* in the promise of revival.

Rees Howell said,
"Bend the Church and Save the World."

How true this statement was then and nothing has changed today. If the Church would humble herself and get right with God, there would be no stopping that mighty, righteous army of prayer warriors who has asked God deal with their own hearts and send revival to the church and an awakening to the land.

You rarely hear it anymore—*REVIVAL* . . .
Is the glory of the former days, the glory that once settled upon the House of God—fading from view?

So much has changed as days, months and years have lapsed into a new decade. I can well remember the early days of revival when it was all the talk of the church among anyone who heard or saw or experienced it.

- **Heard**: to learn by the ear or by being told; be informed of;
- **Saw**: to view; visit or attend as a spectator:
- **Experience**: a particular instance of personally encountering or undergoing something:

It was at my uncle's funeral in a small town in Oregon that my husband and I first ***heard*** of "revival." Someone was trying to encourage us to take "*the trip*" to go with them to take in what God was doing. They had two tickets ready for us to go with them. Though curious about it we declined as being unable to take the trip *"right now."*

At a later date, after having ***seen*** some videos that had been given to us, we made a decision to go and experience for ourselves what was going on. As our feet landed on the grounds of that revival center, we began to experience an expectation of what God might do in our lives. Then when we entered into the first service, after waiting in line with several thousand other *"curious folks and seekers,"* we ***experienced*** for ourselves what the revival was all about.

It was God meeting each one on a very personal level of conviction which led to a lot of soul-searching which led to repentance of sin.

The words of that young deacon in the barn in the Hebrides, *"Oh God, are my hands clean; is my heart pure?"* was resonating once again in a major move of God—one that would sweep the world.

There has never been revival without repentance.

If someone says, *"We're having revival,"* and God is not quickening the hearts of the church and bringing the dross of life to the top for removal, it is not a true revival.

It was surprising to see that this revival, though many unbelievers were coming to Jesus, was really about the church getting right with God. It was backsliders, the cold in heart, the prodigals—and yes, pastors, deacons, evangelists, missionaries and church members thronging the altars.

- ***It was marked*** by preaching that tore at the heart of a person's religion.
- ***It was marked*** by the probing of the Holy Ghost concerning the sin that had crept into the lives of so many people.
- ***It was marked*** by a cry of agony over the sin of one's life.
- ***It was marked*** by the travail of prayer warriors agonizing over the lost souls of the world and church.
- ***It was marked*** by salvation, healing and deliverance.

Oh yes, I can see why some rejected Evangelist Steve Hill. He's in good company as every revival movement from the past had those who were even refused entrance into the church and took the move of God to the fields.

The message of revival is penetrating and assaultive on religion.

Folks whose hearts were melted in the presence of a living and righteous God made their way to the altar in many fiery, truth-filled revivals to *"take care of some very serious business"* between God and themselves.

A great hunger to go and see what it was all about was released by God deep into the hearts of people everywhere, all around the nations of the world. This also was nothing new in our time—it has happened in every great awakening. People flocked to places where God was moving, coming from far and near to see what the rumors were all about.

And it was marked by those who scoffed at the revival as "not being God."
So, just as in Jesus' day, the crowd was a mixture.

- ***Some*** came to scoff while ***others*** came to seek God.
- ***Some*** came to discredit while ***others*** came to validate what they had heard.

So, the years have come and gone and some kind of evolution has taken place as the church world has had to deal with what God started. And from that powerful outpouring, the beginning stages of revival, we now have what is left of what God was doing.

Was it all God? Well, if man was present—it was not ***all*** God. Man is like that; there is a segment of mankind that just has to put their hands on what God is doing and turn it into their show. But, if hungry people seeking God are present, then it is God in humble places wherever people came to worship Him.

And it was God who showed up in response to the cry that had reached His ears!

With the birth of Jesus ***you had Herod*** and ***you had the Magi*** from the East. Both knew about Jesus but each responded in totally different ways. One was manipulating and destructive and the other worshipped.

When Jesus grew up to minister there was also a mixed crowd—those who followed after Him to seek Him and those who followed to entrap and destroy.

If God is moving—man is also moving in response—either to destroy or to worship. Really, nothing has changed.

So, revival was initiated by God on behalf of a praying people and when it happened—it was God, *regardless of man's response to Him.*

And, unfortunately, many in the church have not responded well to God's movement towards His Church.

Oh, folks, He's tried.

- ***He's called*** intercessors to stand in the gap for the church.
- ***He's raised up*** voices crying out on behalf of a worldly and carnal church that has moved on without God's Spirit.
- ***He's moved*** in ways that has challenged the church, releasing His powerful Spirit to stir the hearts of church leaders and congregations.
- ***He's raised up*** prophetic voices to call for repentance and to speak His message to those of His House.
- ***He's shaken*** ministries down to their foundations, trying to extract holy fear in the heart of the Church.
- ***He's placed*** His Spirit in places all over the nations to be a lighthouse in the encroaching darkness that is even trying to put the lights out in His House.
- ***He's s called*** for prayer and worship 24 hours and day, 7 days a week all around the nations, with the cry for revival in the church!

These outposts of God's Grace to many regions dot the landscape—but many yet reject their existence.

Meanwhile, the church is engaging in all kinds of personal renewals—renewals that add to a person's personal worth, self-esteem, prosperity—transformations that can be enacted by man's efforts alone.

So many have chosen alternate paths, going *"another way," "doing it a different way,"*—leaving behind the hard and costly road of a radical return to God.

So, is revival obsolete in this new season—have we moved past that level—have we developed past that need?

I say, *"No!"*

- ***As long as*** God's people are still independent of the Holy Spirit,
- ***As long as*** they are complacent and satisfied with where they are,
- ***As long as*** there are still people who are cold in their love,

- ***As long as*** there is a self-focused religion . . .

We still need revival!

> ***Isaiah 58:1***—*Cry aloud, spare not, lift up thy voice like a trumpet, and show my people their transgression, and the house of Jacob their sins.*

Simply put—do not hold back or restrain yourself, but make a sound like a trumpet to sound the alarm on God's Holy Mountain!

We have stepped right to the brink of this season and time that we have believed God for.

- ***We*** are in a place now of either looking totally foolish for nothing or we are right on the verge of the greatest revival in history.
- ***We*** have either beaten the air or we have moved heaven.
- ***We*** have either muddied the waters with the vanity of our ideas or we have stepped right into the heart of history and are ready to see the Hand of God move in our hour.
- ***We*** have either stepped into insanity or we are right the brink of the promises being fulfilled and a great ingathering of souls coming to Jesus

It takes faith in God to look like fools in a place such as this—to believe God, in the face of religious and social disbelief, that He is a God of His Word and will perform what He has said He will do.

There have been many madmen and women who have made history for their wildly insane ideas that they tried to carry to fulfillment—Adolph Hitler, Mussolini, and Jim Jones—people who dreamed big but walked off a cliff and found nothing to hold them up when it was all said and done.

They are now nothing more than a mar on the pages of our books of history.

Jesus entered into the world, making wild claims that went against the norm but He was right on target and all that was intended to be accomplished by His coming was fulfilled—in spite of the fact people said he was demon possessed and acted for the kingdom of darkness.

He was not in step with religion or man's ideas but made incredible history as one who has changed the world forever.

When a people are called out to do something extraordinary, such as pray for revival and prepare their own hearts, homes and churches, it is to begin to advance against the tide of popular, secular, religious opinion.

We do look foolish but it had better be for something real! It had better be for something that is authenticated by the Holy Spirit.

Are we ready to transition?

- It's all about the plans of God being fulfilled through us in our lifetime.
- It's about leaving this world with a bang—not a fizzle.

Holy Ghost is not flexible about fire—it has to be there!

It's time for the fire on the altar of our hearts to be pressed to white hot, so as to impact our cities, states, the nations, the harvest fields.

I am not talking about those moments in time when you *"feel"* the fire of God . . . but rather when *you are* the fire!

CHAPTER 43

COURAGEOUS REVIVAL

Isaiah 57:15

The high and lofty one who lives in eternity, the Holy One, says this:
"I live in the high and holy place with those whose spirits are
contrite and humble.
I restore the crushed spirit of the humble and revive the courage of those
with repentant hearts. NLT

Psalms 85:6 says, *"Wilt thou not revive us again: that thy people may rejoice in thee?"* This question must have been asked 100's of 1000's of times over the years of history, as people have come to realize how spiritually destitute they have become.

God created space in us which only He can fill. The human spirit, by the nature of being created in the likeness of God, cries out to be filled. Jesus understood that when He came in contact with people on earth. The Samaritan woman (***John 4:9-15)*** met the one who would give her living water with the promise of never thirsting again.

I have a couple of potted fruit trees that have sat in my house for a couple of years. I have noticed some problems with them:

- They are growing in dead soil.
- They are root bound in a pot that is too small with too little soil.
- They wilt easily.
- They are stunted in their growth.
- They are producing no fruit.

I have been meaning to repot the pitiful trees into something that will give them room to grow, to fertilize them, to help them to begin to bear fruit.

Can we not see a great need in the church being described in these two trees?

The word *"revive"* in ***Psalms 85:6*** means, to live, nourish up, preserve alive, quicken, recover, repair, restore to life, be whole.

I ask again, "*Is revival obsolete, past its peak season and out-dated*?" My answer, not one from my lips or opinion, but from a deep place of need in my spirit that cries out for a fresh move of God's Spirit upon the church today, is a resounding, ***"No! It is not obsolete . . ."***

- ***Not as long*** as there is still a dead and dying church;
- ***Not as long*** as sin is still running rampant in the lives of those called by His name;
- ***Not as long*** as a spirit of tolerance for the worldly concepts exists in the hearts and minds of God's people;
- ***Not as long*** as pastors deviate from the Word of God into a lifeless message to appease the masses;
- ***Not as long*** as pride is the covering for that which is done in the church;
- ***Not as long*** as there are schisms and divisions, ripping and shredding the body of Christ;
- ***Not as long*** as people are following their own way, doing what is right in their own eyes . . .

Revival is an action on God's part to deal with His people, to bring to life those that are spiritually dying or dead—those who still go by the name of the Lord but no longer embrace His management of and His image in their lives.

This revival, as preached by Jonathan Goforth in 1908, is one that *"exalts the person of the Lord Jesus Christ as King and Savior who must be reckoned with."* He developed through prayer the firm conviction that revival is born through humility, faith, prayer and the power of the Holy Ghost. He writes, *"If revival is being withheld from us, it is because some idol remains still enthroned; because we still insist in placing our reliance in human schemes; because we still refuse to face the unchangeable truth that 'it is not by might but by My Spirit, says the Lord.'"*

God has always called His church towards *a place* specifically set apart for an encounter with Him.

This encounter is meant to so impact the church that we go forth to the harvest, as carriers of a *God-proportion Anointing* to break the yoke of bondage off people who are caught within the webs of the enemy. The encounter that the church is having with God *is to prepare them* as pure vessels through which His River will flow forth to the nations.

This is a pure revival—when the people of God have had a baptism of fire, purified and full of God's purposes, while dwelling in the place of His calling—your *there!*

This is a powerful combination, people so in love with Jesus who have counted the cost ***and*** who are obedient to the call and the place that God wants them to serve.

There is a move of God across the earth such as has never been seen in our lifetime. We are a part of something bigger than we can imagine. Souls are coming to Jesus in record numbers and being transformed by the Power of the Blood of Jesus!

People in the nations are being brought into the Kingdom of God by the multitudes in a single moment's time in history, in the twinkling of an eye, changed by one encounter with the Living Christ.

Think of it, 1000's, while I write this, have come to Jesus! The Power of His Wonderful Name and the sacrifice of the cross opened heaven for the salvation multitudes of souls. The Move of God upon the earth is opening doors that have never been opened before ***and*** reopening old doors that the devil shut centuries ago. We live in a time when God is raising up an army that was once, as it were, the valley of dry bones similar to Israel.

The breath of God has come into *His* Church and SHE LIVES!!!

She marches forth from victory to victory on the many fronts that lay before her.

The enemy's camp is turning into a place barren of souls that ran to the *Wells of Salvation* that have been opened by a sovereign move of God. Good, clean wells; an oasis with the trees of refreshing shade surrounding them, prepared by a people who not only dug them, but have kept them clean and ready for the thirsty.

Are you there?

There are a lot of wonderful and dedicated people in the *Move of God* and yes, some of them are drawing big crowds who are hungry for God, but also, many of them are also serving in small, remote places around the world.

There are pastors, evangelist, teachers, prophets, apostles, intercessors, church workers, youth and even kids—all with a servant's heart—who have a heart after God, serving Him diligently.

- ***They can be found*** in cities, towns, burgs, villages, jungles, swamplands, village squares, and places that some of us have never heard of—under thatched roofs without walls, brick structures without windows or roofs, wooden benches sat under a tree or standing or sitting room in an open field—in hidden places and in open arenas—God's servants and His people can be found everywhere in every imaginable venue.
- ***They can be found*** preaching the gospel in the prisons, not only as a visitor, but also in many cases as an inmate.
- ***They can be found*** passing out food baskets, and sharing the love of Christ in a tangible and needed way.
- ***They can be found*** in a Sunday school class with a group of 4 and 5 year olds, laying the foundations of faith for those kids and within teen centers, classes and schools.
- ***They can be found*** on the college campuses reaching the nations gathered in those places.
- ***They can be found*** in nursing homes reaching out to those who are almost ready to cross from this life into death.

- ***They can be found*** in hospitals, visiting the sick and wounded, reaching out to those who are hurting.
- ***They can be found*** invading the dark alleys, bars and brothels of the nations, searching for people who are all used up by the world's ways.
- ***They can be found*** in the underground churches of restricted nations and on the city streets of those same nations sharing the love of Jesus for the lost.
- ***They can be found*** leaving their shores to go to foreign places to live within the culture that is totally strange to them, leaving behind family and friends.
- ***They can be found*** in stadiums and coliseums preaching to the masses and working behind the scenes in prayer for those gatherings.

They can be found among and with all people groups of the world—The Church that is alive and well on Planet Earth!

- ***Yes***, there are sincere people who have humbled themselves under God's hand for His use of their lives and are following hard after Him.
- ***Yes***, there are pastors who are leading their flocks into the direct path of God's purpose and movement.
- ***Yes,*** there are prophets that are God-fearing and moving with a call of God on their lives.
- ***Yes***, there are apostolic leaders who break the ground and keeps contact with several flocks at one time, speaking into their lives, visiting, and equipping the Body of Christ.
- ***Yes***, there are teachers who break open the Word of God with integrity and no thought of gain.
- ***Yes***, there are intercessors that are true and faithful servants of the Most High God.
- ***Yes***, there are evangelists and missionaries who are going forth into the harvest fields of the nations and speaking truth and equipping the Body of Christ.
- ***Yes***, there are authors that have written the messages of God, as they have felt the Lord speak into their hearts what He is saying to His church.

- ***Yes***, there are motivators who speak and stir the heart to action.
- ***Yes,*** there are those who rally people around the governments of the world and pray for the leaders.
- **Yes,** there are congregations of people who have sold out to God, holding nothing back and willing to go all the way for Him to the very end of their journey.
- ***Yes***, there is a true move of God and God IS moving powerfully in the midst of a people who are seeking hard after Him, obeying Him, preparing for His coming, and paying the price of discipleship—whatever it may be that the Lord asks of them.

Yes, **it is powerful and yes, IT IS God who is moving upon and through the yielded servants of the King and the Kingdom.**

Are you there?

FORGIVE US LORD!

- ***Forgive us Lord***, for letting the fire on the altar go out and becoming lukewarm towards you.
- ***Forgive us Lord***, for locking prayer up into a side room, for being a prayerless church and people.
- ***Forgive us Lord***, for not keeping our doors shut to worldliness and compromise, for losing ground to the world's values and allowing our foundation of Holiness to erode.
- ***Forgive us Lord***, for being *seeker-friendly* and *performance-oriented.*
- ***Forgive us Lord***, for working so hard to be accepted, for desiring men's admiration and esteem.
- ***Forgive us Lord***, for the years of self-sufficiency, for trusting in riches instead of Your Name.
- ***Forgive us Lord***, for pouring all of our time, energy and money into building a great ministry name for ourselves.
- ***Forgive us Lord***, for Pride of Place and Position.
- ***Forgive us Lord***, for the years of schisms, division, leading to the loss of many hungry souls.
- ***Forgive us Lord***, for the years of manipulation and control; for placing weighty rules of men's doctrines upon the people of God, burdening them down to serve us rather than God.
- ***Forgive us Lord***, for our apathy and slumbering while the world's masses have died in their sin.
- ***Forgive us Lord***, for the years of hypocrisy in preaching, teaching and speaking things in your name that we did not put in to practice.
- ***Forgive us Lord,*** for the lost destiny of our sons and daughters who were born to rule and reign in the Kingdom.

- ***Forgive us Lord***, for not teaching your Word and doctrine to our children and youth, leaving them with no foundation to stand upon when tested.
- ***Forgive us Lord***, for not passing the heritage of a Spirit-filled, Spirit-empowered church down to our children.
- ***Forgive us Lord***, for emptying our altars of the signs of the Holy Spirit's work, His power and the manifestations of God's Glory.
- ***Forgive us Lord,*** for trying to rein in the Holy Spirit in our church services, bringing death to Your movement while we try to keep our order.
- ***Forgive us Lord***, for filling in the vacancy made by the Holy Spirit's absence with *other things.*
- ***Forgive us Lord***, for putting out the Fire of Passionate worship in exchange for years of cold, passionless service and worship.
- ***Forgive us Lord***, for the lack of hunger for Your Word and the moving of your Spirit.
- ***Forgive us Lord***, for saying every time Holy Spirit moves, ***"This isn't God!"***
- ***Forgive us Lord,*** for not being open, honest and of a humble and contrite spirit.

"Until we tell ourselves the truth about *"us"* we will not repent and pray the right prayers—prayers of humility and repentance that restore the heart of God for us, our families and churches."

PART VII

BLAMELESS

Ephesians 5:27

That he might present it to himself a glorious church, not having spot, or wrinkle, or any such thing; but that it should be holy and without blemish.

Refiner's Fire
A Dream

Deuteronomy 4:24

For the Lord thy God is a consuming fire, even a jealous God.

In the dream I saw the hand of God drop a mass of rusty, dirty-looking metal ***(Matthew 6:19-21)*** into a boiling pot of water sitting on an open fire. The water was rich with lye soap, foaming and roiling in the hot water. The dirty metal sunk to the bottom, disappearing out of sight. But, much to my surprise, I saw this beautiful lady, dressed in the most brilliant white and shining gown rise up out of the water. I heard the word, *"chaste."* I felt the strong impression, as I looked at her modest and brilliant garment that she was dressed only for her groom. She came up consecrated and blameless, pure and spotless for her Lord.

No one could rightly accuse her of wrongdoing or having many lovers.

As I awoke the book of Malachi came to me and the refiner's fire.

Malachi 3:1-3 (Emphasis Added)—*Behold, I will send my messenger, and he shall prepare the way before me: and the Lord, whom ye seek,* ***shall suddenly come to his temple****, even the messenger of the covenant, whom ye delight in: behold, he shall come, says the LORD of hosts. But who may abide the day of his coming? And who shall stand when he appears?* ***For he is like a refiner's fire, and like fullers' soap****. And he shall sit as a refiner and purifier of silver: and he shall purify the sons of Levi, and purge them as gold and silver, that they may offer unto the LORD* ***an offering in righteousness.***

This Biblical prophecy tells us ***how*** the Lord is coming—***suddenly.*** It tells us ***in what manner*** He will come—***like a refiner's fire.***

John the Baptist states in ***Matthew 3:11-12,*** *"I'm baptizing you here in the river, turning your old life in for a kingdom life. The real action comes next: The main character in this drama—compared to him I'm a mere stagehand—will ignite the kingdom life within you, a fire within you, the Holy Spirit within you, changing you from the inside out. He's going to clean house—make a clean sweep of your lives. He'll place everything true in its proper place before God; everything false he'll put out with the trash to be burned."* ***The Message*** [3]

He appeared suddenly in a way no one expected and at an inconvenient time—And that is how He enters His House today; as a messenger of His covenant of blood.

- ***The purpose*** of the fire was to **refine:** to bring to a pure state; free from impurities
- ***The purpose*** of the fire was to **purify**: unadulterated; uncontaminated; innocent or holy:
- ***The purpose*** of the fire was to **purge**: to rid of whatever is impure or undesirable;

The purpose **of the fire was to bring forth an offering in righteousness.**

I know with all my heart that God desires and deserves an offering in righteousness! I know His heart must long for His children to be free of all impurities. I know, as you do, Jesus deserves a pure white, spotless, bride of Christ.

May we all yield to the refiner's fire today.

It's time to wash up!

CHAPTER 44

AWAKE MY SOUL!

Psalms 17:15

As for me, I will behold thy face in righteousness: I shall be satisfied, when I awake, with thy likeness.

We are in a time such as has never been seen on the earth. Even though there have been some great and awful times in places around the earth in past history, we are now seeing that this is not just a single place but the whole earth itself that is being impacted. One event today can cause kingdoms, thrones and governments to be moved from where they once were, never to return to their former state.

Events of great magnitude has impacted the earth and sent humanity reeling as they begin to search for the former days of *how it used to be*.

So much comfort and ease has disappeared as people have faced the stark reality of devastating change. From Africa to Indonesia, from China to North Korea, from North America to South America, from the North Pole to the South Pole, from Europe to Australia and New Zealand, to the Islands of the Seas, to every plot of ground where humanity dwells, the world has opened its eyes to the changes that face others and them. The threat of humanity imploding itself in utter Chaos is only a heartbeat away in any region.

Humanity lives with a hair-pin trigger, cocked and ready to snap at any moment, as turmoil abounds and the earth becomes more restless.

The church, meanwhile, is seeking where they are to fit into each event, as disasters bring them out of their doors to *meet the needs* of increasing devastations—tsunamis, fires, floods, storms, earthquakes, terrorism and war.

> ***Romans 13:11*** (Emphasis Added)—*And that, knowing the time, that now it is high time to* ***awake out of sleep****: for now is our salvation nearer than when we believed.*

It doesn't take much of a prophet to figure out the Word of God is being fulfilled and will continue to be fulfilled until the Day of the Lord comes.

So much is already spelled out for us. There are rumblings in every element of the natural and spiritual realm as God utters His voice from His Throne to the thrones of minions and the thrones of mankind, from the highest to the lowest.

The Alpha has spoken down through the ages but now the Omega—*the AMEN*—is rising to speak, possibly some of the last words to humanity in a world as we now know it.

He may be at the beginning of a very long dissertation, or He may be in the middle or on the final pages of history—but He is speaking to the earth's inhabitants even now in very clear tones, including the Church in this present age.

There will be closure to some things when He speaks.

His voice will close a door that will never be able to open again. Mankind in any realm thus affected can try to go behind the door, pry at the door, try to open it with all their might, but when God's hand shuts a door it is shut.

We see this truth in ***Genesis 7:16-18*** where God shut the door of the Ark after Noah and his family had entered, right before the flood came. Jesus declares to the Church of Philadelphia in ***Revelation 3:7***

"He who is holy has the key to open and shut doors."

God's voice resounds over the earth and everything within the sound of His voice is responding—those who bless Him and those who curse Him those who heed His voice and those who ignore it—all are responding to Him in the most pivotal timetable of earth's history.

There are rumblings and shakings and tremors that are unsettling everyone.

Here we are in the middle of history in-the-making, not only earthly history but prophetic history. We are watching things unfold that were foretold of centuries ago and maybe just days ago as prophecies today abound with truth of how and where God's hand is released.

We are in a time when the Past, Present and Future are preparing to converge—prophetically.

While the last pages of Church history are being written, we might ask ourselves, *"What is my testimony and how will I be portrayed on the pages by the eternal scribes?*

Things are heating up all around us so it may as well heat up in the church. If not, then the church will not be ready and positioned for what is to come.

> ***1 Corinthians 15:34***—*Awake to righteousness, and sin not; for some have not the knowledge of God: I speak this to your shame.*

What is God after?
It's us!
It's His church!

So, here we are in the midst of a changing world and we are changing as well. While God has awakened us to so much, this next level is going to release His Glory in ways not yet seen. It is worth it to push in and press and pray in this hour for the rewards are great, *if we faint not.*

> ***Psalms 29:3-4***

3 The voice of the LORD is upon the waters: the God of glory thunders: the LORD is upon many waters.

4 The voice of the LORD is powerful; the voice of the LORD is full of majesty.

It is time that we as a church awaken to the voice and purposes of God in this season.

Our soul is being awakened to the moving and the voice of the spirit of God as it reflects into all the situations—to the reality of the Word, to the events of the world. We are being awakened to our part in interceding the heart of God and in preparing for times *and seasons yet to be unfolded in our lifetime.*

We have had so many people come through our doors over the past years to our bi-annual prayer gathering known as ***Going up to High Places***—all kinds of people but with one thing in common—everyone was hungry and searching for something.

- ***Many*** have come in tattered *garments of spiritual pride and self-accomplishments*, offering God what was left after religion got through with us.
- ***Many***, who had been beaten up, dried up and fed up with religion, were looking for something their souls ached for.

Little did we know at that time how much we needed the processes of God to work in our lives.

- ***Many*** souls were all coming out of a dry place of hunger and thirst.

Lips were parched and hearts were reaching for a lifeline of the Spirit of God. How very much many desired to step into the waters of His presence when they realized where He could be found.

All over the nation watering holes, oases in a dry land opened their doors for thousands. They found these places rich with the anointing that no one had really yet paid a deep price for.

It was God's gift to the sleeping church—a reminder of His sweet presence.

It wafted in upon the spiritual senses and awakened something deeper within people than they had ever known existed. God literally washed over throngs of people seeking Him with an overwhelming and *out-of-this-world-outpouring of Himself.*

- ***Worship*** became more passionate.
- ***Intercession*** erupted as vision for the city and nations began to move our inverted hearts upward and outward.
- ***Zeal for the Word of God*** could not be quenched with casual, mediocre preaching.

People desired the strength of truth! They shouted when people ran to the altars in repentance and then joined them ourselves as they felt undone in the awesome presence of the Lord God Almighty.

God just came down and met with His people in such powerful ways. Altars were full of people crying out to God, answering the call to repentance and preparation.

But at that time, how little we understood the price of deep, heart-felt change that would form us into the image and likeness of Christ for we were only at the beginning of a very long journey, one that would greatly tax our strengths.

Everything was suspect in light of God's holiness as physically, mentally, emotionally and spiritually—our will, our mind, our religion, our attitudes—everything that did not *look like Jesus, smell like Jesus, walk like Jesus, talk like Jesus, worship like Jesus and serve like Jesus* was inspected by the Holy Spirit.

Sometimes God's love is confrontational.
I heard the Lord say, "*Merciful Judgment.*"

Do we understand this part of God's love? Sometime His arrows, *though painful*, are actually ***a lifeline of grace.*** He has not been willing to leave us in the condition that we came to Him in because the baggage we carried was death to the move of God in our lives.

These years since have been made up of *God and people on a collision course* as God has uttered His voice to His Church.

The years have been all about what has happened between Him and us.

- ***Some*** found what they were looking for and allowed God's love to probe deep into their hearts and minds and do a work of restoration, healing, forgiveness and redemption. God's arrows have found soft targets in the hearts of many men and women who have melted at the sound of His voice. There have been many who were deeply impacted by the greatness of God as chains and shackles broke off their lives.
- ***For others***, God's arrows have hit hardness of the heart and been repelled expertly by those who avoid the sound of His voice. We have seen some things that depict the lowest of human nature, revealing the depths to which the enemy has gone to destroy and disable the destiny of God's people and the Church. We have wept for the loss that yet remains and pray for deliverance.
- ***Many*** have come with their hands so full and struggling to lay it all down to follow Jesus, unable to receive the wonderful things that God had in store for them. It breaks our heart and frustrates the grace of God when God wants to work in people's lives but there is *no room.*

We have watched the interaction between God and man from a front row seat.

It has been glorious at times and heartbreaking at other times. Everyone who has entered through the door Jesus in His grace and mercy opened, has been changed—every single person! We are changed by the choices we make one by one. We all decide ***how much, how far, how big, how great a work*** we will allow God to do in our lives.

It is still a time of deep, soul-searching, preparation and God's hand probing into the deepest part of our hearts.

- ***It can be*** rugged, hard and savage.
- ***It can be*** uncomfortable and invasive.

It is a time of war, first on our own flesh and then on the enemy of our churches, family, cities and nations. ***It is a time*** of Worship, Word and Intercession.

There is a sound in intercession that the world is still waiting for, for when this level is hit, the earth will feel the shaking of these prayers.

- ***You have not*** yet prayed like you're going to pray.
- ***You have not*** yet worshipped like you're going to worship.
- ***You have not*** yet eaten the Word like you are going to eat it.
- ***You have not*** yet humbled yourself like you're going to humble yourself.
- ***You have not*** yet sought God's face like you are going to seek Him.
- ***You have not*** yet stood in the Glory of God like you will one day.

***You have not* yet paid the price that you are getting ready to pay to go where you are getting ready to go.**

As God's Winds of Change blow over us, awakening a deeper hunger for God, let us all be prepared to allow God to have His way in our hearts and lives. Then we will truly experience the thing we all search for. Let us all come humbly into the presence of the Lord, realizing that we are in desperate need of change, *yes, even after all these years.*

It is not a time when we waltz our way into the glory of God but a time in which we repent our way into His glory, *prepare* the way for His glory and *die to ourselves* so that we may see His glory come down.

But before that time, there is an old man to kill."
Are we dead yet?

It's our Garden of Gethsemane moment—a time to break our will that opposes the will of the Father. ***(Matt 26:37-42)*** It's our will that we are contending with right now. It's our flesh we contend with—on a level like we never knew before.

It is the spiritual part of our flesh that is now dying—the part that is yielded to serve God, but still does not want to suffer anything to do it.

Lose what you must lose, but keep God in the house.

Isaiah 64:8—*But now, O LORD, thou art our father; we are the clay, and thou our potter; and we all are the work of thy hand.*

To our minds, this is the very gentle hand of Jesus shaping our lives—until he breaks the whole vessel and starts from the beginning. To me this is representative of the fact that . . .

Jesus is totally willing *to break* the vessel *to make* the vessel

This is also the place that many jump from the wheel ***because the Master is identifying the flaws*** in the vessel. We need to hang on and let the processes of God work in our lives to the glory and honor of the Lord.

So, my *old man* is fading from sight—like the invisible man.

Leonard Ravenhill said, *"I don't ask people if they're saved anymore; I look them straight in the eye and say, 'Does Christ live inside you?'"* It is what we have been asking for, isn't it . . . ?

- ***To be*** made in the image of Christ?
- ***To be*** mature?
- ***To be*** used of God?
- ***To see*** the kind of release of power that came at Pentecost?
- ***To see*** the anointing, even in my shadow?
- ***To see*** the deaf hear, the blind see, the lame walk and the dead raised?

We are finally going so far out on a limb that we will either fall or God will bear us up. It is all or nothing right now.

- ***It will be worth it all*** when we see Jesus in us.
- ***It will be worth it all*** when we reach our hand for someone and our hand will look like His.
- ***It will be worth it all*** when we speak and our voice echoes heaven's message, pure and filled with power.

It will be worth it all when the Father says,
"This is my child in whom I am well pleased."

Chapter 45

How far would you be willing to go?

Isaiah 6:1-5

. . . I saw also the Lord sitting upon a throne, high and lifted up, and his train filled the temple. Above it stood the seraphims: each one had six wings; with twain he covered his face, and with twain he covered his feet, and with twain he did fly. And one cried unto another, and said, Holy, holy, holy, is the Lord of hosts: the whole earth is full of his glory. And the posts of the door moved at the voice of him that cried, and the house was filled with smoke. Then said I, Woe is me! for I am undone; because I am a man of unclean lips, and I dwell in the midst of a people of unclean lips: for mine eyes have seen the King, the Lord of hosts.

In God's Glory there is change.

It went from Isaiah seeing the Glory and Majesty of the Lord to "*Woe is me.*" In the light of God's glory we are undone in His presence. Isaiah was quick to realize his condition as he beheld the Lord.

When there is no repentance, there is no vision of the reality of God.

Jesus was . . .

- ***So*** pure
- ***So*** focused
- ***So*** anointed

- ***So*** in tune with His Father's Will
- ***So*** completely favored by His Father

. . . He didn't have a divided heart and mission.

His power came from His purity ***and*** perfect obedience. That mixture was potent and released a level of power that only those who walk on that level of purity and obedience will ever achieve. Jesus' days were walked out in such a way that any moment of need, He was prepared for His Father's Will.

Today we don't walk in the anointing *as we can and should* ; we look for it when we come upon something where it's needed. We want God to use us *"just the way we are."* Is it possible we're satisfied to keep going the way we've been going, so much so that we don't realize our own condition sometimes?

Donald Gee, called the Apostle of Balance, said, *"No revival can continue with the blessing of God upon it that does not have a high standard of holiness."*

We walk with divided hearts, cluttered lives, and busy minds—with distractions of all kinds. And much of the time, unfortunately, *at a time the Father has need of us*, we are not altogether sanctified, set part, holy and ready for God.

Yes we all have ambitions, goals and a bit of pride to go with our desires to *count for something.*

The questions today are these:

- ***Can we*** lay down our personality, language, conduct, attitude, thoughts, and words for His?
- ***Can we*** apply the Sword of the Spirit to our flesh, crucifying the old man?
- ***Can we*** walk in a level of extreme obedience such as Jesus practiced?

- ***Can we*** lay ourselves upon the altar of sacrifice, fully, surrendering our lives to capture His heart, mind, image, Spirit, Glory?

I've always known, *as you have*, there's a place in God that is going to cost more of us than we've yet given.

As sons and daughters of God, we sometimes act like juvenile delinquents, strong-willed, stubborn and determined to *"do it our way."* We are heirs, joint heirs with Christ Jesus, and yet we many times despise our birthright (***Genesis 25:34)*** by reaching outside the fence to satisfy our hunger and thirst.

> ***Romans 8:17****—And if children, then heirs; heirs* (an inheritor and possessor) *of God, and joint-heirs* (participant; we have all things in common) *with Christ; if so be that we suffer with him, that we may be also glorified together.*

Many are so close to entering in, but still stand just outside the realm of His Glory—a place they can enter into as an heir.

I have watched as many have been drawn to a place in God, gladly entering into what He was doing, because they felt good about everything. But what about when it doesn't *feel good*; it hurts and is stretching us beyond ourselves? ***Romans 8:17*** speaks of suffering with Him so that we may be glorified together.

How quickly we can move back to an old comfort zone where it cost us nothing and we gain nothing—*a kind of neutral zone.* It is safe back there—*that place of no cost.*

Are we going to forfeit *for fear, flesh, false, failure, fretting*? Israel simply could not trust God to take them through the difficult passages of the wilderness. And the Glory of the Lord was there all the time, with an invitation to *"come up higher where He was."*

Embrace His Presence!

What does this mean—to you?
And what does it mean to God?

- ***If we are looking for manifestations***—How about the manifestation of repentance?
- ***If we are looking for warfare***—How about the sword to our flesh first?
- ***If we are looking for fire***—How about a hot coal from the altar of God for our tongue?
- ***If we are looking for an altar***—How about one of presenting our body as a living sacrifice, holy and acceptable to the Lord?
- ***If we are looking for an encounter with God's presence on earth***—How about a healthy Fear of God?
- ***If we are looking for a powerful worship experience***—How about clean hands and pure hearts?
- ***If we are looking for a word***—How about first trembling at The Word?
- ***If we are looking for revelation***—How about embracing Truth?
- ***If we are looking for visions***—How about seeing Him high and lifted up?
- ***If we are looking for His Glory***—How about changing from glory to glory?
- ***If we want to experience His Glory***—How about remembering, He will not share it with anyone—not a man—not an angel—not a ministry—not a church.
- ***If we want the Ark of His Presence***—How about fully embracing Jesus Christ?

If we are excited about His presence

How about, *"Lord, Bend me! Break me! Mold me?"*

When we behold His Glory—*self-focus is gone.* Focus on wealth, angels, doctrines, problems, feelings will dissipate like a vapor. Dogmatism about styles of worship and the order of the service will fall away like chaff from wheat.

- ***Moses*** could not enter the tabernacle because of the Glory ***Exodus 40:34-35***
- ***Solomon*** could not stand in the Glory ***2 Chronicles 7:1-2***
- ***Stephen*** knelt in the presence of Jesus. ***Acts 7:56-60***
- ***John*** could not stand in His Glory on the Isle of Patmos ***Revelation 1:17***

If we say we have been in the presence of the Lord, seen and felt His Glory and nothing's changed, then we've seen nothing of His Glory at all—though He was present to change us.

> **2 Corinthians 3:18**—*But we all, with open face beholding as in a glass the glory of the Lord, are changed into the same image from glory to glory, even as by the Spirit of the Lord.*

I know no one truly wants to live on the carnal fringes, *just short of the Glory of God.* I have no doubt in my mind that multitudes are desiring that level in God in which we too see Him high and lifted up and see ourselves in the light of His Glory.

God's Glory is over the earth being made manifest in places we would never think *and* upon and through people we would never choose.

If when the Glory of God filled the earthly tabernacle and it brought man to his knees, and if we being the temple of the Holy Ghost are filled with the very power, presence and glory of God on earth, should we not also be brought to our knees?

Every knee will bow and every tongue will confess that Jesus Christ is Lord.

- ***King's*** will surrender their Crowns.
- ***Pastors*** will surrender their Churches.
- ***Fathers and Mothers*** will surrender their Families.

And every human being will bow their knees and make a long, over-due confession, ***"You are Lord!"*** Even the devil and the empire of demonic powers will surrender on that day . . .

This will be the most overwhelming, glorious, fearful and awestruck moment in history. It will be a time when the Glory of God through Jesus Christ will be revealed in the full intensity of Divine Revelation.

People today can stand in the presence of God, feel the Spirit of God contending with them for their souls and not bend their knees or make confession. But one day the weight of God's Glory will open every eye and loose every tongue and bend every knee and there will be no resistance then.

Why **wait until that day?**

- ***Why not*** loosen our tongues and bend our knees and declare Him ***Lord and King*** of all the kingdoms of our hearts and lives ***now?***
- ***Why not*** embrace the glory of the image of our Lord and Savior, Jesus Christ and draw Him close to our hearts ***now?***

That encounter with the greatness of God's presence is able to not only transform us now, but transform our environment, as it has all down through the ages of time.

God's presence turned a coliseum into a sanctuary.
It made an altar of worship in the dungeon.

And . . . The Glory of God transforms the dead space around us into the Throne Room.

CHAPTER 46

BREAKTHROUGH TO DECREASE

Philippians 2:5-8

Let this mind be in you, which was also in Christ Jesus:
Who, being in the form of God, thought it not robbery to be equal with God:
But made himself of no reputation, and took upon him the form of a servant, and was made in the likeness of men:
And being found in fashion as a man, he humbled himself, and became obedient unto death, even the death of the cross.

The Prophets of old have foretold this day, the day we are living in right now—the day in which we minister, worship and prepare the way of the Lord. There is a culmination of many things in our life span, in our season—one in which we will all play a part.

The decision we will be making is—*"From which side will we view the last days?"*

We have been and still are in a time of choice. Daily, weekly, monthly, yearly—we have been making choices about where we will stand. A challenge will come our way—a trial—a situation—that demands an answer from us and we are thrust right into an arena of choice again and again. Many are choices of eternal value.

- ***We decide*** to what extent we will serve God.
- ***We decide*** what we believe about the messages we hear.

What the old prophets have said is coming to pass right before our eyes, even though there are many yet to be fulfilled.

- ***The Spirit of God*** is moving over the face of the *waters.*
- ***The seas*** are roaring at the mention of His Name.
- ***The younger generation*** of believers is coming together with the older generations of believers in a mighty shout of praise for their deepened revelation of who their King is.
- ***The incense of worship*** is ascending from altars of sacrifice, as people are drawing closer to God in times of worship and intercession.

The aroma of God's people adoring Him is filling the Throne Room of Heaven.

God is stirred to the sounds that are reaching His ears.

We are now, them, in our day. We now have the Mantle being placed upon us as the church. God is laying it upon His Church, those who will ***Prepare the Way of the Lord***, as ***Harbinger Ministries.***

- **Harbinger**—a person who goes ahead and makes known the approach of another; herald. Anything that foreshadows a future event; sign: a person sent in advance.

John the Baptist fulfilled it in his day and there will be a church that will fulfill it in this day.

Think with me for a moment about Elijah—He was a man—human, just like us. And yet, when he came to the place in his ministry to where he was disgusted with the Jezebelian reign that was over Israel and equally disgusted with the impotent king, Ahab, he decided to take a stand. It was not an easy place to be, especially being as *he felt* that he was the *only one* left who would take a stand.

This is so much like many of us in the little towns and big cities and remote villages that make up the worlds harvest fields.

- ***It seems*** as if we are the *only ones* left who will take a stand for anything to do with God, holiness, prayer, revival, and battle against the darkness that is so evident to our eyes.
- **We *feel*** as if the rest of the Christians in our world are maintaining a stance that is safe and unwilling to speak out for injustice, unrighteousness, and the name of Jesus.

But we know that we are called to press in for the harvest. Many have spent years in preparation for the ingathering of souls.

You, reader, have possibly been on your face before God in prayer, fasting, repentance for yourself and stood in the gap for your city. You have no doubt been witnessing to your neighbors, co-workers and family, but feel as if you have made very little ground.

But now, you have sensed that there is a new wind blowing over your soul and you have begun to realize that *it is a time like no other.* You are beginning to feel that God is renewing your vision for your city, increasing your heart for the harvest, pressing you into an even tighter mold of Christ likeness. ***You are ready.***

Ladies and Gentlemen of the Church, you are the fulfillment of prophecy.

Elisha of old, cried out as Elijah was carried up in the fiery chariot from heaven, *"I pray thee, let a double portion of thy spirit be upon me."* ***(2 Kings 2:9)*** He also took up the mantle of Elijah that fell from him, ***(2 Kings 2:13)*** John the Baptist was the next to receive the spirit of Elijah, *in other words,* ***the anointing*** to make ready the way for the coming of Jesus in his day.

The church now is receiving that same anointing to make ready for the coming of Jesus in our day.

We are going to be considering what that means to us. We will be taking some lessons from those who have preceded us with the anointing *in the spirit of Elijah*, so that truly these entrustments can be carried out with holiness and purity.

Elijah was a man who lived in a very perverse world; Ahab and Jezebel's time. A good number of the true prophets of God had been slaughtered and an evil and corrupt empire under Ahab had been established with Jezebel at the head, manipulating and controlling Israel with her witchcraft. The true leader had abdicated his throne and had failed to lead as God's man.

Because of this, the *church,* as it were, was weakened and in hiding. Jezebel had terrorized everyone, so much so, that later on, even Elijah thought that he was the *only one* left who had not bent his knees to Baal. The truth is that seven thousand were there, but unseen, *maybe afraid as well.*

A Jezebelian spirit of control had entered in, displacing the true leaders and scaring the rest into silent acceptance of this tyrannical and ungodly rule.

Simply put, she had been tolerated—and yes, also in our time, in our churches.

Years later, *as a fulfillment of prophecy*, John the Baptist came on the scene into the same type of *church.* Herod now sat upon the throne and he had also allowed, by his own immorality, the kingdom to crumble under his rule, with Herodias and Salome controlling the reins of his heart.

He was not God's man, but theirs.

John the Baptist confronted Herod in the same manner that Elijah confronted Ahab and Jezebel. He called out to Herod the sin that lay in the kingdom. ***(Mark 6:17-18)*** Needless to say, this also didn't go over any better than Elijah's confrontation of Jezebel. Both Ahab and Herod decided, indirectly though it was, (*the true voice that spoke through them was Jezebel and Herodias and Salome*), and each in their own time of rule, to destroy the pure and true voice of God's prophets.

Now it's our turn!

There is, in our time, *as there has been in every season*, a corrupt and a pure church. There are those who, like Ahab and Herod, have allowed others to unseat the true authority of God and replace it with the vile and impure, have tolerated the manipulating, controlling and corrupting of the church. Sadly, any voice that decries its condition will be met with the same response as John the Baptist had. ***(Mark 6:21-27)***

In this kingdom time, there has been no room for
Jesus to sit upon the throne.
He, who is the King, has been unseated by immorality,
corruption and vileness in His House.

This is serious enough that Jesus addressed the church in Thyatira in ***Revelation 2: 20-21*** saying, *"Notwithstanding I have a few things against thee, because you allow that woman Jezebel, which calls herself a prophetess, to teach and to seduce my servants to commit fornication, and to eat things sacrificed unto idols. And I gave her space to repent of her fornication; and she repented not."*

We can narrow the issue down to the very heart of each and
every one of us in this matter.
The church of today is us.
We are the Temple of the Holy Ghost.
And the collective body of Christ is the Church, corporate.

It really matters little which angle you come at this from, but bottom line, many are those who have joined the ranks of the *"rank,"* (defiled) ***or*** the ranks of the *"silent,"* (Tolerant or Fearful).

But a mantle from another fiery chariot is falling, Church!
It is a Mantle of Power and Authority!

It falls on one who has been forged in the fires of adversity, suffering, temptation and the wilderness. The question is, are we in a place to receive it? It is the last days anointing to confront, bring order into our life and church, restore, heal, prepare and make ready for the coming of Jesus.

I had a friend who wrote and gave me her scripture for the day from the ***Song of Solomon 8:5*** with the emphasis on this part: *". . . coming up out of the wilderness, leaning upon my beloved."* This is what has been going on. John the Baptist matured in the wilderness and we will too. We will gain strength and staying power and anointing in the wilderness and when we come out, we will know our Lord well enough and walking close enough to Him to lean upon Him as we come out.

We have gone in to come out!
And, we are coming out!

<u>What kind of person will receive this mantle?</u>

It will be one who will know how to walk in the spirit of humility and service to this move of God and not to themselves. John the Baptist understood this anointing. He was a man of great decrease and yet walked in such preparation, which moved him to a powerful ministry to prepare the way upon which the King of Glory would come in his time. We too can learn from this man what it means to prepare.

We don't fully realize how fortunate we are to live in a day such as this. The magnitude of what God is about to do is going to astound us. If you think the Day of Pentecost was something, then everybody had better get ready.

The Last Day's Church is a powerful Church with a Powerful God who bestows a Powerful Anointing.

John 1:19 "*This is the record of* ________" We are going to make it very personal today. Place your name in this scripture where John's name is.

As John was the forerunner to the coming of Christ in the flesh, so are we the forerunners of Christ, who is coming in His Power and His Glory.

Exactly how does a forerunner conduct himself/herself? The religious leaders of John's day sent a group to ask John, "*Who are you?*" I would ask you today, "*Who are 'you?*" This is an, oftentimes, unspoken question that we have already answered, based upon our unspoken reply. But we do give an answer by our lifestyle and speech. We will surely give an answer out in the open too, at some time down the road.

"Who are you?"

A very interesting question—Very interesting answers.

"I'm and intercessor." I'm a pastor." "I'm a teacher." "I'm a somebody . . ."

We more than likely give an answer for "*who we believe or have been told we are.*"

If Jesus were to reverse the question that He asked His disciples, ***"Who do you say that I am,"*** and ask you, ***"Who do you say that you are,"*** what would your answer be?

In ***John 1:20***, John answers the question of the religious world by "*confessing . . .*" What happens in this instance feels like an interrogation to me, because the men, who came to ask the questions, were coming to drill him for information that they could take back to their bosses. They did not come as friends, but as curious, not to embrace John or his message.

People today will have similar questions for you as you move in deeper with Christ and prepare for His coming. Their questions may sound something like this, "*Who do you* ***'think'*** *you are?*" How do you answer?

"Well, I'm a member of such and such church . . ."

Service men and women are trained to give Name, Rank and Serial Number if the enemy catches them. They are trained to stand there, under any pressure, and to not give anything more than what they have been told to say. In a religious/church/revival world that emphasizes the degrees and experience, titles and notoriety of people, we need to be careful that we not cave to the demand to title ourselves for our status sake. There is a certain way that God is training His army. We're not to give just any old answer, but to give a right answer. We could all take a lesson from John on this.

Here's John's confession: ***"I am not The Christ."*** His first words to them were not who he was, but "*Who he was not.*" Let this sink in. John already knew his answer from the wilderness training.

We have got to know our answer as to **"*who we are not*"** beforehand, lest we begin to boast in and of ourselves and thrust ourselves forward, rather than making way for Jesus.

When John answered, it was out of a heart that had already been established in *"Who he was not."*

This is one of the problems facing the church today—*on every level*—from the board room to the Sunday school class to the pew and the pulpit. There is a lot of fanfare going on, surrounding ministries and people of ministries. When someone asks, "*Who are you*?" our first answer might tend to be who *we think or perceive* ourselves to be.

This is going on and we do need to be forewarned that there is a lot of deception in this area. There is a tremendous *to do* about people; *who they are, what they do, where they've been* and so on and so on . . .

This fanfare was also around John the Baptist. He had large crowds following him—enough that it drew the attention of the religious leaders who sent someone to check him out. John was surrounded by people in a movement that would make some green with envy today. But the one thing about him was that he had his perspective right on target with God's plan being activated through him.

What John was saying by, *"I am not the Christ,"* is *"Don't get your eyes on me—this is not about me."*

His response was instant. With the great following around him, he could have built himself quite a ministry. He was charismatic and appealing enough in his message and style of delivery that he could have had a powerful *man-made* ministry, with little or no effort. But the first and foremost thing was, *"He knew who he was not."*

This is what we've got to get hold of today as forerunners of Christ' coming to the World in salvation, to His Church and ultimately, His actual, physical coming . . .

We Are Not the Christ

As I go on a little further, you'll understand better why I'm pushing so hard on this. Ministry and revival ministry in particular *(including apostles, prophets, pastors, teachers, evangelists)*, though not isolated to those venues only, draws a crowd initially and if you *"play the game right,"* you can keep the crowd.

We are *the voice of one* crying in the wilderness. If we don't keep our perspective on where God's taking us, we will ruin ourselves and what God desires to do through us. Humility will take you along the same path Jesus walked and pride will take you along the same path Lucifer walked.

John was chosen.
We have been chosen.
But we have to know *"Who we are not."*

When ministry is drawing a crowd, one could get the idea that somebody has come because of them. We need to recognize that without the power and presence of Almighty God, Jesus Christ and the Ever-present Holy Ghost, we have no power, except that of human charisma, which is temporary and needs many man-made props to keep it up and in place.

Our voice, without the unction of the Holy Spirit, could not project far enough to do what God is doing today by His Spirit. We cannot call to the four winds or prophecy to the dry bones, or stand on distant lands through our intercession, even entering, through prayer, the dark places of the enemy's camp to get the lost ones home to Jesus, without the empowerment of God's breath.

But, our voice, empowered by God's Spirit and breath, can do it, through us.

Our appreciation of others ministry is not under the microscope here today—it is our appreciation of "***Our Ministry***" that is being scrutinized. Oh folks, may I once again emphasize—this is not about ***the official ministry of brother or sister so and so,*** but is about ***all who are called by His Name!***

Because John had his perspective, all around him was a holy place, full of the drawing power of God. He had nothing more to do than to walk out the call and anointing God had placed on his life.

John the Baptist walked and moved in ministry upon prepared ground because he had been prepared in the wilderness. He had learned humility. The ground had been prepared by his submission, yieldedness, and holiness.

His message of repentance was being preached without hypocrisy.

This attracted true seekers, because they knew something was different here. They had attended the Temple services, made sacrifices, but now this *one* spoke with an intense anointing, honed and shaped by the hand of God.

There are a lot of "*I am*" ministries.
There are not nearly enough of the "*I am not*" ministries.

Let that get deep inside of our spirit and convict those deep places of pride of place, name and position.

Satan had one big problem in the middle of a powerful move of God—he forgot the key rule in heaven—that there was and still is no such thing as "*I will.*" But Satan said, "*I will.*" His end will be our end if we say, "*I will.*" We, too, will not be able to remain in the presence of God if we are of our own will and way.

What is the difference between Satan's fatal flaw of all of his "*I will's*" and the "*I am*" ministries of today? There's nothing, really, that has changed. The same self-exalting spirit is behind it all, because those of today are established on the most satanic foundation that is at the root of every sin known to man—***Pride.***

Here is an acrostic for Pride:

Plummet
Rapidly
Into
Deadly
Ego

Who really knows when Lucifer went from being a submitted, worshipper of God to when he began to raise up *his own throne ministry.* He recognized that there was a lot of fanfare around the throne and he began to desire it for himself. He wanted it and went after it.

***Believe it or not*, this is the same ruling principle of pride behind what goes on today in the religious/church world.**

When people begin to be drawn in by God's voice, His Spirit, His Power—we need to realize that He is the breath, the wind, the fire, the rain, the oil, the anointing, the power and the glory of all that occurs.

People came to John because Holy Spirit in him drew them.

- ***It was the Holy Spirit*** propelling his words that brought conviction when the message of repentance was delivered.
- ***It was Holy Spirit*** that drew them to Jesus, through John.

When God does what He does, it is evident that no one should touch His Glory. Satan tried to touch the Glory of God. He tried to touch His throne, the seat of authority.

We have to have a tremendous amount of integrity so that when the Lord births things of His greatness in our hearts that we will have enough common sense and Godly fear to keep our hands off God's Glory.

God forbid that we should be cast aside—because He will not share His Glory with anyone.
I ask all of us, *"Do we have the capacity to know who we are not?"*

John started his ministry right when he leapt as a baby in his mother's womb at the very presence of Christ. Instantly, at that moment, it was established *"who he was not."* He began his ministry right and he ended it right, always pointing to the One who was coming.

> ***John 1:27***—*He it is, who coming after me is preferred before me, whose shoe's latchet I am not worthy to unloose.*

Get this folks; he positioned himself lower than the feet of Jesus *as far as status goes*. In other words, Jesus was so elevated above him, *in John's own estimation*, that he would have needed to promote or elevate himself to have touched the feet of Jesus to tie His shoes.

Here's the problem for some—*too many* are building ministries on how they estimate themselves. We are very good at estimates. Jewelry, cars, houses, jobs, ministries, titles . . . we seek the estimation of others for our ministries. We also estimate others ministries by what we see, know, rank . . .

A *John the Baptist ministry* will never get caught up in the estimation game of ministry.
It will only focus on the One who is to come.

In ***John 1:23***, John is firmly stating who he is, not by name or position, but by this:

- ***I am a voice*** *. . . of one crying in the wilderness—to prepare the way.*
- ***I am a voice*** *to declare that The King is coming.*
- ***I am a voice*** *to preach repentance.*
- ***I am but a voice!***

If we could all just be a voice . . .

John came preaching repentance, one of the most despised messages to a proud and rebellious people. He knew that the road he was preparing was the hearts of men and women, youth and children.

It's our turn now!
He cried out and we will too, *"Get the road ready, folks— The King IS coming."*

Be a voice crying from your wilderness, ***"Make it straight!"*** Let the first cry be into your own ears. Tell yourself, ***"The King is coming."*** Then we can tell others out of a heart of wilderness preparation the message of repentance and restoration and mean it without hypocrisy.

We don't become a voice for God because of *who we are*, but because of the redeeming blood that touches our lives every day that we live.

Lucifer forgot that he was *just a voice*. He wanted to be the I ***AM***. Focus, *for Lucifer*, shifted from God. He had been worshipping Him. He was there as a covering cherub.

This is one of the dangers in revival—when God begins to move, *(and He always does move,)* we get to looking at it and begin to think, *"Wow, look at all of this."* Lucifer shifted the focus from God and suddenly he no longer wanted to be *just a voice of worship*, but he now wanted it for himself.

A healthy appreciation and awe is warranted when God is doing something special or great, but this is also fertile ground for pride . . . if we do not remember, *"Who we are not."*

Lucifer's voice of worship stopped.
His focus shifted.
He lost perspective of *"who he was not."*

This is one the fastest ways for your worship to end. He wanted God's movement for himself. Lucifer, instead of bathing the throne with his worship, prepared out of a heart of love for God, began to prepare his own road and to walk upon it. He began to move separate from God.

John understood the Law of Decrease.

> ***James 4:10***—*Humble yourselves in the sight of the Lord, and he shall lift you up.*

We too need to understand the Law of Decrease. Humility has to happen in our hearts before we see Jesus higher than ourselves. John didn't mind *not being seen*. He, though a public and much-sought-after figure, understood how to make and keep Christ visible—the center point of all He did. *Oh that we today would learn this.*

Even the angels of heaven understand the Law of Decrease—
"Don't bow down to us . . . we are not The Christ."

The earth and its ministers must understand this message of humility. The Church must understand. The Ministers must understand. The intercessors must understand. The prophets and apostles must understand. Board members, treasurers, church leaders must understand.

You and I must understand—*lest we move into vainglory and get busy building our own kingdoms.*

- ***John the Baptist*** came from the wilderness into His ministry.
- ***Jesus*** came from the wilderness into His ministry.
- ***The church*** will come from the wilderness into her ministry.

John's message was uncompromisingly, repentance.
Jesus preached repentance.
We will preach repentance in our coming from the wilderness.

Some may say, *"Oh, but we've made way for Jesus in our church. We've let Him come in. We've prepared a road for Him. We feel His power in our services."*

My question is not to be provocative, but sincere in asking . . .

"If He's come into your church, has He overturned your tables yet? And if He has, what was the response?"

The Church may be *remodeled*, but is it cleansed? Has the . . .

- o ***Dry Rot*** *of Self-Government,*
- o ***Termites*** *of Division,*
- o ***Closed Closets*** *of Secret Sins,*
- o ***Skeletons*** *of Wrong Deeds Done,*
- o ***Buried Treasures*** *of Greed,*

. . . all been addressed, opened for the Lord to come in and cleanse?

What if we all just laid our soul bare before the Lord and said, "*Come in Jesus and be King here?*"

The ***"I Am's"*** are a dime a dozen. Far too many want to get in on the act if God is going to show up. Unfortunately, while the True Church is making way for the King of Glory to come, by laborious intercession and sacrifice, the ***"I Am's"*** are busy making their own way, preceding the King of Glory. They create their own roads upon which they will walk and all the while mislead the unsuspecting church into believing that they act on behalf of Him Who is to come.

We give more honor to the latest prophet or apostle and clamor to them quicker than Jesus Christ who walks among the candlesticks. *(Revelation 1:13)*

We prepare and extol their greatness and give them honor in their coming, *most of the time because they feed our ego.* This may be the ultimate reason why a message of repentance offends so much—*it assaults our ego.*

If we will humble ourselves, God will take care of our ministries and how we are used. This is a truth that, *if we get hold of it*, we will have a God movement upon the thrones of our hearts, lives and churches, which will then spill out the temple doors into the city streets.

That is what the River of God—Holy Spirit in us—is all about.

One of the reasons that revival has not fully broke over the banks of the church and flooded the land, is that God is still *resisting the proud* in the church.

James 4:6-7

6 But he giveth more grace. Wherefore he saith, God resisteth the proud, but giveth grace unto the humble.

7 Submit yourselves therefore to God. Resist the devil, and he will flee from you.

When we humble ourselves, God's resistance will be gone, and then you can resist the devil and he will flee.

There is already a powerful voice being raised from many ***"I am not's"*** ministries, calling for preparation and repentance. Will you join the anthem of the servants of the Kingdom, those who declare as an *"I am not person/church/ministry,"* that Jesus Christ is preeminent, above all?

The Highest Seat does not belong to us—it belongs to the One who is worthy, Jesus Christ.

When Jesus came to be baptized of John, John recognized him instantly, as the One he had been preparing the road for. It wasn't long after that John slipped from the forefront as his head rolled off in prison.

But, it had already rolled, long before his death.

Pride was dead in his life, as he had allowed no place for it to dwell.

- ***How quiet*** can we be when Jesus is being glorified?
- ***How invisible*** can we get when Jesus is being lifted up?
- ***How, not there*** can we be when the Lord wants to manifest His presence?

God, not only desires, but requires, a humble church, one that won't try to outshine the Son. As Jesus was baptized of John, it was all about Jesus, but one little point I would like to make—John experienced the encounter with Him, *because he knew Who Christ was.* But what about you and me—*here and now*—today—Where do we stand in preparation for the coming of The King? In the presence of Jesus, there is no rank, no ministry, titles, no big or little, because—***He is and we are not.***

Only humble people can get close enough to Jesus to baptize him with tears of repentance and love and submissive devotion.

CHAPTER 47

ANOINTED

Ephesians 5:26-27

That he might sanctify and cleanse it with the washing of water by the word, That he might present it to himself a glorious church, not having spot, or wrinkle, or any such thing; but that it should be holy and without blemish.

There's a church that is going to run the final lap on planet earth on home; going forward to cross the final finish line. This church will not limp her way across, will not crawl her way into glory—she will be a brilliant and beautiful lady—***a Great Lady***—The Bride of Christ.

She is going to look and be like the first church that was birthed in power and she will go out in power.

In the *last* of the Last Days there is a church, the one bought by the blood of the Lamb that will move with the power and authority of God. They will have a Rod of authority in their hand as surely as Moses had one in his.

The battle for the souls of the Last Days will be fierce but will result in multitudes being swept into the Kingdom of God.

This Last Church on Planet Earth will be a power houses of God's Glory and will be filled with His Spirit, move in His Authority and act with His Power. The Word of God records common people who carried an incredible anointing with powerful results following them everywhere they went.

Peter was such a man who dripped with the anointing—he exuded it so much so that even those in his shadow were healed.

He was not worried about the other things that followed him—*persecution, conflict with the religious world and the secular governments, jail time or the stir that went on in the cities that he entered or the damage he did to the enemy's camp* as people were set free. This was a normal part of his ministry—to be expected for one who was responsible for the supernatural things that were occurring.

He was followed by crowds who came with many problems—demonic activity, infirmity, disease, blindness and lame people—and it was not a bit intimidating. He did what Jesus said he was to do—*"preach the kingdom of God is here, heal the sick, cast out demons, raise the dead and cleanse the lepers."****(Matthew 10:7-8)***

It was a normal part of his ministry—and was to be expected by one who knew when his encounter with Jesus Christ hit him so hard it changed him forever.

Everywhere he went the waters were stirred, currents were created and waves rippled outward. It was just a normal day in the life of a Holy Ghost, Fire-filled believer who stepped into a moment in history when God exploded on man.

If he had been any other place, had missed his hour of visitation, his life would have been so different.

There were others like Peter who, with holy boldness shook their world because of the powerful message and the powerful miracles that they did in the name of Jesus Christ.

I took time to look at the Azusa Street Revival and search for the evidences of their revival.

What I found should be in any revival when it reaches its peak—true Pentecost with signs and wonders following those who believe—The Acts Church at its finest manifestation of God's power on earth!

Here is the evidence of their revival in the late 1800's:

- ***People*** left idolatrous religious systems—completely.
- ***Racial and denominational walls*** came down, removing every dividing wall in a segregated world.
- ***Love*** grew in the hearts of the people towards humanity and each other.
- ***People*** were ready to do His will, no matter the cost or where they were called to serve.
- ***Humility*** was evidenced in everyone, including pastors and other Christian workers.
- ***Restitution*** was made by people, debts repaid, wrongs made right, crimes confessed to, adulterous relationships broken, and hard feelings being dealt with.
- ***Power*** was evident.
- ***People*** had faith for provision.
- ***Healings*** abounded.
- ***People*** began to anticipate and preach about the soon coming of Jesus.
- ***Salvations*** were evidence in every meeting.
- ***Persecution,*** mockery, ill-treatment and arrest were evidence.
- ***Missions*** expanded all over the world and the states as people answered the call to go.
- ***Prodigals*** came home in record number and were welcomed back.
- ***The Word*** was alive from Genesis to Revelation as understanding broke upon people.
- ***People*** had holy boldness without fear.
- ***Holy living*** came to the church, separation from the world, the flesh and the devil.
- ***An ever-lengthening altar*** was evidence as people in growing numbers were seeking God.
- ***Expectation*** of answers to prayer when praying was evident.
- ***Burdens*** for the lost developed in the hearts of people.
- ***Hunger*** for more of Jesus grew in the hearts of people.
- ***Prayer Warriors*** continued to pray for revival to come to their homes, families and cities.
- ***Children*** were baptized with Holy Ghost fire, with many of them being called to preach the gospel.

- ***Believers*** were equipped to do what God called them to do.
- ***Spiritual stamina*** in the face of persecution grew in the hearts of the devoted.
- ***Sanctification*** was a part of the church as *"people stayed on the anvil of God, 'til we reflect the master."*
- ***One church*** was being born out of many denominations and the unsaved world benefited.
- ***Unity*** was evident.
- ***Evidence*** of the *"Fruit of the Spirit"* in people's lives developed.
- ***Supernatural*** occurrences were a normal part of life.
- ***Secret doors*** were pried open by the Spirit of God so deliverance could come.
- ***Prayer*** for others was made to see that they made it through their struggles.
- ***People*** believed the Word of God.
- ***The church*** *"took it to the streets,"* to brothels, bars and neighborhoods, seeing souls saved, healed and delivered.
- ***Restoration*** of the gifts to the church grew and manifested—all of them.
- ***Truth*** was evident and love of truth was the norm.
- ***Ministers and congregations*** were kicked out of denominations that renounced the work of the Spirit in their lives.
- ***Visions, dreams, prophecy and revelation*** were evident.
- ***Communities*** were shaken and transformed.
- ***People*** were Spirit-led, listening and moving accordingly.
- ***Conviction*** was strong in the streets and in the church.
- ***People*** were faithful.
- ***Full surrender*** to Jesus was evidence.
- ***Biblical doctrine*** replaced Man-made doctrine.
- ***Pocket books*** got converted as evidence that people were sold out.
- ***Obedience*** was evident as people did what the Lord told them to do.
- ***People*** trusted God—took Him at His Word and believed Him.
- ***Manifestations and crowds*** were normal evidence of God's presence.
- ***Gifts*** in full operation were evident.

This remarkable list was accomplished by a mixture of yielded people, the rich and poor, many races and creeds. There were no named stars of the revival. Holy Spirit was honored greatly and room was always made for Him to do it His way.

This kind of righteous living was the key to the anointing that was upon the average believer, the pastor, evangelist, missionary, doctors and nurses, prayer warriors and yes, even whole communities.

So, now here we are in our world. The Azusa Street building still stands but those people are gone onto their reward.

- ***Now,*** what about us?
- ***Can we*** accomplish such things in the name of Jesus?

The early church had the Holy Spirit gifted to them at the beginning of the church age. Since that day, there have been seekers—people who have received not only their salvation, but a Holy Spirit baptism. They have been endued with power from on high—walking in authority in their time—doing great exploits in the Name of Jesus.

They not only walked their talk—they talked their walk. ***Acts 1:1*** tells us that Jesus ***said and did***—taught it and walked it out in His life. He didn't recline at His leisure in Nazareth and then take a trip to Capernaum and suddenly was powerful. Every place He laid His head and took His meals was an anointed place of separation unto the Father's purpose for Him.

He lived the yielded life, one that was laid down to die for the cause long before the nails were struck through His hands and feet. His life was anointed and no matter where He found Himself, He did not have to work up an anointing by having a prayer meeting—He walked, lived, ministered and even slept in that level of the Holy Spirit anointing twenty-four/seven—***(twenty-four hours a day, seven days a week.)***

<u>**This was exampled in His life when He stood before Lazarus' tomb preparing to raise him from the dead.**</u>

John 11:42-44 (Emphasis Added)

> *42 And I knew that thou hearest me always: but* ***because of the people which stand by I said it,*** *that they may believe that thou hast sent me.*
>
> *43 And when he thus had spoken, he cried with a loud voice,* ***Lazarus, come forth.***
>
> *44 And he that was dead came forth, bound hand and foot with grave clothes: and his face was bound about with a napkin. Jesus saith unto them,* ***Loose him, and let him go.***

Jesus didn't need to *work up* the anointing—He *was* anointed.

When He raised Lazarus, He was ministering from the Spirit of the Lord which was upon Him, as recorded in ***Luke 4:18*** (Emphasis Added).

- ***He had no doubt*** His Father heard Him when He said, *"Lazarus, come forth!"*
- ***He had no doubt*** of His friend's freedom when He said, *"Loose him and let him go."*

And now, here we are, desiring to be used of God to see people set free, brought into salvation and healed and we are going to need exactly what Jesus needed.

It seems fairly silly to me for any of us to assume that we can do what Jesus did without the same Spirit that rested upon His life. Yes, we can do religion without the Spirit of God—but we will never see people set free without the anointing of the Holy Spirit.

Jesus set the pattern for ministry that we are to follow to *"do the things that He did."* We oftentimes state the actions of the early church and declare that *we need to be like them* and this is only partly true.

The full truth is that they, and everyone after them, had to be like Jesus to fulfill their call. They had to obey His command to *"Preach that the Kingdom of God is here, heal the sick, raise the dead, cleanse the lepers, cast* *out demons," **(Matthew 10:7-8)*** to go forth with the promise that *"signs will follow those who believe." **(Matthew 16:17)***

We are on the verge of a greater move of God's Spirit than has ever been seen.

We have stepped *right to the brink* of this season and time that we have believed God for. We are in a place now of either looking totally foolish for nothing or we are right on the verge of the greatest revival in history.

- ***We have*** either beaten the air ***or*** we have moved heaven.
- ***We have*** either muddied the waters with the vanity of our ideas ***or*** we have stepped right into the heart of history and are ready to see the Hand of God move in our hour.
- ***We have*** either stepped into insanity ***or*** we are right the brink of the promises being fulfilled and a great ingathering of souls coming to Jesus.

There have been many madmen and women who have made history for their wildly insane ideas they tried to carry to fulfillment—kings, queens, dictators, despots and a plethora of religious leaders, too many to name. This space would not hold the multitude of unbalanced, ruthless people—men and women alike—who affected history; people who dreamed big but walked off a cliff and found nothing to hold them up when it was all said and done.

They are now nothing more than a mar on the pages of our books of history.

Jesus entered into the world, making wild claims that went against the norm but He was right on target and all that was intended to be accomplished by His coming was fulfilled—in spite of the fact people said he was demon possessed and acted for the kingdom of darkness. ***(Luke 11:14-18)***

He was not in step with religion or man's ideas but made incredible history as one who has changed the world forever.

When a people are called out to do something extraordinary, such as pray for revival and prepare their own hearts, homes and churches, it is to begin to stride against the tide of humanity. We do look foolish but it had better be for something real! It had better be for something that is authenticated by the Holy Spirit.

Are we ready to transition?
We, like Peter, are not what we are going to be.

Yes, we established beachheads in warfare, but we are now getting ready to go beyond maintaining our ground.

***It is about* pushing into a convergence—a place where everything comes together.**

- ***It's about*** the plans of God being fulfilled through us in our lifetime.
- ***It's about*** leaving this world with a bang—*not a fizzle.*

Holy Ghost is not flexible about fire—it has to be there!

It's time for *"our Pentecost"* to impact our cities, states, the nations, the harvest fields. I'm talking about a pure sacrifice presented before a Holy God who takes a coal from the Altar of Heaven as He did on the Day of Pentecost and ignites our hearts ablaze with His passion.

I am not talking about those moments in time when you *"feel"* the fire of God . . . but rather when *"you are the fire."*

***I'm talking* about . . .**

- ***When*** you walk into the midst of the forces of hell and have them scramble to get out of your way . . .
- ***When*** demons flee, the sick are healed, the dead are raised, and leprosy is cleansed . . .
- ***When*** you speak words that do not fall to the ground powerless but establish the Kingdom of God and defeat the enemy's kingdom in the hearts of men and women.

***I'm talking* about an anointing that will . . .**

Luke 4:18

- ***Preach*** the gospel to the poor
- ***Heal*** the brokenhearted
- ***Preach*** deliverance to the captives
- ***Recovering*** of sight to the blind
- ***To set at liberty*** them that are bruised,

***I'm talking* about an anointing that . . .**

- ***Sings*** when you are in prison,
- ***Sees*** Jesus when you are being stoned,
- ***Receives*** the revelation of the Lord while in exile,
- ***Enters*** into fiery furnace trials because you will not bend your knees to the gods of the world,
- ***Refuses*** to lie down with Potiphar's wife, spending time in prison for your integrity,
- ***Speaks***, *"It is written,"* when Satan tries to tempt you to follow after his flattering words,

What would you be willing to lay down for the anointing—your reputation—your pride?

You are a runner of the *"Last Lap,"* of the race.
It is time to run it home!
There is no stopping, *"UNTIL we are taken up."*

It's Our Turn Now!

CHAPTER 48

EXPONENTIAL

Ephesians 3:17-21

That Christ may dwell in your hearts by faith; that ye, being rooted and grounded in love,
May be able to comprehend with all saints what is the breadth, and length, and depth, and height;
And to know the love of Christ, which passes knowledge, that ye might be filled with all the fullness of God.
Now unto him that is able to do exceeding abundantly above all that we ask or think, according to the power that works in us,
Unto him be glory in the church by Christ Jesus throughout all ages, world without end. Amen.

"Until we strip ourselves of our mantle—our pride—our identity . . . we have no place for God's mantle."
Loren Dummer

Many in the church all over the nations have fallen to their knees in repentance and moved into intercession and preparation and have battled long and hard on this rugged front of religious spirits. It has been a warfare that has taken a toll but for those who have been determined, it has been a war they are not willing to lose. Major beachheads have been established and held. Even though it *feels* like ground gained has been lost, they have held onto the promises of God.

Their bull-dog tenacity to believe God has caused them to hang on when others lost grip with the reality of what God, not only desires to do, but can and will do.

He has always chosen a people of ***extreme faith, obedience and sacrifice*** to step into the impossible and believe God against all the odds.

These are the people of this hour—an army of rugged warriors who walked out of the fog of religion and into the glorious light of the Gospel of Jesus Christ.

Yes, they have been Christians, but they have risen to a new level of discipleship!

- ***They have*** plunged deep into their flesh the Sword of the Spirit which is the Word of God.
- ***They have*** pierced their hearts through with truth in a spiritual world of lies, seduction, hypocrisy and deception.

They are Warriors of Truth

It is at this juncture that the Spirit of God rises to meet this army for they are now ready for the arsenal of Holy Ghost power.

***This is* where the Word in us, *met on His terms*, meets the Spirit on His terms.**

- ***This is*** a place where a Spiritual collision of great power and authority is going to explode upon the Upper Room fanatics.
- ***This is*** where the *Come up Higher Crowd* gets a view from a different plain.
- ***This is*** where we believe Jesus enough to *go the extra mile for the extra fuel* that it's going to take to turn our world upside-down."
- ***This is*** where we step into a different dimension of Spiritual revolution, starting with ourselves and moving outward.
- ***This is*** where those who have sat at Jesus feet and learned of Him are commissioned to the harvest field with signs and wonders following.

- ***This is*** where these people find the release of the Promises of God.

Really what God has been waiting for is for the Word to work mightily in us so Holy Spirit has a resource from which to draw. ***Hebrews 4:12-13***

This is where Rivers of Living Water flow from our bellies, a river made of the Word and Spirit, with healing and life for a dying world.

The time is ripe for a visitation such as has not been seen in our lifetime. Early revival and the developing prayer movement may have been great, but this is the time of the exponential move of God.

God is moving us onto the purpose for which we have been called.

We believe God for an outpouring of the Spirit of God that goes beyond manifestations in our flesh bodies, the kind of outpouring that changes us spiritually into bold harvesters like it did the early disciples. ***Acts 2-3***

I know there are those who will say that they are out in the field working hard to win souls and it is true, but ***there is still a missing blend of fuel*** that has yet to infuse into the church and its people. We are still sailing at half-mast and it is about time to hoist the sails to catch the gale-force wind of God's Spirit that will all but rip the sails from our ship if we don't move with it.

God's Spirit is moving!

I feel deep within my heart that there are many sitting in churches, or other meeting places where Christians gather, all around the world that are feeling dissatisfaction with where they are spiritually because the Word is calling for the Spirit of God to come forth."

It is Deep calling to Deep.
It is the Word crying out in us for the Spirit to use it and us.
The Word can never set dormant while people need saved, healed or delivered.

We have come to *a Saturation Point* in the church where *we use it or lose it.* My heart is desperate for this outpouring because I know that it is the next step for a mighty army of believers who will declare with me . . .

***"I am no longer satisfied with yesterdays anointing.
I need fresh fire in my belly."***

I feel the cry of many hearts calling for God to break us open as vessels of anointing.

It is time for the Word and Spirit to marry for the explosion of power that will fill us to overflow into the harvest fields of our world.

Deep in your heart there is still hunger and desire for the real, the genuine—the non-manufactured brand of Holy Ghost and Fire. I wish for all of us to lift our eyes off this earthly plain and believe that God is . . .

- ***Greater than*** our church or denomination
- ***Greater than*** what we have believed about Holy Spirit
- ***Greater than*** the revival we've already had
- ***Greater than*** what we have already believed Him for

It's time to get filled with the fuel of the Spirit of God so there is something to ignite us with the power to go forward on a level unattainable without Him.

If **we can measure it,** ***it's too small.***
If **we can pump it up,** ***it's not God.***

**Our hot-air balloons are not enough to attract heaven's attention.
He is enough all on His own!**

What man can ever tell God *"what"* He's going to do or *"how"* He's going to do a thing?

- ***I cannot guarantee*** the Spirit or what He will do in your life, but I can say that if you are available, He is ever present.

- ***I will not decree*** His movement, how or when He will do what He desires to do, but I will stand with you all and decree my movement towards Him as you move toward Him.
- ***I cannot schedule*** Him to show up on demand, but I can cry out with you for a fresh Holy Spirit Outpouring of Fire and Glory.
- ***I cannot empty you*** to make room for God's Spirit nor can you empty me but I will empty myself to make room and invite you to do the same.

Seek with a passionate heart for more of God and see if God won't meet your preparation and hunger!

CHAPTER 49

THE LAST CHURCH ON PLANET EARTH . . . . AND WHAT IF WE ARE IT?

Revelation 22:13

I am Alpha and Omega, the beginning and the end, the first and the last.

History can be divided into three parts . . .

- ***What was***—History past
- ***What is***—Today
- ***What is to come***—Unfolding Prophecy

Where there is no time-line concerning Jesus—*He is the I AM that I AM—Who Was, Who is and Who is to come*—and this description states an eternal value in regards to Him—**With Earth** there are historical and prophetic values that have a beginning and an ending.

History Past teaches us what Jesus put into motion—*His Church*—and reveals to us the contrast of where we are today by comparison. All we have to do is to return to the Word of God to discover the truth of what God intended His Church to be.

When Jesus said, ***"I will build MY church and the gates of hell shall not prevail against it,"*** in ***Matthew 16:18***, He was talking about a people who would be bound together by a common denominator, Himself. He set things in motion for an unending lineage of believers who would walk out their faith in Him in every generation.

We can also see from history past, beginning at the inception of the church, those who began to redraft the original blueprint handed to the Apostles by Jesus. They began to reconfigure key parts of the doctrines of Jesus and thereby created, for all intents and purposes, ***"The church that man built."***

As a consequence of man's failure to thrive and live by God's plan for them, God has intervened in history at many intersections. He has seen the captivity of His people and heard the cries that come from earth once the weight of sin and failure begin to reap a crop of sorrows. In His grace and mercy and tenderheartedness, He has sent revivals, renewals and awakenings to restore His House back to its former glory.

Revivals are God's attempt to bring the church back to Him, to restore it to its original pattern—to take it back from what the years and human choices have done to it—have done to us.

The difference between *"What was"* and *"What is"* is stark.

When we place the two spiritual pictures, the original and the copy-cat, side by side and are asked to *find the differences*, it is not all that hard. If we want to look and see it is fairly easy to search out truth, the obvious deviations from the original picture.

Am I the only one that had gone into an office of some kind and found the children's magazine in which such a puzzle can be found? I think not. We all want to solve problems.

But, invariably, when I have attempted to do these kinds of picture searches, I can find the most obvious, very quickly only to suddenly stall. I begin to take the picture apart, line by line to see the miniscule or very craftily hidden problems.

I look at the bottom of the page where the icons can be found, showing me the undiscovered elements I have not seen. I then look back to the picture that lies next to the original to see what I am missing. I compare the angles, the dots and lines, the curves and the color, searching with my eyes from top to bottom, side to side. It doesn't matter or change truth because I have not found all of them. I just need to search more diligently for the less obvious because they are there.

There are some discrepancies that exist between the church of "*What was*" and the church of "*What is,*" and God is trying to return His church to original condition so there will be a "*What is to*

Come," a last day's church of power, purity, anointing and authority moving upon the land.

And yes, there are discrepancies that exist between believers of "*what was,*" and "*what is,*" but Jesus is going to do His best work to restore a people who will follow Him into "*What is to come,*" to be that glorious church.

"What is"—we don't have to look very hard to pick out the obvious, but can we see the more disguised and hidden places, the differences. We are personally at a point where ***we need to look more carefully to see the more obscure and hidden "differences,"*** because Jesus already knows the original pattern He's working from to revive, reform and restore His Church—His people.

The Last church
The Last disciples
The last responsible parties
The last chance for the lost

Has God got His church, His people if the time of His return is just around the corner and the harvest is still in the fields?

Just as there was a beginning, there will be an end and someone has to wrap up the last season for the church, to bring it on home to Jesus.

- ***There will be*** a generation of believers who will comprise the last of the last.
- ***There will be*** a culmination; one in which the finality of all things pertaining to the church and the believer is accomplished and what is done is done, finished.

You must decide today what caliber of believer you will be

<u>The last day's church that Jesus has will not be . . .</u>

- ***Willful***—she will be fully surrendered
- ***Wayward***—she will follow His voice
- ***Wanton***—She will be pure, without spot or wrinkle

Jesus said, ***"He will build His Church,"*** and we know that everything being built is not of Jesus' doing.

> ***Psalms 127:1a****—Except the Lord build the house, they labor in vain that build it.*

Jesus built *His Church* to last until the Last Days.

He build it to stand against the gates of hell, a place that from which would come every evil thing to assault Jesus' Church, but Jesus said it would be impossible to stop ***His Church!***

David, pre-dating the church, asked the question, *"Can man build a house for God on earth,"* referencing a physical building in which the presence of God would dwell. David was only able to build the earthly house according to pattern.

Jesus built and is yet building His church according to pattern. It would not be housed in sticks and stones but in flesh and blood. The laws would not be written on tables of stone, but on the hearts of flesh and blood.

> ***2 Corinthians 3:3b***—*. . . written not with ink, but with the Spirit of the living God; not in tables of stone, but in fleshy tables of the heart.*

But today man has reduced the church to sticks and stone, setting in place houses of traditions where it has been all about man.

These are temporal, having no eternal value, but the Temple of the Holy Ghost, *(you and me,)* is eternal. ***II Cor. 6:16-18***

Jesus' church is not about the weak-hearted and weak-kneed. It is comprised of brave hearts that are not afraid to meet God, ***on His terms***

- ***They*** are an army of people that are tired of all compromise, all half-hearted attempts to serve God and just call anything that we offer Him, *"good enough."*
- ***They*** are a people who understand the value of pure and holy strength that endures through the test of time and circumstances.
- ***They*** are those who understand that obedience is mandatory with no room for leaning left or right or looking back.
- ***They*** are a people who understand that God has required *all that they are* and *all that they have* as His own.
- ***They*** have eyes and ears are open spiritually to hear the Holy Spirit speak and are obedient to any call that He makes.
- ***Their*** ears are attuned to the Clarion Call that summons God's army to a certain place for God's sovereign purposes.

Jesus' Church—the one He built—is comprised of a people who are not afraid to be numbered among those who have sold all to follow Jesus.

- ***They have*** laid down their nets to become *fishers of men.*
- ***They have*** no fear of the Body or the Blood of Jesus Christ and His call to *eat and drink all of it.*
- ***They have*** stayed when others have walked away because they know that Jesus alone has the *Words of Eternal Life.*
- ***They have*** embraced the Sword of The Lord, which is The Word of God and *revel in its truth.*
- ***They have*** no fear of criticism and persecution but have determined to pay the price to keep on going *when the going gets tough.*
- ***They have*** picked up the Sword of the Lord and *know they are battling to win.*
- ***They have*** an understanding for Worship with a cutting edge, laying aside even the religion of music *to worship in Spirit and in Truth.*

Their dignity is unimportant when it is time to humble themselves to dance as David did or get on their faces prostrate in the Presence of King Jesus.

They are a people who are so hungry for God that little else matters.

<u>They are a people . . .</u>

- ***Who have*** witnessed the power of God time and time again and are aware of a deepening intensity of the Spirit, taking them to a new level of encounter.
- ***Who have*** battled together for cities and ministries.
- ***Who have*** searched for the priceless treasures of God's Word, enriching their lives, beyond measure.
- ***Who have*** sought after God's heart for souls to be saved, healed and delivered.
- ***Who have*** seen God move in power and majesty until the roof seemed to have risen with the praises of God's people.
- ***Who know*** that there is no point to anything if God is not with us.

What is being built is not a man or woman's idea—it is Jesus idea of His Church, fashioned after patterns of heaven.

I believe this is bigger than any of us. Only eternity will tell what God is getting ready to do across the region in the lives, cities and churches of those who have entered into God's purposes for His Church in this hour.

**Nothing is an accident.
Everything is strategic in timing and the preparation of us for God's purposes.**

We do not need to make any path for ourselves, but listen and prepare to meet Heaven's blueprints, for it is He who builds ***His*** Church, according to His plans.

Jesus, when He laid down the pre-requisites, left no stones unturned.

- ***He spoke*** with clear definition of what He was looking for in His disciples.

- ***He offered*** little more than the Cross, along with His Body and Blood to those who gathered around Him.

  2 Timothy 3:1*—This know also, that in the last days perilous times shall come.*

We are entering the Harvest Time and it is truly growing late. The storm clouds are all around us and some are not aware that a flood is coming, that the dam has broken.

- ***We must*** prepare ourselves so that we can prepare others who have never known the Lord.
- ***We must*** come out of the wilderness as John the Baptist did, with a word in our mouths and prepared hearts to meet the multitudes standing in the Valley of Decision.

Be a hold-out for the real

The last church on planet earth:

- ***They will*** walk in the power and anointing of the Holy Ghost
- ***They will*** be watchmen of the most excellent kind.
- ***Their garments*** will be washed in the blood of the Lamb
- ***Their message*** will be bold and radical and many times offending to the flesh
- ***Their sound*** will be the sound of high praise, war, a rugged sound that comes from seasoned warriors.
- ***Their passion*** will be deep and fiery for their Lord

All people—all nations—will be drawn to a final conclusion that has long-ago been written by the finger of God.
Could it be that we are that generation of believers?

- ***There will be*** a generation that will see the culmination of time and life as we have known it.
- ***There will be*** a people who unknowingly are a part of the last act on the stage of earth's history.

- ***There will be the*** good guys and the bad guys in this unfolding drama.

Everyone living will take part as a character—they will have no choice, for prophecy will demand it of all humanity.

The secular world and the apostate church that has been drawn into the vice grip of last days deception will continue to write their own history before God and man. They will *do it their way*—but they too are already a part of the whole picture and stand upon the stage of time as well.

The pull of this fallen world is increasing and applying pressure on people everywhere to yield to being poured into the one-world mold of thinking about science, government, money and religion.

All is not lost, *yet* . . . all is not hopeless, *yet* . . . There is a light that shines in the darkness of this age—The light of Jesus Christ shines through His Church—His people.

> ***Matthew 5:14***—*Ye are the light of the world. A city that is set on an hill cannot be hid.*

These are those of a different spirit—The Body and Bride of Christ—making her mark on the closing pages of history as well. They are rising in greater and greater numbers; much feared by the enemy for they are granted and endued with heavenly power and authority, filled with the Spirit of the Living God and have filled their bellies with the Word of God. They have ears to hear what the Spirit of God is saying to them.

They do more than just hang around Jesus—they are following the One who leads them as the Lord of Hosts!

They are the Redeemed ***(Revelation 5:9-10)***, those who wait for His appearing, ***(2 Timothy 4:8)*** keeping the oil in their lamps ***(Matthew 25:4)*** and their garments washed in the Blood of the Lamb ***(Ephesians 5:26-27)***! They are the Church of the Lord Jesus Christ, of whom He is the head. ***(Colossians 1:18)***

Christ's Church is brilliant, fierce, strong, loyal, pure, true and holy.
(2 Peter 3:13-14)

- ***She marches*** upon the soil of the nations of the earth, taking ground for Her King.
- ***She works*** in multiplied harvest fields of the nations, cities and town, villages, mountains and valleys, deserts and seasides for the souls of humanity—as many as she can bring to crown Her Lord and Savior, Jesus Christ.

We need to address the times we live in—a time that is locked in the battle for the souls of mankind—one in which two kingdoms are clashing before our eyes in prophetic fulfillment. We must look closely at how we are to walk out our faith and live *"In times like these,"*—to not fall away from the faith on any level but to further establish our lives and ministries deeper into truth.

The times are perilous and a further look at these times, in the light of God's Word is the order of the day. We need to expose any level of darkness in our thinking that will lead to deception.

It is a Holy War!

- ***It is time*** for Holy Ghost, Word-Filled Truth Serum.
- ***It is time*** for a wake-up call—the kind of call that will put us in tune with what God is actually doing in this season.

The closer we get to the end, the more our survival will depend on a marriage between the Word of God and Holy Spirit. The father of Lies, deception, error and the mirage is loosed to deceive you.

- ***He's after*** your faith.
- ***He's after*** your prayers.
- ***He's after*** your stand.
- ***He's after*** your spiritual eyes and ears.
- ***He's after*** your gifts.

He's not after your sticks and stone buildings—***he's after*** the flesh and blood of the people of God. He wants to spill your holy blood in an unholy sacrifice upon his last day's altar. He would rather you be a martyr than a survivor . . .

You are the biggest threat he will ever face—the Last Days Church of the Most High God, filled with the Spirit of the Living God, on the March, fearless, focused and faithful. We want to be a people of truth, to walk in the Light of God's Word—and to do that we must be willing to allow God to probe our hearts by a work of the Holy Spirit.

The Church came in Glory and She will depart with Glory!
God started with the Church and He will finish with Her.

God has brought you to life for a reason. His expectations of you are great because the destiny He has for you is far greater than anything you can ever imagine.

The Acts Church is ALIVE—She yet lives because you are a part of the living lineage of the Church of today!

EPILOGUE

HITHERTO IS THE END OF THE MATTER

Daniel 7:27-28a

And the kingdom and dominion, and the greatness of the kingdom under the whole heaven, shall be given to the people of the saints of the most High, whose kingdom is an everlasting kingdom, and all dominions shall serve and obey him.

Hitherto is the end of the matter . . .

I love the words, *"Hitherto is the end of the matter."* There is such a ring of finality with those words—as if there is nothing left to say—end of the matter.

With God, when it's done—it's done!
When it's said—it's said.

Think of the worst-case scenario that could ever happen—The world that humanity lives in coming under the evil rule of an antichrist man/god who has the most intense hatred for God that could ever be manifested. This one will be so impacted with Lucifer's hatred for God that he, in return, will impact a whole world of people to turn to him as their *redeemer* from the world's problems.

Consider that he is a total mockery of everything that is holy, eternal and pure by exalting hatred for God, Jesus Christ and the Work of the Holy Spirit in reaching out for the souls of mankind.

In light of such a plan that is being developed now to destroy humanity and remove all traces of God, we can better understand the problems that are being faced right now in our world. These problems are complex and many in number but they all fit into a *planned displacement and overthrow* of Jesus by Satan.

He will use anyone and anything to have his way with man and the earth.

Every perversion, lie, and evil scheme is clutched in his fists that he has shaken and is shaking against God's Kingdom and God's people. The antichrist spirit is already at work and has been increasing in power and position for the final thrust of the Satanic Kingdom. Out of this movement flows all the past-hidden-agendas that are becoming arrogantly unveiled for the world to consider. What was hatched behind closed doors is now boiling up out of the pits of hell, escalating the spirit realm into a major battle with the Church of the Living God.

We see, even now, the gates of hell being opened over our nations—with your nation and my nation of America no exception.

America *(and many other great nations)*, once a stronghold of God, it now *appears* to be fast turning into a chamber of satanic agenda. Powerful men, women and devils are moving rapidly to attempt to unseat God once again, *just as Lucifer attempted in the days of his creation.*

It is still all about thrones and who will sit, ruling and reigning.

We, as *God's Divine Intercepting Force,*—intercessors of all kinds, from all rank and file of the church, from the head down, are positioned right in the middle of the most deadly battle that the earth will ever face—possibly the last great revival and ingathering of the souls of men and women, boys and girls.

The devil is not going down easy—*not yet anyway* . . .

Currently we have many battlefronts as varied as man's thoughts, but all are certainly a part of a single, but multifaceted satanic plan to displace God's Son, Jesus, and His followers, Christians, from planet earth.

Remember, I am talking about the plans of the devil, not the weakness of our stance or acting as defeatist for that certainly is far from what I am presenting to you. I believe in the victorious, overcoming Church of Jesus Christ, that we are conquerors, more than conquerors through Christ Jesus . . .

Romans 8:35-39

35 Who shall separate us from the love of Christ? Shall tribulation, or distress, or persecution, or famine, or nakedness, or peril, or sword?

36 As it is written, For thy sake we are killed all the day long; we are accounted as sheep for the slaughter.

37 Nay, in all these things we are more than conquerors through him that loved us.

38 For I am persuaded, that neither death, nor life, nor angels, nor principalities, nor powers, nor things present, nor things to come,

39 Nor height, nor depth, nor any other creature, shall be able to separate us from the love of God, which is in Christ Jesus our Lord.

But, we should not be fooled into believing in some *glitzy religion* that is soft, easy and cushy—it will not exist in the season ahead—for it will be a time of two distinct sides with two kingdoms developing, one to God, the Father of Light and one to Satan, the father of lies.

We see that even now the point of division is Jesus Christ.

Matthew 10:34—*Think not that I am come to send peace on earth: I came not to send peace but a sword.*

Only the rough warriors of the faith, those full of determination and the Word of God will stand the test. Lines are being drawn for the church by the Finger of God. *"Step to a side and choose"* is the message of this hour. Every move of God has been full of choices as to where one will stand, but stand we will—*one side or the other.*

The powers of darkness are already challenging the Church.
The world will hate you if you love Jesus!
Count on it.

John 15:18-19

18 If the world hates you, ye know that it hated me before it hated you.

19 If ye were of the world, the world would love his own: but because ye are not of the world, but I have chosen you out of the world, therefore the world hates you.

I pray that we will never minimalize the season we are in; as if *this too shall pass* and we will soon get back to normal.

We must not be those who hide our faces in a hole in the ground and trust that if we don't look that it is not real.

The world, under the current rule, will never be *normal* again. This is not *a single storm cloud* that has blown our way—this is *a darkening cloud* that is attempting to cover the face of the earth—to blot out the Light of God's Kingdom and His Glory that is prophesied to *"cover the face of the earth."*

We are sliding down the slope to Armageddon and nothing can stop what God has ordained for this world or the time-table that he holds in His Mighty Hand for this world.

Folks, the devil is ***NOT*** in control but he is raging. He still has to watch for God's clues as to what is to happen next; he then quickly, jumps in with both feet to try to catch up and make something work for him. He too has a plan, but his is secondary to God's.

- ***Remember****—the devil's miscalculations began in heaven and are still a big flaw in him—he still thinks that he can outsmart God somehow and actually make it work.*

But then, there is God who never miscalculates, misinterprets, misfires or misinforms—a big foe of the liar who always misleads.

**God's Son shall rule and reign and literally rule from Jerusalem—
but not yet . . .**

Even with satanic power such as has never yet been seen on our earth and is yet to come, even with all that the devil will employ to serve him in his grand *Scheme of the Ages*, remember that God Himself has the *Plan of the Ages* that He enacted even before Lucifer was created and could even think of how to oppose God.

The Ancient of Days that is seated upon a Throne that is eternal and shall not pass away, one who has already decided the end of the matter, it is His Christ who shall sit upon the Throne and for all intents and purposes already does.

**When we think of thrones, we think of those that match our own
human government, based upon our own thoughts,
but this throne is not a chair.
It is a position.**

Satan can touch it all he wants in this season, but it will ***NEVER*** be his! It is God's to possess and He does! If God has decreed that Jesus will sit and rule from the New Jerusalem, then He already does—the matter is sealed eternally.

Timing is everything with God.

Time only allows humanity to make a decision about Christ, move things into place for the end of the ages and for the devil to dig a deeper pit for himself in which he will soon be taken.

When God prophesies a matter—it is done. His Word shall be accomplished—just as He said it would be.

So, Israel, watch out—for your Messiah is on His Way!

World, watch out—for King Jesus is soon to arrive on Planet Earth!

What a sight that will be!

> ***Revelation 19:11-16*** (Emphasis Added)—*And I saw heaven opened, and behold a white horse; and He that sat upon him was called Faithful and True, and in righteousness doth he judge and make war. His eyes were as a flame of fire, and on his head were many crowns, and he had a name written, that no man knew, but He himself. And he was clothed with vesture dipped in blood: and his name is called The Word of God. And the armies which were with Him in heaven followed him upon white horses, clothed in fine linen, white and clean. And out of His mouth goeth a sharp sword, that with it He should smite the nations: and shall rule them with a rod of iron: and He treadeth the winepress of the fierceness and wrath of Almighty God. And He hath on His vesture and on His thigh a name written,* ***"KING OF KINGS, AND LORD OF LORDS."***

If everyone thought that the earthquake at the cross was something—think about the magnitude of the earthquake—*spiritually and physically*—that will rock this planet and the city of Jerusalem as Jesus touches down His Holy feet right into the center of the plans of a dirty devil.

The unholy trio will be feeling fairly confident and suddenly, Jesus comes to town.

All hell is going to break loose, really break loose. The grip of Satan will be broken, not a finger at a time, but ripped off by the Power of Jesus Christ. He has come to declare war and hitherto is the end of the matter! It is going to be glorious and earthshaking. All the plans of the devil and men are going to dissolve in a heartbeat. The heads of all will bow and confess that Jesus Christ is Lord!

> ***Revelation 17:12***—*These shall make war with the Lamb, and the Lamb shall overcome them: for he is Lord of lords, and King of kings: and they that are with him are called, and chosen, and faithful.*

When Jesus sits down for that first time, in the eyes of all mankind, that seat will establish more than we can ever begin to comprehend.

Every nuance of filth, debauchery, and rebellion will be erased and in an instant be no more.

> ***Revelation 19:20***—*And the beast was taken, and with him the false prophet that wrought miracles before him, with which he deceived them that had received the mark of the beast, and them that worshipped his image. They both were cast alive into a lake of fire burning with brimstone.*

It will be the end of the matter and not one soul on planet earth will be able to argue, for Jesus is Lord! The devil will be thrust from the scene as rapidly as he was thrust from heaven on the day of his transgression—He will once again be cast as lightning, but this time, from the earth.

> ***Revelation 20:1-3***—*And I saw an angel come down from heaven, having the key to the bottomless pit and a great chain in his hand. And he laid hold on the dragon, that old serpent, which is the Devil, and Satan, and bound him a thousand years. And cast him into the bottomless pit, and shut him up, and set a seal upon him . . ."*

Think just for one moment about the bottomless pit. My mother, Pastor Mary Seaton, received a revelation on this pit:

She said, *"It is bottomless! Satan will find in this place no end—he will be falling for one thousand years! Can you imagine the fallen angel, not just being cast out of heaven and falling from grace, but the fallen angel falling without end for one thousand years with no way of escape.?"*

Amazing! Now who has the power? Satan's power that was permitted for a season will be banished and Jesus will reign supreme and immortal.

When He first raises those nail-scarred hands and decrees a thing—it will be established—for He is the King!

How can I talk about a King such as He is?

How can my mind even begin to understand the rule of Heaven's King, the One who is seated right now to the right hand of the Father and making intercession for me, even as I write this letter to you?

How can I speak of such majesty and power?

How can any human being on the earth begin to understand His Kingship when all we have to compare it to is earthly kings that are rising and falling all the time, presidents who are elected in and out, prime ministers who are here today and gone tomorrow, men who die and are no more, seats that have a revolving door behind them, evil rulers and good rulers, those who are seated by popular opinion and those who are seated by dominance?

Who can **understand a King such as Jesus Christ,**
the Son of the Living God?
Who can **comprehend Him or even worship**
Him as He is worthy to be worshipped?

Who can?

God help us all to do it now for surely on a day in the future, *having no choice, no matter on which side we stand,* we will worship Him. Our eyes will behold Him and our heart will be captured by who He is, regardless of where we stood in relationship to Him in our lifetime.

Oh that everyone would worship Him now!

Can I bring this message home to you, *up close and personal*? In making application for how we live and fit within the incredible plan of God, we still live in flesh bodies striving for spiritual excellence. We know that we all face some terrific odds in living out our faith and at times are seemingly tested beyond our endurance.

Consider the worst thing that you are currently facing, *personally*. Think of the magnitude of such terror, loss, pain, agony, confusion, disappointments, false accusations, difficulties and such that you may be going through and meditate on this:

God is still on the Throne!

The Ancient of Days has already settled matters, decreed it from His throne and is enacting His plan even now, within the confines of His plan and timing. It is a matter of us moving in harmony with God's plan for our lives.

We battle our own minds and flesh when trials come our way and eventually turn to God in desperation, because, really, we don't know how to fix anything.

How very little we understand the thoughts and ways of God and how often we override them with our own thoughts and ways. Oh, faith is a tough thing when it's tough. It is easy when everything is smooth, but when the whole earth is shaking and our own little world is shaking, how do we stand?

We still have a tendency to remove Jesus from the Throne and take the seat to rule and hold the reins of our own lives.

We too, even though we believe that He is, act as if He isn't. So much of our own weakness is revealed in times of difficulties and persecutions.

Prayerfully, we *softer, modern Christians* who have yet to really be tested in a fiery trial of God-proportion will eventually get it—He is in the fire with us.

Daniel was troubled by what he saw, just as we too are troubled by what we see and are going through. But the matter is settled with God.

When all the breath is knocked out of us,
God is still full of breath.

When our anchors have slipped and we feel like we are
wafting upon uncertain seas,
God is still our anchor.

The cross of Christ defeated the Devil.

> ***Colossians 2:15**—And having spoiled principalities and powers, he made a show of them openly, triumphing over them in it.*

Jesus has already mocked him and put him to an open shame. Imagine all of hell who had placed their hope in Lucifer, had hoped that the crucifixion was the end of the matter, had believed that the world belonged to them and all the people in the world were theirs to do with as they pleased.

When the blows were placed upon the back of the Jesus of Nazareth, and the spikes were driven into his hands and feet and he was crucified, it may have given hell a moment of relief and belief, but that was soon crushed.

***You see,* Jesus did not even wait for the resurrection to mess up the devil's day, He did it while the devil though he was still dead.**

The shock and dismay on the devil's face must have been great to behold as he realized that Jesus was still there and still very much in control.

We have to be willing to also mess up the devil's day and let him know that even though he thought that we were dead that we are still very much alive and kicking—not in our own power, but in the might and power of our risen Lord and Savior, Jesus Christ. We may not see the look of dismay on the devil's face when we are victorious in the midst of our trials, but we do know that it is there.

Better yet, shock him;
Blow his mind;

Trust Jesus and watch his face when Jesus comes to town—to you, your family, your church, your town and messes up the devil's plans for you.

Isaiah 46:9-10

Remember the former things of old: for I am God, and there is none else; I am God, and there is none like me,

Declaring the end from the beginning, and from ancient times the things that are not yet done, saying, My counsel shall stand, and I will do all my pleasure:

AFTERWORD

The Grand Finale'

By Pastor/Teacher Mary R. Dollar-Seaton, Morning Star Worship Center, Scappoose, Oregon

There has been an endless parade of humanity going on for over six thousand years.
It has trailed its way through the centuries, moving unended through the history of mankind.

Though many human parades have taken place, there is one that dwarfs every parade man has conceived to display. As bright and colorful as they have been and are, when man's parades are over all that remains is the garbage that litters the streets.

But God's parade of millions of faithful and grounded souls who believe in the One True God, this parade of the godly move upon the streets, highways and byways of this world, leaving in its wake salvation, healing and deliverance, preaching the Kingdom of God is here. These who have trod upon the earth in *times past* and those who march *today* have left and are yet leaving an indelible imprint on the face of history.

Every life lived for the Glory of God still resounds and echoes from the mountain tops to the depths of the valleys today.

The voices of the millions today connect to the voices of the millions of yesterday, spanning the globe with a deep-held conviction that Jesus Christ is the Son of the Living God. These who have placed their faith in the

Lord Jesus Christ, who have anchored their lives deep into the soil of that confession, continue to live consecrated and holy lives.

This is *Bedrock Faith at its finest.*

It is as true today, as it was since time began for mankind, this parade will continue through the coming generations. It will continue unbroken in the march because it is not fixed or imbedded in the momentary glory of colors, lights, blowing horns, waving of flags, emotions rising and tears shed in patriotism for all it represents.

It is a parade of worshippers who live, sing, work, and pray in holiness to their King. This continuing parade will keep marching, singing, waving flags of victory over the obstacles of life, triumphantly anchored in the Rock of their Salvation.

"Their faith is built on nothing less than Jesus blood and His righteousness."
They settle for *nothing less* than the best!

With man's parades, people gather in places around the world, on lakes, hillsides and homes on the Fourth of July or some other national holiday in other nations of the world, to watch the fireworks shot into the night sky. They *ooh and aah* as the skies light up with the exploding cannons and powerful booms of temporary thunder.

This display of man's wonder may go on for a half an hour or an hour or so, ending with a massive Grand Finale' as everything man has is launched to impress the crowds gathered. Though a beautiful display the skies grow dark again with fading glory.

All that is left is the smell of smoke and gun powder.
Empty Wonder!

Looking back in history, we see a gathering of those who witnessed the ascension of the One who was dead, buried and resurrected from the dead, laying aside the burial garments. Jesus Christ was clothed in garments of glory and stood before His disciples on that day. He left them with a promise of coming again and then He lit up the sky like never before. They, *as we yet do*, anchored their faith to the promise He made that day.

> ***1 Thessalonians 4:16-17***
>
> *16 For the Lord himself shall descend from heaven with a shout, with the voice of the archangel, and with the trump of God: and the dead in Christ shall rise first:*
>
> *17 Then we which are alive and remain shall be caught up together with them in the clouds, to meet the Lord in the air: and so shall we ever be with the Lord.*

The Grand Finale' to the everlasting parade of *Bedrock believers*, for they will hear a trumpet sound and see the ground explode with a multitude of the Bedrock Faithful rising up out of their graves.

Those who remain will see a sky lit up with the Son of God waiting. Gravity will suddenly lose its hold on all who were anchored to that Eternal Rock. They too shall rise, because they believed, obeyed their Lord and Master, and established their lives on the ***Bedrock of Faith in Jesus Christ alone.***

Faith that is at Bedrock level, when taken hold of, will not leave you empty, sitting in the dark. Like the cloud by day and the fire by night, it's constant, sure, solid, not because we have faith, but in whom that faith is anchored.

When Jesus makes a promise to return for His Church—it shall not be moved out of its place in history—it will come to pass. This is truly ***Bedrock Faith*** in the One and Only True Word!

Bedrock Faith! Yes!

Outside the Box Revolution

- ***We will*** get out of the boat *(church)* and walk upon the water *(humanity).*
- ***We will*** move into the power and authority of the Holy Spirit, with signs and wonders following those who believe.
- ***We will*** pray until the ground around us shakes, until principalities throne's crumble and the prison doors swing open on the enemy's camp to release the captives.
- ***We will*** strive to create a habitation for the Ark of the Living God, a resting place for His Shekinah Glory to dwell.
- ***We will*** do whatever it takes to bring the church into alignment with the model that is set forth in scripture to govern ourselves, send forth workers, discipline ourselves, and evangelize and disciple.
- ***We will*** persevere through the tough times with a spirit that allows for no compromise, so that we may attain to the fullest all the promises of God for this hour that we live in.
- ***We will*** rise up to the full stature of Jesus Christ, growing into mature men, women and children of God, who will express the wisdom and grace of God in our lives.
- ***We will*** grip the Word of God with all of our hearts, embracing its life-giving words, so that we will be no longer tossed about by every wind of doctrine, judging all things by the Word of God, which is our only true plumb line, that which lights our path so that we will not stumble.
- ***We will*** keep our spiritual eyes and ears alert to the voice of Jesus, learning to know His voice so that we will follow Him and not another.
- ***We will*** stand upon the walls of our homes, churches, cities and regions as watchmen, sounding the alarm upon the approach of the enemy.

- ***We will*** be alert, sober and vigilant to the deceiving spirits of this age, understanding that the enemy is relentless in his efforts to lead us astray.
- ***We will*** judge prophecies, revelation and words by the Word of God, so that we will not be misled by smooth-talking false prophets who are bent on deceiving and drawing a following unto themselves.
- ***We will*** set our own lives in order according to the principles of the Kingdom of God as taught by Jesus Christ Himself.
- ***We will*** establish our churches place of meeting as a House of Prayer for all the Nations, lifting up intercession on behalf of the believers, pastors, leaders and the harvest world-wide.
- ***We will*** allow God, by His Holy Spirit, to flow freely in worship, building again the House of David.

ENDORSEMENTS FOR BOOK ONE ELUSIVE FAITH

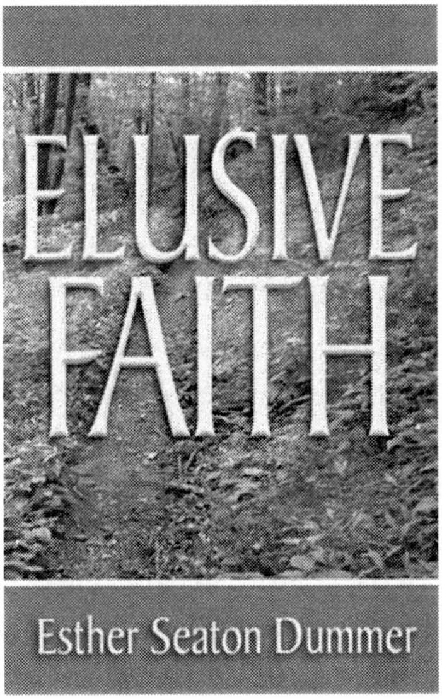

***Elusive Faith** is among the most heart-touching and faith-lifting books that I have ever read. As I read, my faith kept on growing. It fertilized and watered my faith. The book imparts supernatural faith—unstoppable faith—unusual, uncommon fire-invoking faith; faith for unusual miracles, supernatural boldness; courage and unusual ability to stand and face anything and anybody. My ministry will never be the same.*

- Pastor Erick Ondicho ~ Harvest Worship Church, Nairobi Kenya.

*Oh the wonderful drink of life **Elusive Faith** provides. It nourishes, it comforts, it re-kindles the fading embers of one's finest dreams, and most impossible callings. This fresh reminder of the glories of true faith is a gift to the lame, the used-up, the tossed aside, the mistake—ridden believers. And,* *it is a powerful wake-up call to those who deem themselves to be doing 'just fine'.*

- Pattie Thompson—author of two books. *Ashes to Gold* and *Dance of the Broken Heart*, Oklahoma

*Faith. It is key to everything in the Christian life: salvation, answered prayer, miracles, and pleasing God. Yet, so many Christians struggle understanding the elusive concept of faith. That does not need to be the case anymore as Esther Dummer's book, **Elusive Faith**, shows through a comprehensive biblical study of faith how we can all see the faith God has placed in each bring good fruit in every area of our lives.*

- Alan Ehler, DMin, Associate Professor of Pastoral Ministries, Northwest University, Kirkland, Washington

*As you explore this unique book it will surely stir the depths of your soul! As you re-live and explore with the giants of faith; Abraham, Sarah, Moses, Noah, and Gideon, their perspective of experiencing **"Elusive Faith"**, you will be uniquely surprised; your heart will be confronted and even shaken by the many misnomers of **"genuine faith".** An excellent and riveting explanation of faith that will draw you to the place of desperately knowing your God.*!

- Gary S. Huenke, Evangelist, Closer to Him Ministries, Oregon

*Faith is indeed a "dusty road" littered with the bodies of those who have reached out to man-made teachings of the "do's and don'ts" of faith rather than the person of Jesus Christ. **Elusive Faith** will help take you on a fresh journey alternately tearing down and building a more sure foundation built on Christ Himself; alive with new passion and new hope to see the promises of God fulfilled in your life and ministry.*

- Pat Huenke, Evangelist, Closer to Him Ministries, Oregon

***Elusive Faith** gives hope and promise of acquiring enduring faith, while moving into a deeper relationship with our Living God. It is our prophetic destiny.... given to us from the foundation of the world... as a measure of faith.... a homing device that leads us to our Beloved, when we answer the call.*

- Lucinda Waddell, pastor, New Harvest Fellowship, Oregon

*I thank God for Esther's words of wisdom in **Elusive Faith** that have impacted my life as I strive to champion my faith in God and conquer by the words of my mouth in agreement with the Word of God.*

- Bishop Desmond Tyman Richard—Word of Life Ministries—Guyana South America

***"Elusive Faith"** is a tremendous help to all who struggle to lay hold on the insurmountable riches of God's grace, giving insights that make God's abundance more available to every true believer.*

- Lester Askland—Minister—Washington

*I am impacted by the depth of Esther's revelation and her ability to convey that to others. I believe anyone who will read **Elusive Faith** with an open mind and heart will be blessed and best of all, changed!*

- Alice Reames—California

***Elusive Faith** is an awesome read, anointed and easy to understand, and a good reminder of God's love and plan for our lives. It is just what I needed and when I needed it most. I highly recommend this book!*

- Brenda Sanborn—Missionary

Elusive Faith is available in Kindle through _Amazon_ and in Nook through _Barnes&Noble_

WAY TO HELP SPREAD THE WORD ABOUT THE AUTHOR'S BOOKS

1. Check with your book store to see if they stock ***Bedrock Faith*** and ***Elusive Faith***, book one and two of the Outside the Box series.
2. Ask your church bookstore to carry the author's books.
3. If you are a Christian leader, recommend the book to those you come in contact with. Also, if you are a ministry that is itinerant, consider carrying the books to display in venues to which you are invited to speak.

About the Author

Esther Seaton-Dummer, veteran pastor, author and teacher, resides in Oregon with her husband, Loren Dummer. They have co-pastored Gateway Worship Center for twenty years. She and her husband have been married for forty-three years and have three grown children, Donna, (husband Neal) Debra (husband Mark) and Daniel, (wife Erin). They have been blessed with fourteen grandchildren—Christopher, Brian, Dante, Michael, Timothy, Tessa, Eden, Tehilla, Gideon, Dana, Lucy, Briana, Benjamin and Ruthie. She is the daughter of veteran pastors, Delbert and Mary Seaton, also of Oregon.

In the last fifteen years she began to share her gifts of writing and teaching with others on a greater scale than the church she serves in. She authored and released ***Elusive Faith***, on January 1, 2010. She is also author of ***Check Point,*** an on-line ministry of timely messages. In addition, she founded and leads a ministry that is in its fifteenth year called, ***Going Up to High Places.*** She teaches an adult discipleship class weekly and leads the intercessory ministry in her home church.

While she understands the season we live, in which there are spiritual conflicts between kingdoms, she also holds to a strong faith that God has His Church of which His dear Son, Jesus Christ is the Head. She writes to expose, but also to equip, with a desire to edify truth and thereby release others to live on a plain and a level that is far above all the conflicts of the heart, the church and the world at large.

Esther is known for her deep and revelatory presentation of the Word of God, mining the depths of God's heart and mind to His people.

Outside the Box Series

Outside the Box is a term the author has coined to describe people who, *though a part of a church or fellowship*, have embraced an extreme faith in and obedience to Christ that takes them beyond the four walls of their church and homes, beyond their comfort zones and religion—into the harvest fields.

Book One—*Elusive Faith*—Believe

Book Two—*Bedrock Faith*—Stand

Coming Soon

Book Three—*Fluid Faith*—Go

CONTACT INFORMATION

Write to:

Esther Seaton-Dummer
P.O. Box 345
Clatskanie, Oregon 97016
USA

Or

Email to:
estherseatondummer@gmail.com

Order Books At:

http://www.outsidetheboxonline.com

To Suscribe to CheckPoint,
a semi-monthly ministry message:

harvester@charter.net

CPSIA information can be obtained at www.ICGtesting.com
Printed in the USA
BVOW080153011012

301701BV00002B/2/P

9 781449 762469